The Best American Sports Writing 2008

The Best AMERICAN SPORTS WRITING™ 2008

Edited and with an Introduction
by William Nack

Glenn Stout, *Series Editor*

all best,
Will Nack

HOUGHTON MIFFLIN COMPANY
BOSTON • NEW YORK 2008

www.houghtonmifflinbooks.com

ISSN 1056-8034
ISBN 978-0-618-75117-4
ISBN 978-0-618-75118-1 (pbk.)

Printed in the United States of America

VB 10 9 8 7 6 5 4 3 2 1

Contents

Foreword

NOW I CAN tell the story.

This is the eighteenth edition of *The Best American Sports Writing*, and it has been my pleasure and honor to sit in at this keyboard for all eighteen. As the twentieth anniversary of the series has approached, I've often thought of how I'd like to mark that milestone, because at the start there was no assurance whatsoever that after edition number one, *The Best American Sports Writing 1991*, there would even be a number two.

In fact, there very nearly wasn't even edition number one. Although I had planned to save that story for the introduction to number twenty of this series, which will appear in the year 2010, there is no longer any reason to wait. The story involves the first guest editor of *The Best American Sports Writing*, David Halberstam, who I hoped to ask to serve as guest editor for number twenty. Sadly, David was killed in a car accident on April 27, 2007.

The story of this book begins in the summer of 1991 when, almost by accident, I was first approached to do this series. An editor at Houghton Mifflin asked an agent of cookbook authors whether she knew of an agent who might have an author who would be interested in serving as series editor of another *Best American* title, this one a collection of writing about sports. The agent did not, but she had just taken me on as a client, not because of my culinary skills, but, I think, as more or less of a favor to a mutual friend. I had published a couple dozen magazine stories about sports history and thought I had a few ideas for a book.

I met with the editor, and we discussed the parameters and process of creating this title. I was instantly interested, as I was already familiar with what were then the only two other titles in the *Best American* series, those on short stories and essays, and I knew the level of respect each volume had among not only readers but writers. I remembered that it took two or three shelves in my small-town library to hold every edition of *The Best American Short Stories*, and I envisioned that one day this sports writing series would hold a similar place in the library as first one, then five, then ten, and then twenty annual volumes were published. That vision, remarkably, has come true.

But I was the unknown commodity in this fantasy, and untested. So, before committing to a contract, my editor sent me out in the field and asked me to gather a sampler of sorts — a collection of stories written over the past five years or so that would be representative of the kind of stories I would select for the proposed series.

No problem. I was a vigorous reader of almost everything, including sports writing, and I worked at a library — not just any library but the Boston Public Library, then one of the greatest public libraries in the world. I was also — ahem — a *real* librarian armed with a library degree funded by the largesse of the City of Boston. A few years earlier, when I was working as a lowly library aide I was able to take advantage of a program that has long since gone defunct — the city actually paid me to get a master's degree in library science and paid me more while doing so (and gave me more vacation time), then paid me even more after I received the degree. God bless big government.

So finding fifteen or twenty representative stories was a gimme. I mined preexisting anthologies and the *Reader's Guide* not just for stories by sportswriters but also for writing about sports by writers who expanded that definition, people like Frank Deford, Pat Jordan, Tom Boswell, Ira Berkow, and George Plimpton.

I also thought of David Halberstam, who a decade before had a bestseller in *The Breaks of the Game* and had just published *The Summer of '49*. In fact, a few years earlier he had sought me out at the library, and I had given him some assistance as he researched the book. He had subsequently contacted me once or twice more, and I thought that counted for something. Not only did I include a story by Halberstam in my sampler — an account of attending a

rowing camp with his wife, Jean, that I found in *Vogue* magazine —
but when I next met with my editor to discuss the project I allowed
that I knew David Halberstam and thought he might be the perfect
guest editor for our inaugural volume.

My sampler was a success — I recall the editor being particularly
impressed that I had found something from *Vogue* — but my ac-
quaintanceship with David Halberstam may well have been the
clincher. They signed me up and a few weeks later asked Halberstam to serve as guest editor. He remembered me and, to my ever-
lasting gratitude, agreed to serve as guest editor, a coup of the
highest order.

It was already toward the end of the summer, so I spent the rest
of the year canvassing every magazine and newspaper I could get
my hands on and sending hundreds and hundreds of postcards to
editors of the same, begging for submissions; I was soon buried in a
deluge. Then, as now, my task was to deliver to the guest editor
some seventy-five stories or so, from which the final selection of stories would be made. Shortly after the first of the year, I dutifully
called David Halberstam to make arrangements for delivery, and
he indicated that, owing to his schedule, he preferred to receive
the seventy-five stories in two batches, one sooner and one later,
rather than all at once. I sorted through the pile and soon sent off a
batch of about thirty stories.

A few weeks later, just as I finished making my selections for the
second batch and was, quite literally, packing them up to send
them off, the phone rang. It was David Halberstam. I started to
speak, to tell him that a second batch of material was about to be
sent on its way, but he had not called to chat. He started speaking,
not rudely, but in one long run-on hurried sentence that gave me
no chance to interrupt and ended, "so I really don't think there's
enough to make a book it was a good idea and you've done a good
job but I really don't think this is a book good-bye."

Click . . .

Gulp.

In my mind I saw that library shelf full of *The Best American Sports
Writing* come tumbling down and turning to dust. I also saw myself
working nights in a convenience store for the next year to pay
back my advance, which of course had already been spent, and my
fledgling career in ruins. What had looked to be a wonderful break

now looked to be a disaster. I imagined myself sitting in bars for the next several decades, the Terry Malloy of sports writing, endlessly lamenting all the "coulda-beens" of my fate.

So now . . . what to do? I had no choice. I called my editor and told him, bluntly, that after reading my initial selections the Pulitzer Prize–winning journalist and bestselling author David Halberstam did not think there was enough there to make a book. He was off the project.

I do not know, have never asked, and do not care what happened next. All I know is that a short time later my editor called and told me all was well and that I should send my second batch of material to David Halberstam. I did as I was told, and a few weeks later, Halberstam called again.

Perhaps he had just had a bad day, or was burdened by deadlines or some private matter, but it was as if our previous conversation had never taken place. He made no mention of it but wanted to discuss some of the stories I had sent him. To my surprise, he loved the stories now and wanted to know which I liked, and more so than any other guest editor this series has enjoyed, he enthusiastically solicited my involvement in the selection process. Over the next few days we arrived at the twenty-four stories that made up the first volume of this series — the first story we selected, in fact, was "Pure Heart," a story about the death of Secretariat from *Sports Illustrated*, still one of the very best stories ever to appear in this series, written by the guest editor of this volume, the immensely talented William Nack.

The books all flew back onto the shelves, I was saved from my fate behind a cash register, and a lucky bartender missed out on my self-loathing. The book appeared in the fall and was well received by both readers and reviewers. As the rest of my life has taken place, this series, like a slow-growing tree that one sees out of the same window season after season and that changes yet stays the same, has remained a constant in my life. David Halberstam remained a great friend of the book, suggesting stories and other guest editors, later serving as guest editor of *The Best American Sports Writing of the Century*, and, as I learned, serving as a terrific example and mentor to a generation of young writers and journalists.

Earlier this year I was honored to serve as the editor of a collection of his sports writing, *Everything They Had*. Needless to say, as I put that book together in the same fashion in which I build this one each year, I never thought there were not enough stories to make a book. I do admit, however, that shortly after David Halberstam and I selected the twenty-four stories that made up volume one of this series, I did go back and check to see how many stories from each of those two batches of material actually made it into the book.

I don't believe he would mind if I told you it was a dead heat.

If David Halberstam was in some way one of the spiritual fathers of this series, then W. C. (Bill) Heinz was one of its grandfathers. In many ways Halberstam's own literary model, Heinz has also passed away since I last sat here, on February 27, 2008.

I only had the pleasure of speaking with him once, shortly after Halberstam selected several of his stories to appear in *The Best American Sports Writing of the Century*, and he once sent me a note so kind that I framed it and have it hanging on the wall of my office — as far as I am concerned the best writing award I have ever won, or really ever care to. If I can pull at a thread that leads me here, to this book, it may well have begun when I was twelve or thirteen and read Bill Heinz's work in the old *Best Sports Stories* series, those wonderful, unforgettable narratives from now-defunct magazines like *True* and the *Saturday Evening Post*, where Bill published many of his stories in the 1940s and 1950s. Not until I met David Halberstam did I become aware of just how groundbreaking and influential those stories were to others, and how many writers they inspired.

I did know, however, that reading those stories made me want to write. Each year as I try to put this series together, I think of that, for as much as these books are for the readers, I cannot help but think of them as primarily for writers, and those who wish to write. My hope every year is that within these pages there is at least a story or two that will inspire a writer to aspire to find his or her place here, just as the work of David Halberstam and W. C. Heinz inspired me.

I dedicate this volume not just to their memory but to their example.

Every season I read every issue of hundreds of general interest and sports magazines in search of writing that might merit inclusion in

The Best American Sports Writing. I also actively survey the Internet and contact the sports editors of some three hundred newspapers and hundreds of magazine editors and request their submissions. That process is, of course, overwhelming and insufficient, so everyone reading this is encouraged to send me stories they've written or read in the past year that they would like to see reprinted in this volume. Writers, readers, and all other interested parties should feel free to alert me to either your own work or that of someone else for consideration in *The Best American Sports Writing 2009* according to the following criteria. Each story:

- must be column-length or longer;
- must have been published in 2008;
- must not be a reprint or book excerpt;
- must be published in the United States or Canada; and
- must be received by February 1, 2009.

All submissions should include the name of the author, the date of publication, and the publication name and address. Photocopies, tear sheets, or clean copies are fine. Readable reductions to 8½-by-11 are preferred. Submissions from online publications must be made in hard copy, and those who submit stories from newspapers should submit the story in hard copy as published. Since newsprint generally suffers in transit, newspaper stories are best copied and then mounted on 8½-by-11 paper and, if the story also appeared online, with the appropriate URL attached. There is no limit to the number of submissions either an individual or a publication may make, but please use common sense. Owing to the volume of material I receive, no submission can be returned or acknowledged. I also believe it is inappropriate for me to comment on or critique any individual submission. Publications that want to be absolutely certain their contributions are considered are advised to provide a complimentary subscription to the address listed below. Those that already do so should make sure to extend the subscription.

No electronic submissions will be accepted, although stories that only appeared online are eligible. Please send all submissions by U.S. mail — midwinter weather conditions here at BASW headquarters often prevent me from receiving UPS or FedEx submissions — and please try to hit the deadline. This past year I received dozens of stories too late to be considered, some of them quite

good; you'll even find a few of them listed in the "Notables" section
at the back of this book, instead of in the front where they probably
should have been, but they didn't arrive on my doorstep until
April. I cannot overstate the obvious but will try to do so again — a
story cannot be considered for this volume if it does not find its way
to me.

Please submit either an original or clear paper copy of each
story, including publication name, author, and date the story appeared, to:

Glenn Stout
P.O. Box 549
Alburgh, VT 05440

Those with questions or comments may contact me at basw
editor@yahoo.com. Copies of previous editions of this book can
be ordered through most bookstores or online book dealers. An in-
dex of stories that have appeared in this series can be found at
my website, glennstout.net.

Thanks again go out to Houghton Mifflin for allowing me to
continue to work on this book, particularly my editor, Susan
Canavan, Will Vincent, and Elizabeth Lee. Thanks also to William
Nack for his enthusiasm and the care he expressed for this project
— during the throes of the selection process he once e-mailed me
that "I go to sleep thinking about them and wake up thinking
about them." I hope the reader has that same experience. I also
thank the website sportsjournalists.com for posting submission
guidelines, and to Siobhan and Saorla for putting up with all that
gazing I do each year at that slow-growing tree whose roots and
branches usually begin as piles of magazines and mail scattered all
over the house, then somehow turn into these few leaves. And
thanks again to the writers who, season after season, create such a
strong and lasting vision.

GLENN STOUT
Alburgh, Vermont

Introduction

LATE IN April of 1958, while I was doing time as a seventeen-year-old junior at Niles East High School north of Chicago, my mother's congenial younger brother, Edward Feeney, called from his home in nearby Park Ridge and made me an offer that no larval horse-player could possibly refuse.

Ed was a frontline sports photographer with the *Chicago Tribune*, a kind of celebrity in such haunts as Wrigley Field and Chicago Stadium, and he had long known that the ponies had become the ruling passion of my world — that I had begun to case all the finer gambling salons around Chicago; that I had, like some rare new genus of idiot savant, memorized all the Kentucky Derby winners, from little Aristides in 1875 to lissome Iron Liege in 1957; and that I carried, behind a hidden flap of my wallet, a snapshot of the 1955 Derby winner, Swaps, a surpassingly handsome dude who was the closest thing to an enduring boyhood hero that I would ever have. Ed himself was a longtime tracker of the running horse, and I suspected that he meant to observe my behavior around them up close; to that end, and in a way that would ultimately shape the journalistic contours of my life, he decided to invite me to that great racing laboratory of Churchill Downs, home of America's most famous horse race.

"I'm going to Kentucky to shoot the Derby in a couple of weeks," Ed said. "Would you like to go?"

How else could a teenage kid with the comely mug of a horse in his wallet respond to that?

And so it came about, on the Thursday morning of May 1, that I climbed aboard a train at the old Union Station in Chicago and began the long downhill roll toward River City. It was among the great adventures of my youth, my first foray alone away from home. All these fifty years later, I can still hear the rhythmic click of its iron wheels as the *City of New Orleans* plunged through the farmlands of eastern Illinois, swept across the Ohio River, until at last, in a steamy vale of snorts and sighs, it stopped to deposit its hundreds of Derby-bound pilgrims in that nineteenth-century metropolis known by native wags as LOO-ville. Just hours after pulling into its crowded railroad station, I felt as though I'd been transported to this magical kingdom, a sort of Blue Grass Brigadoon, which awakened once a year to throw a five-day bacchanal crowned by the hairiest stampede on earth — with reporters and columnists invited from all over America to chronicle the event.

That very Thursday night, in fact, I was sitting on a bed in a room of the old Brown Hotel when Ed's roommate, *Tribune* sports columnist David Condon, a notebook and a sheaf of papers in his hands, came huffing through the door. Those days during Derby Week rooms were as rare in Louisville as honest touts, and working newsmen commonly shared ceiling fans with each other; all visiting freeloaders slept on foldup army cots borrowed from the head bellman's basement collection. Condon plopped down at a desk by the window — dressed only in an undershirt and pair of boxer shorts — and launched into writing his Derby column for Friday's paper. He would look trancelike out the window, light the end of one Camel off the burning stub of another, then lean forward and attack the keys of his Underwood with a fury, stopping only to shift in his seat, or sift through the papers and notebook, or stare out the window again — at the revelers on the street below, at the merry bustle of punters back from the races, at the scene he had witnessed that morning at the barns.

Next day I charged downstairs to buy a *Trib*, and there discovered that the Derby favorite, Calumet Farm's Tim Tam, was listed at odds of 9–5, that his already celebrated stretch-running rival, Silky Sullivan, was second choice at 2–1, and that Condon's "In the Wake of the News" column, the one I'd watched him write the day before, was tucked right under the large banner headline in the sports section. The headline announced that the National League's first-place Chicago Cubs, in yet another miracle on Clark Street, had just beaten the Milwaukee Braves, 3–2, though we cynical Northsiders all knew the Cubs were merely flashing their vaunted early foot as a prelude to the inevitable summer collapse — the swoon that had long ago served to drive me from the ivied walls of Wrigley Field to the tree-shaded paddock at Arlington Park.

Here's how Condon broke from the gate in the next day's *Tribune*:

LOUISVILLE, MAY 1 — The man sitting solidly in the saddle gazed for a moment at the twin spires of Churchill Downs. Two devil's red jackets blazed against the sun. Finally, trainer Jimmy Jones — the man solidly in the saddle — swept his hand thru the morning air. And Calumet Farm's horses and horsemen, moving as majestically as cavalry, filed toward the racing strip where the 84th Kentucky Derby will be run Saturday.

The only thing I recall about reading that little piece back then, aside from my astonishment that it had traveled so far so fast — it went by foot on copy paper from the room in the Brown Hotel to Western Union, and thence by wire to Chicago, and thence back to Louisville by plane or train, arriving at last as a finished broadsheet — is that it appeared to suggest a hell of a fine way to make a living, and that it sure beat my father's daily slog as an electrical engineer who read blueprints almost as fluently as he did the morning line at Arlington.

That Friday morning, tagging along behind David and Ed, I hitched a ride on what was known by then as the Dawn Patrol, the circuitous trail of writers in gray fedoras who moved in packs from barn to barn, from Derby horse to Derby horse, stopping to gather round the chestier trainers and their charges. I see now, in a glance at old library clippings, that the longtime sports editor of the *Washington Post*, Shirley Povich, was there that morning, and so was the *New York Times'* Arthur Daley, who had a column in that morning's paper about Jewel's Reward, a well-regarded Derby prospect who belonged to the famously daffy cosmetician Elizabeth Arden Graham. In a scene that had her slender fingerprints all over it, stable hands had set a phonograph in front of Jewel's stall so he could listen to a recording of "My Old Kentucky Home," the ditty played during the post parade, in hopes he would not panic when he heard it on Saturday. "When the band plays that just before the Derby," his handler, Pat Linton, said, "this colt will not only be able to whistle the tune, he'll even know the words."

The inimitable Red Smith of the *New York Herald Tribune* showed up that morning too, a day after filing a story on Thursday from Henry Clay's hometown in the heart of the Blue Grass, some seventy miles to the east of the Downs:

LEXINGTON, KY., MAY 1 — When you've got Silky Sullivan in your hair, Tim Tam on your mind and juleps on your conscience, the treatment is to flee Louisville to this land of rolling green pastures and white rail fences, and freshen up the metabolism. It was a shock to find Lexington more crowded than Derbytown itself, with one hotel crawling with delegates to a convention of cemetery tycoons and the other stuffed with lawyers at a State Bar conference. For a corpse or a felon, it was ideal, but tough on the constitution.

It was a warm, bright, devil's red and blue world that I found myself wandering into during those two days at Churchill Downs, and I can still close my eyes and see Charlie Whittingham's little gray colt, Gone Fishin', posing for my uncle at the gap leading out to the track; see the herd of writers gathered around that muscular, penny-bright chestnut, Silky Sullivan, as he took his soapy morning bath; and recall that little rug of sunlight out by the Longfield Avenue fence, where I spent at least a half-hour either stroking the neck of Gen. Duke, the '57 Derby favorite until he hurt himself, or harassing the greatest of all American horse trainers, Calumet's retired Ben A. Jones, as he sat nearby on a large white horse. I had heard so much about the long line of Calumet champions, especially the 1948 Triple Crown winner, Citation, that I couldn't resist passing myself off as a reporter.

"Who's the greatest Calumet horse ever?" I asked.

Ben didn't flinch. "Armed," he said, referring to the mighty gelding of the mid-1940s.

"Armed?" I blurted. "What about Citation?"

"Armed could do anything," the old man growled, "and carry weight doin' it."

So could I, in those far-off days, and bear a load too. At 3:45 on Saturday afternoon, lugging a satchel of Ed's equipment and film, I made my way gingerly along a stretch of wooden planks set across the deep, muddy track under the finish line. Ed set up his camera by the fence. I held his film. Glancing up, I beheld the sight of a young lifetime. The vaulted Churchill grandstand rose before us like the Pyramid of Cheops, and the vast crowds of people swarmed everywhere around it, in and out of its little nesting holes, sounding like white noise thrumming in your inner ear. And then, at precisely 4:32, at the top of the stretch a quarter-mile away, the fourteen horses burst as one out of the gate. The whole of the Downs came alive in one thunderous din, and suddenly all these 1,000-pound animals were charging past us fifteen feet away, mud flying and jockeys yelling, with little Lincoln Road in front, Tim Tam and Jewel's Reward caught in the middle of the pack, Silky trailing far back. Ninety seconds later came again that unearthly roar rising from the stands as Tim Tam, on the outside, bounded past Lincoln Road to win it by a half-length, with Jewel's Reward fourth and Silky twelfth, beaten by twenty lengths. And moments later, as we policed up the gear, a heaving Tim Tam strode by, with the face of his jockey, Ismael Valenzuela, caked in mud, and at the horse's head was Ben Jones and his son Jimmy, all walking fast toward that garland of roses.

For a kid like me this was — not to sound too delirious — a truly stupendous experience, and it had what I suppose now was an inevitable sequel. In 1963, five years later, I was in journalism school at the University of Illinois and the sports editor of the *Daily Illini*, of which a nurturing Roger Ebert, later the nonpareil *Sun-Times* film critic, was then editor-in-chief. And by 1972 — after soldierly diversions through the U.S. Army and Vietnam, after journalistic detours at *Newsday* along the wetlands and sewer mains of Long Island, and following one magical evening in which the paper's editor, David Laventhol, overheard me recite all those Kentucky Derby winners I had memorized as a kid — I was on the Dawn Patrol in May at Churchill Downs, trooping from barn to barn with Red Smith and Condon, with Povich and Daley, and at night sitting by an open window in my hotel room, now and then turning to look at that seventeen-year-old ghost cackling over my shoulder, and writing it for the next day.

Red Smith was the best sports columnist in America throughout the three decades that I was reading sports prior to his death in 1982. There were many notable U.S. sports columnists who had grand runs and loyal followings in their times — from Jim Murray at the *Los Angeles Times* to Jimmy Cannon at the *New York Post*, to name just two — but over the years, setting one sportswriter against another, none wrote so consistently with the wit, the style, and the elegance of Walter Wellesley Smith. Of course, one of the things that set him apart, as anyone can attest who ever covered an event with him, was his surpassing skill as a reporter — his unerring eye for detail, his perfectly tuned ear for the telling phrase, his talent for seeing humor where others saw none.

This volume is dedicated to two other writers, W. C. Heinz and David Halberstam, both of whom died in the last year, who shared Red's gifts and enthusiasms for the craft of reporting. Heinz and Halberstam knew, just as Red and all the other great ones have always known, that the quality of a piece of journalism ultimately traces to the depth and quality of the reporting, to the energy and skill of the reporter — to his willingness to rap the pavement and make that extra call, to his acuity as an interviewer and observer, to his ability to listen patiently and well. First in his Pulitzer Prize–winning reporting from Vietnam for the *New York Times*, later in books such as *The Best and the Brightest*, then later still in his sporting books on Michael Jordan and Bill Belichick, Halberstam's respect for the reporting process both informed and shone through his work. Heinz, Smith's longtime colleague and friend, was an admirer of Ernest Hemingway and had cultivated the master's feel for dialogue, his spare and unadorned prose style, and his eye for the germane detail. All of these qualities emerge with abundant clarity in *What a Time It Was*, an anthology of Bill's old *New York Sun* newspaper stories and his magazine work.

Virtually all of the 2007 stories offered here fairly brim with the kind of reporting that honors the memories of Halberstam and Heinz. The permanent editor of this collection, Glenn Stout, dispatched to me some seventy stories as candidates for the book and suggested that I cut them down to my favorite twenty-five. It was agony. Nearing deadline, I had sliced the original list down to forty, but by then I had trimmed away what little fat remained on it and begun to cut into muscle, even touched bone. I had also begun to feel, with considerable discomfort, like a professor grading term papers, doling out grades that ranged from A+++ down to A−, with an occasional B+. It is not easy judging the work of friends and peers, particularly when you know how hard this work can be and know the long days and hours spent reporting, organizing the notes, then sitting down and shaping on a keyboard a cohesive, perhaps even artful, piece of work. At last, tying on a lobster bib, I pared the forty stories down to thirty-seven, then to thirty-five, then to thirty-three, and finally to twenty-nine. There I stopped, threw up my arms in surrender, and called Glenn to plead that the list could be cut no further. So what remains here are, at least to these eyes, the best sports stories of 2007.

In the end, looking back on the experience, I was struck by the strong work being done in the dot-com world, particularly in the realm of long-form narrative nonfiction, and to see and understand this, all you need to do is read the three exceptional pieces harvested from ESPN.com: "Murder by Cricket" by Patrick Hruby, about the mysterious death last year of Pakistan cricket coach Bob Woolmer in Kingston, Jamaica; "Bo Knows Best" by Michael Weinreb, a wonderful tale that takes the reader into the very private world of the greatest athlete of our time, Bo Jackson; and "Behind the Bamboo Curtain" by a brilliant Mississippi sportswriter named Wright Thompson, who turned his automobile journey through China, in the year before it hosted the Olympic Games, into a riveting diary that reveals a grim landscape the Beijing authorities would rather you not see, one coated with the soot of change and human suffering. In one diary entry, "Descent into Hell," Thompson writes:

> There is a tunnel ahead.
>
> Coal dust and smog block out the sun. It's morning but it feels like dusk. Kilometer by kilometer, we close on Linfen, the most polluted city in the world. Smokestacks line the road like telephone poles. The white road markers are stained black. The red bricks are stained black. The faces of the people we pass are stained black.
>
> The tunnel gets closer.
>
> We pass a cement factory. Then a brick factory, one of many we've seen in the past hour, some of them known to be manned by children kidnapped and forced into grueling labor. Every so often, an impromptu Delta Force of angry fathers rescue their children. The hours are long and hellish here in the place hope forgot.

The dot-com world, with its myriad websites and bloggers, with its limitless space and infinite reach, has threatened the very survival of newspapers and magazines, but the vast majority of pieces in this book were first published on paper, most of them in magazines like my alma mater, *Sports Illustrated*, or in *Esquire*, *GQ*, and *Men's Journal*. Their budgets may have grown tighter, but this was certainly not reflected in the quality of the stories that they and others ran in 2007. Steve Friedman's piece in *Runner's World*, called "Dogged," has it all — a woman, her dog, and the hovering specter of death. Here Friedman tells the story of a world-class endurance runner, Danelle Ballengee, who was saved by her devoted mutt after she'd been injured and stranded in the desert, alone and helpless in the cold, for three days and two nights. Chip Brown's story about Steve Nash on tour, which appeared in *Play*, is simply superb, as is John Brant's saga retracing the footsteps of Canada's national folk hero Terry Fox in *Runner's World*; with one leg already lost to cancer, Fox attempted to run across the length of his native land, all 5,100 miles, only to die of the disease before he could finish.

Michael Lewis is one of the country's most accomplished sportswriters — his *Moneyball: The Art of Winning an Unfair Game* is a classic — and here in "The Kick Is Up and It's . . . a Career Killer," which first appeared in *Play*, he deftly tells the story of the precarious lives that place kickers lead in the NFL. And speaking of originality, here is J. R. Moehringer's long but utterly fascinating study, from *Los Angeles* magazine, of USC football coach Pete Carroll. Carroll is at least as strange and intriguing as the title of this story, "Twenty-three Reasons Why a Profile of Pete Carroll Does Not Appear in This Space." But then it does appear. And memorably so.

In my last days at *SI*, I wrote a cover story on the terrible suffering endured by aging men who had played in the National Football League, identifying the slings and agonies caused by everything from slipped discs to broken joints to brain concussions. As a consequence, I was drawn immediately to Paul Solotaroff's excellent and very hard-edged take, as it appeared in *Men's Journal*, on how this small army of crippled men have been shunned, not only by the owners of this multibillion-dollar sport but also by the NFL players' union, whose $6.7-million-a-year chief, Gene Upshaw, is bled like a bull under Solotaroff's lance. Nor does Vanessa Bryant, Kobe's wife, come away unmarked in Mike Sager's compellingly written profile of Bryant that ran in *Esquire.*

> Vanessa's dark beauty and silken coal-black hair bring to mind the kind of idealized Mexicana frequently seen in tattoos sported by Latino gangbangers. She is known by some as Kobe's Yoko. I have seen her, purring and demure, at Kobe's side in her four-inch heels, her makeup

and wardrobe obviously the work of someone with ample time and money on her hands, bringing to mind the image of a tower-kept princess before her mirror, primped to the last eyelash, the last curl, the last bangle.

After writing how "Splenda sweet" Vanessa's smile can be, Sager then tells how she cursed out a fat guy who was leering at her daughter outside the Lakers' dressing room. He ends the graph: "She might well own the record for the most *motherfuckers* in one sentence."

And do not miss Jeanne Marie Laskas's *GQ* story on the Cincinnati Bengals cheerleaders, one of my favorite offerings in this whole collection. I first approached it with a cautious curiosity, wondering where Laskas might be going with this, but she won me instantly, on the very first page, and I enjoyed it so much — its pace, its italicized mini-profiles of the women, its original voice and style — that I ended up sharing it with friends, female and male alike. Here she paints a scene she saw before a Bengals game: "Cheerleaders are all over the place, half-naked, shrieking, sitting, squatting, kneeling in front of mirrors in the panic of an NFL Thursday night. National television! The game starts in just over an hour. This is crunch time, hair-spray time, false-eyelash time. Revlon-Orange-Flip-lipstick time. '*WOULD SOMEBODY PLEASE HELP ME? I CANNOT FIND MY MULTIPLICITY ESCALATE VOLUME WHIP!*'"

What also surprised me, as I look back, was that I came to like so many offbeat stories, so many absorbing tales about sports I'd never heard of, including Eli Saslow's story in the *Washington Post* called "The Old Ba' Game," a seventeenth-century sport that is like a giant rugby scrum involving hundreds of men divided into two teams, all of them pushing and shoving a ball back and forth across the Scottish town of Kirkwall; you must read Saslow's story to believe it. And do not pass on Alec Wilkinson's story in *The New Yorker* called "No Obstacles," a sophisticated story about an activity called parkour. Wilkinson describes it as "a quasi commando system of leaps, vaults, rolls, and landings designed to help a person avoid or surmount whatever lies in his path." If you cannot imagine what this might be, watch the opening minutes of the recent James Bond film, *Casino Royale,* in which our hero leaps and vaults, in rapid pursuit of a villain, over everything short of the French Alps. Just as fascinating, to be sure, were three other pieces on sports that fall well beyond the range of the traditional: from *Skiing* magazine, Tim Neville's neat story about the growing sport of speed flying, in which a winged skier can literally fly over obstacles in his descent; from *Harper's Magazine*, Sam Shaw's beautifully crafted story about the world's longest human footrace, the Self-Transcendence 3,100, in which about fifteen brave souls circle a single block in Queens exactly 5,649 times, for a total of 3,100 miles, never doing less than 50 miles a day; and from *Backpacker*, a well-spun yarn from Tom Clynes about his trek through California's Redwood National Park in search of Hyperion, at forty stories the world's tallest known tree.

Southerner Rick Bragg's *Sports Illustrated* profile of the new Alabama coach, Nick Saban, is rich with good ol' boy humor. On the matter of Saban's arrival in Tuscaloosa, Bragg writes: "They have welcomed him as Caesar, as pharaoh, and paid him enough money to burn a wet dog." And on the hiring of Alabama's greatest coach ever, in 1958, Bragg writes: "His name was Paul Bryant, and he was popular here. They named an animal after him." And do not pass by Alexander Wolff's story in *SI* about former marathoner Alberto Salazar and his near-fatal heart attack.

Indeed, *Sports Illustrated* is still producing some of the best sports writing in the country, and no story the magazine ran in 2007 makes that point more eloquently than S. L. Price's piece "A Death in the Baseball Family." The story grew out of a freakish accident that occurred when a baseball player named Tino Sanchez struck a sizzling foul ball down the first-base line that struck Mike Coolbaugh, a minor league coach, and killed him almost instantly. Less than three weeks later, Price went down to Texas to report what he figured would be a two-page story, perhaps a four-pager. At forty-six, with fourteen years at *SI* and nearly as many years as a newspaperman before that, Price was a sharp, seasoned reporter with a keen eye and an inquiring nature. He had barely arrived in Texas when he learned that this was a far larger and more complex story than one involving the death of a man. In fact, as he uncovered it, he found the story layered with eerie coincidences, a premonition of death, and a touching human drama. Price is one of the strongest writers of sports in America, and he turned this story into another gem.

No doubt the single most controversial sports story to appear this year, the one that raised the most dust when it was printed, is the tale that Franz Lidz told in a new Condé Nast magazine, *Portfolio*, called "Baseball After the Boss." *Portfolio* asked Lidz to find out what had happened to George Steinbrenner, the brash, blustering, and often abusive owner of the New York Yankees. So unlike the Steinbrenner of old, the Boss had grown strangely quiet, even invisible, in a New York sporting scene he had commanded for years atop Cape Scowl, his glassed-in box at Yankee Stadium. George was seventy-seven, Lidz knew, and no doubt was paving the way for someone to succeed him as the head of the Yankees, the richest and most important sporting franchise in America. Lidz wanted to ask him, *Who will that be?*

In the company of one of Steinbrenner's oldest friends, Tom McEwen, the eighty-four-year-old former sports editor of the *Tampa Tribune*, Lidz drove his rental car out to Steinbrenner's home. They entered the Steinbrenner compound after the front gate opened and another car left. They asked a front-yard gardener to inform George that McEwen, who had not seen Steinbrenner for a year, was there to visit. Moments later, Steinbrenner came out the front door. In all his twenty-nine years as a journalist, says Lidz, he was never more surprised than he was when he encountered George that day. This is no time to give away the story, but Franz did say: "He didn't even look like George Steinbrenner. It was as if I were talking to a Steinbrenner impersonator." The only thing that shocked Lidz more was the reaction the story elicited when *Portfolio* hit the stands. The *New York Post* ran it under bold headlines, as though the *Titanic* had struck a berg, and in the world of New York sports, perhaps it had. The biggest boat in that harbor appeared to be sinking. Lidz took a lot of blogger heat for this story, but in truth he did absolutely nothing wrong — unless working within the law, as an enterprising reporter, has somehow become a journalistic sin — and he pulled off the scoop of the year.

Long-form narrative nonfiction is not the only ale on tap here. Five newspaper-grown columns, the most endangered of all journalistic species, offer respites from the magazine stuff. There is the nifty story of Bo Jackson by *Kansas City Star* columnist Joe Posnanski, which runs here as a companion piece to Weinreb's longer and far different take on Jackson; Rick Telander's vivid and poignant column, as it appeared in the *Chicago Sun-Times*, on the legendary Doug Atkins of the Chicago Bears, perhaps the greatest defensive end of all time; and T. J. Simers's tale about a beloved father, the head of a family, keeling over and dying in his seat near the end of the Rose Bowl game.

If you like pure commentaries as much as I do, writers swinging from their heels for the fences, do not miss *Washington Post* columnist Thomas Boswell's indignant take on Roger Clemens and Slate.com's Tommy Craggs on how Henry Aaron has been trotted out by writers and used and used and used . . . I also very much liked, as I suspect you will, Rick Reilly's *SI* column about the suicide death of a female athlete, her parents' decision to donate her organs, and how her donated lungs saved the life of a man who ended up connecting and running with her father.

Finally, and in part because I have always favored such things, I chose three memoirs for this collection. One of them, Dan Jenkins's "Golf in Geezerdom," which appeared in *Golf Digest*, is in part the writer's lighthearted look at the pains of a golfer growing old. "I don't even want to hit a green," Jenkins writes. "It'll mean bending over to mark the ball. . . Every time I'm forced to do it today, I tend to stagger a few steps and mumble, 'Paging Mister Ritis . . . Mister Arth Ritis.'" The second memoir, which ran in the *Great River Review* under the title "Joining the Club," is Mark Lucius's sweet reminiscence built around the time he caddied in a 1967 tournament for Patty Berg, the LPGA's Hall of Fame golfer of the 1940s to 1960s. And the third, a finale as good as any, is Mark Kram Jr.'s touching, probing attempt to come to terms with the life, legacies, and sins of his late father, Mark Kram Sr., a brilliant *Sports Illustrated* writer of the 1960s and 1970s, a poet in prose, who was fired from *SI* in 1977 after an internal investigation led to three charges of gross misconduct, including two claiming that he took money from men about whom he had written stories. Years later, he also admitted taking money from boxing promoter Don King, another subject of his writing.

Young Mark, a gifted sportswriter with the *Philadelphia Daily News*, lived with that legacy of shame for almost thirty years. This memoir, which ran on Drexel University's website, TheSmartSet.com, represents his courageous effort to deal with old demons, exorcise old ghosts, and come to terms with some very old and painful business — the anger and regrets, the resentments and disappointments, that colored life with his father, even after his death in 2002. Of the writing of this memoir, Kram says, "It was a painful surgery, let me tell you. There were a lot of things I had suppressed because I loved him dearly. Here I looked at him with a journalist's eyes, and if I was going to be honest, I really had to address these things head on. After I finished it, I sobbed for half an hour. It was a very tough thing to do."

Heinz and Halberstam would have applauded the honesty. And, for sure, his father would have been proud.

WILLIAM NACK

The Best American
Sports Writing
2008

S. L. PRICE

A Death in the Baseball Family

FROM SPORTS ILLUSTRATED

AT FIRST Tino Sanchez figured he had no choice but to quit base-ball cold. Would anyone have blamed him if he'd stayed holed up in his hometown of Yauco, Puerto Rico, for the rest of the season? Forever? He'd gone there to be with his wife, Maria, for the birth of their first child, and as they waited he tried to take in the soothing words of friends and family. *Come on, Tino, it wasn't your fault.* The Colorado Rockies' front office told him not to hurry back, but the game that had been his life kept exerting its pull. So even though the baby — due to arrive on the same July day they rolled Mike Coolbaugh away in a hearse — stayed in Maria's belly, and even though his nerves still jangled, Sanchez returned. To the blast-furnace heat of a Texas League afternoon. To the visitors' club-house in the Dallas suburb of Frisco. To another dusty dugout, seventeen days after he hit the foul ball that killed his coach.

A breeze wafts through the quaint confines of Dr. Pepper Ball-park, promising a cool that never comes. Sanchez sits on the far right side of the vinyl-covered bench, three of his Double A Tulsa Drillers teammates hovering. It's 4:42 P.M., more than two hours from the first pitch, but already the same terrifying guilt that had left Sanchez buckled is at work again. In his first game since pulling the line drive that fatally struck the thirty-five-year-old Coolbaugh in the first-base coaching box, Sanchez is still getting accustomed to a macho subculture's clumsy stabs at sensitivity, to his bewilder-ing new identity as both perp and victim. No one has yet informed Sanchez that Coolbaugh's older brother, Scott, is at the park today — and that he's the coach on the mound in a gray T-shirt throwing batting practice for the Frisco RoughRiders.

Scott grooves a pitch, a batter swings, and the ball flies into shallow right field, toward a cluster of Drillers. "Heads up!" someone shouts, and then two more voices say it again. Sanchez flinches, his gut twisting until he sees the ball plop in the grass. His teammates notice his reaction. They act as if they don't.

"How are you, Tino?" asks one. "Daughter?"

"Not yet," Sanchez says. "And my wife, she's big. She's forty weeks."

Someone somewhere flips the stadium's speakers on; cheery pop music muffles the grunts and cracks, and for twenty-five minutes the day seems almost routine. Sanchez is the second man up for Drillers batting practice. Hitting right-handed, he bunts twice, runs to first base. The music stops. Two teenage girls start singing into a microphone next to the stands, practicing "The Star-Spangled Banner." Sanchez rounds third base as they harmonize about the flag forever waving, then hops back in the cage. Batting lefty, he pulls a ball foul along the first-base line. Everyone tries to ignore that too.

Sanchez is a utility man, at twenty-eight the oldest player on the team, so it's no shock that he doesn't start. In the bottom of the first inning he sits in the dugout, gauging whether the coaches are taking their positions farther from home plate. When the Rough-Riders' first-base coach turns, Sanchez sees the name COOLBAUGH on his back.

"Is that Mike's brother?" he asks a teammate.

"Yeah, that's Scott."

Sanchez had written a letter to Mike's widow, Mandy, and asked a teammate to deliver it at the funeral, but heard nothing back. Now he feels a slight panic: *What do I do? What should I say? How will Scott react?* But in this dugout, this stadium — in this world, really — there's no one who has the answers. In the top of the eighth a Driller is ejected, and manager Stu Cole tells Sanchez to get ready. He has never reached the majors and probably never will. In eleven minor league seasons he has played in games that decided championships, games that seemed vital to his career, games during which he was distracted by family troubles. But nothing like this.

In the bottom of the eighth Sanchez trots out to first base and fields a few grounders. Then the moment he's been dreading comes; before he looks he can feel Scott Coolbaugh walking up the line to the coach's box. The Drillers lead 3–2, and the crowd of 6,853 has thinned. A man eats peanuts; a child sleeps on his mother's shoulder. On any field, anywhere, there could be no more emotionally charged moment than this one, but the fans don't seem to notice. While Coolbaugh takes his position in the box, Sanchez readies himself not fifteen feet away. In the Tulsa dugout, two pitchers shake their heads at the eerie sight of two men yoked by tragedy and separated by one thin line of chalk. One of the pitchers thinks, *This whole thing is just unreal.*

For a moment or two, Sanchez and Coolbaugh are close enough to hear each other whisper. But Coolbaugh doesn't want to distract Sanchez during the game, and Sanchez, with no idea what Scott is thinking, can't stop his mind from racing. He wants to apologize, grieve, console, be consoled, say something, anything. He steals a glance at Mike Coolbaugh's brother. He fields the first out, a pop-up. The bases load, then Frisco ties the game, but Sanchez can't focus. Mostly he looks at the dirt by his feet. The inning ends. The two men run off in different directions without saying a word.

Coolbaugh doesn't go out to the field in the bottom of the ninth. At first that's a relief to Sanchez, but then he wonders if Scott can't bear to be near him, if the Coolbaugh family will ever forgive him, if his future seems doomed to unfold in the space between two unanswerable questions.

"Why me?" Tino Sanchez asks. "Why him?"

News of the accident at Dickey-Stephens Park in North Little Rock generated shock and horror across the nation. Mike Coolbaugh's death in the ninth inning of Tulsa's 7–3 loss to the Arkansas Travelers had every earmark of a freak event, a lightning strike: no way to stop it, no way to explain it. The last fatality caused by a baseball in a professional game — the pitch that killed Cleveland Indians shortstop Ray Chapman in 1920 — still serves as a cautionary tale of how quickly a toy can turn into a deadly projectile. But in that case the ball had been doctored. Coolbaugh's death seemed more random, a feeling compounded by the presence of three people all too familiar with the impact a ball can have.

Up in the press box and doing color commentary for the Travelers was general manager Bill Valentine, a former major league umpire who, forty summers before, had been behind the plate in Fenway Park when a fastball from California Angels pitcher Jack Hamilton pulped the face of Boston Red Sox outfielder Tony Conigliaro, damaging Tony C's eyesight forever. Drillers pitching coach Bo McLaughlin had his major league career effectively ended in 1981 when a Harold Baines line drive caved in his left cheek. And two months earlier Tulsa pitcher Jon Asahina suffered a fractured skull and a shattered eardrum when a batter at the same Little Rock park drove a ball into the left side of his head. If the impact had been an inch or two in another direction, Asahina was told by neurosurgeons who viewed his CAT scans, he might not be standing today.

Some observers suggest — and Asahina insists — that Coolbaugh, in just his eighteenth game as a first-base coach, was focusing on the lead of Drillers base runner Matt Miller and not on the batter in the second before Sanchez made contact. Inexperience might have been a factor, but one seemingly offset by the fact that Coolbaugh constantly preached about the dangers posed by foul balls. "He was more worried about it than anybody I've ever met," says Mandy. In 2005, when Mike was playing with Triple A Round Rock, he was about to settle into his crouch at third when he noticed Mandy visiting a friend in the seats behind the base. Before the pitcher could wind up, Coolbaugh walked off the field and insisted that she move somewhere safer. "So when people say he was turned the wrong way, I just can't believe it," she says. "He was so aware of what a ball could do. God plucked him. There's no way he would've let a foul ball kill him."

For those closest to Coolbaugh, "God plucked him" is the most palatable explanation for what happened in Little Rock. Within the game itself that Sunday night, so many things had to line up: hits, runs, calls. Heading into the eighth inning the Travelers held a one-run lead, a choice situation for their sidearming closer, right-hander Darren O'Day. But Arkansas scored three in the bottom of the inning to erase the save opportunity. Bill Edwards, a more conventional righty, took the mound. Would O'Day have thrown the same pitches as Edwards? No. Would it have mattered?

Miller led off the ninth for Tulsa with a single to right. Up to the plate came Sanchez. Edwards threw three consecutive balls; one more and everyone would be safe. "The 3–0 pitch," recalls Drillers play-by-play man Mark Neely, "was a very borderline strike on the outside corner. I'm not blaming this on the umpire. But with all the strange things that had occurred to get to that moment . . . Many times — though umpires would never say this — on a 3–0 count the strike zone does expand. That was a perfect example: a borderline pitch on the outside corner that was called a strike and made it 3–1."

It was 8:53 P.M. Coolbaugh leaned over to Miller, standing on first. "We're down a couple runs, so don't get picked off," he said. "Freeze on a line drive." Then Mike Coolbaugh said his last words: "If you're going first to third, you've got to be sure."

Miller took a lead. Edwards brought back his arm. Miller took another step.

A fastball inside, the kind of pitch that always gave Coolbaugh trouble as a hitter. Sanchez, batting lefty, swung a fraction of a second too soon, and the ball blasted off his bat. "A rocket!" Neely shouted into his microphone.

"I don't remember a ball being hit that hard, that fast," says Valentine, who has been working in baseball for fifty-six years. "He really got every bit of it."

Even though he knew the ball was foul, Sanchez kept watching as it hooked behind first. Coolbaugh threw up his hands as if to defend himself, and tilted his body slightly back.

"It's so crazy," Sanchez says. "It seemed like the ball followed him."

Mike Coolbaugh's baseball career began with an accident. Football was his first love. As a highly touted senior quarterback for San Antonio's Roosevelt High, he was sitting in the locker room when his head coach, hurling a clipboard in what was meant to be a motivational rage, hit him square in the face. His nose deeply gashed, Coolbaugh couldn't wear a helmet and missed vital games; the coach was fired, Coolbaugh's family sued and settled out of court. Recruiters from Texas, LSU, and Wisconsin stopped calling. Coolbaugh turned to baseball, became a power-hitting third baseman, and was drafted 433rd by the Toronto Blue Jays in 1990.

He spent his first ten and a half years bouncing among six organizations: four years in A ball, three in Double A, nearly four in Triple A. He made three All-Star teams, was voted a team MVP, broke the Southern League record for RBIs in a season. He sat and

watched as callow talents, bad teammates, and, yes, plenty of superior players elbowed past him. Soon Coolbaugh was twenty-nine
and thinking his chance at the majors would never come. "Just one
day," he would tell Scott. "To get called up for just one day."

God knows, he had worked for it. When Mike was in high school
and Scott in college at Texas, teammates had come to work out in
the family backyard in San Antonio once or twice, never to return.
"Camp Coolbaugh" they dubbed it, and they didn't mean days
spent dangling a toe out of a canoe. The boys' dad, Bob, a precision tool-and-die man, was a onetime high school talent from
Binghamton, New York, who'd turned down an invitation to a New
York Yankees tryout because he knew he wasn't good enough. He
would make sure his sons never felt that way. The boys loved sports,
all sports, but Dad knew baseball, and his rule about playing it was
simple: if you won't help yourself by practicing 100 percent, then
you'll help me pull weeds or wash the car — 100 percent.

Scott began running a three-mile course at age twelve, and when
the smaller, wiry six-year-old Mike would bolt ahead of him, Scott
would gasp, "Don't you beat me or I'll kick your tail!" Bob set up a
pitching machine in the backyard, tinkering with it until it could
fire at 110 mph, and each boy would take three hundred, four hundred cuts — to start the day. Their sisters, Lisa and Linda, were put
to use fielding grounders, feeding balls. "Sprint work, running,
swinging an ax into a tree stump," Scott says of the workouts. "He'd
have us hit into a stump two hundred times before we went to bed.
We got through the stumps so quick, he dulled the blade. There
were a lot of hard times, but it created a work ethic."

Bob couldn't help trying to make his young tools ever more precise. If Mike or Scott went 3-for-4, Bob needed to know what went
wrong that one at bat. Scott absorbed the constant analysis and
prodding quietly, but Mike couldn't. He was hard enough on himself already. "That's what kept those two going," Scott says. "You'd
put them in a room together, and they'd argue like they were about
to fight, but that's what made their relationship, and they accepted
it. They both said their piece and walked away."

Bob will forever be bitter about his boys' small-time careers —
Scott, a corner infielder, played 167 big league games from 1989
through '94 — certain they were jobbed by the powers that be.
Baseball? "A curse on the Coolbaugh family, as far as I'm con-

cerned," Bob says. Mike hit 256 home runs in the minors, and if he agonized over not getting his break, he never resented the good players who got a shot. He could be dour: "a lovable grouch," Astros second baseman Chris Burke, a former minor league teammate, called him. But Coolbaugh's dark moods would always pass. "Listen to me complain," he would say. "Like I've got it bad."

Finally, on the afternoon of July 15, 2001, he got his day. Coolbaugh was heading for the batting cage in Durham, North Carolina, when Indianapolis Indians manager Wendell Kim stopped him. "I don't think that's a good idea," Kim said. "It wouldn't be good for you to get hurt just before you go to Milwaukee."

Coolbaugh warned him not to joke. "Better get packed," Kim said. "You're going to be late for the plane."

Mandy and Mike had been a couple since 1996 and married since 2000. She knew him to have cried only four times: on their wedding day, on the days their two sons were born, and on the day he got called up, after 1,165 games in places like St. Catharines, Ontario; Knoxville, Tennessee; and Huntsville, Alabama. "We did it," Mike said in a voice mail, between sobs. "We finally did it. We're going to be up there."

The next day Coolbaugh had a cab drop him at Milwaukee County Stadium at 9:00 A.M. A security guard told him no one would arrive until 11:00. He had nowhere to go. So the guard gave him a tour: up and down the concourses in a golf cart, out to the perfect field, into the hushed clubhouse. Coolbaugh found his locker, with a Brewers jersey hanging in it: number 14, his name stitched with care across the back.

He played thirty-nine games with the Brewers. None were as sweet as the first two. In his first at bat, with Mandy in the stands, he smacked a pinch-hit double. The next morning the couple woke to find that Mike's father, his mother Mary Lu, and his sisters had arrived after an all-night drive from upstate New York. "My dad's here today," Mike told one sportswriter. "I'm going to have a good game." In his second major league at bat he drove a 3-and-1 pitch from the Chicago White Sox's Jon Garland into the left-field stands and ran around the bases as if it were the most normal thing in the world. The whole Coolbaugh family was crying. "Just that one at bat," Mandy says. "He didn't need anything else."

*

No, Coolbaugh needed what all competitors need: more. Milwaukee gave him a taste of playing at the pinnacle, with its plush hotel rooms, a $320,000 salary, and, most of all, respect. He finished the season with two home runs and a .200 average, and now, it seemed, all those years of work might pay off. Even after the Brewers released him that October, Coolbaugh felt he belonged in the majors. He hooked on with St. Louis the next spring, ravaged Grapefruit League pitching, and seemed sure to head west with the Cardinals. Instead, the St. Louis brass opted for the multidimensional, if less productive, Eduardo Perez — a decision that shocks Perez to this day. When manager Tony La Russa called Coolbaugh over with the news that he was being sent down again, Coolbaugh began to jog away. "You're not going to catch me," he said, laughing outside and groaning within. "This is not going to happen."

But it did. Coolbaugh played five games for St. Louis as a September call-up, hit .083, and would never appear in a major league city again. "To me it's one word: opportunity," says former Houston Astros general manager Tim Purpura. "It just never came for him at the right time. He had the talent. There just wasn't the opening."

It's a truism of minor league ball that anyone who plays it for a long time must be a team guy, good for clubhouse chemistry. Coolbaugh played seventeen seasons in the bushes for nine organizations, and no one ever said a harsh word about him. Clubs gave him chances well past his sell-by date. He played in Korea in 2003, got hurt, then surfaced in the Astros' farm system. In '04 he reached Triple A New Orleans, only to get off to a poor start. One night in Omaha he struck out three times, and the team bus passed him walking the ten miles from ballpark to hotel. "He's got his head down and he's talking to himself," Burke recalls. "Here he is, with a thousand games in his career, but he couldn't handle the fact that he was in a bad rut."

Coolbaugh climbed out and hit 30 home runs that season. It wasn't nearly enough: Morgan Ensberg had a lock on third base in Houston. Coolbaugh was back in Triple A in 2005, hitting 27 homers and driving in 101 runs for Round Rock. "I'm not going to let them beat me," he told Scott. The Astros had every intention of calling him up in September, but in late August, Coolbaugh took an inside pitch on his left hand, breaking a bone. In the spring of '06, on the first day of big league camp with the Kansas City Royals, a fastball shattered his left wrist. He toyed with playing in Mexico this spring but gave it up after a week. His playing career was done.

Still, Coolbaugh wanted to keep his battered hand in. He tried to land a rookie league coaching job with Houston, but execs there felt his demeanor, while fine for seasoned players, might not be right for fresh-faced youngsters. Coolbaugh didn't have, as Burke says, a "warm-and-fuzzy *Field of Dreams* love of baseball." There were times when Coolbaugh, like any self-respecting player, hated the game for its politics, all the gut-wrenching failure. He took business courses online, but baseball was what he knew; he had a family to feed and a baby on the way. His sons, five-year-old Joseph and four-year-old Jacob, wanted to see him in uniform again. When hitting coach Orlando Merced left Tulsa for personal reasons and the job opened up in May, Mike interviewed and waited — but didn't say a word about it to Mandy until he actually got hired.

"He didn't want to jinx things," she says. "It felt like we were always being jinxed in his career."

Coolbaugh joined the Drillers on July 4, introducing himself at the batting cage in San Antonio. "I always had trouble getting away from inside pitches," he told the players. The team's hitting improved almost instantly. With his quiet sincerity, Coolbaugh gained the players' trust. "You just felt him," says Asahina. "He had that warrior energy, very stoic. I was very careful: I would only ask him crisp questions. I wanted to let him know I'm not here talking about last night or women in the stands. No: it's baseball."

Here was a guy who wanted them to succeed, like "a family member," says Sanchez, who had worked as the de facto hitting and first-base coach before Coolbaugh's arrival. "When somebody got a hit, it was like he got a hit. When somebody struggled, he said, 'Hey, let's do this or that.'" Like Coolbaugh, Sanchez had been victimized by injuries and the numbers game. Like Sanchez, whose daughter, Isabella Sophia, was born on August 18, Coolbaugh was expecting a child — and was sure it would be a girl. On July 21, the day before he died, Coolbaugh took Sanchez out to lunch at a Mexican restaurant. "We couldn't stop talking about baseball," Sanchez says. "After I told him I was going to have a baby, his face changed. He told me that it's the most beautiful experience I would go through. That's when I knew how much he really loved his family."

The last time Scott Coolbaugh saw his brother, he stopped by

Mike's house in San Antonio. Mike had been with the Drillers less than a week. It's really starting to click, he told Scott. They spoke of the Drillers' August 8 game in Frisco, and how cool it would be to face each other on the field again. "I'm looking forward to seeing you," Mike said.

When a bat hits a pitch flush, the ball gains speed. Asahina's sinker ranges from 88 to 91 mph, but a field-level radar gun measured the speed of the ball at 101 mph just before it struck the side of his head. The ball that crushed Bo McLaughlin's cheekbone hit him at 104 mph. McLaughlin has a tape of that game and swears that the microphone hanging from the press box picked up the sound of bones breaking. He needed two operations to reconstruct his face. His left eye socket is wired in five places. McLaughlin lives in Phoenix, and whenever temperatures hit 113 or 114 degrees, the metal gets so hot that the whites of his eyes turn red.

Did Mike Coolbaugh know what hit him? McLaughlin remembers every instant of his accident. Asahina, on the other hand, seems to have experienced a protective amnesia. "I don't recall seeing the ball off the bat or anything else," he says. "It's like something in your deep subconscious says, *No, you're not supposed to see this.* So I don't."

Eyewitnesses declared that they saw the ball strike Coolbaugh in the temple. But the sound of impact wasn't that of ball on bone; it was more muffled, and a preliminary autopsy released two days later found that the ball hit Coolbaugh about half an inch below and behind his left ear. The impact crushed his left vertebral artery — which carries blood from the spinal column to the brain — against the left first cervical vertebra, at the base of Coolbaugh's skull. Squeezed almost literally between a rock and a hard place, the artery burst. A severe brain hemorrhage ensued. Mark Malcolm, the Pulaski County coroner who performed the autopsy, says he's never seen a case like it in his twenty-one years of work. "Man, that's a one-in-bazillion chance," Malcolm says. "A half a hair in either direction and it wouldn't have killed him."

Coolbaugh fell to his back, his hands landing on either side of his head. Sanchez bolted out of the batter's box and up the first-base line, reaching Coolbaugh first. Coolbaugh's eyes were rolling up into his head. His mouth spewed a whitish foam; his body convulsed. Sanchez backed up, sank to his knees, and dropped his head into his hands.

The two team trainers and the three doctors who came out of the stands raced to the prone figure. Within seconds Coolbaugh had stopped breathing. He was given oxygen and hooked up to a defibrillator. An ambulance was called, and Cole had Asahina run into the clubhouse, retrieve a trainer's first-aid pack, and carry it out to first base. It was the first time Asahina had stepped on a field during a game since his own accident twelve weeks before.

Sanchez was standing now, praying for Coolbaugh to be okay. He also begged God, *Please don't do this to me.* Then he heard someone near Coolbaugh say, "Don't go, Mike! Come back!"

The ambulance took him. Though Coolbaugh still had a pulse when he arrived at Baptist Health Medical Center, doctors determined that his life ended at the moment of impact. "He may have heard the crack of the bat, but that's it," Malcolm says. "I think he had no knowledge."

Cole received the news soon after in his office but didn't inform the players until a good ninety minutes later, after he'd been to the hospital and back. In the meantime Sanchez buttonholed everyone he could, asking if they'd heard anything. When the manager finally announced that Coolbaugh was dead, Sanchez started flailing. "I think I fractured my hand here," he says, pointing to the bottom of his right hand, "because I couldn't control it; I started punching everything. I hit the floor. I walked away and I went down, because I couldn't stop myself. I went down."

The phone rang in the Coolbaugh house in San Antonio around 9:15 P.M. Mandy had friends over to watch a movie, and when she saw it was Mike's cell phone, she answered quite appropriately for a pregnant woman whose mile-a-minute boys were finally down for the night. "Mike, you know I have people over here," she said instead of hello. "What do you *want?*"

The instant she heard the voice of Drillers trainer Austin O'Shea, Mandy knew the news was bad. Mike called himself whenever he got hurt. O'Shea told her only that Mike was at the hospital. He didn't want some insensitive MD telling her out of the blue that her husband was already dead. "You need to come up here," O'Shea said.

But a doctor phoned before she left for Little Rock. For Mandy the rest of the night was a blur. She got up early and saw that reports of Mike's death were on TV; the first camera crew came to her door at 7:00 A.M. Mandy knew she had to tell the boys quickly. When they woke up, she and Mike's mother sat in their bedroom, with the baseballs listing their birth weight and height, and their dad's Milwaukee and St. Louis jerseys on the wall. Mandy told them Daddy was hit by a ball, and God took him to heaven. "Well, if Daddy's up in heaven now, can I play with his bats?" Joey asked.

Mandy Coolbaugh is still irked by the way she answered the phone that night. But it's just like baseball to leave her with regret on top of grief. "This game will step on your neck and keep stepping on it," Burke says. "But something like this is almost too much to take."

Tino Sanchez kept sinking. There was a five-hour bus ride back to Tulsa, a tearful team meeting the next day, a night of torment in his apartment. He didn't sleep. He turned off his cell phone. Everyone kept repeating that it wasn't his fault. "People don't understand," Sanchez says. "They're still telling me that it was an accident, and that's been very supportive. But whether it was my fault or not, literally I killed a human being."

He would stare off, having clear flashbacks of his lunch with Coolbaugh, of looking to the coach for reassurance during his next-to-last at bat — every image from the moment they met to when the ambulance rolled away. Too many thoughts: *Coolbaugh's family. His sons. His wife, his wife, his wife.* Guilt engulfed Sanchez those first forty-eight hours. He felt as if he were drowning. "Mike is dragging me," he told a friend. "He's taking me with him."

The Rockies sent him home to Yauco. Sanchez began to calm, to sleep. He decided to go back to the Drillers because he felt he owed the organization and his teammates for standing by him, because he wanted to honor baseball and Coolbaugh. When he rejoined the team in Frisco, he almost felt ready.

But then came that strange dance with Scott Coolbaugh at first base, the silence, the guilt flooding back into his gut. The game ended, and as Sanchez was gathering his glove, a teammate pointed to two women along the rail who wanted a word. The stands emptied as he walked to a spot just by the on-deck circle. Scott's wife,

Susan, introduced herself and Mike's sister Lisa. Sanchez removed his hat and put out his hand, eyes stinging. Lisa's knees wobbled; she wasn't sure she could speak. Mike had spoken to the family, had said how proud he was of this one player on the team named Tino. She wanted him to know that. She reached out, crying too, and they grabbed each other tight.

It was about 10:30, two strangers touched by mercy. Lisa told Tino that the family was doing well. She said they didn't blame him. She cried again and said they would all get through this together. The stadium lights went dark. And for the first time since Coolbaugh died, Sanchez felt lighter.

He'll never be completely free. "I took his life away," Sanchez says, "and he took a part of my heart with him." But when Scott Coolbaugh stopped Sanchez during batting practice the next afternoon and repeated his sister's words and told him to call whenever he needed, it helped. When Mandy approached him outside the clubhouse in Tulsa in mid-August, it helped even more. That the Coolbaughs could push past their profound pain to comfort — no, absolve — him seems like a miracle, proof of grace. "Everything that's got to do with love is God," Sanchez says, "and that was pure love."

They saved him. Of that alone he's sure.

In the baseball world, the reaction to Coolbaugh's death went far beyond what would be expected for a player so obscure. It wasn't just because of the accident's freakish nature. Coolbaugh had played for so many organizations that, for many people, he'd become emblematic of how arbitrary the sport could be. More than $100,000 in donations has poured into the foundation formed to help his family. Not just from fans, but also from major leaguers who know that just one broken hand could have derailed their careers too — players who fear what Coolbaugh represented. He was the guy who always gets a flat tire on the way to the job interview, the one who never could get a break. He was minor league baseball, and who grew up wanting to be that?

Yet off the field Coolbaugh was an object of envy. He took his two boys with him everywhere, couldn't seem to breathe without holding them. And when O'Shea frantically scrolled through Coolbaugh's cell-phone directory that Sunday, it wasn't hard for him to find Mandy's number. He came upon the nickname "Gorgeous" and knew to hit Send.

"As a husband? He was perfect," Mandy says. "He just did everything right. He was the one who made sure we got to church every Sunday, who made sure the kids prayed before every meal, who tucked them in at night. He would leave me surprises everywhere. If he left before me for the season, he would leave handwritten notes, but he would hide them under pillows, in shorts, drawers, suitcases, a book I was reading. Saying things like, 'I'm going to miss you, but we'll be together soon. I love you.' He would call every night no matter how late it was just to tell me he loved me. When we had our kids, he wrote two songs describing our life. I was in labor, and he sat in the hospital and took out a notepad and wrote them down and would sing them to me. He sang all the time."

Mike built the crib and the changing table from scratch and installed the catcher's-mitt light in the boys' room. The only time in ten years that Mandy and he disagreed, she says, was over the third child. Mandy wanted one, while Mike worried that they couldn't afford another. She figured that the battle was lost, but on the day she learned she was pregnant, he couldn't have been happier. Money would be tight; he didn't care. Tears roll down her face as she speaks of it: Mike always put her first. "But I know you want this," he said.

"So there are days I question it," she says of his death. "Why would God want this to happen to the kids? I have no doubt it would've been easier for everybody if it had been me instead of him, because Mike would know where to go from here. He would know what to do."

He always made the decisions, after all, which is why his behavior this past spring seemed so jarring. Mike turned thirty-five in June, and indulged in midlife-crisis standards like calling old friends he hadn't spoken to in years. But he also had become fixated on death. Cancer had killed Mandy's mother in 2003, but not until recently had Mike wanted to know details of the moment she passed, how much pain she endured. He talked about buying burial plots for himself and Mandy. He insisted that Mandy, who never even knew his salary, learn how to handle the household finances in case "something happens to me." Just weeks before Little Rock, he spoke about her having a baby after he died. For the first time too he wanted her to sit out in the front yard and watch while he showed Joey and Jake how to play baseball. "If something ever happens to me," he said, "I want you to remember how to teach them to hit."

"Mike, you're not playing anymore," Mandy told him. "We're home. Nothing's going to happen to us."

Mike never let the boys mess with his equipment. Now Joey puts on his father's spikes and refuses to take them off. Now he wears his dad's oversized T-shirts all day. One day recently when Joey was hitting the ball, he told Jake, "Get out of the way. I don't want you to get killed." That was about the time he started badgering Mandy about Mike's black bat, the one in the attic. She didn't know what Joey was talking about, but, finally worn down, she climbed up there the night of August 10. Joey followed her and pointed to a black Louisville Slugger. "There it is!" he cried. A scrawl on a piece of masking tape wound around the handle identified it: the bat Mike used for his first major league hit, July 16, 2001.

The next morning Joey stands in the front yard swinging the black bat that's nearly as long as he is tall. His father taught him well. His swing is smooth. He lines the first three pitches twenty feet over the grass.

At times like these, Coolbaugh's death makes almost no sense. It's easy to see the accident as merely a random occurrence. For believers, though, the coincidences, premonitions, and precursors are signs of a plan: causal lines and connections revealed only after the fact, like a spider web after rain.

Or maybe it's nothing so grandiose. Mandy mentions all the tributes from Mike's peers, the hundreds of e-mails from around the world, the fact that the Drillers have retired his jersey. "If he went out any other way, would he have gotten all the respect he has from this?" she asks. "If he was in a car crash? When he wasn't called back to play, he said, 'I put in so many good years. I wish I could at least have the respect that I was a good player.' And by dying on the field, he did."

Now a DVD tribute is playing on the TV, and she's identifying the images as they fade in and out: Mike with his grandfather, Mike and Mandy mugging in a photo booth, Mike and Mandy dancing at their wedding, the last family photo, Mike's first home run, Mike walking in the surf with his sons. "His last day with the kids," she says. "He took us to Corpus Christi beach. Then he took a long walk with me. He hated sand between his toes, but he wanted to take a long walk. We walked for about an hour, the kids running in front."

It seems a brutal trade: a husband and father dies prematurely in return for a little respect. Mike Coolbaugh's wife, expecting a third child in October, is alone. His sons cling to empty clothes and the fading echo of a summer sea. Who can say why? It will have to be enough to know that in the most obscure corners, compassion lives and success has nothing to do with fame or money or even greatness. It will have to be enough to understand that such a notion is easy to forget, until a good man's dying forces the world to pay attention at last.

G-L-O-R-Y!

FROM GQ

RIGHT NOW ADRIENNE might be sick. It isn't funny. It isn't her stomach so much as her nerves, her heart, her history. Rhoneé, one of her closest cheerleader friends, has her eyes bugged out, standing outside the stall door, *"Adrienne? Adrienne, are you okay?"*

"I'm good," Adrienne is saying. "No, I'm good. I'm good."

She vomits. This is not good. Something is seriously wrong with Adrienne. At pregame practice in the gym an hour ago, she ran off crying — twice. Ran to the bathroom and slammed her fist into the stall door to get ahold of herself, to reclaim herself, to remember who she is: a Ben-Gal. Both times she returned to the gym with a smile, got in formation, front row, left center. "C-I-N!" she roared. "C-I-N! N-A-T-I! LET'S GO!"

She seemed *fine*. She seemed *Adrienne* again, five feet nine, a thoroughbred of a woman, broad shoulders, booming voice, the biceps and forearms of a sailor. She is not the drama queen of the squad, not even close, not one of the girlie-girls, with the super-yummy cleavages and the wee, wee waists and the sugary smiles. She is the iron-willed, no-nonsense, no-curls straight shooter of the squad — six-pack abs, forlorn eyes, too busy with her own too busy life to deal with a lot of crap.

"Is Adrienne okay?" shouts Shannon from the other end of the locker room. Shannon is perhaps best known for her extreme volume of sandy blond hair.

"What happened?" asks Shannon's very best friend and protégée, the demure Sarah.

"Is something wrong?" asks another, as news of Adrienne's nausea filters through the din of cheerleader chatter.

Cheerleaders are all over the place, half-naked, shrieking, sitting, squatting, kneeling in front of mirrors in the panic of an NFL Thursday night. National television! The game starts in just over an hour. This is crunch time, hair-spray time, false-eyelash time, Revlon-Orange-Flip-lipstick time. *"WOULD SOMEBODY PLEASE HELP ME? I CANNOT FIND MY MULTIPLICITY ESCALATE VOLUME WHIP!"* Some cheerleaders are in curlers the size of Budweiser cans. The locker room, reserved just for them, is hardly equipped for the machinery of glamour, and so most have brought their own full-length mirrors, power strips, extension cords, suitcases of makeup, curling irons, hose. *"Try my Bouncy Spray Curl Activator. You can totally glop it on."* The cheerleaders are all scream and shout, jazzed with beauty adrenaline, in thongs and hose and push-up bras, stretching, bopping, bouncing, assisting one another with hair extensions, pasting over tattoos, spraying tans, announcing newly discovered cleavage-engineering solutions — "Duct tape, girls!" — hooting and hollering in a primpfest worthy of Miss Universe.

"We look so awesome."

"Oh, my God, we do!"

Perhaps fittingly, there is a big storm coming, right now a cold front dumping rain and snow on Chicago, moving swiftly east, headed exactly for Cincinnati, promising to turn a balmy sixty-eight-degree evening into instant winter in a way that no one anywhere near Paul Brown Stadium is prepared to believe. *Maybe the storm will be late? Maybe it will get . . . delayed?* Charlotte, the mother superior of the Ben-Gals, the one responsible for all the rules — all the line formations, all the dances, all the praise, all the punishments, all the outfits — has to make a difficult decision: teeny-weeny skirts with white go-go boots and halter tops, or catsuits that hardly provide any better winter cover. The gals vote: catsuits. *"Please! Please! Please!"* They love the catsuits. There is nothing sexier than the catsuits.

"Is Adrienne *okay?*"

"Did you hear she is throwing up?"

"Oh, my God!"

*

Now, the men. The men are just super. Oh, the men think this whole thing is about them. That is so cute. That is enough to make any Ben-Gal roll her head to one side and get teary with admiration. *That is so sweet!*

Hello, men. Meet the cheerleaders. There are a lot of them. At first they are hard to tell apart in the same way kittens playing with a ball of yarn in a basket are hard to tell apart. Every single one of them you want to pick up and stroke and pinch and poke and take home. How can you *choose?* And what if you did take one home? Think it through. Where would you put the cheerleader? What would you feed it? Would you have time to play with it? Play with it in the way it longs to be played with? Yeah, that is one luscious volume of girl flesh.

The cheerleader is a fantasy. Let it go.

It. The cheerleader is an it. Are you aware that you have been thinking of this person as an *it?* Does that make you a pig? Nah. Or no more so than the next person, but that's not even the point. This is about the cheerleader. She is not trying to get your attention so much as she knows she has it. God, you're easy. You are not the real reason she has been up since five working on her hair, spraying on her tan, squishing her breasts together, and forcing them upward into a double-mushroom formation with the assistance of all manner of wired undergarments. Of course, you play a role in it. Of course. When you catch a glimpse. For barely a second on the TV. There on the sideline. Right after some blitz resulting in a crushing sack. She's there for you. Sharing your moment of glee. Bouncing up and down for you with her pom-poms, beckoning you to, yeah, pump-fake your way into her itty-bitty shorts.

Right. She knows you think this way, but there is more to the story: you are sorta beside the point. Oh, your weakness is *precious.*

This is good old-fashioned sex appeal. This is straight-up Marilyn Monroe pinup-girl shtick. Sexy-happy, happy-sexy. It's family-values sex appeal. Other than that, it has nothing to do with you.

People assume a lot. People assume cheering in the NFL is mostly about a girl trying to snag herself a big, beefy, stinkin' rich football player. That is not the case. The Ben-Gals are not even permitted to socialize with players, except at officially sanctioned appearances. This rule is strictly enforced. Zero tolerance. As for football itself, the game, the players, the stats, the formations — that stuff rarely rises to the level of actual conversation. For most of them, this whole thing has nothing to do with football.

Money? No, no, no. This is really, really, *really* not about money either. People assume NFL cheerleaders are within some vague sniffing distance of the good life, but a Ben-Gal is paid seventy-five bucks per game. That is correct: seventy-five bucks for each of ten home games. The grand cash total per season does not keep most of them flush in hair spray, let alone gas money to and from practice. "We have a rule book that's like *this thick*," Charlotte will explain to any woman interested in becoming a Ben-Gal, holding her hands four inches apart. "If you can demonstrate commitment and dedication and following-the-rules, you're good to go." It is not as easy as it sounds. Practices are Tuesdays and Thursdays at 7:00 P.M. — sharp — at which time a Ben-Gal must be in full uniform, full hair, full makeup, a state of readiness that can take two hours to achieve. She must then step on the scale. If she is more than three pounds over the target poundage assigned to her by Charlotte, she will have to attend the after-practice "fat camp," doing crunches and running laps for a half-hour after everyone else is gone, and she may not be able to cheer in that week's game. There are many other reasons a cheerleader can get benched: If she misses a single mandatory practice, she will not cheer at that week's game. If she misses four practices, she's off the squad. She is permitted just two tardies per season. Within fifteen minutes, it's a tardy, but sixteen is a miss. Two tardies equal a miss. No excuse is greater than another. Death won't get you a free pass, unless it's your own.

Given all the rules and the lack of distinct perks, it is difficult to understand why so many beautiful young women would eagerly and longingly choose any of this.

Charlotte sees it as a gift. Charlotte sees herself as a fairy godmother with a magic wand under which only a few select gals earn the privilege of the wave. "My most precious thing I can do is take a person and give them the tools that the program offers and watch them grasp it and watch them mature," she says. "Now, not everyone does that. But you take a girl like Adrienne. I mean, she was . . . *whew*! She was kind of . . . alternate for a while. You know what I mean? And now to watch her mature and develop into the program — she's a real special girl. She's had a hard life. She's the only single mom we have on the squad. Oh, I don't know why I'm talking about Adrienne. I mean she's not *Pro Bowl* yet. But still."

Contrary to popular mythology, not all NFL cheerleaders are bimbos or strippers or bored pretty girls looking to get rich. The Ben-Gals offer proof. Neither a bimbo nor a stripper nor a bored pretty girl would survive the rigorous life of a Ben-Gal. The Ben-Gals all have jobs or school or both. Kat and Sarah are sales reps. Sunshine is a database administrator. Shannon works at a law firm. Tara is a cancer researcher working toward her PhD. Adrienne works construction, pouring cement.

They have full and complicated lives. They don't need all this nonsense. They completely crave it.

Meet the Cheerleader: Rhoneé

This is my second year as a Ben-Gal. The first year, I commuted three hours from Liberty, Kentucky. That's how bad I wanted to cheer. I had never even heard of a switch leap before — where you do a leap and do splits and then switch legs? The first time I tried that, I felt like Peter Pan.

I have a bachelor's in chemistry and a bachelor's in biology. I just finished my master's in public health with an emphasis in environmental-health science. For two years, I worked on a project dealing with air quality within chemical-fume hoods. We came up with something called the smoke-particle-challenge method. I did monoclonal-antibody research for BD Transduction Laboratories. I worked for the U.S. government at the Center for Health Promotion and Preventative Medicine. We did soil sampling, water sampling, at military bases throughout Europe. That was the very best job I ever had.

When I first took my new job at PPD's global central labs, I didn't tell anybody I was a Ben-Gal.

I met my boyfriend when I was fourteen. He was sixteen and I was fourteen. We took our time. We got engaged in 1998. He asked me to marry him in Paris, at the Eiffel Tower. I was like, "I'm melting!" That's been a long time ago. He's going to have to, you know, renew that. His job takes him to Chicago a lot, so I don't see him a whole lot.

I don't feel thirty-two. I keep telling everybody you're only as old as you feel, and I don't feel thirty-two at all.

For me the Ben-Gals is about fulfilling a dream. Not many people out there can say they're an NFL cheerleader. I have never been so proud to wear such an ugly color of lipstick.

In Kentucky, cheerleading is big. But when a small-town girl tries out for

NFL cheerleading and makes it, that's huge. I made the front page of our local newspaper. Last year I was Miss November in the Ben-Gals calendar. Everyone kept telling me they wanted a calendar. I didn't tell a lot of people I had them. Word of mouth, people asked. I ended up bringing over 350 calendars back to my hometown. This year I'm not a month, but I'm still in the calendar. You feel like a superstar. I had trouble doing the sexy look. They teach you how to do that, to look like you're mad at somebody. This year I don't look mad. Just like I'm halfway smiling. I'm wearing a Rudi Johnson youth size small jersey that they cut up and made into a bathing suit. A youth size small.

The Reindog Parade is this Saturday. There will be five hundred dogs dressed like reindeer. I have to be there at one. Judging begins no later than one-thirty. The parade starts at two. I'll be walking in the parade with a reindog.

Adrienne comes flying out of the stall. She is not done throwing up but refuses to continue. She will not give in to a day of senseless, stupid puking. She is: Cheerleader of the Week! Okay, that news came days ago. So it's not *news* news, but tonight is the night, and so you could say reality is settling in. This is almost certainly at the center of the nausea Adrienne must conquer.

There are so many things that may or may not happen tonight. The storm may or may not come. The Bengals could score very many touchdowns. The Ravens could be called for holding or do an onsides-whatever kick. All kinds of . . . *football* things could or could not happen on this electrifying NFL Thursday night. But one thing is certain: Adrienne is going to be Cheerleader of the Week. She'll get her face on the JumboTron during the second quarter. Just her, dancing live, beside a sign listing her name and her hometown and her hobbies — in front of sixty thousand people in Paul Brown Stadium — for perhaps five or six or seven seconds.

Okay, listen. Adrienne poured the cement in Paul Brown Stadium. Way before she became a Ben-Gal. When she was just a regular person working under a hard hat in the freezing-cold wind blowing off the Ohio River. *She poured the forms.*

She does not feel worthy to be Cheerleader of the Week, and yet, at the same time, she does. (When in this life does *she* get a turn?) She is looking into the mirror, trying to get color into her cheeks.

She is trying to get ahold of herself. *She is a Ben-Gal!* A good Ben-Gal. An obedient Ben-Gal. She stays in her target-weight zone, 144–147, higher than most because of her muscle, her height. She does not smoke. She does not chew gum. She has no visible tattoos or naughty piercings. She curls her hair when Charlotte or Mary tells her to curl it, sprays it when they say it needs to stand taller or wider, slaps on more makeup when they demand bigger glamour. She works as hard as any other Ben-Gal at becoming what the coaches call "the total-package."

But Cheerleader of the Week? It is overwhelming.

"Come here," Rhoneé tells her. "Look in this mirror. Isn't this a great mirror? It makes you look so skinny. It's an awesome esteem booster!"

"All right," says Adrienne.

"Oh, you look awesome," Shannon tells Adrienne.

"You *always* look awesome," Sarah tells her. "I wish I had your abs."

"I wish I had your boobs," Adrienne tells her.

"I wish I had your hair," Rhoneé tells Shannon.

"*Everyone* wishes they had Shannon's hair," Sarah says.

"I wish I had your brains!" Shannon tells Rhoneé.

"Oh, you girls are so awesome," Adrienne says.

Cheerleader of the Week. It is not something most people in the world ever get even close to being. For that matter, most people don't get close to being a regular Ben-Gal — just thirty per year, out of a field of a couple of hundred who try out. Chief among the characteristics required to make the squad — beyond raw dance talent, a degree of physical beauty, a soldierlike level of self-discipline — is a specific consciousness. It is so obvious to those who have it and yet so fleeting, if at all attainable, to others. Ask a person who does not have it why she wants to be a Ben-Gal and she will say things like, "Because I love to cheer," or, "I have cheered my whole life," or, "For the camaraderie," or blah blah blah.

Now try this same question on a person who has within her the consciousness, the essence of what it is to become a Ben-Gal.

"So why do you want to be a Ben-Gal?"

She will look at you. She will look at you blankly, keeping her smile in place while her eyes tell the story: *What, are you from Transylvania or something?*

"Because it's a *Ben-Gal*," she will say, wondering politely and in her own generous way if you have perhaps suffered some brain injury at some point in your tragic life and if there is anything she can do to help make your world just a tiny bit brighter. Everyone, she thinks, wants to be a Ben-Gal. Pity the president of the United States, the queen of England, the winner of the Nobel Peace Prize, for not having the attributes necessary to become a Ben-Gal. It is difficult to accept that not everyone in this world has what it takes to become a Ben-Gal, and for those people, all she can do is pray.

That's what it takes to become a Ben-Gal. If a woman has any lesser sense of the glory, she will not make it.

Charlotte and her assistants, Mary and Tracy, and the captain, Deanna, maintain and constantly feed the glorification. Each Tuesday at practice, they decide who will cheer that week and who will not. Six people per corner, four corners, twenty-four cheerleaders. Six get cut. It depends on weight, glamour-readiness, dance-preparedness, all the factors of the total-package. Each Tuesday, as nonchalantly as possible, Charlotte reveals her choices for those who will cheer and those who will not, for those who have earned a coveted spot in the front of the formation and those who must go to the rear. "Sarah, you are in the back," Deanna will say, or, "Shannon, I want you up front." *Nonchalantly.* Because it's stressful enough. It's devastating enough to be left out or put in the back, even though most girls sort of *know,* can sense, can see the signs in Charlotte's eyes or see the way Mary is whispering to Charlotte and nodding and pointing and wondering, *Who told Sunshine she could dye her hair that dark?!?!*

The choosing goes on all season. Everything is about the choosing. Whose picture will make the Ben-Gals calendar? Who will be Miss January? Who will make the front cover and who will make the back? These choices are revealed Academy Award–style at a special ceremony in September, with slide shows, at a restaurant, with families invited, and lots of hugs and lots of tears, celebration, consolation, grieving.

There is more choosing. There is the biggest honor of all: the Pro Bowl. One cheerleader per season per NFL squad is chosen to attend the Pro Bowl in Hawaii. All season long, the cheerleaders speculate about who will be chosen. Charlotte will tell no one until it is time — she is the decider. No one understands the total-package better than she, herself a Ben-Gal from 1978 to 1989, a Pro Bowler, and a coach for thirteen years.

The choosing is the bait that keeps any Ben worth her Gal reaching toward her total-package goal. And each week there comes this choice: Cheerleader of the Week.

Who among the living would not vomit?

Now, the men. The men are super-adorable. The game has not yet started, and some of the cheerleaders are glamour-ready, so they have left the locker room to sign calendars by the stadium gift shops. "Who-dey!" some of the men chant, soldiers coming to battle, stomping up stadium steps toward nachos, hot dogs, beer. *"Who-*dey!" The idiosyncratic growl is a Bengal original and all the more popular now that the team is actually semicompetitive. Marvin Lewis came in 2003, turned the team around, gave football back to a woefully depressed Cincinnati. From a cheerleader point of view, it's been super.

Who-dey!

The men are dressed in orange and black, some with striped faces, crazy wigs, naked bellies pouring over Bengals pajamas, furry tails hanging from their asses. Soon this platoon rounds a corner, comes upon a table behind which four cheerleaders sit. Daphne, Sunshine, Kat, Tiffany. Glimmery and shimmery kitty-cat babes signing calendars, $10 a pop. The men say OH, MY GOD with their eyes, stop dead in their tracks.

"Who-dey!" the cheerleaders say, all sex and sweetness and growl.

The men suck in air, seem to have trouble releasing it. These gals are, well, *whoa.* These gals are — fuckin' A.

The cheerleaders give a thumbs-up. "Awesome outfits, guys!"

The men look at each other, at face paint, tails, fur. *Oh, sweet Jesus . . . we look like fucking idiots.*

"Who-dey!" the cheerleaders say.

The men dart away like roosters.

Outside in the parking lot, the men are more serious. Businessmen, banker types, tailgating, bonding. Somebody knew somebody and arranged for two cheerleaders, yeah, two real cheerleaders to come to the tailgate party for two hundred bucks. Heh heh. *Where they at? Are they coming? Where they at?*

Holly (blond ringlets) and Stephanie (brunette innocence) arrive.

"Hi!" They have doe eyes and dewy smiles. They wear little string backpacks in which they carry pom-poms. They slip off their backpacks. They slip off their white satin Ben-Gals jackets. "Ooh, it's chilly!" Holly says, revealing her naked arms and abundant bosom. "Ooh, that storm is coming!"

"I've been looking at you girls on the Internet," one of the businessmen says.

"Dude," says his colleague. *"Dude."*

"I'm Holly," says Holly. "Nice to meet you. Thanks for having us."

"You want some beef-barley soup?" one says to her. "Some kielbasy?"

"We have Chips Ahoy," says another.

"I'm good," says Holly.

"We're good," says Stephanie.

The conversation is not flowing. Just what *is* the purpose of this meeting?

The men give up trying to talk to the cheerleaders, turn to one another, laugh, grunt. Holly and Stephanie stand there smiling. Stephanie is shy, is a first-year, is taking lessons from Holly, who is also a first-year but who has so much more experience feeling gorgeous. "Would you guys like to learn a cheer?" Holly asks them.

"Uh, yeah."

"Come on, do it with us."

"Uh, no."

"Well, will you say it if we do it?"

"All right."

Of course, it starts to rain. The men dart under a tarp. Holly and Stephanie stay out in the rain, just a sprinkle, a trickle, a tickle, droplets for the cheeks.

"Let's go Bengals — ooh, aah!" the cheerleaders chant. "Let's go Bengals — ooh, aah!" They spin, throw their heads, offer ass. The men learn the words quickly. "Let's go Bengals — ooh, aah!" The men hold up their beer cans, toast one another. Heh heh.

The cheerleaders finish and wave, taking their jackets and pom-poms with them.

"Well, that was worth it," says one of the men.

Meet the Cheerleaders: Sarah and Shannon

Sarah: I work for Pepsi. I'm pretty much on call twenty-four–seven, so it's stressful. If somebody runs out of Mountain Dew and they're having a sale on it, they're calling me to get out there. I'm like, I know, I know.

Shannon: This apartment is two bedrooms, two baths. We met pretty much through Bath & Body Works in Lexington. We both went to the University of Kentucky.

Sarah: I called Shannon "Miss Hair." I was like, "Do you know Miss Hair?" That was my first meeting of Shannon. We've been best friends ever since then. We're so laid-back. Nothing gets us really fired up too much.

Shannon: I thought it would be awesome to be a Ben-Gal. You just put it way up here. You never really think you can get there.

Sarah: We dared each other to try out. To be an NFL cheerleader, I think every girl dreams.

Shannon: We use a great bra by Victoria's Secret. Body by Victoria Push-up Bra. We all had to get a bra that has a fixture that's real low. It's spandex and it's definitely tight, so it squishes and pulls. And then we have bronzing stuff to make it look more. . . . You do it, like, right here in the V. It makes it look like there's a shadow, so it makes your chest look bigger.

Sarah: Being a female, you gain water weight. You can go in there and think you're so thin, and it'll weigh you five pounds over. It gets frustrating. I eat lots of asparagus.

Shannon: There's, like, seven or eight things on our grocery list. For breakfast it's egg whites and oats — dried oats.

Sarah: People think we're so weird. You have to be very disciplined. And you have to get in that mind-set, because it is hard to follow. Very, very hard to follow. Like, a guy will ask you out on a date on a Wednesday night, and you can't say, "I can't eat, because I have to weigh in tomorrow." But you can't go and not eat either. So it is hard.

Shannon: I've been in situations with people who think, like, Oh, you're not having fun. Or, Why won't you go out? Because I don't want to eat.

Sarah: I usually say to a guy, "Let's wait until Friday night, because I have four days to get my weight back down after that."

Shannon: You saw us in practice in the short booty shorts and, like, a sports bra or bikini top? That's so they can see your fitness level. The stomach, the legs, the butt.

Sarah: They stand right in front of you with a clipboard. I don't like it, but it's a good idea. It has to be done.

Shannon: It's about glamour, fitness, and always being ready: full hair, full makeup, giving 110 percent.

Sarah: Of course, guys look at it as some type of sex symbol. But I don't think it's a thing that guys want their girlfriend to look like, you know what I mean? It's like a costume. It's not something I think a guy would like to look at every day.

Shannon: Egg yolk is actually what carries most of the fat. I'll usually put one yolk and about six egg whites just to have some fat and not just the protein.

Sarah: This month has been good. I mean, we gained a few pounds, but that helps you start again.

Shannon: I'm not usually this color. I tanned yesterday.

Sarah: If Shannon has her hair up in a ponytail, I swear, ninety-nine out of a hundred people would bet it's fake. It looks so perfect, and it's so big and thick. I bet ninety-nine out of a hundred would think it's fake. It's that good.

Shannon: You want some water?

There's more. For Adrienne, so much more. You have to understand at least one more important beat of the backstory: this is not the first time Adrienne has been named Cheerleader of the Week. The first time, she blew it. She may be the only Ben-Gal in history to screw up so royally. It happened three weeks earlier. Charlotte had told Adrienne, "This is it! You're going to be Cheerleader of the Week!" The night before the game, Adrienne was so excited she could barely sleep. Well, she did sleep. And sleep, and sleep, and sleep.

She awakened to the sound of her phone ringing. It was Missy, calling from the parking lot, where all the other cheerleaders had already gathered. *"Where are you?"* Adrienne hoped this was a bad dream. But, no, it was true. She had overslept. She threw on her clothes and rushed into the stadium, arriving not exactly Ben-Gal ready and more than sixteen minutes late.

"Tardy!"

The Cheerleader of the Week was . . . *tardy?* She was immediately dethroned. She would not be allowed to cheer, let alone be Cheerleader of the Week, and she would be penalized two games. Hey, late is late. Rules are rules. All the gals, including Charlotte, embraced her, grieved with her, over the tragedy that seemed for her so typical, so many almosts, so much dumb luck, so much stupid, rotten, dumb luck.

"It's my own fault," Adrienne told her teammates on that dismal day. "It's nobody's fault but my own."

For all her mother-superior-style discipline, Charlotte is a kind soul. Now here it is, just three weeks after Adrienne's disaster, and Charlotte is giving her a second chance at being Cheerleader of the Week. Here you go, Adrienne. Your sins are forgiven.

So maybe it's the generosity that is making Adrienne sick. The outpouring of love. The second chance that in so many ways feels like the last. The thought of going out there, in front of all those screaming fans, appearing on the JumboTron in the stadium whose concrete you yourself once poured.

After serious consultation with Mary and Tracy, Charlotte has an announcement. "Catsuits!" she bellows out into the locker room that by now is held in tight under a hanging cloud of aerosol. "Okay, girls, *catsuits!*"

"Catsuits!" the women shriek. There is nothing sexier than the catsuits.

Adrienne throws her head in the sink, runs the water at full blast, plunges. "Catsuits!" several tell her. "Catsuits!" They throw their arms around her, leap tiny leaps. "Catsuits!"

"Adrienne, honey, are you okay?"

Meet the Cheerleader: Adrienne

My mom was killed. She was murdered by my stepdad. I had just turned one year old. I break down sometimes. You can't think: why me? Things happen for a reason. You just can't think about the unknown.

This right here is a mud mat. It's just so we have a flat area to set our forms on. We poured all this today. We started back in the corner. Last pour, we did over three hundred yards.

The finishers finish the concrete and make it look pretty. And the laborers, which would be us, rake it and pull it close to grade. The rod busters are the ones that put all the rebar in. They are just totally rebar. Oh God, I would never want to be a rod buster.

Cement is not the same as concrete. Cement's an ingredient in concrete. Cement is the glue in concrete.

Working with all men, you realize that they really act like girls. They whine and cry. I'm not trying to be stereotypical, but they act different. I don't think of myself as a female at work. I think of myself as an employee. As a guy. Well, I don't want to be a guy. But I let them know: you're not allowed to call me names or treat me like dog crap.

With the Ben-Gals, with thirty girls in one group, you'd think it'd be a bunch of backstabbers, cliques, but it's not like that. They say I'm this role model because I have a little girl I'm raising on my own and I work construction. They say I'm an inspiration. They say that they're amazed I do all this.

I went to college, a full ride in track. I chose criminal justice. Afterward, I took a test in Lexington to become a cop. I got all the way to what they call the "rule of five," when they compare you to four other applicants. I had four speeding tickets, because I commute a lot. That ruined my chances. That kinda bummed me out. I was like, Screw this.

Then I took the county exam and failed by two points. I did bad because the whole time I'm thinking how I'm gonna kill my boyfriend because he made me late. He had my car, didn't get it back to me in time. The whole time I was thinking about him.

I had a change of heart. I decided I didn't want to be a cop. I didn't want someone to have to tell my kids someday that I'd been shot.

In the beginning, when I started working construction, the guys were horrible. The first day, my boss said I was a lawsuit waiting to happen. He made me bust up a twelve-by-twelve slab of concrete alone, with a sledgehammer. Then I had to carry four-by-fours, one after another. But I stuck it out. I've been doing this eight years. My body goes through a lot.

After my mom was killed, my aunt Pam wanted me. She really wanted me. After two years, she hitched a ride to Florida in the back of a truck to get me. People were upset with my grandma for letting me go. Pam was sixteen at the time. I call her my mom now. She ended up being a single mom with six kids. I think that's why I am the way I am today, because I was raised on love.

I told Pam I wanted to go on Ricki Lake and find my dad. I said I want to know who made me. She didn't want me to do that, but she talked to my aunts. I met him at a benefit. It was weird. I cried. Like, Wow. We went out to dinner the next night, to F&N Steak House, in Dayton. I ate chicken, and he was so mad. "I bring you to a steak house, and you order chicken?" I didn't want him to think I was money-hungry. He told me how beautiful my mom was, how much he loved her. He said he remembered the last time they made love was 1975, World Series Game 7. He followed newspaper stuff about me through high school but didn't know for sure that I was his.

I don't regret anything that's ever happened. I did get the shit end of the deal with Mom dying, but that was out of my control.

I never get hit on. A lot of my friends say I'm intimidating. Women who are successful or independent, guys are too scared to talk to. Which I hate. Because I'm a person.

My one fear is failing at being a mother. I don't want her to go through the things I went through. I'm afraid she'll be a priss. Her dad spoils her, which I hate because it makes me look bad.

Being a Ben-Gal in general is just awesome.

Being Cheerleader of the Week is awesome.

Taking photos for the calendar was awesome. It's a day that's all about you. Last year I ended up being Miss October. This year I was Miss December. It's heartbreaking when you don't make a month. People say, "Why didn't you get a month?" We don't know. But when you are a month, you feel great. Awesome. Sexy. Amazing. You feel like you're somebody.

Underneath this, I have jeans and long johns. And then I have two long-sleeves on, a sweatshirt, a sweater, and one of the poly sweatshirts that, like, covers you, and my Carhartts. You get cold. Your hands and feet and face and your nose. I'll thaw out later on tonight, like, a couple hours after I'm home I'll start thawing out.

I've always wanted to be a nurse. Ever since I graduated from high school. So I'm just gonna go back and give it a shot. I'm a people person. That's my calling. I get home, and normally I pick up my daughter, and we usually do homework. I have to study. I'm taking chemistry. In a couple years, I should be a nurse. I should graduate in three years. August 3, 2010.

You're not supposed to put a lot of stickers on your hard hat, because sometimes OSHA will think that you're covering up a hole. If these get a hole, you can't use them, because something might land on your head and kill you. But I have this sticker that says HOTTIE. *And* DEWALT *tools. The twin towers — one of the guys from the company, he was killed, so I have a sticker from him. And I have one that says* BITCH GODDESS.

I spit, too, like boys. Oh yeah. Just 'cause, I don't know. Your mouth gets dry or whatever. The guys are like, "Quit spittin'. That's not ladylike." And I'm like, I'm not a lady at work. Charlotte doesn't know I spit. Charlotte would kill me.

*

"Who-dey! Who-dey! Who-dey think gonna beat dem Bengals?"

"Nobody!"

It is time. The gals have pranced like a pride of lions out of the locker room and are standing in the tunnel, peering out. There are enormous Bengals walking around back here, but the gals notice only one another. They are cold. Sarah is holding on to Shannon for warmth; she always seems to disappear next to Shannon, mostly due to Shannon's hair, currently a celebration, a testament to extremes, curls streaming like Niagara Falls down her back, crashing into the bend of her bottom. "I'm so freezing!" Sarah is saying.

"Get a grip, girl!" Shannon says. "It's showtime!"

The catsuits are sleek, sleeveless, with necklines plunging deep and tight, allowing for blasts of perfectly spherical honeydew breasts. Each gal wears a thin glitter belt around her hips and a pair of white satin wrist cuffs crisscrossed with orange laces. Hair is high, broad, glued in place. Makeup is paint, pasted on thick. Tans are air-sprayed, darker in the V to accentuate the total-package. Perfect. Exactly perfect.

Of course, it might not *really* rain and ruin all their hard work. It might not. The storm is probably still over Indiana or something. It could hold off. The balmy sixty-eight degrees has gone kerplunk to fifty-two. Outside, in the stands, ponchos are starting to come out.

"I don't know about the eighties look, with all this hair," Lauren says. "Do you think we look like poodles?"

"I can't brush my hair after," Tiffany says. "I have to wash it."

"I have to soak it," Brooke says.

"You guys!" team captain Deanna interrupts. "Think how lucky we are to be here, and savor every moment!"

"Sexy, ladies!" Rhoneé shouts. "SEXY!"

"SEXY!"

"Wooo!"

With that, they fire out of the tunnel like bullets out of the barrel of a gun. One arm up, pom-pom shaking, "Let's Get It Started" blaring, "Who-dey!" "Who-dey!" Fireworks shooting into the night sky. Any one of them could burst into tears of excitement. Some of them will. Adrienne will absolutely not. Adrienne is all game face, determination from a twisted gut. She's on the five-yard line, next to Maja and Tiffany, all the cheerleaders lined up forming a chute, a welcome path for the football players, who come chugging out like beefy boxcars. "Who-dey! Who-dey!" The gals stand like ponies, one knee up, one arm down. Pom-poms shimmering.

They take to their corners, and the kicker kicks off, and the stadium erupts into "Welcome to the Jungle," Axl Rose crooning his timeless anthem, gals dancing stripper moves with hips, ass, roll head, whip hair. Then they just as quickly retreat into sweet pom-pom action. Sloopy. Feelgood. Hicktown. Worm. Tweety. All the dances have code names.

"We're on Pump, right?"

"We're on Worm!"

"Oh, my God!"

Four sets of cheerleaders, one set in each stadium corner, Charlotte and Mary and Tracy with walkie-talkies, demanding coordination, demanding precision: "Lines, ladies, *LINES!*"

Six minutes into a scoreless first quarter, most of the hair is . . . flat. That was quick. That is a shame. But that's okay. At halftime they'll charge back to the locker room and drop to their knees in front of mirrors waiting like lonesome cousins. Hot rollers. Curling irons. Makeup. Spray tan. Primp! There is not much time to re-create perfection, but they'll do their best.

Six-yard line. The football players are trying to pound the ball in. *Come on, football players!* The cheerleaders hold their arms up, smile, keep their arms high, and jiggle their pom-poms, shimmer shimmer shimmer. They have turned themselves into candles burning flames of hope.

A field goal. Okay, we'll take it. Who-dey! "Jungle Boogie." Celebrate with the cheerleaders; watch them bounce like balls.

It isn't until three minutes twenty-six seconds into the third quarter that Carson Palmer completes a forty-yard flea-flicker touchdown pass to T. J. Houshmandzadeh, but that is not even the point. The sky has done it, finally opened up — sheets of rain. The gals valiantly bump and grind to "Bang on the Drums," the touchdown song, in the glimmery downpour. Forget hair spray, forget makeup. It is all washing off now, washing down, soaking them. Wet cheerleaders! The JumboTron appears itself to experience the orgasm. Exploding wet cheerleaders! The cameras are all over the cheerleaders. The gals are screaming, laughing, howling, forgetting everything. Forgetting the fucking construction site, the man who murdered your mother, the store calling for more Mountain

Dew, the chemical-fume hoods and the smoke-particle-challenge method, the men who don't call, and all those egg whites and protein shakes that have made this moment possible. Forget it all! This is it. This is a rain dance, a joy dance, a jet-propulsion explosion of cheerleader love, love to the crowd, love from the crowd, men in striped pajamas, wigs, tails, painted bellies washing clean, oh, those men are super, super-duper adorable. Who-dey drunk.

In the stands cheering for Adrienne is Pam, the woman who hitchhiked decades ago to Florida to scoop her up. Also, Adrienne's cousin Leslie, her aunt Nancy, her little aunt Sandy, and her regular aunt Sandy — the one who takes the picture. It is the first time they get a picture of Adrienne on the JumboTron. In the picture, Adrienne is smiling and looking up. It's just her face next to her name and her hometown and her hobbies. In that moment, she doesn't even know she is on the JumboTron. She is damp, out-of-her-mind joyful. Free.

Weeks go by, months, a year. Adrienne is looking at the picture. She keeps it in a storage box in her spare bedroom. She doesn't know what else to do with it. She thinks she looks awesome. She thinks she looks like a real girl. She thinks she looks happy. Probably she should display the picture, downstairs with her collection of tiny ceramic angels. She can't believe this is happening.

MARK KRAM JR.

Forgive Some Sinner

FROM THESMARTSET.COM

HEAVYWEIGHT CHAMPION Lennox Lewis had just beaten a suddenly old Mike Tyson that evening at The Pyramid, and now Dad
and I were back in the courtyard of our hotel in suburban Memphis, far from the crowds that spilled from the arena and choked
the highways leading from downtown. I remember thinking as we
sat there how the years had accumulated on him, how he had been
unable to walk even short distances in the clammy haze that June
week without breathing hard; I had to drop him off at the door
wherever we went. But even so it had been a busy trip, full of big
meals and good cigars and long conversations punctuated with
laughter. He had never been in better spirits than when he had
work to do, nor happier than when he had some jingle in his kick.

He'd come to Memphis to begin a book on Tyson, whom he had
profiled for *Esquire* and later interviewed for *Playboy*. I had picked
him up at the airport that Monday, and we spent the week on
the go, slipping out of crowded press conferences and going off
in search of local color. We stopped by Graceland, the National
Civil Rights Museum, and the crossroads in Mississippi where the
bluesman Robert Johnson supposedly sold his soul to the devil —
only to end up dead by the hand of a jealous husband who poisoned him. I had come along because I always did in these later
years, if only to drive the car and serve as a sounding board for his
ideas, plans, and assorted gripes. We were close that way. Given that
we both also wrote under the same byline — I am not technically a
junior — I sometimes wondered where he left off and I began. So I
was not surprised when there was only one credential waiting for us

at the press center, where the bewildered young man behind the counter looked at us and said: "So there are two of you." Stuff like that was always happening.

With age seventy bearing down hard upon him as we convened in Memphis in 2002, Dad had by then written for better than forty years, during which he had become celebrated, later disgraced, and I would like to think ultimately redeemed. While some of his contemporaries were better known, few surpassed his virtuosity with the language. For thirteen years during the golden era of *Sports Illustrated* in the 1960s and 1970s, he followed Muhammad Ali and others on the boxing beat across the world, a journey highlighted by his classic coverage of "The Thrilla in Manila" between Ali and Joe Frazier in 1975. That story has been widely anthologized — including in *The Best American Sports Writing of the Century* — and is looked upon by the keepers of the canon as one of the finest pieces of sports reportage ever. A friend told me that, even today, a famous comedian he knows is able to extemporaneously recite the lyrical opening passage: "*It was only a moment, sliding past the eyes like the sudden shifting of light and shadow, but long years from now it will remain a pure and moving glimpse of hard reality, and if Muhammad Ali could have turned his eyes upon himself, what first and final truth would he have seen?*"

Good as some of his old stories are, it always seemed to me that his own was better than any of them; I only wish he had written it himself. Growing up in a working-class section of East Baltimore, where his father had punched a clock for forty years at Chevrolet, he played some baseball, discovered books, and hustled a newspaper job that led him to *Sports Illustrated* in 1964. I would like to be able to say that the work he did was the sum of his experience there, but the truth is more complicated than that, and perhaps ultimately irretrievable. I can only piece it together so far. But I do know that by the spring day in 1977 when he was called in and fired, he had wandered far from who he had been to a place walled in by shadows. He overcame some very long rounds to piece together a comeback with *Esquire* and fashion a lively finish in 2001 with his contrarian take on the Ali-Frazier trilogy, *Ghosts of Manila*. By then, he had turned an unforgiving eye upon himself.

"Novels, short stories, plays — I had those things in me, but I just never got down to work, did I?" he asked as we sat at the hotel. "Creatively, I just never grew the way I should have."

I just looked at him, uncertain exactly what to say. Then: "You still have plenty of time."

Carefully, he held a lighter to the bowl of his pipe. "Well," he said, letting the word hang there. "What it comes down to is discipline. I just never had it. You have far more than I ever did."

I changed the subject. "So, what did you think of Graceland? Elvis had some place. You should have gone onto his jet with me. You could have used it in the book."

Clouds of smoke curled in the air as he said, "If there is a book."

Given where he'd started, you'd have to admit he'd come far. Without any experience, he strolled into the *Baltimore Sun* in 1959 at age twenty-six and asked to see the sports editor, Bob Maisel, who just happened to have a job opening that summer day. Newspapers were like that then, especially sports departments; you could walk in off the street and see someone without an appointment. Dad handed Maisel a crumpled piece of typescript as a sample of his writing and told him, yeah, he had attended the University of Georgia. Fine, Maisel supposedly replied: the job is yours if you can prove it. Dad walked out of the building, went to Western Union, and wired himself a telegram that read, in part: THIS IS TO INFORM YOU THAT MR. KRAM HAS SUCCESSFULLY COMPLETED THREE YEARS OF UNDERGRADUATE STUDY. Signed: Dean of Men, University of Georgia. Dad doctored it up some and took it back to Maisel, who glanced at it casually and gave him the job. "Could have happened that way," says Maisel. "Probably did, 'cause I know I would have asked if he had any college."

Baltimore became the subject of a cranky yet affectionate piece by Dad seven years later, on the eve of the 1966 World Series between the Orioles and Dodgers. The story was called "A Wink at a Homely Girl," the title drawn from the epitaph of fellow Baltimorean H. L. Mencken, the cigar-chewing, self-proclaimed agnostic who had waxed with loveliness: "If, after I depart this vale, you ever remember me and have thought to please my ghost, forgive some sinner and wink your eye at some homely girl." "Wink" told of a Baltimore that has long vanished, the insular world Dad knew as a boy in the Canton section of East Baltimore, where men sat in the shadows of corner saloons reading the racing page and women wiled the summer evenings away on the stoop exchanging gossip. With a hard edge that assailed his old hometown as a "*tunnel between*

Washington and Philadelphia," the Baltimore piece ended with a special poignancy if you knew the circumstances from which he sprang. *"Sonny, change will come here, too,' said Uncle one day by a pier, while the nephew stared vacantly at a freighter crawling through the water, and wondered where it came from, where it was going and if he would ever go."*

I think back on that old row house on Hudson Street in East Baltimore as a place of reassuring rhythms, of large beds and candy bowls and the cheerful presence of my uncles: Gordon, who sold chewing gum for a living; and Gerard, who still cuts hair at his barbershop in Canton. But the house I remember is far from how Dad experienced it in the 1930s and 1940s, when the two-story, three-bedroom affair was occupied by thirteen warring members of the Kram-Arthur clan. Funerals were always gala events for the women of the family, who commented cheerfully on the expert preparation of the deceased, usually over a piece of crumb cake in the dining room. Beer and hard liquor flowed under clouds of cigar and cigarette smoke in the adjoining parlor, consumed with ascending glee by men with sagging bellies. Dad still went by his birth name back then, "George," though he was better known as "Sonny" or "Otts" and — curiously — "Randy," which he later picked up as a baseball player because, as his former army buddy Vince Stankewitz told me: "It made him sound like he could run faster."

For an athletic young man who graduated high school 134th in a class of 144, the only escape from Hudson Street was playing ball. A three-sport star at all-boys Calvert Hall High School, Dad won second All-City honors in baseball his senior year, during which he played against Southern High School sophomore Al Kaline, later a Hall of Fame player for the Tigers. He *did* attend Georgia, but only for part of one semester, when he dropped out and was promptly drafted into the army. But instead of being shipped off to Korea, he slipped into a special services unit and played baseball at Fort Benning. There, he once slammed two home runs in a game off of Cardinals pitcher Vinegar Bend Mizell, who later became a Republican Congressman from North Carolina. Ex-big leaguer Tito Francona played with Dad there. "Good second baseman," says Francona, whose son Terry manages the Red Sox. "George could have batted leadoff in the big leagues if he had caught a break. Did he ever sign?"

I have an old contract in a box somewhere that he signed with the Pittsburgh organization upon his discharge from the army in February 1955. But it remains unclear what happened that year, just as it remains unclear how his career ended a year later with the Queen City Packers in the Man-Dak League in North Dakota.

He always said he had been beaned.

But I wonder.

"Otts showed up at a party that spring with Mercurochrome on his temple, and I said to him, 'What happened to you?'" says old friend Charlie Hartman, who grew up not far from Hudson Street. "He told me he had gotten beaned. But there was no swelling underneath, so I said, 'Otts, I think you just got cut out there, and you had to come up with a story.' Oh boy, did he get angry! He said, 'You SOB, we'll settle this tomorrow in the ring. Meet me at the Y at noon.' So for three rounds we pounded away at each other, then he threw his gloves down and said he was never talking to me again. But he got over it."

Whatever happened out in North Dakota, it had to have been a letdown for him to come back to Baltimore in the spring of 1956. Married the previous December to my mother, Joan, he settled in with her in a small room above a fish store her grandparents owned in South Baltimore — and that July I was born. He once told me he stopped by the Lord Baltimore Hotel to see Francona, then a rising player with the Orioles. "I took a bus downtown and we had lunch," said Dad, then employed at Maryland Dry Dock. "I asked him, 'What happened, Tito? Why you and not me?' Then he took a cab to Memorial Stadium and I took a bus back down to the fish house." But it was during this period that he began reading for hours on end, given books early on by his old high school friend John "Jack" Sherwood, later a fine writer for the *Washington Star*. "Reading a book is not something Otts would have done back in school," says Sherwood, who also cultivated in Dad the notion of writing for a newspaper. "They were pals," says my mother. "So when Jack got a job on a newspaper, your father figured he would give it try." Sherwood even helped Dad "fix" the telegram he gave to Maisel, saying now: "He showed it to me and I said, 'Otts, no one is going to believe that.'"

It was not until then that Dad shed "George," "Sonny," "Otts," and "Randy" and adopted the name he and my mother had given me three years before: Mark. By virtue of the fact that he had become a palindrome — his name spelled the same backward as forward — he immediately became somewhat of an oddity at the *Sun*, where the newsroom was still the way you've seen them in old B-movies: noisy typewriters, gin bottles in the bottom drawer, and card games between editions. For $65 a week he worked the copy desk and covered high school games. Within a year he was doing features and later a twice-a-week column, "Another Day," gorgeously impressionistic pieces such as one on the perils of boxing called "All Gone and Quite Forgotten," the beginning of which read: *"For the faceless and the nameless, for those who know the smell of squalor and poverty, the fight game can be an exit . . . a light in a moonless world . . . a ride on a golden elephant."* A *Sun* copy editor forwarded his clips to a former colleague at *Sports Illustrated*, and in January 1964, the young man who just a few years before had been scented vaguely of smoked eels suddenly found himself there in a stable of emerging stars.

One of them was fellow Baltimorean Frank Deford, who had been a copyboy at the *Evening Sun* before Dad worked there. "I remember thinking: 'Where in the hell did this guy come from?'" says Deford. "From the day he arrived at *Sports Illustrated*, he was looked upon as sort of a mad genius." Early on they became close friends, even taking a stab at a screenplay together. Inevitably, they would talk about their old hometown, the characters there, the burlesque houses on The Block and so on. And yet as Deford observes pointedly: "We never talked about *his* Baltimore." But I think I can understand why. That Baltimore stood in his psyche as if it were a downed airplane entombed in some uncharted jungle. Strip away the vines clinging to the wreckage and it is there you would find *his* Baltimore, a place where one day as a small boy he tiptoed down the narrow stairs of that Canton row house and came upon the cold body of his deceased grandfather, arranged in a wooden coffin and bathed in an amber light. For years, Dad held that memory close, only telling me when I had grown and he began letting go of some of his secrets.

What I remember now is his back, the way it dampened with an enlarging oval of perspiration as he sat with his big shoulders crouched over the typewriter. Steeped in piles of newspapers and

assorted coffee cups corroded with tobacco ash, he labored amid a
drifting cloud of pipe smoke in Room 2072 wrapping up a piece on
the National Marbles Tournament, which would later be included
in *The Norton Reader.* I remember him chasing away a young woman
that day who'd come early for his copy. Even at seventeen I had to
laugh, because he used every second allotted to him by a deadline,
be it an hour or weeks. He'd get up, jam his pipe into his pocket,
and pace, up this corridor, down the other, light his pipe and end
up back at his office, where his typewriter remained with the same
piece of paper in it on which twelve words had been written. His editor Pat Ryan refers to this as "stall walking" — what jittery thor-
oughbreds do to calm down — but eventually that sweat and tobacco paid off in prose that was like slipping into a velvet boxing
robe.

Managing editor Andre Laguerre unlatched whatever raw abili-
ties Dad possessed. The legendary Frenchman did not care if he
had been to Georgia for three years or even three hours; in fact, a
"Letter from the Publisher" in March 1968 played up the phony
telegram he concocted at the *Sun* as the act of a resourceful imagination. Laguerre divined in him a deep reservoir of moody sensi-
tivities that could swell into uncommonly seductive prose. That became abundantly clear as his work developed in the ensuing years
in an array of sharply observed pieces, none better than his 1973
profile of the forgotten Negro League star Cool Papa Bell called
"No Place in the Shade." That story begins: *"In the language of jazz,
the word gig is an evening of work: sometimes sweet, sometimes sour, take the
gig as it comes, for who knows when the next will be. It means bread and
butter first, but a whole lot of things have always seemed to ride with the
word: drifting blue light, the bouquet of leftover drinks, spells of odd dialogue and most of all a sense of pain and limbo. For more than anything the
word means black, down-and-out black, leavin'-home black, gonna-find-me-
a-place-in-the-shade black. "* Dad would come to think of that piece as
his finest effort at *SI.*

But it would be his work on the boxing beat that would bring
him acclaim. Down through the years, few in that Runyonesque
galaxy of unrepentant rogues were spared the sharp point of his
critical lance, including Ali, his entourage, the new Madison
Square Garden, and rival promoters Bob Arum and Don King.
"Boxing is a world of freebooters," says Mort Sharnik, who covered

boxing with Dad at *SI.* "And in that realm Mark was looked upon with much apprehension." And yet as cynical as Dad could be, I think Sharnik is on to something when he says that he was oddly naive. "Whenever you told him something, he would draw on his pipe and cock his eye in this skeptical way," says Sharnik. "But a true cynic would not have allowed himself to be drawn in by some of the questionable characters Mark did. In that way there was always some rube in him."

From the old Madison Square Garden to Mexico to Europe, Dad found his voice in the bold personalities that populated boxing back in the 1960s. But it was his coverage of a young Muhammad Ali that captured the eye of the public, which occasionally flogged him with letters accompanied by small boxes packed with animal excrement. Such were the passions that followed Ali into his government-imposed exile from the ring in 1967 for his position on the Vietnam War. By the end of it three and a half years later, the unjustness of that ordeal and the emergence of Joe Frazier set the stage at the new Madison Square Garden for "The Fight of the Century" in March 1971. With the jammed streets surrounding the Garden buzzing over the upset by Frazier, Dad hopped a subway back to the Time-Life Building, where the issue was being held open for his story at a considerable sum per minute. But in the one hour he had been allotted, he composed a story brimming with lyrical imagery that observed of Ali: *"He has always wanted the world as his audience, wanted the kind of attention that few men in history ever receive. So on Monday night it was his, all of it, the intense hate and love of his own nation, the singular concentration and concern of multitudes in every corner of the earth, all of it suddenly blowing across a squared patch of light like a relentless wind."* Dad used to say those one-hour jobs were "ball breakers": "Editors pacing outside your door; you could feel their blood pressure go up whenever you stopped typing." He did it again three years later for Ali-Frazier II.

I have a photograph of him from the old days. In it he is standing on a train platform at Penn Station in New York with his bag by his side and leather coat folded over his hands. Sharply dressed in blazer and turtleneck, sideburns descending in the fashion of the day, he appears as Sharnik remembers him: "Like an escapee from a Dutch fishing fleet." Dad had become an ambassador of rail travel in 1969, when engine trouble forced a jet he was on to return to Heathrow Airport, where the passengers were evacuated through a chute onto a foam-covered runway. He later told me, "I went to the bar and said: 'Give me a triple, and work your way down. And then work your way back up again.'" Overseas journeys were then effected by passage on the *QE2*, during which he'd indulge in cold vodka and caviar and delve into Schopenhauer, who'd become an object of envy ever since he learned that the nineteenth-century German philosopher had withdrawn from society into a cork-lined room. Once, upon his return from Europe, I am told he submitted an expense account that included a charge and explanation that became legendary. Boat: $10,000.

But fear of flying was just a piece of his psyche on display for colleagues, who would come to think of him as beset by demons. I used to see it unravel whenever the summer sky would blacken, the way he would scurry to the basement for cover at the sign of lightning. Down there he would stay, the blood gone from his face, hands atremble. Going to the doctor was also out of the question for fear of hearing that he had cancer, and he simply could not bring himself to attend a funeral — including his own father's. But as a young boy, none of this appeared strange to me. Nor did it seem curious that he was juggling two lives that very seldom intersected: one in Baltimore, where I lived with my mother and two younger sisters; and the other in New York, where he constructed a world disconnected from the four of us. I simply looked forward to his appearance back home: a slam of the cab door, footsteps up the walk, and there he would be, his bag spilling over with the New York papers and perhaps the typescript of a story he just completed.

"Here," he would say, handing the piece to me as he poured himself a J&B. "See what you think of this."

I would later hand it back to him and say, "Really good. Is it running soon?"

"Couple of weeks," he said. He poured himself another then said, "Do me a favor, would you, champ?"

"What is it?"

"Never become a writer."

"Why?"

He sighed and said, "It changes you."

Even then I knew he drank too hard. As a teenager, I would sit up with him at the dining room as he dissolved into disjointed soliloquy. In other settings he would become abrasive, and I have been told stories of how combative he could be. For years a story has been told how he and Norman Mailer once exchanged blows at a Manhattan cocktail party, which Dad years later described in an interview with *Philadelphia Magazine*: "He made some uncalled-for remark and then head-butted me. It became a full-scale battle. While we were on the floor, he bit my arm. Jesus. It was one of those things." Colleague Bud Shrake told me Dad even challenged Laguerre at the bar one evening: "I remember Mark standing there and telling Andre, 'Get off your stool, fatty, and I'll knock you on your ass.' Andre just looked at me and a few others and said, 'Would you please get him out of here?'" Shrake says Dad expressed profound remorse the following day — he always did. He would shake his head and ask, "Did I really do that?"

Edgy gloom engulfed Dad when Laguerre was forced into retirement in early 1974. Says Ray Cave, an executive editor under new editor Roy Terrell: "Mark simply could not adjust." With the safe harbor that Laguerre had provided him gone, the panic disorder that had plagued Dad since his young adulthood had begun weighing in again, striking him at random and leaving him reeling with rubbery legs, lightheadedness, cold sweats, and nausea. Years later he would describe these episodes in an essay for *Men's Health*: *"The overall feeling is that you are going to die, instantly — not tomorrow, right now."* A psychiatrist could have helped with this, but his fear of doctors coupled with what he called the *"embarrassment of being looked upon as a blazing neurotic"* propelled him deeper into the embrace of alcohol, which only caused his symptoms *"to rebound more fiercely the next day."* Editors who admired him would come to regard him as unreliable, understandably so given the fact that his ever worsening terror of flying rendered him incapable of accepting two events for which he had been slotted: the Evil Knievel canyon jump in Idaho and Ali–George Foreman in Africa.

But he had to go to Manila for Ali-Frazier III. "It was a war getting him over there," says Cave, who remembers that he and Pat Ryan were perpetually waging a rear-guard action in defense of Dad. "You always had to account for his eccentricities, and say to the people who were bothered by him: 'Shut up!'" Cave remembers Terrell had "every conceivable feeling that it was a really bad idea to send

Mark to Manila," but Cave persuaded him otherwise, in part because he would be sitting in that week as managing editor while Terrell was on vacation. Says Cave: "I had a great deal at stake in that issue." So Dad gulped down some tranquilizers and flew to Manila on the same plane with Ali, who would slip into the row behind him and rattle the back of his seat, intoning: "Ali and Mark Kram, we're going to die, die, you hear!" George Plimpton — who had stepped in to cover Ali-Foreman — noted in his book *Shadowbox* that the trip was so traumatic for Dad that "all that was left of him to unload in Manila were a few flakes of dandruff."

People have told me that they can remember where they were when they read his coverage of "The Thrilla in Manila." I only remember that I was at the University of Maryland, unaware that, on the other side of the world, Dad had become romantically involved with a young woman who later became his second wife. But that did not prevent him from doing his job: his six-page advance included a Q&A with Philippines President Ferdinand Marcos. From what Dad later told me, he then attended the "Thrilla," supplemented his own reporting with the aid of *Newsweek* correspondent Peter Bonventre and others, downed some more tranquilizers, and flew back to New York. There, he handed in a story that Cave played with photographs by Neil Leifer across eight pages, which opened with stirring side-by-side head shots of the battered rivals that led perfectly into the text. The lead portrayed Ali at a dinner held in his honor at the presidential palace, then cut to Frazier in the bedroom of his villa: *"The scene cannot be forgotten: this good and gallant man lying there, embodying the remains of a will never before seen in the ring, a will that had carried him far — now surely too far."*

"Mark came through in spectacular fashion," says Cave. "The story he did was more than splendid. He rose to the occasion. And it was the last occasion."

I would like to be able to say that Dad did not have a hand in what followed, that he was undone by the Machiavellian creatures that have always populated *SI*. But that would be letting him off the hook. Living a separate life in New York had led to continual money problems — "the shorts" — he attempted to alleviate by drawing advances on his expense account, always a wink-and-nod proposition he abused. He also played the horses as if he knew what he was doing; I can just see him sitting there drawing up betting slips for some senseless exotic wager at Roosevelt Raceway. While he still delivered some very fine pieces — including a profile of Herbert Muhammad, the power broker behind Ali — he grew increasingly irritable as he paced the corridors, especially when Cave departed to *Time* and Ryan to *People*. By then he had also accumulated a legion of adversaries in boxing — which Sharnik calls "a stewpot in which everyone is mixing in the venom." But Dad acted as if he were beyond scrutiny, steered by the incalculably wrongheaded belief that how he comported himself with King and others was irrelevant just so long as he remained unbiased in his copy. The only explanation I can think of is that alcohol joined with his increasing desperation to cloud his judgment.

The end came in the spring of 1977 on the heels of a crooked boxing tournament promoted by Don King, whom Dad profiled two years before for a cover story. When it was revealed that the records of some of the boxers in the draw were cooked, rumors began circulating that certain New York sportswriters were "on the take" — including Dad. *Sports Illustrated* conducted an internal investigation and alleged three episodes of what it labeled "gross misconduct": Dad accepted $1,100 from Ali corner man Dr. Ferdie Pacheco, one-half of his fee from *Sports Illustrated* for publishing excerpts from his book; he accepted $5,000 from Rocky Aoki, the Benihana founder and speed boat enthusiast Dad had profiled in March 1976; and he utilized a researcher on that story who was not employed by *Sports Illustrated*. (Dad always said the payments from Pacheco and Aoki were part of book arrangements; the researcher was a young man he was then trying to help.) While there was no formal finding of a financial link with King, Dad conceded years later that he did receive payments from King for some screen work he had done; King was then looking into expanding his interests into Hollywood.

Terrell called him in. "Really a mixed-up guy," Terrell told me before his death. "I was very fond of him personally. It killed me to fire him . . . but it was all I could do."

"Where are you *going*?"

I had just parked the car and found him crossing the lawn of his apartment building in Washington to his bedroom window, which he always left open a crack for air. He stepped over a hedge, shoved the window higher, and hiked himself up on the sill. Then he slipped inside.

"Get a key, would you?" I said when he opened the door for me. "You could have hurt yourself."

"The guy at the front desk usually lets me in," he said with a laugh. "Either that or somebody just leaves the door open."

I looked at him and said, "In Washington?"

"What have I got to steal?"

"Jesus, you need a keeper."

But I should not have been surprised that he did not carry a house key. He did not carry a wallet either. Whatever he had on him could be found in his trouser pockets: a few crumpled-up dollar bills, his pipe and some tobacco, a pill bottle, and several packages of Sweet'N Low that he had purloined from the coffee shop. He did not own a house because living in apartments allowed him to pick up and go. Nor did he know how to drive a car — a good thing, given his drinking. Others did that for him, along with a variety of small tasks that seemed beyond him: getting books from the library, chasing down copies of his old stories. He probably had them somewhere, but they were buried beneath haphazard piles of papers, under which I inexplicably found an old car battery. I remember he used to stay up until 4:00 A.M. or later and not climb out of bed until 3:00 P.M. It was useless to even think you could reach him by telephone before then.

For years it seemed that Dad had disappeared. With the usual expenses that come with divorce and the demands of a second family, he eventually found himself tossed into the suburban sprawl of Staten Island, where one hungover morning he peered out the kitchen window and told me: "Another beautiful day in the Petrified Forest." Immediately upon his dismissal from *Sports Illustrated*, he coauthored a book with an alleged hit man, called *Blow Away*, and wrote a novel, *Miles to Go*, on the quest to shatter the two-hour barrier in the marathon. Neither sold. Some assignments came from a talented young editor at *Playboy*, Rob Fleder, who had wondered what happened to him, but it was not enough to keep him from calling an old colleague and asking if he could use a connection to line him up at *National Enquirer*. By then he had become a sad story, which former baseball owner Bill Veeck, an old friend, commented on to Thomas Boswell in a story in *Inside Sports*: "I wish, just once in my life, I could write five hundred words as well as that man. Journalism prefers a simon-pure mediocrity to a touch of tarnished genius."

I remember how Dad used to seethe back then, how furious he would become at the success of others. Why *him* and not *me?* While I did not look upon him as a cruel person, it was not unusual for him to say cruel things, philosophically ruminating that "no writer should have this many children." I remember thinking: *Is he trying to tell me something?* Broke, he accepted a sports columnist job for the start-up *Washington Times*, owned by the Reverend Sun Myung Moon. He stayed a year, grew bored, and began writing screenplays for a few thousand here and there. None were produced. Increasingly, he became obsessed with money — with not having it — and that locked him up creatively, leaving him disinclined to tug at the tiny threads that might lead to rewarding projects. For him to become interested, it had to possess the potential to bring a windfall. By now into his fifties — and looking it, with that gray, untrimmed beard — he had no patience for picking up an occasional assignment for low pay, especially from a generation of editors who would invariably ask him: "Are you using a PC or a Mac?" He still used a typewriter.

By then I had also become a writer, ignoring his advice of so long ago. I think I did it in part to draw closer to him, to get a leg up over the wall he remained behind. As a boy and into adulthood, I looked upon him with wide and pardoning eyes, even as I knew that he had behaved poorly in certain ways. But as the years passed I became worn down by his continually sour disposition, the apparent indifference he had toward my young family and our aspirations. I also became increasingly weary of our shared identity, given the fact that it carried with it a patina of shame. Occasionally, I would overhear conversations where the subject would come up, eighth-hand gossip that welled up from the psychotic delight journalists take in the troubles of others. One story that circulated even had it that the Manila piece was actually written by Bonventre, who told me with a laugh: "Nowhere near it. I gave him some cold, bare facts on the dinner at the palace, which I know he would have done for me. And he turned it into poetry." But Dad never summoned a defense for any of it, which only underscored the validity of whatever crazy rumors bubbled up in his chaotic wake.

God, how I brooded over this.

For years.

And then one day I developed pneumonia.

I was so weakened by fever that I was unable to climb from under the covers.

Three weeks passed, and as I began feeling better, it occurred to me that I had not heard from him. I wondered how long it would take.

I gave it another week. It became a standoff.

Months elapsed before the phone finally rang one July evening.

"Where have you been? Is something wrong?"

"Nothing," I said. "But you know, I was sick and never heard from you and well . . . I just wanted to see how long it would take you to pick up the phone and call."

There was a long pause. Then he said quietly, "I know."

Subtly, his outlook began to change for the better. Not coincidentally, he began seeing a psychiatrist and taking antidepressants, which capped his panic attacks and allowed him to open up. Revelations began spilling from him, of fears that had preyed upon him as a boy during World War II and beyond — of young children his age crippled by polio and of anti-aircraft batteries lined up in Patterson Park in East Baltimore. He became obsessed with lightning strikes because a player on an opposing sandlot team was struck dead before his eyes by one in center field. And he remembered some advice he had once gotten from Laguerre, who had gotten it from Raymond Chandler years before over drinks in London: "Always try to leave three things on each page that matter to you as a writer. A word, a phrase, a line of dialogue, an observation of character. By the end of a story, these tracks of craft will lead to quality." I remember thinking what an education our conversations had become.

Wild tigers stalked him during his sleep, yet in the light of day he gradually gained stronger footing. Not to say that he stopped bitching — especially when his assignments dried up — but he began showing up in places that he once would have avoided. When my grandmother died, we attended the funeral and later sat at the now-abandoned house on Hudson Street, where he passed up a drink himself but poured one for me and slid it across the table, saying: "To better days." He stopped by to see his brother, Gordon, then dying of cancer, and the two of them sat in the cool shade of a tree and reminisced in a way that had always been so hard for them. He became progressively less irritable with his second family, and endeavored — albeit belatedly and with some awkwardness — to begin trying to build a bridge back into the lives of his first. Cooking became a hobby for him, and it was common for him to bake pies during the holidays for the checkout ladies at the supermarket. And I remember that he was always losing his pipe, which he once looked for high and low with some noisy aggravation, only to discover it at the bottom of a simmering saucepan of chili. He had placed it on the edge of the pot and it had fallen in when he went to answer the phone.

By then he had also recovered his bearings as a writer. David Hirshey, then an editor at *Esquire* and long an admirer, began assigning him pieces that, if they did not solve his unending financial crisis, gave him a place to exercise his talent. Of the subjects he profiled for *Esquire* — including actor Marlon Brando and drug enforcement agent Michael Levine — none were better than his incisive piece on Ali, called "Great Men Die Twice," during which he attended a blood-cleansing procedure Ali underwent at a South Carolina hospital. That 1989 piece began: *"There is a feel of a cold off-shore mist to the hospital room, a life-is-a-bitch feel, made sharp by the hostile ganglia of medical technology, plasma bags dripping, vile tubing snaking in and out of the body, blinking monitors leveling illusion, muffling existence down to a sort of digital bingo. The Champ, Muhammad Ali, lies there now . . ."* For years Dad had struggled with a biography of Ali, piling up pages that shuttled from publisher to publisher, but only when Hirshey landed as an editor at HarperCollins did it occur to Dad to look at both Ali *and* Frazier.

Going back into that world was not easy for him, if only because it was the very place that so long ago had been the scene of what he now viewed as his own foolish behavior. But he had a unique understanding of both Ali and Frazier; I think he saw some of himself in both. He had an appreciation of the struggle Frazier had endured, of how he had come out of the South Carolina low country and carved an identity out of his flabby body. Far more complex was his view of Ali: Dad yielded to no one in his appreciation of his ability in the ring — and wrote that again and again — yet it irritated him that even this astonishing talent alone was not enough, that it had to be invested and elevated in ways that were to him so perplexing. The Ali he had encountered had been a flesh-and-blood figure, given the same corrosive foibles and appealing decencies as other men. And that is precisely how Dad portrayed him in *Ghosts of Manila* in 2001. In a comment aimed less at Ali than his chroniclers, he observed in the introduction to the book: *"Of worldly significance? Well . . . countless hagiographers never tire of trying to persuade us that he ranked second only to Martin Luther King, but have no compelling argument with which to support that claim. Ali was no more of a social force than Frank Sinatra."* A large percentage of the reviews were glowing, even if the Ali bloc weighed in with no small degree of animus.

So Dad had a hop in his step when we hooked up in Tennessee for Tyson-Lewis. Tyson had exploded in fury at Dad during the *Playboy* interview in November 1998, saying at one point: *"Please, sir, don't take it personally. I'm a very hateful motherfucker right now . . . I know I'm going to blow one day."* But Dad looked upon Tyson with a certain empathy and hoped to get a closer look at him in Memphis. Better than twenty years had passed since he had been to a live boxing match, yet he slipped into gear that week just like the old days, jotting down ideas as they occurred to him on scraps of paper and jamming them into his pocket. Seated in an auxiliary press section in the upper deck at The Pyramid, he looked upon the exchanges in the far-off ring with an increasingly disinterested eye, as if he had just uncovered his plate in a fine restaurant and found a peanut butter sandwich. Back at the hotel, he entered the elevator and happened to run into Leifer, whom he had covered "The Thrilla in Manila" with and whom he had not seen since their days together at *Sports Illustrated*. Leifer did not recognize him until Dad finally spoke up, "Hey, Neil! Don't you remember Mark Kram?" Embarrassed, Leifer says now, "He just looked so different from the Mark Kram I remember."

We both had planes out the following day: I had an early one back to Philadelphia; he could not get one back to Washington until well into the evening. Increasing concern for his health had prompted me to ask him: "Should I stay with you tomorrow and catch a later flight?" He waved me off as he had earlier that week, when he blamed the suffocating heat for his difficulty breathing. I had asked if he wanted to go to a hospital and get checked out. But

he said he was fine, and I wanted to believe him. As we sat by ourselves in the hotel courtyard, we puffed on cigars and talked of the
plans we each had at home. He had an assignment for *GQ.* "Jesus,
can you believe it?" he said wearily. "Sixty-nine years old. And still
out there scratching." Small bugs swarmed in the spotlights that
flooded the pool area a few feet away. Both of us were dripping with
perspiration and thinking of going upstairs to our rooms when suddenly the sprinkler system came on. We sat there in the cooling
spray. And we had a long laugh.

There was no book. Five days later, I got a call at 3:30 A.M. that he
had died of a heart attack. Given his uneasiness with funerals, he
probably would have cringed at his own. But we had one in spite of
him. A friend flew in from California for it, and a group of his old
high school pals drove down from Baltimore the previous evening
for the wake. Near the end of the service, I had a friend read the
closing passage from "A Wink at a Homely Girl," and as the words
washed over me, I pictured a young man on that deck of that
freighter as it plowed out to sea, hands braced firmly on the railing
as the shoreline faded before his eyes. The *New York Times* carried a
very kind obit. *SI* printed nothing.

I have had a lot of time to think of him since then, of our days together that now seem to have been so brief. A popular online
sports columnist has since written, in a piece that applauded the
virtues of *Ghosts of Manila,* that Kram should have had a better career. I think Dad probably would have agreed with him (albeit
probably not in the ways that the writer supposed). But I am entirely unclear how you quantify any of this. Journalists today are
judged less by their actual writing than by their presence on television; Dad did not even appear on live TV until a year before his
death, when the publishers asked him to promote *Ghosts of Manila.*
Uneasy in the advancing age of talking heads, he remained an-
chored in a long-ago world that placed a premium on what appeared on a piece of typescript, always full of crossed-out words in
what would always be a forlorn search for eloquence. I am sad-
dened that he did not feel it added up to much, because I certainly
think it did, that in forty years behind that clanking Royal that was
always overdue for a new ribbon, he produced a body of work that
still stands up.

I have since ended up with his papers, box upon box of folders jammed with tobacco-scented old clippings and yellow legal pads busy with notations, the bare bones of projects that always just remained good ideas. I found it interesting that one of them also contained a long list of vocabulary words that he had come across in his reading. Opening up the boxes one by one, I have come across an array of other items: snapshots of his children, the crinkled-up dismissal letter from *SI*, and a column from the *London Times* that I cannot help thinking I was supposed to find. The piece concerns the funeral of the playwright John Osborne, who had apparently harbored some old grudges that his family would not forgive. Four people were forbidden entrance to the church, an act that columnist Libby Purves found inexplicable. "Who are you to presume that the glorified John still hates anybody?" Purves observed. "In the clear dawn of eternity, all things are reconciled." That would be good.

TOM CLYNES

Above and Beyond

FROM BACKPACKER

NORMALLY, I WOULDN'T LET a few downed trees get in the way of a good bushwhack. But as I surveyed the wall of redwood trunks lying across the creek that had been my pathway into the mountains, I had to consider the possibility that I had met my match. Each of these trees was at least 10 feet in diameter, and more than 250 feet long. Piled up like pickup sticks hurled by a livid giant, the fallen trunks created a formidable barrier to further ascent.

My two companions and I sat down on mossy rocks to assess the situation. Going over the wall of wood was likely impossible without climbing gear, which is not allowed in the park. Going under might have worked, had we brought along snorkels and wetsuits. Going around would entail a battle with head-high nettles that ran up and down the 50 percent grade at creekside. From recent experience, we knew that the climb could take hours, and several pints of our blood.

We had come to this remote basin in northern California's Redwood National Park to hunt for the world's tallest living tree, a coast redwood nearly 380 feet in height. Explorers had discovered it last summer, in a remnant stand of old growth in the southern section of the park. Growing quietly on a mountainside for centuries, the newly crowned giant is some 70 feet taller than the Statue of Liberty, or about as tall as a 40-story building. Its discoverers christened it Hyperion, after the Titan (of Greek mythology) who fathered the sun.

The news was followed, as these things must be nowadays, by a press release. E-mailed from the tourism people in Humboldt County, the message claimed that Hyperion "is too far from any trail to visit." But, it consoled, "adventurers piqued by the discovery have plenty of other opportunities to explore old-growth redwood groves in Humboldt County, the tallest, largest and most pristine in the world."

Having spent time in Humboldt, I knew the superlatives were well deserved. But among my several inveterate weaknesses is an attraction to extremes. I'm a sucker for the biggest and tallest and fastest, the super-jumbo jets and Everests and top-fuel dragsters. I hit the Reply button and typed a message to Richard Stenger, author of the press release. "Why couldn't an ambitious backpacker visit Hyperion?" I asked.

A few minutes later, Stenger was on the phone. "I gotta tell you," he said, "this one is really off the beaten path. They say it's on an incredibly steep slope with thick underbrush that you'd have to bushwhack through. If you knew where to go. But the park folks aren't telling anyone where it is. Everyone who knows anything about this tree is sworn to secrecy."

All of which sounded, to me, like a pretty good challenge. And so a few weeks later, I found myself driving up the Redwood Highway with photographer Mark Katzman and photo assistant Derek Southard. From San Francisco north to the Oregon border, California's coastal population thins out and the forests and fogs thicken. Lacking good harbors, far-northern California had little to grip the roots of settlers. Fortune-seekers came and moved on, following the boom-and-bust cycles of the gold rush and the timber stampede.

We overnighted in Eureka, 225 miles north of San Francisco. There, in an Irish pub, Katzman revealed that he was less than confident about our mission. "So we're just going to show up," he asked, "with no credentials and no notice, and try to find this tree that no one wants us to find?"

That was essentially the plan — although I had put a call in to the park's interpretive specialist, Jim Wheeler. Chief ranger Pat Grediagin was supposedly the only Park Service employee who knew the exact location of Hyperion. The *New Yorker* had quoted Grediagin as saying "there's been a lot of talk about this discovery. I'm just worried that someone will get a wild idea to try to find this tree."

That would be us. But I reassured Wheeler, on a drizzly Thursday morning when we met him at park headquarters in the town of Orick, that ours was a responsible quest. If we managed to find the tree, I told Wheeler, we wouldn't reveal its location, either in print or in conversation. But Wheeler, and the other rangers we would meet, didn't seem overly concerned about our intentions.

"Mostly," Wheeler shrugged, "nobody around here thinks you have any chance of finding it."

According to the rangers and tree researchers, Hyperion's location needed to remain secret for the tree's own protection. In the past, vandals and over-adoring fans had injured other champion trees whose locations had been publicized. In the early 1960s, rangers signposted what was then believed to be the world's tallest tree, making it the centerpiece of the park's Tall Trees Grove. Ten years and thousands of visitors later, names had been carved in the trunk and the top of the tree had died — an outcome attributed, by at least one scientist, to soil compaction around the roots. Researchers found damage in the crown of another champion redwood, the Mendocino Tree, that suggested it had been clandestinely climbed. Even Luna, the redwood made famous by Julia Butterfly Hill, was deeply gouged by a chain saw a year after Hill had saved it from loggers.

But those trees are near roads and populated areas. Hyperion, by contrast, is far off-trail. Along the Redwood Highway, motorists will happily pay to drive through a tree, but only a small percentage will actually get out of the car and hike more than a few yards from a road, no matter what the attraction. Still, I reiterated to Wheeler that Hyperion's secret would remain safe with us, if we managed to find it.

"You won't," he said.

Jim Wheeler, still boyish at fifty-one, came up to this area in 1978, "looking for Bigfoot," he jokes. He has worked at Redwood National Park for twenty years, long enough to be known as a "homesteader" among the service's mostly itinerant staff. Wheeler offered to take us out to some of the park's representative areas. We drove up Bald Hills Road, then walked down a steep trail to the Tall Trees Grove.

"The old-growth redwood forest in Humboldt County is the tallest tree canopy in the world," Wheeler said, beginning what sounded like a well-practiced spiel. Even though all but 4 percent of that old growth has been logged, the thirty-nine state and national parks in redwood country retain much of the diversity of the original forest. In deep valleys and hidden ravines that the loggers' machines couldn't reach, there remain thousands of acres of undisturbed old growth.

Set inside a hairpin turn on Redwood Creek, Tall Trees Grove is a treasure of the national park system. Below the top canopy of mature redwoods are subcanopies of moss-draped western hemlocks, Douglas firs, big-leaf maples, and tan oaks — many of which would be considered massive if they were anywhere else. The spot has a timeless quality that's reinforced by the sweet smell of California laurel leaves.

Industrial logging started in far-northern California as early as the 1820s. Using axes and crosscut saws, it took the first lumberjacks nearly a week to bring down a giant redwood. But with the introduction of chain saws, bulldozers, and skidders, the pace of harvesting increased. The opening of the Redwood Highway (CA 101) made it easier to ship the lumber out, and towns like Orick boomed.

In 1917, a few prominent conservationists traveled to Humboldt and Del Norte Counties along a highway littered with felled giants. It wasn't until they reached the area that is now Redwoods State Park that they stood in pristine forests. Realizing that all the big trees could be lost in the not-so-distant future, they founded the Save-the-Redwoods League to fund land acquisition, education, and research.

We followed Wheeler onto a gravel bar in the middle of Redwood Creek and dug our lunches out of our packs. It was here that a National Geographic Society naturalist named Paul Zahl wandered in 1963, following rumors of "great timber" in this still-unlogged part of the valley. Zahl recalled that he walked out onto the gravel bar for a rest.

"While catching my breath," Zahl wrote, "I scanned the treetops before me and suddenly started. One particular redwood rose above the others like a giant candle."

At 367.8 feet high, the tree — at first called the Libbey Tree, then simply the Tall Tree — would hold the record from 1963 until the late eighties. More importantly, its discovery would energize conservationists' effort to establish a national park.

As Wheeler described the park's beginnings, I turned discreetly and scanned the steep, mazelike country upstream. Somewhere up there, Hyperion had been quietly holding forth for decades, while lesser trees hogged the limelight. The next day, we would try to find it.

Paul Zahl's discovery attracted worldwide attention, including a *National Geographic* cover story. But the region's newfound fame would accelerate the economic decline of towns like Orick. In 1968, President Lyndon Johnson signed a bill authorizing the acquisition of 58,000 acres for the creation of Redwood National Park. A decade later, Congress expanded the park by 48,000 acres, effectively forcing out most of the timber mills.

According to silviculturists, the area that became the park could have supported only two more years of logging before the harvestable timber was gone. But as 2,500 jobs vanished, the park and federal government became scapegoats.

In 1977, Orick loggers put their chain saws to an old-growth redwood log and carved out a nine-ton peanut, as a sarcastic gift for President Jimmy Carter, who had approved the park's expansion. They loaded the sculpture onto a truck and drove it to the White House with a sign reading, "IT MAY BE PEANUTS TO YOU, BUT IT'S JOBS TO US." Carter's aides refused the hunk of wood, and it made the long trip back to Orick.

Over the next two decades, Orick's population dwindled, businesses shuttered, and lumber mills were eventually outnumbered by backwoods methadone labs. In 2000, the NPS outlawed camping on the beach south of town, exacerbating the bitter feelings. Park property has been targeted by pipe bombers and arsonists, and rangers have been threatened.

That night, we passed the peanut sculpture near the southern edge of town, lying in a yard near an abandoned hotel. Farther north, the Lumberjack Tavern beckoned, its neon sign depicting an ax-carrying logger eyeing a pink martini glass.

During boom times, locals apparently stood three and four deep at the bar. But on this night, maybe fifteen patrons were inside, most drinking beer through thick beards. Bartender and owner Mark Rochester greeted us warmly. He wore a LIVESTRONG bracelet on one wrist, and a tattoo of a LIVESTRONG bracelet on the other wrist. Over his shoulder, the Commander-in-Chief peered at us from a picture hung behind the bar. I asked Rochester if he knew anything about Hyperion.

"That *#*&# tree!" he bellowed, setting down a pitcher of local microbrew in front of us. "Don't get me started!" Rochester had recently purchased the tavern, and was changing its name to Hawg Wild, to attract more bikers.

"The Park Service won't tell us where it is. They're sitting in their multimillion-dollar headquarters, made of redwood that they can cut down and we can't, and they don't want us to know where the tree is, even though we supposedly own it. And you know what? When the liberals get in power there's going to be even more rules."

Rochester popped a packaged chicken pie in the microwave, then came back over. "We had no decision in anything the Park Service has done," he said. "They have systematically choked the life out of this town."

As he grabbed a Budweiser for another patron, a woman waiting for her shot at the pool table came over to our end of the bar. "I got a different take on it," she said. "I'm pro-park, and I love trees. But I work at the mill. Sometimes it feels like working in a graveyard. But it pays the rent. And no, I don't know where that tree is."

Moments later, a woman in the corner of the room caught my eye. She came over and leaned close to my ear. "I work for the parks," she whispered. "And I know too much to even talk to you."

The next day, I sat down to breakfast with Katzman, Southard, and Jerry Rohde, an educator and author who's written several hiking guides to redwood country with his wife, Gisela. Thin, bearded, and bright-eyed, Rohde had agreed to accompany us on our tree hunt, though he cheerfully warned us that the bushwhacking would be "brutal."

We pushed aside coffee mugs and plates of eggs, and laid out Rohde's collection of maps. Triangulating various rumors and hunches, we narrowed our focus down to a few sections of old growth that flanked a couple of small streams that empty into Redwood Creek.

We drove to a trailhead, then hiked down to Redwood Creek. The seasonal bridge had been removed for the winter, so we pulled off boots and gaiters to wade barefooted through the frigid water.

On the other side, we put them back on again — only to soak them almost immediately as we headed up a feeder stream.

As we waded upstream, the trees on either side got larger, and the notch that the creek had cut into the mountain got deeper. After an hour of sloshing, Katzman spotted a small piece of orange loggers' tape, attached to a bush. We scrambled up the steep bank and found that the tape marked the beginning of a short trail, still fairly fresh. It led through thick stands of rhododendron into a grove of redwoods.

We were surrounded by tremendously tall, thick-trunked redwoods — trees that you really have to see to believe. Though the bases were spread across the hillside, the crowns were intertwined in a nearly unbroken canopy, starting about 150 feet above our heads. From the ground it was impossible to tell if any one tree was taller than any other.

On one tree, Southard found a metal tag stamped with three digits. We had assumed that Hyperion would have a tag on it, to mark it as a research specimen. This trunk did seem fatter than the rest, but it was hard to tell whether it was taller. I had brought along a laser rangefinder, which uses a laser beam to calculate the height of a target object. But without a clear shot at the top of the tree, the device was useless.

Rohde, who had heard there was a clear-cut within a few hundred feet of Hyperion, headed up the slope to try to find a vantage point. He returned and confirmed that there was indeed a clear-cut but that it offered no unobstructed sight line to the tree.

Could we have found Hyperion? It seemed too easy. Would the researchers have marked their path with something as obvious as loggers' tape, visible from a creek — even a creek as little-traveled as the one we were on? Probably not, we concluded, as we hiked back to the trailhead.

Chris Atkins, an amateur naturalist who lives in Santa Rosa, first visited the redwoods in the 1980s. "I was in awe of their size, their beauty, and their longevity," said Atkins. He found himself drawn back to redwood country again and again, and eventually he got in touch with a McKinleyville postal worker named Ron Hildebrant, who kept a database of tall-tree measurements. (Jim Wheeler, the ranger, told me that he once came across Hildebrant counting rings on a downed redwood, using a magnifying glass. "He was up to 1,300 when I came along, and it wasn't an estimate. He was counting every single ring.")

When Hildebrant's work schedule left little time for exploring forests, Atkins teamed up with Michael Taylor, who shared his craving for fresh air and biological extremes. Eventually, Atkins and Taylor blew $3,000 apiece on high-end laser rangefinders. (Atkins described our rangefinder, which cost only $500, as "pretty much useless.")

Prior to the advent of these devices, measuring a redwood could take all day — if you could even manage to get surveying gear into position. The rangefinders allowed Atkins and Taylor to focus their energies instead on the logistics of getting deeper into the parks, to explore the patches of old growth hidden in remote basins.

In the late 1990s, the pair decided to search the entire range of the coast redwood, to document every living tree taller than 350 feet. When they began, only about twenty-five such trees were identified. As of early 2007, Hildebrant's database contained 136 individual redwood trees exceeding that height — most of which had been discovered by Atkins and/or Taylor. In 2000, Atkins made it into the *Guinness Book* when he found the 369-foot Stratosphere Giant in Humboldt Redwoods State Park.

"After the discovery," Atkins said, "someone asked me if we might ever find a taller one. I said the odds were pretty low. We thought we had pretty well mopped it up."

Redwood National Park has no car-camping sites, and backcountry camping is allowed only on gravel bars in Redwood Creek — not a good idea during rainy season. So we bedded down at the Palm Motel, a seen-better-days place that's one of two lodging options in Orick. Owner Martha Peals, a Tennessean whose card introduces her as "pie-maker, entertainer, bed tucker," said she hadn't had "too many up here looking for that tree, but I've had people from all over the world come here to see Bigfoot."

Still, she offered to help. "I'll tell the waitress in the morning," Peals said. "Her husband works for the park. Her name is Betsy." As we headed to our rooms, she called out, "Don't you worry, I'll find out where that tree is for ya."

The next morning dawned sunny and calm. As I sat at the counter in the Palm Diner, Betsy came over with a coffeepot and met my hopeful eyes. "I wouldn't have a clue," she said. "And my husband doesn't know either. They won't tell him where it is."

I was halfway through my lumberjack omelet when Rohde called to say that his knee, which he had tweaked yesterday, couldn't take another day of bushwhacking. He was staying home.

Indeed, our party had taken a few good hits. Katzman, recovering from rotator-cuff surgery, had jerked his shoulder while hoisting himself over a behemoth log. I had dislodged a waterlogged burl that was my foothold while climbing over a downed tree, and fallen through a brittle web of branches, bruising my hip. Only Southard was unscathed.

"I hope you boys find that tree," Martha Peals sang out to us as we packed up the truck. "But it'd be even better if you ran into Bigfoot out there. Then you could bring me lots of customers and make me lots of money."

We stopped by the park's information center to grab a better map. Wheeler, who was raising the American flag, saw us and shouted out, "Did you find the tree?"

I told him about the tree with the metal tag. Wheeler just smiled and said that there are several trees tagged with numbers, identifying them as subjects of various studies by experts at Humboldt State University.

Before crossing Redwood Creek, we reviewed our clues and concluded that we had probably been up the correct drainage, but on the wrong side of the feeder stream. A green-shaded area on the map identified an extensive grove of old growth on the other side, a little farther upstream. But judging from the bunched-up contour lines, Hyperion's potential location would be steeper. Much steeper.

The day before, Redwood Creek had been up to our ankles. Now, after a night of rain, it was knee-high. If we got more rain, we would need to hightail it back before the rising water cut off our retreat. As we plunged in, a salmon jumped next to Katzman. Carrying his pack full of lenses and camera bodies, Katzman picked his way over slippery rocks through the swift current, balancing with a walking stick in one hand and a carbon-fiber tripod in the other. I followed him, scanning the mountainside above us. Somewhere up there, the world's tallest living thing was quietly growing ever taller.

Sixty million years ago, redwood forests covered much of the Northern Hemisphere. But as a result of climate change, and then harvesting, the three species of redwood are now found in only three small areas. The giant sequoia, the world's largest tree in terms of total volume, grows in seventy isolated groves in California. The dawn redwood, once thought to have been extinct for 20 million years, has been discovered in remote valleys in central China. The object of our quest, the coast redwood, is found along a 40-mile-wide, 470-mile-long strip in northern California and southern Oregon.

The coast redwood is no mere mortal tree, and I mean that in the most literal sense. Its scientific name, *Sequoia sempervirens* (forever-living sequoia), refers to its ability to regenerate. Under the right conditions, a single tree can live for two thousand years or longer, protected by a foot-thick bark layer that is fire- and insect-resistant. Like other conifers, a redwood can regenerate from seeds. Should it topple, it can also regenerate from sprouts that shoot up from fallen trunks, thereby keeping its genetic line unbroken over millennia.

But the coast redwood has an Achilles' heel: a shallow root system that grows only a few feet under the surface. The trees that blocked our ascent up the creek had most likely been on the losing end of an epic wrestling match with the wind. As a gust levered one tree's roots free of the earth and sent it hurling toward the ground, the falling giant would have bumped into one or more of its neighbors, setting off a domino effect that would, within a few seconds, bring millions of pounds of wood down across the creek.

As Katzman, Southard, and I sat on the mossy rocks, we could see small green shoots coming up at intervals along the trunk, making tentative forays into the misty air. We considered our options. The prospects of going over, under, or around looked equally unpalatable. So we decided to go through the middle. Beginning with Southard, we burrowed through a convoluted series of gaps that formed a rough passageway, pausing at intervals to relay the camera gear.

Then we continued climbing up the stream until, at a bend, we began ascending the steep bank. We pushed through sword ferns seven feet high, getting soaked in the insanely humid environment. We struggled through fields of brambles, scrambled over the debris of more fallen trees, and found little solid ground to stand on. At one point, Katzman slipped and his camera crashed down, lens-first.

As he and Southard continued to barge their way through the prickers, I tried my luck at walking atop the inclined trunk of a downed redwood. It had looked like a viable route up the hill, but halfway along I was reduced to shimmying, riding the slippery tree like a horse. Eventually, the tree bucked me off and sent me sliding sideways down a carpet of moss and decaying slime. I fell through a mat of sticks and leaves and into a hidden void. After thudding to the ground, it occurred to me that if Hyperion really was anywhere nearby, it was in little danger of being overrun by bushwhacking throngs.

In the late 1970s, as Congress debated expanding Redwood National Park, the pace of logging picked up dramatically. Pushing ever deeper into the area that would soon be off-limits, timber crews set up floodlights powered by mobile generators, allowing around-the-clock work. By the time President Carter signed the expansion legislation, about 80 percent of the soon-to-be-annexed land had been logged. On March 27, 1978, the chain saws finally fell silent, less than two hundred feet from Hyperion. The tallest known tree on earth had been two weeks, maybe less, from its demise.

It would take three decades for anyone to notice the tree. On August 25, 2006, Atkins and Taylor were bushwhacking through a remote basin that neither had previously visited. They had recently found two huge trees — 371.2-foot Icarus and record-breaking 375.3-foot Helios — in a nearby grove.

After many years of tree-hunting, Atkins and Taylor had developed a keen intuition. They knew with a glance which trees might be worth a two-hour bushwhack; they knew how to find the "sweet spots," as Atkins describes them, from which a laser shot might be possible.

Taylor was walking about one hundred feet ahead when Atkins noticed a redwood crown looming above its neighbors. Atkins recalls that he got his rangefinder out of his backpack and shot at a point just below the top of the tree. He couldn't see the base, but he estimated that the tree had to be at least 360 feet tall.

"Michael," Atkins yelled. "Get over here. This tree's incredibly tall."

While Atkins crossed the creek to bushwhack up the slope, Taylor went to the tree and began calculating the elevation of the base. Atkins eventually found a window through the foliage and lay down to get the laser as steady as possible. From that position, he shot the tree's top. Then he began working his way back to Taylor, adding and subtracting the elevations of intermediate targets along the way. After all that, they wound up with a preliminary height — 377.8 feet — that would make the tree the tallest living thing on earth.

Katzman, Southard, and I spent an hour struggling through a maze of brambles and downed trees to reach our target grove. Then we labored farther to rise above the redwoods, hoping that the clear-cut would provide a good vantage point. But it turns out that a thirty-year-old clear-cut in a rainforest isn't a smart place to go for visibility, or mobility. Amid the dense saplings and underbrush, we quickly lost our bearings and momentum. We decided to head back down into the old growth.

Our own cheap rangefinder was proving fickle, due partly to limitations of the technology, and perhaps mostly to user inexperience. Trees that were obviously well over 250 feet were showing up as 82 feet. The GPS, too, was useless. Under the dense canopy, I could pick up only one satellite. I stowed the devices in my pack, where they would stay for the rest of the trip.

Keeping the clear-cut line a couple of hundred feet above us, we traversed the mountainside, three humans dwarfed by the mind-boggling scale of the trees. We thought we had been in big-tree country before, but as we walked farther into the grove, we realized that we had now entered a new realm. All around us, twenty-foot-wide trunks rose in great grooved columns that stretched upward for two hundred feet before the lowest limbs appeared. Katzman tried to photograph one particularly massive trunk, but he didn't have a lens wide enough.

Despite the hard going, the environment was surprisingly hospitable. Once, falling through a false floor of sticks and leaves, I landed softly on my back, cushioned by a bed of spongy moss and pine needles. There were no biting or buzzing insects. And, had we found ourselves in need of a dry and cozy bivouac, there were plenty of accommodating caves that had been burned into the bottoms of living trees.

Under the shade of the immense trees, the ground vegetation thinned out and the walking got easier. Occasional shafts of sunlight penetrated the canopy, angling into the gallery like spotlights, illuminating lush beds of moss and twenty-foot-high stumps whose charred tops formed jagged maws. The solitude and the sense of timelessness were so complete that none of us would have been surprised to get a tap on the shoulder from a brontosaur. It was, without reservation, the most startlingly beautiful forest I have ever encountered.

Among the first people Atkins and Taylor told of their discovery was their friend Stephen C. Sillett, a professor of botany at Humboldt State. Sillett was the first scientist to climb into the redwood canopy, and he is considered by many to be the world's foremost authority on the redwood forest.

When Taylor told Sillett that he and Atkins had found a tree that they estimated to be higher than 378 feet, Sillett was floored. Having been out in the forest many times with Atkins and Taylor, the botanist had total confidence in their measurements. But, said Sillett, "nobody expected a tree that tall to be growing that far up the mountainside, in conditions that were less than optimal." It was, Sillett said, "the most significant discovery in tree height in seventy-five years."

The only absolutely accurate method of measuring a tree's height is to climb into its crown and drop a tape measure from the top. Sillett delayed his ascent for two weeks, until the end of the nesting season of the marbled murrelet, an endangered seabird that inhabits the area. Then he assembled a team to climb Hyperion and verify its status as the world's tallest tree.

With Atkins, Taylor, and Sillett's wife, Marie Antoine, beside him, Sillett tied fishing line to an arrow. Using a crossbow, he shot the arrow over a branch in the lower crown of the tree. Then he tied a nylon cord to one end of the fishing line and, pulling on the other end, hoisted the cord over the branch. Finally, he attached a climbing rope to the cord and pulled the rope over the branch. After tying off one end to a nearby tree, Sillett attached mechanical ascenders to the hanging end of the rope, and began to pull himself up toward the first branch.

"The lowest branch in a big redwood," said Sillett, "is higher than the tallest branch of almost any other tree in any other forest on earth. And once you get up there, you realize you've got almost another two hundred feet to reach the top."

The crown of such a giant is a gnarled mass of limbs, with bridges of living and dead wood running horizontally from branch to branch, forming a natural structure of struts and girders. Upon reaching the first branch, Sillett set up an elaborate rig of ropes and carabineers, which he used to pull himself up from limb to limb, into the heart of the crown. There, Sillett found blackened chambers in the trunk, hollowed out by an ancient, high-reaching forest fire.

"It's another world, almost another planet up there," Sillett told me. "There's a lot of biological diversity that's unexpected. On limbs and in crotches, you get these huge accumulations of rich, wet soil, hundreds of feet off the ground. We found salamanders, earthworms, aquatic crustaceans, huge huckleberry bushes, even other trees growing on soil mats. It's literally a hanging rainforest garden."

Before Taylor and Atkins began finding exceptionally tall specimens high on mountainsides, Sillett and most other experts believed that the tallest redwoods would grow only in alluvial flats, the silty floodplains near creeks.

"There were taller trees up higher all along, of course," Atkins said. "But the ones in the low, flat areas were what people happened to see, because getting onto the remote mountainsides was so challenging."

The fact that Hyperion is located in such an unlikely place suggests to researchers that its height was not such an anomaly. Of particular interest to Sillett is the question of the physiological limits of a tree's height. In other words, how high can a redwood grow?

Trees suck water upward through microscopic pipes called xylem. As water molecules evaporate from the pores of leaves at the top of the tree, other molecules are pulled up from the roots to replace them, in a journey that takes a few weeks from root to treetop. Redwoods, more than any other tree, can move water to great heights, against tremendous forces of gravity and frictional resistance. But at a certain height, the tension of the water column begins to overstress the tree.

Sillett's team has used centrifuges to artificially create tension in xylem, and has demonstrated that the limit to a redwood's height is about 410 feet in southern Humboldt County. In the wetter, cooler northern part of the county, where Redwood National Park is located, Sillett's preliminary research indicates that the limit may be considerably higher.

"What we've discovered about the redwoods' physiology indicates that they can grow a lot higher than the ones we've found," said Sillett. "Which brings up a sobering thought. Now that 96 percent of the old-growth redwood landscape is lost, we understand that, even in our lifetimes, we almost certainly had trees over four hundred feet. And we cut them down."

According to Sillett's measurements, Hyperion's height is 379.1 feet. Chris Atkins believes that the chance of finding an even taller tree is less than 1 percent. "There are so few places we haven't been through," he told me. "Then again, there are a couple of basins we haven't seen yet, and there are rumors of tall trees up there. We're hoping to get in there in the next few months."

We were talking over the phone, a couple of weeks after my trip to Humboldt County. Toward the end of a long conversation, Atkins asked me where we had hiked. I named the creek basin we had explored on our last day.

"Wow," he said. "You managed to find your way into one of the most spectacular groves on earth." He asked a few more questions, regarding how far up the creek we went, which side we climbed, how high we went. After I described the location, Atkins was silent for what seemed like a long time.

"You were in the right place," he said finally. "You probably walked right past it."

I shivered when I heard that. Later, as I looked at some of Katzman's pictures, I recalled that final day when, pausing to rest on a bed of pine needles, I was overcome by a feeling of insignificance that grew until it became strangely ecstatic.

For all I know, I was sitting in Hyperion's shadow. But at that moment, the pursuit of a single tree — even the tallest one on earth — seemed inconsequential. The real object of my quest was all around me, a mass of immortal columns strong and generous enough to support the sky.

I'd come here looking for a tree, and discovered a forest.

Dogged

FROM RUNNER'S WORLD

HE WAS A BAD DOG. That was an awful thing for the runner to think as she lay dying. He had curled next to her that first night in the hidden canyon, after the accident. He had put his snout on her belly, and licked her face as she stared up at more shooting stars than she had ever dreamed. And that first morning — could it have been just the day before? — when it was so cold she had to crack the ice on top of the miraculous puddle, he had played with a stick, run in little circles, and barked with what she thought was happiness, and he was such a good dog then. He made her think that maybe things weren't so bad. She saw an eagle glide overhead that morning. It was beautiful. It was a beautiful morning. She was in a beautiful spot. Red rock and sandy soil and a juniper tree and the soft sighing of the high desert wind, and to lope through it would have been a wonder for a runner whose body wasn't broken and bleeding inside.

All she had was the puddle, and her dog. And then she didn't have the dog, because when she was screaming, when it took her two hours to reach behind her head to fill a water bottle from the puddle, the dog ran away. She couldn't stop screaming. She screamed because she hurt, and because she needed help, and because she was afraid that help might not come in time. The dog came back, but he wouldn't lie down next to her that second night. It was just last night, but it seemed so long ago. There were no shooting stars the second night. The second night, she saw things in the sky that made no sense, and heard a strange voice from the dark, and it made no sense either.

Today, the third day, the dog was gone. Then he was back. Then he was gone again. Maybe she was hallucinating. Even though she was well known for enduring things others could not, for persevering through heat and cold and all manner of punishing climate and topography — even though she was one of the most accomplished endurance runners in the world — she still had her limits. On the third day, in the hidden canyon, her body broken, she discovered them.

And then the dog was back, and now he was coming closer, and now he was lapping at the puddle, her only water source, and she couldn't help it, she yelled at him. It was the only water she could reach. Couldn't he find another puddle? Bad dog!

No one knew where she was. It would be dark again, and cold. No one could hear her scream. No one was coming. Today, her third day on the rock by the puddle, she allowed herself to see the truth.

She had won the Pikes Peak Marathon four times. She had raced up all fifty-four of Colorado's 14,000-foot peaks in less than fifteen days, faster than any woman in history. She had competed in 441 endurance events (races that took from an hour to ten days to finish) since 1995 and finished in the top three in 390 of them. Three times she was part of a four-person team that won one of the most punishing endurance events in the world, Primal Quest, a 400-mile trek over land and water, mountain and desert terrain. She had earned six "U.S. Athlete of the Year" titles in four different endurance sports. She had kept going when others had told her she had to stop. Now, she couldn't move.

It was midafternoon on a Friday. She had degrees in biology and kinesiology, and as much as she had invested, personally and professionally, in the awesome power of the human spirit, she also possessed grim knowledge regarding the limits of flesh and bone. It was ten days before Christmas. That's when Danelle Ballengee, just thirty-five years old, prepared to die. That's when the runner who never gave up, gave up. It really was a beautiful spot. She felt peace. And then she heard another sound. And it didn't make sense either.

Two days earlier, on Wednesday, December 13, Ballengee had spent the early part of the morning e-mailing with sponsors, writing articles, answering questions from clients who had hired her as a personal trainer. She left her house on Cliffview Drive in Moab, Utah, at 10:00 A.M. She also had landlord duties to attend to. She owned three rental properties in Colorado, and she rented out space in her Moab house, and one of her tenant's friends had stolen some money, so she had to go to the bank to file a fraud report. Only then could she begin the highlight of her morning — the run.

With her dog, Taz, a three-year-old reddish-brown mutt with a long jaw and a broad chest, she climbed in her white Ford Ranger truck, her kayak on top of the roof. She stopped at a Burger King for a chicken sandwich and French fries and a large coffee, because she had forgotten to eat breakfast. The dog got a bite, because the dog always got a bite. She had spoiled him since the day she got him from the pound, when he was just a few weeks old.

It was a good day for a run, cloudy but not too cold. She listened to "Beautiful Day," by U2. She thought about the guy she had met a few weeks earlier at a race in Leadville, Colorado, and smiled because she thought there was potential. When she got to the parking area at the Amasa Back Trail, five miles out of town, she kept driving, continued a quarter-mile north on the road to a turnoff near a cliff. She did it because she wanted to shave a quarter-mile off her run. The endurance runner was feeling lazy.

She put on a pair of cheap orange sunglasses, grabbed her MP3 player and a large plastic bottle filled with water and a raspberry-flavored energy gel. She wore running pants, a fleece hat, silk long underwear, a polypropylene shirt, and a thin fleece jacket. The temperature was in the forties, but she wanted to be prepared. She invested as much in preparation as she did in the power of positive thinking. Just before she locked her wallet and cell phone in the car, she spotted a fanny pack in the backseat. She had forgotten it was there. She grabbed it, stuck her water bottle in, and took off.

Her plan was to run and hike an eight-mile loop. She would start on the Amasa Back Trail, popular among bikers and hikers, especially in spring and fall. But she would veer off of it after just a few miles, just before the top of a mesa, where she would follow a seldom-used jeep trail known to the locals as the Mine Sweeper and into a hidden canyon, then she would scramble up the rocks of that canyon, toward Hurrah Pass, onto another seldom-used jeep trail, through another canyon, up some more rocks, and she would eventually land back on another jeep trail that would take her back to a road that led to her truck. Taz ran alongside her, panting happily. An hour in, she had covered five miles. She had drunk half her water bottle. She was scrambling up the rocks in the first hidden canyon, Taz just behind her. It really was a beautiful day.

If you stopped to think about the things that could kill you, you could drive yourself crazy. Another second in an intersection. Another inch on a highway. One misstep on some ice-covered slickrock. Or maybe it was just slippery lichen.

One second she was one of the best endurance runners in the world, out for a late autumn loop in the high desert, breathing in the soft, juniper-scented air, barely paying attention to the low, grayish clouds scudding by. One second she was a world champion out for a light workout.

And then the second was gone. Now she was sliding, like a kid down a giant water slide. That's what she thought at the time, that it felt like a water slide. Past lichen, past rocks, past sand. She slid on her butt, hit "a little bump," then "another little bump." Then she came to "a little ledge."

People hear Primal Quest and they see adrenaline junkies. People read about Danelle Ballengee and they think risk seeker. But in her kayak, she steered clear of white water. On skis, she descended carefully, avoided steep out-of-bounds areas. She had no interest in bungee jumping. Other adventure racers yipped with glee at sections that demanded hanging from ropes. That was the point in the race when Ballengee frowned and gritted her teeth.

She kept picking up speed. According to a newspaper account published a week after the accident, she flew off a cliff and plummeted the equivalent of two stories, landing on her feet. The reality was messier, and more plain. She ended up halfway down the hill, prone. She caught her breath. She had once survived eight sunbaked days in the Morocco Eco-Challenge, a race equally as fearsome as Primal Quest. A leech had attached itself to her eyelid in another race, given her a corneal ulcer, blinded her for three days. That was punishing. This was just a nasty tumble. But she was smart, and careful. She had her two degrees from the University of Colorado. She would be methodical. She put her right hand on her right leg, her left hand on her left leg. *Whew.* That was the word she thought. *Whew.* She wasn't paralyzed. This was her next thought:

Man, it's gonna be a long walk out of here. A moment later she realized she couldn't stand up.

She would crawl thirty feet to the bottom of the canyon. She would drag herself over rocks and through scrub. Then she would crawl the three miles to the Amasa Back Trail and hope that someone would see her. It was noon when she started.

Her left leg wouldn't move. She scooted forward on her right knee, balanced, then reached back with both hands and pulled her left leg forward. She knew things were broken. She knew she was in trouble. When she reached the bottom of the canyon, she looked in her fanny pack to see if there might be something to help. She found another pack of raspberry energy gel, a shower cap, and two ibuprofen. She swallowed the pills, kept crawling. She crawled through sand and brush and some snow — the canyon floor was not just sand — and by the time she arrived at a flat rock, and a sinkhole filled with water, the air was getting cold and shadows in the canyon were lengthening. It was 5:00 P.M. She had crawled a quarter of a mile, and it had taken five hours.

She lay down on her back, drank the remaining half of her water bottle, put her hands between her legs because they were so cold. She decided she would refill the water bottle from the sinkhole — she didn't care about parasites. But it hurt too much to turn over. So she reached backward over her right shoulder and filled the water bottle without looking.

She did crunches with her head and neck to keep warm. Her knees were bent, and she tapped her feet on the rock. She rubbed her hands together. She reached for the shower cap in the fanny pack, but she couldn't find it. Taz curled up next to her. He put his chin on her stomach and looked at her. The temperature dipped into the twenties. She lay on her back, freezing, exhausted, and looked at the moonless sky. She saw the Milky Way and shooting stars. She had never in her life seen so many shooting stars.

She wondered what the guy in Leadville was doing. She wondered if someone would see that her truck was missing from her house. Then she realized how dumb that was. She loved working with others in the endurance challenges, but she hadn't told anyone where she was going. And what she was most famous for was enduring. Why would anyone worry about her?

It was so cold. She didn't want to die. She *couldn't* die. There were friends and family she wasn't ready to leave. She continued her crunches, her feet-tapping, her finger-curling.

At first light, she saw Taz playing with a stick. That cheered her. She ate one of the energy gels. She tried to refill her water bottle, but the water in the sinkhole had frozen. She reached over her shoulder and broke through it with the cap of the bottle.

She decided that today she would crawl out of the canyon. She tried to roll over, to get on her hands and knees, and she screamed. She felt pain radiating down her legs, up her back. Taz licked her face and she lay back down, on her back, to gather her strength. And she screamed for help, in case anyone could hear her, and when she looked up, Taz had gone.

Then it was three o'clock and he was back. She wasn't sure how so much time had passed, but it had. The temperature had risen into the forties, and that felt good, but it would be dark again soon, and the cold would come. She screamed for help, even though she knew no one was coming. That's when she saw the shower cap — it was just a couple feet away. It was too far. She raised her head, lowered her voice. She looked at Taz.

"I'm hurt," she said. He looked at her and tilted his head, first to the left, then to the right. She knew it was ridiculous, but it looked like he understood.

"Taz," she said, "you know, maybe you could go and get some help for me."

He tilted his head again, didn't move. She told herself not to be stupid, that he was a dog. Just a dog. And then Taz ran away again, down the hidden canyon.

Now it was four o'clock. She had to get the shower cap. She would need it for the night, to keep what meager body heat she still had. Two feet. It took an hour to get it.

And now the sun had left the hidden little canyon, and it was getting colder again, and she felt a swelling in her midsection, a lump the size of a water bottle, and she knew she was broken inside. Then Taz was back, which was comforting, but it meant that he wasn't magic, he didn't understand English, he was a good dog, but he was just a dog. No one would be coming down the hidden canyon to rescue her.

She started the crunches again, the feet-tapping, the hand-rubbing. Taz refused to curl up next to her. Was it an animal's instinctive recoiling at imminent death? Did he want softer ground? It made no sense to her. Every so often, though, he would place a paw on her chest, lick her face. "Good dog," she would say.

It got colder, and colder, and darker. She gazed up, looking for shooting stars, for the Milky Way, for evidence that the world hadn't ended. That she hadn't ended. She saw only stripes. Long, white stripes slicing through the black night sky. She knew her body was shutting down, her brain malfunctioning. She was seeing things. She cried. She cried for her family and her friends and the nascent romance with the guy from Leadville that would never go anywhere. She is not religious, and she did not pray. What she did was plead.

"Please," she pleaded. "Please, somebody, notice that I'm gone."

Dorothy Rossignol is seventy-six years old, a "nosy neighbor" by her own account. Others in Moab call her a "piece of work," a "little old lady," and "the busybody of the neighborhood." She is childless, a widow since 1990. She loves mining, and if there is a town in the American West that ever produced a significant amount of any valuable mineral, whether gold, silver, or lead, she can name the town, along with its mineral. Chances are she lived there with her husband, Robert, who mined it. "My husband would rather mine than eat," she says. They first came through Moab in 1957, a young bride and her husband, a miner looking for work during the uranium boom. They returned in 1969 and settled there for good. Moab was something in the boom years. "Parties you wouldn't believe," she says, ". . . dancing girls from Spain."

Life is slower now, nights quieter, days longer. She volunteers at the Dan O'Laurie Museum, eats lunch four days a week at the Moab senior center ("I'd eat there five days, but they're closed on Thursdays"), tends to the five peachcot trees (peach trees with apricot fruit grafted on) in her yard. Rossignol liked the young woman who moved next door five years ago, which is saying a lot. "I don't rush over to meet new neighbors right away," she says, "because you don't know what kind of people they are."

But the young woman seemed nice, and quiet, and she bought a puppy who jumped over the little metal fence separating the yards so often and scratched at the widow's door so relentlessly that she finally gave up and bought a bag of dog biscuits. Every day Taz would come over, and every day Rossignol would give the mutt two biscuits. He'd eat one there and take the other one home. Ballengee was gone a lot — "training for one of those adventure things" — so Rossignol fetched her mail, made sure her pipes didn't freeze in the winter when she was traveling.

They would do yard work together and chat "about everything in general and nothing in particular." As nice as Ballengee was, she wasn't so great on following leash laws. "So when I see the police or the dog catcher," Rossignol says, "I tie him up."

Taz didn't come to visit on Wednesday, December 13, and that night Rossignol looked outside and saw that Ballengee's truck wasn't there. She also saw that Ballengee had left her drapes open, her lights on. She saw Ballengee's laptop computer on. She knew that Ballengee was a free spirit, that when she wasn't training or visiting her parents in Evergreen, Colorado, she sometimes left to visit friends. She knew that Ballengee sometimes didn't tell anyone where she was going. The widow didn't exactly approve of all that gallivanting. On the other hand, she had to admit, she admired it. They weren't all that different, the endurance runner and the miner's widow. Self-sufficient women in a man's world. Rossignol might have been a nosy neighbor, but she wasn't a scaredy-cat. She would feel foolish calling the police if her young neighbor was out just having fun. She went to bed.

On Thursday afternoon, Rossignol looked again and saw the open drapes, the blazing lights, the computer. That's when she called Gary and Peggy Ballengee, in Evergreen, Colorado. She told Danelle's parents she was worried.

She was so tired. And cold. What was the point of tapping her feet? No one was coming down the hidden canyon. She stopped tapping. Then she heard a strange voice, commanding her. She knew she was alone. She knew there was no one telling her anything. She didn't believe in God. She knew there couldn't be a voice. But there was. And it wouldn't shut up. Keep tapping, the voice said. She kept tapping.

Word had spread through town, along with rumors, and someone from the bicycle shop called someone else who called the guy from Leadville. "I promise," the guy told Ballengee's parents over the phone. "I did not take your daughter to Mexico. I don't know where she is."

Police spent three hours inside Ballengee's house that Thursday. When they arrived, Rossignol was waiting. She told them her neighbor was in trouble, that they should be looking for her truck, and her dog. She told them she would show them where things were inside the house, where to find important clues. When they refused her entry, she stood on the sidewalk outside. She stood on the sidewalk for three hours.

One of the police officers was a woman. She listened to the widow's requests and suggestions and urgent entreaties. Then the officer gave her a card. It was dark now. If Rossignol heard anything, the cop said, feel free to call. Then the cops left.

The strange voice had stopped. The stripes were gone. It was light and she was alive. But the water in the puddle was frozen again and Taz was gone. She broke through, filled her bottle. She ate the other raspberry energy gel, the last one. No one was coming. She estimated she couldn't make it more than a few feet an hour, and wondered if it was worse to die trying or to die next to her little puddle. She started crawling.

She dragged herself off the rock, and her pants came off, because she couldn't lift her pelvis off the ground. She found herself in a shallow depression. She was stuck. She saw the stupidity of her decision and crawled back onto the rock. A round trip of four feet. It took two hours. Now she was hyperventilating. Now she felt the ball of clotted blood and swollen flesh moving inside her. And now it was 1:30 P.M. She would never leave this hidden canyon. Why had she wasted hours, and time, and precious energy to go four feet? Why hadn't she told someone where she was going? Why hadn't she told more people she loved them? And where the hell was Taz? What was wrong with that dog?

Craig Shumway grew up in Moab, dug in its soil for uranium during the last years of the boom. He loves the high desert, the wide-open spaces. He has been in law enforcement for seventeen years, a Moab detective for four. On Friday morning, December 15, he was sitting in his office at the police department on East Center Street when Sergeant Mike Wiler walked in and sat down.

Wiler told Shumway there had been a missing-person report the previous night. He said it looked like someone had left a house unsecured. He said he had given the information to the Grand County Sheriff's Department and that they would be checking trailheads to see if the truck might be there. In the meantime, Moab police had put out an Attempt To Locate (ATL). In Moab, a magnet for the young, the adventurous, and the risk-seeking, an ATL is not exactly a red alert. "You just don't jump out and go look for every one of 'em," Shumway says.

Shumway nodded, plowed through some paperwork, then decided, before lunch, he would take a drive. No one was too alarmed about the missing woman — people took off for days without telling anyone all the time in Moab, and she was a world-class athlete. And it wasn't his job. It wasn't his jurisdiction either. But he knew how big the desert was, how many trails crisscrossed the canyons and rivers of southern Utah. First he stopped at Ballengee's house, took a quick look. Then he drove ten miles north to the Sovereign Trail and checked the trailhead, and found nothing.

Law enforcement officers often talk about intuition and gut feelings and how important it is to recognize them. On the way back to Moab, though, Shumway felt something unfamiliar.

He drove down Kane Creek Road, to the parking lot of the Amasa Back Trail. He's not sure why, but he passed it, kept going, to the top of the hill, to the little spot near the cliff. That's where he saw the white Ford Ranger. He wanted to document things, in case there had been a crime. He pulled out his eight-megapixel Canon digital camera and took pictures. Later, he would look at the receipt that the runner had left inside the car. It was from Burger King, for a chicken sandwich and large fries and a large coffee. It was dated Wednesday, December 13, at 11:00 A.M. Now it was 1:30 in the afternoon, two days and two cold nights later. Shumway had another feeling, a bad one.

It was the effort she had expended crawling into and out of the little depression. It was her body shutting down. It was fear. She knew she needed to stop hyperventilating. She forced herself to breathe more slowly, and it worked. She breathed. She didn't know where her dog was, and soon it would be cold and dark, and she was broken and bleeding inside, and no one was coming, but at least she was breathing. So she breathed. She breathed and she waited to die.

By midafternoon, when the Grand County Search and Rescue team gathered at the Amasa Back trailhead, they knew who they were looking for. John Marshall, the officer in charge of the team that day, had met Ballengee once before, when he worked as a volunteer at the 2006 Primal Quest in Utah. When he had first seen her then, she had just finished a 46-mile trek across the desert. The temperature had been 105 degrees. She had been without water for the past four hours. Her feet were more blisters than flesh. Marshall suggested an IV drip that day. Ballengee declined. She was in a hurry.

And now she had disappeared. "I'm thinking," Marshall says, "this was a world-class, I-eat-nails-for-breakfast person we're looking for. I'm thinking she's been out there for two nights.

"I'm thinking she didn't twist an ankle. I'm thinking there's something very, very serious going on."

As soon as Marshall and the others got near Ballengee's truck, they saw the dog. It was running in circles, "going a million miles an hour." Marshall suspected it was the runner's dog.

"Most dogs won't leave their master as long as their master has a pulse," he told a newspaper reporter. "To see that dog was a truly saddening sight."

He called Taz, tried to coax him over. But Taz wouldn't come. The dog circled Marshall and the others, then dashed toward town. Marshall thought they should try to grab him, but no one could. Then the dog stopped, looked back over its shoulder. Then the dog was gone.

Marshall sent Melissa Fletcher, a team member who works as a backcountry mountain bike guide, running up Jackson's Trail, a narrow, steep, single track, because it was the most difficult and she was the most fit member of the team. He stayed near the truck to coordinate the search. Though he wasn't a Search and Rescue team member, Craig Shumway had, after calling his discovery in, gone home, changed into hiking clothes, and trekked up the Cable Arch Trail to make sure Ballengee wasn't there. She wasn't. Marshall sent two men and a woman up the Amasa Back Trail in ATVs. Riding the second ATV were Mike Coronella and Barb Fincham. In the first ATV was a sixty-year-old commercial heating and refrigeration installer named Bego Gerhart.

Gerhart is five-feet-eight-inches tall, weighs 180 pounds. He has a full gray beard and piercing blue eyes and a potbelly. He looks like he'd be more at home in front of a cheeseburger than driving an ATV through the backcountry, looking for a woman about to die. He hitchhiked to Moab in 1970, a onetime California Eagle Scout with no particular direction. A Moab cop asked him for identification, and Gerhart asked if the cop knew anyone looking for work. That's how he ended up as a trucker, "with guys who had two-hundred-word vocabularies, and a hundred of 'em were obscene."

Gerhart has volunteered for the Grand County Search and Rescue squad for eleven years. He rigged ropes in New Zealand for filmmakers shooting *Vertical Limit* in 1999. He served as a consultant to a television show called *I Shouldn't Be Alive* in 2006. In 2003, he was on the team that hiked into Blue John Canyon, where he winched a boulder and retrieved the hand of Aron Ralston, who had hacked it off in order to free himself. Others might have broader shoulders and younger legs, but of the ninety-one calls that went out to the Grand County Search and Rescue team in 2006, Gerhart responded to eighty-eight of them, more than anyone else.

A lot of men and women who run (and hike and bike) in wilderness-rich areas like Moab speak of the majesty of the outdoors, the intoxicating consequences of fresh air. Many submit that the majestic sweep of the sky and the exquisite desolation of the desert serve as prima facie evidence of a loving spirit. But those tend to be the younger, leaner runners. Gerhart sees things a little differently.

"What happened to someone like Danelle is pretty good evidence against the existence of a benevolent God," he says. Regarding the secret to survival, he says, "It's all about knowing how to suffer."

Gerhart was a mile down the Amasa Back Trail, puttering along in his ATV, when his two-way radio sputtered to life.

"The dog! The dog!" It was Marshall. Taz had come back. He had sprinted up the trail, passing Coronella and Fincham's ATV. Fincham had gotten out of his ATV to follow the dog on foot, and the dog had promptly disappeared.

The dog dashed by Gerhart's ATV, and it stopped. It looked at

Gerhart, then it dashed off the trail, up to a little mesa. Gerhart clambered out of the ATV, walked up the mesa, where the dog was waiting. Gerhart stared at the dog. The dog stared at Gerhart. And the dog was gone again.

People journey into the desert without enough water or the proper clothing every year, and people die. People slip, and they never rise. People get lost, and they stay lost. Search and Rescue team members do their best, but when someone is gone for three days and two nights, on the fringe of winter, help often consists of a recovery mission. It often includes a body bag. Less than a month earlier, two men had died near Moab. They had frozen to death. Both were wearing heavier clothes than Ballengee. Gerhart knew all that. But he had a feeling. Gerhart is not a sentimental man, nor prone to a lot of religio-mystical mumbo jumbo. This is about as close as he gets: "My mind said, *Follow the dog.*"

But the dog was gone. So Gerhart backtracked to where he had first spotted Taz. A few years earlier, he had taken a tracking course from U.S. Marshals, and now he studied the ground. He looked for dog tracks, next to footprints of a woman runner. When he saw them, he followed them, away from the main road, down a little spur, toward a hidden canyon. He saw that the trail got rockier and more and more rugged. He hopped into his ATV, and he drove toward the hidden canyon, the sounds of his engine echoing off the red-rock walls. And he drove, and drove some more. And then he stopped. He thought he had heard something.

The dog had been disappearing all day. This time, when he got back, he ran straight to the puddle and he started drinking. And he drank and drank. And as much as the runner loved the dog, as inured to pain and loss as she was, she was still human. Bad dog! She yelled at Taz, "Can't you drink out of another pothole?"

And there they lay, less than a week before the shortest day of the year, a woman broken and bleeding inside, a dog lapping up her precious water. She cried. She thought again of the people to whom she hadn't said, "I love you." And then something shifted. It wasn't the dog's fault. It wasn't anyone's. Is this what acceptance felt like? She wasn't angry anymore. Now, she was ready to die. Now, she was at peace. And then she heard a sound that didn't make sense.

*

Later, a lot of people would invoke divine mysteries, seek answers in the supernatural. Shumway would reflect on the strange feelings that led him to search for the missing truck, the inexplicable and powerful urges that guided him up the Kane Creek Road and to the little patch of dirt on top of the hill, near the cliff. "You can call it whatever you want," he says. "Call it coincidence, or fate, or whatever. I'm a God-fearing person and I can't explain it. It was a sense of urgency. I had never felt it before." Marshall would ask out loud how someone with virtually no body fat could possibly live through two cold nights in the high desert, "how her internal metabolism defied the laws of physics." People referred to the entire episode as a "Christmas miracle." When it came to myth-making, though, no one beat the dog lovers. In the news accounts and stories of the accident, Taz morphed into a furry genius, a four-legged phantasm, a kind of barking, galloping Gandalf. Some Search and Rescue team members talked about how, in hindsight, it looked like Taz had planned the rescue the whole time. "It was like he was trying to get us to pay attention to him, so when he showed up later, he could lead us to her," Marshall says. (Marshall is a dog lover.) Even academics sang the praises of the wonderdog. Marc Bekoff, a biology professor at the University of Colorado and author of *The Emotional Lives of Animals*, says there's a good chance Taz knew what he was doing. "I don't know what his doggy brain was saying, but it was probably something like, 'There's something novel, there's something new here.' I bet you that dog was just going, 'This is new, this is different, I gotta do something.' There's no doubt that [Ballengee's] scent was changing. At some point, he was picking that up. At some point, I'm sure the dog realized there was some opportunity to save her. I know people will laugh at me, but I don't care. I believe that."

But that was all later.

First, Gerhart had to drive toward the sound. That's when he saw them. There, on a rock, in the little hidden canyon, was a woman on her back. And there, lying next to her, with his snout on her chest, the mutt.

"I'm so glad to see you," Ballengee cried, weeping.

"I'm glad you're glad to see me, and that you can say so," Gerhart replied. At least that's the way he tells the story. The way he remembers, she was lucid, but emotional. He was amazed she was so articulate, but he was concerned about keeping her core temperature from falling, so he fetched from his ATV a heavy sleeping bag with Velcro straps, what Search and Rescue team members call Doctor Down. The way he remembers it, he kept her talking, even as he was radioing for help, scanning the landscape for a place where a rescue helicopter might safely land, shoving her hands into heavy gloves. All of that, according to Ballengee, is accurate, but incomplete. The way she remembers it, Gerhart was weeping too.

Taz ran to Gerhart and licked him. Then the commercial heating and refrigeration installer said something to the runner that people have said to other people as long as there have been pets. "You got one heck of a dog," Gerhart said.

She didn't sleep well last night. Every time she shut her eyes, she was tumbling down the slickrock, picking up speed. Every time she opened them, she was on her back, halfway down the steep wall, cold and alone, broken and bleeding inside. And if she did sleep, then what? She was afraid of the nightmares. She didn't want to find herself back in the hidden canyon, cold and alone and dying.

It was midafternoon, January 23, almost six weeks after she fell, and she was tired, and she hurt, and though she was lying on the couch in the basement of her parents' house in Evergreen, and they were upstairs, and she was safe, and though Taz was lying on the floor next to her, and even though she and her dog had been on the *Today Show*, even though she and Taz had ascended in the popular consciousness to Christmas Miracle and Wonderdog status, the reality was messier, more difficult.

She didn't have complete control of her left hand. She wasn't sure if she ever would. Her feet felt as if she were standing in an icy stream. She wasn't sure if they would ever feel differently. Both were consequences of frostbite.

She was taking six Neurontin pills a day to help reduce the pain. She was taking three 600-milligram tablets of ibuprofen for inflammation, four 30-milligram iron pills to help increase her red-blood-cell count, and Percocet for more pain. And anti-anxiety pills, for the nights she had trouble sleeping, like last night. And stool softener. Until a few days ago, her father had been injecting her every day, in her stomach, with a drug to lessen the chances of her blood clotting. After she complained about the pain, her doctor finally relented. Now she was taking 325 milligrams of aspirin daily.

She is almost five-feet-five-inches tall, and weighed 120 pounds before the accident. Now she weighed 100. She has dirty blond hair, blue eyes, and anyone who has spent any time around her comments on her impishness and how she can't stay still. Today, she was squinting with pain and exhaustion. Her pelvis had broken in four places. At one spot, it splintered into too many pieces for doctors to count. She cracked three vertebrae. She lost a third of her blood. Doctors at Denver Health Medical Center had operated on her for six hours, inserting a titanium plate in her pelvis.

When the *Today Show* called afterward, she wasn't all that interested. Of course she was grateful to be alive, but in the hospital, she hurt, and she was tired, and hungry and — truth be told — scared about what the injuries would mean. Then the *Today Show* people said they wanted Taz on the air too. She hadn't seen the dog since the Search and Rescue helicopter had lifted her into the sky, right after she scratched him behind the ears and said, "It'll be okay, boy," and Taz had gone home with John Marshall, who couldn't live with himself if he let animal control take the dog. If agreeing to be interviewed by the *Today Show* meant she'd be able to see Taz, she was on board.

Now she was talking about how after the shooting for the *Today Show* was done, and how after Taz had gone home with Ballengee's sister, Michelle, to her home in Denver, a quarter-mile from the hospital, the dog had escaped, and how her sister knew where he was going, so she walked to the hospital, and there was Taz.

She was a miracle, and Taz was a hero. Cards came from all over. One day, a box filled with dry ice arrived. It was from a woman in Michigan who had seen the *Today Show.* Inside were five pounds of hormone-free aged rib steaks and a red-and-white Christmas stocking with a stuffed Santa inside. On the top, embroidered in green, was the name of the intended recipient — Taz.

Ballengee had visitors — including the guy from Leadville — and heard from friends and relatives and strangers. She wouldn't make the same mistake again — this time, she told everyone how much she loved them. There were a lot of them. And love was great, and maybe she was a Christmas miracle, but she was still human, and this was life.

She couldn't walk. She stayed in the hospital for fifteen days, and the first week, her biggest accomplishment was forcing herself to sit up in bed without passing out. Ten seconds was a good day. Just a week ago, she tried to get out of bed to use a portable commode that was just a few feet away, and fainted. Now she could make it to the bathroom, using a wheelchair, by herself. That was a big deal. She couldn't afford all the medical bills. At the moment, the bill from Grand Junction, where she had been taken by the helicopter, totaled $45,000, and the insurance policy that had sounded so good when she bought it turned out to be not so good, and she hadn't even received her bill for surgery or her Denver hospital stay yet. She had managed a lap and a half around a West Denver mall in her wheelchair yesterday, and that had felt great, "just to get the blood flowing," and runners and endurance athletes she had competed with were holding fundraising events for her, and that was great too, but she knew she wouldn't be able to walk for at least two months, and after that, it would be another few months before she could run, and then it would be "how to run fast, then how to run aggressively. On trails and up and down mountains. Whether I'll be able to do it at the levels I used to — I'm gonna try. But if I can run again at all, I'll be so happy."

She works hard at planning to be happy. But she is scared too, and she has nightmares.

She talks about those nightmares, and about Bego Gerhart (whose name, when she first heard it in the canyon, she thought was Bagel, "probably because I was so hungry"). She talks about Dorothy Rossignol who, unbeknownst to Ballengee, has promised that when the runner moves back to Moab, she will be watched with special vigilance — even for a nosy neighbor — and nagged about where she's going, "even when it's just a trip to the mailbox." She talks about how much she misses being outside, "just being with Taz, running through the woods."

She talks a lot about Taz, how people ask if he gets extra treats now, or extra attention. He doesn't. "He's always been spoiled," she says. "I treated him pretty well before."

Mostly, she talks about her days in the hidden canyon, and the cold, and how she was sure she was going to die, and about the way she saw the white stripes in the sky, and heard the strange voice that commanded her to keep tapping her feet.

Daniel Smith, author of *Muses, Madmen, and Prophets,* a book on auditory hallucination, says the strange sounds Ballengee experienced were likely caused by "the abuse the body takes and the exhaustion. [They] often occur in that twilight moment between sleep and wakefulness."

Ballengee knows that. She earned degrees in biology and kinesiology, after all, not philosophy and religion. But she's not sure. "As far as I'm concerned," she says, "I'm going to be the best person I can . . . I'm okay without an answer."

She has been watching movies at night. She recently watched *Touching the Void,* the story of a man who had to crawl his way off a mountain in the Peruvian Andes and through a crevasse with a broken leg, and *Eight Below,* the tale of eight sled dogs who faced death by freezing in Antarctica. A visitor suggests a few comedies, considering the nightmares.

Then Taz starts barking. He sees a squirrel outside. Ballengee's father walks down the steps when he hears the barking and tells his daughter he'll take her mutt for a walk.

"He's kind of dumb," Gary Ballengee says, patting Taz on the head. "Brilliant at saving lives, but he'll chase that squirrel all day. He's just kind of dumb."

Her father and her dog are behind her, and it's not easy to turn her head, but that's what Danelle Ballengee does. She's done more difficult things. She turns and looks first at her father, who doesn't notice, then at her dog, who tilts his head and looks back at her. He tilts his head first to the left, then to the right, side to side, just like he did that terrible afternoon when Danelle Ballengee lay dying. And then the runner smiles at her dog and she puts her head back on her pillow, and she rests.

JOHN BRANT

Following Terry Fox

FROM RUNNER'S WORLD

"YOU MIGHT NOT BE able to find many people who saw him,"
Darrell Fox warns me as he drops me off at my Toronto hotel.
"Twenty-six years is a long time. People die; people move away."

Darrell has reason to be a bit skeptical. Where do you start to
write a story about Terry Fox, to many the most influential distance
runner of the last half-century or, as 32 million Canadians politely but passionately maintain, of any era? How do you compete
with the biographies, the feature films, the TV documentaries, the
narratives in school textbooks? Highways and stadiums have been
named after Terry Fox; in a 2004 poll among Canadians, he was
voted the second-greatest Canadian of all time in any field.

During the spring and summer of 1980, on one good leg and
one prosthetic leg, Terry Fox ran more than halfway across Canada, a total of 3,339 miles, logging nearly a marathon a day over
143 days, and through his Marathon of Hope raised more than $23
million for cancer research. On the 143rd day, he was forced to
stop; the cancer that took his leg had spread to his lungs and would
kill him in the summer of 1981 at age twenty-two. Each year since,
on a Sunday in September, Terry Fox Runs have been held, growing to more than four thousand venues in fifty-six nations. These
noncompetitive 5-Ks and 10-Ks, along with other efforts by the
Terry Fox Foundation, have raised close to $370 million.

Thus far the Canadians I've talked to about Terry, like his
younger brother Darrell, have supported my project, but with a sardonic undertone. *Don't come waltzing up from the States, mister, and try
to tell us something new about Terry.*

My plan is to drive a portion of the Marathon of Hope route west from Toronto, call the directors of the Terry Fox Runs in the towns along the way, and see what sorts of memories, influences, ripples, and reverberations turn up. I already know that, regardless of age, almost everyone in Canada has a Terry story to tell and that, a quarter-century after his death, he is almost always referred to in the present tense. During this week in mid-August, I will go all the way to the end of the line, to the statue of Terry by the Trans-Canada Highway in Thunder Bay, the city where he ran his last mile.

That's a round-trip distance of more than 1,700 miles. On the night before departing, over a cold Molson in my hotel near the Toronto airport, I study a map of Ontario, a province so wide that it encompasses two time zones. And I first voice the question I will repeat a hundred times over the next several days.

How in God's name did he run this far?

I recite the names of the towns I will encounter — Parry Sound, Sudbury, Blind River, Sault Ste. Marie (known in Canada as the Soo), Marathon (Marathon!), and my favorite, the one I keep whispering because of its homely but soulful sound and its remote location on a distant corner of Lake Superior: Wawa.

An unnatural stillness seemed to have come over the town on that August day in 1980. As sixteen-year-old Shelly Skryba walked across Wawa, Ontario, she wondered where everyone could be. Men should be punching out from the day shift at the Algoma Ore mill, women should be out weeding their gardens, and kids should be out riding their bikes. At this point in the summer, on the far northeast corner of the cold lake, you seldom wasted a sunny day.

About 3,700 people lived in Wawa, which was known for its twenty-eight-foot-high metal goose welcoming motorists off the Trans-Canada Highway; the word *wawa* means "wild goose" in the Ojibway language. Embarrassed by its rather silly sound in English, civic leaders had changed the name to the more dignified "Jamestown" in the 1950s. The new name failed to catch on, however, and it soon reverted back to the original.

From October through April, and some years well into May, winter seized the town. Snow often closed the highway, isolating Wawa on a bleak edge between ice-locked Lake Superior and Canada's vast, granite-studded Precambrian Shield. In the summer, dense morning fog drifted off the lake, forcing truckers to inch up and down the steep Montreal River grade east of town.

The town, the lake, the highway, summer's dwindling days: as she neared her boyfriend Earl Dereski's house, the dime dropped for Shelly. She suddenly remembered why the streets were empty today. Terry Fox had run into Wawa.

Shelly had not been granted a carefree childhood. Her father had worked at Algoma Ore. When her mother was stricken by multiple sclerosis, Shelly and the rest of the family moved to Sault Ste. Marie, the nearest urban center, for medical care. There, unfortunately, the couple's marriage foundered. Following the divorce, Shelly moved back to Wawa where she lived with her grandmother.

Shelly daydreamed often during that summer of 1980, thinking about the house that she and Earl, also a mill worker, would live in one day after they got married. She imagined having a daughter who would graduate from college and accomplish great things. But all that dreaming almost kept her from seeing the fantasy running in her direction.

She had been late jumping onto the Terry Fox bandwagon. One day a few months earlier, Shelly got home from her summer job at the local tourist agency, eager to change clothes and go meet Earl. "Hello," she called as she walked into her house.

"In the kitchen," her grandmother, Elma, responded. Shelly headed that way. Her grandmother was listening to a news report on the radio. "He's made it to Toronto," she announced. Elma pointed to a map of Canada spread out on the table, running her finger from St. John's, Newfoundland, where Terry had started to run in April by dipping his prosthesis in the Atlantic Ocean, over to Ontario, and then all the way to Vancouver, near his hometown of Port Coquitlam, British Columbia, where he was due to arrive in September. When finished, he would have run a total of more than 5,300 miles. "Just look at what this young man is doing!"

Terry had trained years for the run, preparing his legs — both the good one and prosthetic one — for what was in store. The prosthetic was a standard model, outfitted with a few primitive modifications for running; a metal valve, for instance, had been replaced with one of stainless steel so it wouldn't rust from sweat. During the Marathon of Hope, he would start running most mornings at five, moving with a stride that consisted of two hops of his whole leg and one of his prosthesis, moving at roughly an eleven-minute-per-mile pace. Terry would turn testy sometimes when challenged on his athletic integrity.

"Some people can't figure out what I'm doing," he had said in June. "It's not a walk-hop, it's not a trot. It's running, or as close as I can get to running, and it's harder than doing it on two legs. It makes me mad when people call this a walk. If I was walking, it wouldn't be anything."

He would run two miles, take a brief water break at the van that his best friend, Doug Alward, drove beside him, run another two miles, and then take another break. Terry continued this routine until he covered fourteen to sixteen miles, usually finishing his morning stint by eight. He would rest for three hours, then run another ten to twelve miles, regardless of heat, cold, crowds, or head-winds.

In the afternoons and evenings, he gave interviews and addressed audiences in community halls and school gyms. As he spoke, a representative of the Canadian Cancer Society would move among the crowd, collecting bills and change in plastic trash bags and wrinkled grocery sacks. Every cent went directly to fighting cancer; all expenses for the Marathon of Hope were separately donated. He declined all sponsorship offers and displayed no advertising logos, not even a T-shirt with the name of a college or hockey team. The only hint of a corporation's presence were the three parallel stripes on Terry's dark-blue Adidas Orions.

He and Doug would spend the night in the van or, as they moved through Ontario and Terry's fame grew, in donated motel rooms. At five the next morning, they would return to the spot where he had stopped running the day before, which Doug had marked with a small stack of rocks piled by the highway. Making sure to set out from behind the rocks, Terry began the ordeal over again. He was determined to run every inch of the distance across Canada.

As he came closer to Wawa, millions of Terry Fox fans assumed that he was only halfway through his journey. No one could imagine that he actually approached the end: both of his epic road trip and of his brief life. But in terms of impact and influence, of inspiring hope and courage, of achieving fundamental progress in the fight against cancer, Terry was just getting started. "The way I think about Terry," says Alward, speaking not altogether metaphorically, "is that he's not really dead."

In 1976, Dick Traum became the first person to finish the New York City Marathon on a prosthetic leg. A few months later, in early 1977, in Port Coquitlam, British Columbia, eighteen-year-old Terry Fox developed osteogenic sarcoma, a rare type of bone cancer, which required his right leg to be amputated six inches above the knee. The day before the amputation, Terry's former high school basketball coach happened across a copy of Runner's World *with a story about Traum running New York. The coach brought the magazine to Terry that night, thinking the story might encourage him. The kid looked at the story but didn't say anything. The coach worried that he'd committed a terrible gaffe. But Terry kept studying Traum's photo. Finally, he said, "Thanks, Coach," and put the magazine aside.*

Terry had a dream that night. He dreamed that if some old walrus like Traum could run the New York City Marathon, well . . .

Four years passed. Terry became world famous; then he died. He was honored with a memorial distance run, and because he had inspired the kid, Dick Traum was invited to Toronto to participate. At most American road races, Traum was the only disabled runner; he was astonished by the number of disabled athletes running the Canadian event.

He went home and reported the experience to Fred Lebow, the New York City Marathon race director. Lebow encouraged Traum to recruit disabled runners for the marathon, and thus was born the Achilles Track Club, which has grown into the largest and most influential organization of its kind in the world. "It didn't really come from me or that magazine story," says Traum, who remains president of the Achilles Club. "It all came from Terry's dream."

Leaving Toronto and heading west, I get held up in morning traffic. It takes me more than an hour to cover ten miles — not a great deal faster than Terry's pace. Two hours north of the city, I approach Parry Sound, the hometown of hockey legend Bobby Orr. When they met during the run, Terry showed Orr his prosthesis, and Orr showed Terry the scars from his knee surgeries.

The expressway narrows to a two-lane highway and the traffic calms. I catch glimpses of Georgian Bay — shards of a blue dream — and listen to a CBC call-in show about minor league hockey goons. Most days during the Marathon of Hope, despite his excruciating effort (at times, for instance, the chafing of his prosthesis rubbed his stump so raw that blood dripped into his shoe), Terry also had a blast.

"I loved it," he told a reporter after the run. "I enjoyed myself so much, and that was what people couldn't realize. They thought I was going through a nightmare, running all day long . . . Maybe I was, partly, but still I was doing what I wanted . . . Even though it was so difficult, there was not another thing in the world I would rather have been doing."

As the summer wore on, as Terry's story percolated across the nation, Shelly grew more interested in Terry and his run. She wasn't nearly as consumed by the Marathon of Hope as Dory, Earl's sister, was. Dory had filled scrapbooks with pictures and stories of Terry, as if he were a rock star. Still, Shelly sensed that he wasn't just a media darling. He wasn't doing this to stoke his ego or strike it rich. Terry reminded Shelly of the Ontario pioneers she had studied in school, who had paddled across Superior to deliver medicine to sick children. They weren't trying to be heroes; they were just doing what was necessary. Terry seemed to have the same attitude. He was just a plodding Canadian kid — average in school, average as an athlete — who had somehow been chosen for a wonderful, terrible mission. Before Terry, people died from cancer, but they were ashamed to talk about it. This boy from Port Coquitlam wasn't ashamed. Every day, Terry showed his cancer to the world, and the world would never be the same.

Millions of Canadians were drawing similar conclusions. Once Terry had moved through Quebec, there were no more pudgy lifestyle-section reporters puffing alongside him so they could write what running with Terry felt like. The flavor of the news reports changed. The stories took on a respectful, almost reverent tone. The TV showed thousands of people massed in Nathan Phillips Square welcoming him to downtown Toronto. Women in hair curlers hustled out from beauty parlors to watch him run past. Little kids shoved pennies into his hand. NHL superstar Darryl Sittler, Terry's own hero, looked starstruck as he stood beside Terry.

Shelly watched the TV news reports with growing fascination as the Marathon of Hope parade — an Ontario Provincial Police cruiser, Doug Alward and other crew members in their smelly van, an RV carrying a staffer from the Canadian Cancer Society, and, on foot, a one-legged man wearing ragged gray shorts — lurched west toward Wawa.

Lyndon Fournier is a forty-seven-year-old executive for the financial firm ScotiaMcLeod in Mississauga, Ontario. His corner office is filled with Terry Fox memorabilia: photos, newspaper clippings, and certificates of appreciation from the Terry Fox Foundation. Each year Fournier leads the office fund drive for the Terry Fox Run. One of his most prized possessions is a pair of Adidas Orion TFs. In 2005, to help commemorate the twenty-fifth anniversary of the Marathon of Hope, Adidas came out with the TFs, a retro model of the original Orions Terry wore on his run. One of his used shoes — a right-footed one, which he wore over the foot of his prosthesis — sits under glass at an exhibit at the Terry Fox Public Library in Port Coquitlam. Battered, stained, torn, worn down to the midsole, the shoe seems like a relic of a medieval saint. The foot bed of the commemorative TF was embossed with a color map of Terry's marathon route and sold for $100. Adidas donated all proceeds to the Terry Fox Foundation. It wasn't easy to find a pair. Nationwide, 40 percent of retail locations sold out on the first day, and 75 percent in the first week. Fournier had to pull a few strings to get his pair. He looks at the shoes every so often, for inspiration. They have never touched the ground, of course, and Fournier wouldn't dream of running in them.

In Sudbury, I have lunch with a man named Lou Fine, who, in 1980, as district supervisor for the Canadian Cancer Society, accompanied the Marathon of Hope over its final six weeks. "I told one lie to Terry," Fine confesses to me. "When we got to the town of Marathon, halfway between Wawa and Thunder Bay, he got tendonitis so bad in his good leg that he couldn't go another step. One of Terry's supporters got us a small plane, and we flew to the Soo to see a doctor. The doc looks at his leg and says, 'You gotta take a day or two off, son, or at least cut down to thirteen miles a day.' Terry, of course, says the hell with that.

"We were all set to fly back to Marathon, and that's when I told Terry my lie. I made up a story that fog had closed the airport in Marathon. We would have to catch a bus, and wouldn't you know it, there wasn't another bus coming through town until the next day."

Lou gives a dry laugh. "To my amazement, Terry bought my BS.

He let himself rest for two days — two of the three days he took off out of the 143 days on the road."

On his way to Wawa, Terry had followed a convoluted course through heavily populated southern Ontario, adding hundreds of draining miles to his route in order to collect as much money as possible for cancer research. Finally, in mid-July, he worked clear of the Toronto megalopolis and began running up Highway 69 along the eastern shore of Lake Huron, onto the edge of the rocky Precambrian Shield and the great boreal forest carrying north to the Arctic.

At Sudbury, Terry picked up Highway 17, the southern arm of the Trans-Canada Highway, which carried him due west, into the morning fog and muskeg, along the blue deeps of Huron and Superior, through Blind River and the Soo and finally, in mid-August, to Wawa. Now, late on that Monday afternoon, he was about to speak at the Community Center. Shelly raced across town and squeezed into the arena as Terry took the stage.

In front of seven hundred citizens, Terry looked exhausted. On this day, number 129 of his run, he had completed one of the hilliest portions of his cross-country expedition, and yet was only thirty minutes off his scheduled 3:00 P.M. arrival. "I guess I was spurred on by the challenge of it. Everybody kept talking about the hills — Montreal River, Old Woman Bay, especially Montreal River," Terry told the crowd. Shelly listened intently. "But when I got to the top of it, I said, 'Is that it?'" Shelly broke into a smile. Watching him, her first thought was that this must be what it was like seeing the Beatles. He had curly hair, a deep tan, and a white smile. He was pure muscle from all the running. At the same time, the angular machinery of his prosthetic leg made him seem like a vulnerable little boy. Shelly and her girlfriends were practically passing out looking at him. And besides being gorgeous, he was modest.

"I'm not the one who is important here," Terry told the crowd. "This whole thing isn't about me at all."

The people in and around Wawa raised more than $15,000. Donations included $500 from a Wawa motel, $88 from the sale of homemade blueberry pies, and the donation of a gold-plated goose. Another $1,000 or so came from motorists who donated directly to the caravan. Terry told the people of Wawa, before leaving the center, why every dollar was important. "I've been on the road four months and I'm sore. It's hard for people to comprehend what it's like getting up and running every single day. All we're trying to do is help this cause."

In early 1993, fourteen-year-old Nikki Parkinson developed a sharp pain in her shoulder. She assumed it was due to tendonitis caused by the stress of being a competitive swimmer. The pain persisted, however, and specialists in her hometown of Toronto discovered that a malignant tumor had invaded her shoulder joint. Parkinson had been stricken by osteogenic sarcoma, the same type of cancer that afflicted Terry Fox. If, as in Terry's case, Parkinson's tumor metastasized, it would spread to vital organs and kill her. But that was where the similarities between Terry's cancer and Parkinson's ended. "When I came out of the biopsy and got the diagnosis, I asked my mother if I was going to die," Parkinson says. "She looked me in the eye and told me no."

Instead of a 50 percent chance of survival, which was what Terry faced, Parkinson's chances stood at 85 percent. At the end of March, instead of amputating her arm, surgeons at a Toronto hospital performed reconstructive surgery in which Parkinson's malignant shoulder joint was replaced by one from a cadaver and reinforced with steel rods. It was an innovative surgical technique unheard of in Terry's time, and developed in large part due to funding from the Terry Fox Foundation.

After surgery, she underwent a chemotherapy regimen, at the end of which she was diagnosed cancer-free. She went on to graduate from high school and college and earn an advanced degree in human genetics. One day, Parkinson says, she hopes to work with cancer patients at the same hospital in which she was cured. "Terry is the reason that I'm alive," she says. "In more ways than I can count, he is my hero."

I stop one night in Blind River, about 250 miles southeast of Wawa, on the northern lip of Lake Huron, and stay at a motel on Highway 17, the same one Terry stayed in when he came through the town. The owner tells me that guests often ask about him. The waiter at the Chinese restaurant across the highway remembers the day Terry ran through Blind River, and so does Wayne Rivers, the local taxi dispatcher.

"He makes me proud to be a Canadian," Wayne told me, as if Terry were due in Blind River tonight.

I plan to get up just before five tomorrow morning and run a few miles in Terry's footsteps. I watch the sun set over the lake, go to bed early, but sleep poorly. On some nights during his run, despite his exhaustion, Terry also had trouble sleeping. By the time he reached Blind River, in what turned out to be the marathon's final few hundred miles, the signs of decline must have been undeniable — the dry cough and double vision that Doug and Darrell assumed were symptoms of the flu.

The next day I rise as planned. The same hour that Terry rose. He would have gotten out of bed and likely said a quick prayer. (Although he never made a show of his faith, he had read through the entire New Testament during his final months of training for the run.) He would have stepped into his prosthesis the way another man steps into his jeans. He would have washed and dressed and stuffed his gear into his pack and then headed out to the parking lot where Doug and Darrell, Lou Fine, and the OPP trooper waited by their respective vehicles.

"If Terry said, 'Good morning, Lou, are you still fine?' then I knew he had slept well and we were in for a smooth ride," Lou had told me in Sudbury. "But if he just walked right past without a word, I knew that our morning was going to be interesting."

I turn left outside the motel and run past the twenty-four-hour coffee shop, the dark Chinese restaurant, and the park by the mouth of Blind River. Terry's sea-to-shining-sea marathon appears possible at this hour. When he ran this stretch of road twenty-six years ago, it must have seemed a sure thing. He was twenty-two years old, and the cough and double vision had to be symptoms of the flu. He was more than halfway across Canada now, more than halfway home.

I had learned, however, that Terry rarely thought in such abstract terms. When he reached the streetlight, he thought about making it to the gas station. When he reached the station, he thought about running to the water tower on the edge of town.

But no matter how iron your discipline, sometimes your mind drifts. On this morning there are no dogs howling or monster semis batting past with a back draft that knocks you halfway across the highway. The fog lies softly over the muskeg in the last of the moonlight. The breeze is cool off Lake Huron, and the dawn light lacks the day's punishing glare.

Sometimes a farm family would be out at dawn to greet Terry and offer a doughnut or a cup of tea. But not today. It's just the OPP cruiser up front and Doug and Darrell in the van beside him and Lou in the RV, riding sweep. No sweaty crowds, no reporters asking why. The springs on his prosthesis make a steady mechanical squeak. Now the light is rising. A half-mile up the highway, a granite outcropping takes shape out of the fog. Terry sets aim at the rock, emptying his mind, keeping his pace, moving west.

Shelly Skryba cried on the day Terry Fox died, June 10, 1981. It had been nearly ten months since he had come through Wawa. She saw him leave town that evening, and then two weeks and 293 miles later — after running through cities like Thessalon and Marathon — he came to a spot on the highway a few miles east of Thunder Bay and stopped, brought to a halt by crushing chest pains. Three years earlier, when the surgeons had sawed off his leg at the hospital in British Columbia, Terry had convinced himself they had also cut out his cancer; he had willed himself inside that charmed circle of osteogenic sarcoma survivors, the 50 percent who were cured.

But it was now plain that, to his and the world's grief, he'd been running outside that circle all along. Before the amputation, seeds of carcinogenic bone had migrated to Terry's lungs, and had now bloomed into an inoperable secondary cancer. The Marathon of Hope was suspended in midstride. Terry was flown to a hospital not far from his home, where, after a ten-month decline, he died.

Since his death, the Terry Fox Foundation has continued to raise money for treatment-based cancer research chiefly through donations gathered at the Terry Fox Runs. Over the years, the foundation, led by Darrell Fox, has maintained tight control over Terry's name and brand and has shown the same kind of disciplined focus for fundraising that Terry displayed. For instance, in 2000, Darrell turned down a request by the Canadian mint to sell a Terry Fox commemorative coin set marking the twentieth anniversary of the Marathon of Hope; portions of the profits would go to the foundation. Only after the mint came forward with a new proposal in 2005 — it would produce a general-circulation silver dollar embossed with Terry's image — did Darrell say yes. "Terry's original goal was to raise a dollar from every Canadian," Darrell had told me before I set out on my trip, "so the symbolism was perfect."

Like Shelly, much of Canada was in tears the day Terry was buried. The CBC televised the funeral live from Port Coquitlam. By that time, Terry was already half-legend. There had been a telethon with Gordon Lightfoot and other stars. Canadian Prime Minister Pierre Trudeau made a speech. Millions of dollars had poured in from every province in Canada and around the world. Plans formed for the first Terry Fox Run that September.

After his funeral, the media stories about Terry worked down to a trickle. Life returned to normal in Wawa. The men punched in for their shifts at Algoma Ore, the big trucks boomed by on the Trans-Canada Highway. In the summer the fog drifted off the lake, and in the winter the iron cold clamped down. In September, just after the start of the school year, the kids ran around the playground in memory of Terry Fox.

Jason Bielas answers the phone guardedly. Why would a sportswriter be calling? But when Bielas, a thirty-one-year-old postdoctoral fellow in the Department of Pathology at the University of Washington Medical School in Seattle, hears the name Terry Fox, he relaxes. Somehow, whenever Terry is involved, no connection is too far-fetched. There always seems to be a thread to follow.

So Bielas discusses his recent work. He is helping develop a reliable laboratory test for measuring the level of cancer-associated mutations in DNA. With an accurate mutation-level test, Bielas explains, thousands of unnecessary surgeries could be avoided each year. But Bielas also talks about his challenges: federal funding to the lab has just about dried up. Only 10 percent or so of the NIH grants his department applied for this year in the United States have been approved. Which leads the conversation back to Terry. Because Bielas is the recipient of a $40,000 Terry Fox Foundation research grant, Bielas doesn't share his colleagues' anxieties. He can continue his work in the way he sees fit. This makes Bielas feel lucky, and somewhat guilty, and also, especially at this time of year, a little homesick for Canada. Each September, when he was growing up in Toronto, Bielas would do the Terry Fox Run at school. Of the four thousand Terry Fox Runs, only a few are held in the United States. When Bielas mentions Terry Fox to his American friends, he rarely gets more than a blank look in return.

In 1981, at the age of seventeen, Shelly married Earl Dereski, and they soon had two daughters. Shelly worked on being a mother for ten years, then went to college and earned a nursing degree.

Life was fine except for one thing: Taylor, the couple's second child, was always sick. She was constantly missing school; she didn't have the same energy as other kids. Shelly took her to the doctor and they ran tests, but they couldn't find anything wrong. The pattern continued through the summer of 1998. Taylor was sick when she started high school in September, and by Halloween she was too weak to get out of bed. Shelly took her to the hospital in Wawa, but the doctors still couldn't find anything wrong. Taylor went home and collapsed into bed. In the middle of the night she was burning up with fever and her pulse was racing. Her mother put her in a cold tub. They got through the night, and at first light Shelly drove Taylor down to the emergency room. X-rays revealed a foggy mass in Taylor's left lung. The doctors diagnosed pneumonia and put her on antibiotics. But Taylor's condition worsened.

Over the next week, Taylor grew increasingly delirious. One night, Taylor lay quietly in bed, when she said to her mother, "I know why I'm sick."

Shelly didn't like this. "Why?"

"Grandma Myrna wants me to come visit." Shelly went cold. Her mother, Myrna, who had suffered from MS, had died before Taylor was born. Shelly hardly ever talked about her.

At the end of the week it was decided that Taylor should be seen by specialists in the Soo. There, doctors detected a tumor sitting at the opening of her left lung. The next day a medevac helicopter flew Taylor and her mother down to the Hospital for Sick Children in Toronto, one of the world's leading pediatric hospitals, which was popularly known by its nickname, Sick Kids. Specialists verified that the tumor was malignant and had gradually cut off the blood and oxygen supply to the organ. The lung had stagnated, collapsed, and filled with pus. The simmering infection was what had made Taylor sick all her life and was now threatening to kill her.

"At the time, I was too scared and worried to remember that secondary lung cancer was what killed Terry," Shelly would later tell me. "But at the same time, I couldn't help but think of him. Terry Fox was all over Sick Kids."

On a practical level, Terry's influence was tangible in the hospital's radiology and chemotherapy, its surgery and physical therapy: over the last decade, these and other healing arts had dramatically advanced due to support from the Terry Fox Foundation.

But Terry was also present in other ways. His picture, for instance, looked out from the T-shirts of the young patients on the oncology floor. These kids had grown up with Terry Fox. They had listened to their parents tell stories about him around the dinner table, had studied him in the classroom, and had run in his memory on the playground. Now, as they engaged cancer themselves, Terry was their guide and companion.

Driving Highway 17, I approach Wawa seemingly by the inch. Bombing rain eclipses the Montreal River grade, and the CBC drifts out of range on the radio. The eighteen-wheelers throw up fiendish curtains of water. Over the last day or so behind the wheel, I've begun thinking out loud, but not exactly talking to myself. *Terry*, I complain, as, semi-blindly, I pass another truck on the rain-swept highway, *why did you have to run so damn far?*

A hundred miles west of the Soo, I stop for gas, coffee, and to call ahead to Wawa on a pay phone; my cell phone doesn't work in Canada. I dial the race director of the annual Terry Fox Run in Wawa, but I'm doubtful she'll be home on a Saturday afternoon. I'm right; a young voice answers, her daughter's voice. Her mother and father are down in the Soo for the weekend, she says. She would normally be there too, but on the spur of the moment she decided to drive up to Wawa for a fishing derby, which is currently suspended by rain. Purely by chance she had answered my call.

I stammer out my case anyway . . . *magazine in the States, traveling through, thought I'd take a shot* . . . the kid must think I'm a lunatic. But she hears me out calmly and says she'd be happy to talk with me. In fact, Taylor Dereski says, she has her own Terry story to tell.

On November 23, 1998, surgeons removed most of Taylor's lung, leaving a long, hook-shaped scar across her back. She returned home to Wawa, where she missed the remainder of her freshman year in high school. Taylor quickly caught up, however, and in ensuing years, short of some type of vigorous exercise, savored all the pleasures that her disease previously had denied her. She developed a passion for fishing. She graduated from high school and immediately settled on a profession. "Because of the model of my mother, I hope to become a nurse," Taylor says, sitting in her parents' apartment. "Due to my own experience with cancer," she adds, "I'd like to one day work with kids with cancer."

Taylor pauses. At twenty-two, she is the same age that Terry was when he ran through Wawa, and radiates the same sense of life that jumps out from his photos. "My mother talked about Terry a lot, and we learned all about him in school," she continues. "I don't mean to sound spooky or cornball, but having gone through the same thing as he did, and with him actually visiting Wawa, I feel like I know him."

In September 2002, Shelly Dereski noticed that something had changed about her hometown. For the first time since 1981, Wawa lacked a Terry Fox Run. There had been no deliberate slight; people hadn't forgotten Terry. The run organizer had simply moved away, and nobody picked up the ball. Shelly was horrified.

"How could there not be a Terry Fox Run in Wawa?" she says. "With my daughter being a cancer survivor, I had a direct connection to him. And Terry ran through Wawa. I *saw* him."

So Shelly volunteered to become the town's Terry Fox Run director. She didn't know anything about the job. She called the run director in Thunder Bay to get advice and sent away to the Terry Fox Foundation for an organizer's kit. Soon Terry's photo appeared on the same bulletin boards and store windows where the original Terry Fox posters had hung during that golden month of August 1980, when millions of people followed each mile of his magical run through northern Ontario, step by syncopated step. Shelly was young then, and she dreamed of having a beautiful daughter someday. Something profound had touched this cold little town, delivered by a one-legged man who paused here during his long run home.

Shelly had Earl lay out a 5-K course around the high school, while she organized a barbecue at the finish line, and a few hundred people came out, raising $2,600 for the foundation. For the next few years the turnout grew, and in 2005, during the Marathon of Hope's twenty-fifth anniversary, townspeople contributed more than $5,000. Taylor's diminished lung capacity did not allow her to run or walk at the event, but one year, as a cancer survivor, she cut the ribbon at the starting line.

Her mother smiled. Terry Fox had returned to Wawa.

On the third Saturday in September, a month after my trip through Ontario, I drive north from my home in Portland through Washington State, under the Peace Arch border crossing, and into British Columbia. I spend the night at a motel in Port Coquitlam, just outside of Vancouver, watching the replay of a 2005 TV movie about Terry Fox and the Marathon of Hope. I'm impressed by the actor playing Doug Alward. The next morning I meet the real Doug Alward, a shy, intensely private man, and together we go to the Terry Fox Hometown Run in Port Coquitlam.

Near the starting line before the run, Alward shows me the various memories of Terry that have been gathered on a bulletin board. Noting Alward's interest, but having no idea who he is, a race volunteer asks him if he has any stories to share. Alward starts to speak, then catches himself, gives an awkward smile, and decides to walk away. I follow him.

At this same hour, in their respective time zones around the planet, Terry Fox Runs are rolling in hundreds of towns and cities, including Toronto, where I picked up Terry's trail, and Wawa, where for reasons beyond my ken, the trail always seemed to lead me. There are still a few minutes before the start, and to pass the time I ask Alward about his memories of Wawa.

"Everything about that day was a blur," he recalls. "I vaguely remember the big white letters etched into a hillside on the highway."

Doug explains that their start that morning had been delayed because a film crew wanted to get a shot of Terry running up the nearby Montreal River grade. At his habitual 5:00 A.M. starting time, however, Terry would have been climbing the hill in darkness. So they waited an hour so the crew could shoot in daylight. "At the end of the day we had to pay the price," Doug tells me. "After leaving Wawa, Terry still had to run another ninety minutes to reach his quota for the day."

At that moment the ribbon is cut at the starting line. Alward, a 2:45 marathoner at age forty-eight, takes off into the morning drizzle. I chug along in the middle of the pack, connecting Alward's story with my own memories of the town, the lake, the highway, and summer's dwindling days.

JOE POSNANSKI

The Legend of Bo

FROM THE KANSAS CITY STAR

OKAY, SO ONE DAY IN NEW YORK, Bo Jackson complained in the dugout before a game. Reporters surrounded Bo, which never made him happy anyway. Reporters wanted to explain things, and Bo Jackson wasn't about explaining. Bo was about doing.

"Everything I do, people tend to exaggerate it," he moaned. "With me, they want to make things bigger than they are."

Bo said he was just another guy. He wasn't some sort of folk hero, like John Henry or Pecos Bill. No, he hurt like other players. He made mistakes like other players. He struck out a lot. He wasn't forged out of steel, and he couldn't outrun locomotives, and he couldn't turn back time by flying around the world and reversing the rotation of the earth.

"I'm just another player, you know?" he said.

Then the game began, Royals versus Yankees at Yankee Stadium.

First time up, Bo hit a 412-foot homer to center field.

Second time up, Bo smashed a 464-foot opposite-field home run. Longtime Yankees fans said that ball landed in a far-off place where only home runs by Ruth, Gehrig, and Mantle from the left side ever reached.

"Colossal," teammate George Brett would say. "I had to stop and watch."

Third time up, Yankees manager Stump Merrill walked out to the mound to ask pitcher Andy Hawkins how he intended to get Bo out this time.

"I'll pitch it outside," Hawkins said.

"It better be *way* outside," Merrill replied.

Hawkins threw it way outside. Jackson poked the ball over the right-field fence for his third homer. The New York crowd went bananas.

Bo never got a fourth time up that day. Instead, Bo hurt his shoulder while diving and almost making one of the great catches in baseball history. New Yorkers stood and cheered Bo as he walked off the field. It's possible that no opposing player ever heard those sorts of cheers at Yankee Stadium.

"You know what?" Royals Hall of Famer Frank White would say almost twenty years later. "I really did play baseball with Superman."

Yes, you read that right — it has been twenty years since Bo Jackson was a rookie. That means there is an entire generation of young baseball fans who never experienced that incomparable thrill of watching Bo play baseball.

How can you explain Bo Jackson to a kid today? Old-time baseball fans and scouts are always telling tall tales about players — they will say, "Oh, you should have seen Mickey Mantle before he hurt his knees; he ran so fast he could bunt for doubles." They will say: "Before Pete Reiser started running into walls, he could play left field and center field at the same time." They will say, "There was nobody quite like Monte Irvin before he went to war; he used to hit for the cycle three times a week."

So what makes Bo different? Well, for one thing, it's all on video. Bo really did break a baseball bat over his thigh after striking out. Bo really did throw a ball from left field all the way to first base on a fly to double up Hall of Fame catcher Carlton Fisk. Bo really did, in his spare time, transform into the most sensational running back the NFL has ever seen. He really did . . . well, he really did a lot of stuff.

First time I ever saw Bo Jackson was in 1986 in a makeshift ballpark in Charlotte, North Carolina. He had just started his pro baseball career, and even then it seemed a bit surreal. Bo had won the Heisman Trophy at Auburn. The Tampa Bay Buccaneers picked him number one overall, of course, sent a limo to pick him up and drive him to Canton, where sculptors were already working on his Pro Football Hall of Fame bust.

Instead, he signed to play baseball with the Royals.

"That day we signed Bo was one of my greatest days in professional baseball," says Art Stewart, now the Royals' senior adviser to the general manager. "There was just nobody like this guy."

On the day Bo signed, he asked whether he could take batting practice. Bo had not swung a bat in months. He hit the first pitch he saw off the base of the crown scoreboard in center field. It had to fly 450 feet. Avron Fogelman, who co-owned the Royals, shouted: "Get me that baseball." Bo promptly hit the second ball he saw to almost the exact same spot, off the base of the scoreboard.

"Get me that ball too," Fogelman said.

That was the day that Buck O'Neil heard the sound — a crack of the bat he heard only three times in his life. The first time he heard it was as a boy, when he watched Babe Ruth take batting practice. The second time was as a player in the Negro Leagues, and the player was Josh Gibson. The third time was Bo that first day in Kansas City.

"You had to rub your eyes," Art Stewart said. "Because you couldn't believe what you were seeing."

A short while later Bo was playing for the Memphis Chicks in that little park in Charlotte. He muscled a long fly ball over the Krispy Kreme sign in left field.

"That was Bo Jackson's first professional home run," the public-address announcer said.

Everybody cheered. And then someone pointed and shouted, "He broke his bat."

Yes, kids. Bo Jackson broke his bat on his first professional home run.

That's the kind of guy we're talking about here.

Bo Jackson was always grouchily unimpressed with himself. Michael Jordan thought that was part of Bo's magic. "Neither of us is very easily amazed," Jordan told *Newsweek* in those days when he and Bo were the two greatest athletes in the world. "You have to expect things of yourself before you can do them."

So when Bo Jackson was called up to the big leagues that September after only fifty-three minor league games, he shrugged. When he had his first four-hit game in only his fifth game, he announced, "It's just another night." Two days after that, he faced Seattle's Mike Moore, a power pitcher who would win 161 games in the big leagues. Before the game, Bo went over to Willie Wilson's bats, liked the feel of one, and announced, "This is mine."

With Willie's bat, Bo Jackson hit a 475-foot blast to left-center. It was the longest home run ever hit at Royals Stadium.

Yes, kids. Bo Jackson's first major league home run flew 475 feet.

"It felt good," Bo said. "But it can only last a couple of minutes. Everybody was oohing and ahhing and giving me high-fives. You know, the usual stuff that goes on."

You know. The usual stuff.

"There's something about Bo," Royals general manager John Schuerholz said then. "Call it mystical or magical."

Nobody had any idea what to make of Bo Jackson. On the one hand, he really didn't know how to play baseball. He was striking out nearly every other at bat. Fly balls were an adventure. He needed time to learn . . . but there was no time. He was playing football. He was a Nike icon — Bo Knows commercials were the hottest thing in sports. He was too big a star to ride minor league buses.

"I think if Bo had been able to stay healthy and been given time to learn the game, he would have been a Hall of Famer," says Allard Baird, who was working as a scout for the Royals at the time. "I have no doubt in my mind about that. He had everything you could want in a player. Everything. But that just wasn't Bo's destiny."

No, instead, Bo's destiny was to become a comic book hero.

September 2, 1986: Bo's first game. His first at bat was against Hall of Famer Steve Carlton. He hit a ground ball to second base, and Tim Hulett picked it up and threw to first — only Bo was already past the bag.

"Oh man, nothing that big should move that fast," said Royals Hall of Famer and former hitting coach John Mayberry.

April 14, 1987: Bo Jackson faced Detroit's Nate Snell with the bases loaded. In spring training that year, Snell had forced Bo to pop out with the bases loaded and Bo threw his bat and glared at Snell.

"Bo was the kind of guy who wanted to prove you wrong," Frank White says. "If you told him he couldn't do something, he would do it."

Snell threw a fastball, and Bo crushed it. Grand slam. It was his fourth hit of the day, his second homer, seventh RBI. He also stole a base. When the bat boy picked up the bat, he realized something. Bo had broken his bat on the homer again.

July 29, 1988: Bo Jackson was facing Baltimore's Jeff Ballard. He called time-out and stepped out of the box. He adjusted his batting glove when he realized that the umpire did not actually grant his time-out, and Ballard was throwing the ball. Jackson jumped back into the box, swung that bat, and . . . yeah. He hit a home run.

"Most amazing thing I've ever seen in my life," says Bob Schaeffer, Kansas City's first-base coach at the time.

May 15, 1989: Legendary baseball writer Peter Gammons was in Minnesota to write a *Sports Illustrated* cover story about Jackson, so he watched Bo take batting practice. It was a typical Bo hitting session — he cracked rockets all over the field. Then it was time for his last swing. Bo jumped into the cage and hit left-handed.

He hit a titanic shot 450 feet off the Hardware Hank sign in right field.

Left-handed.

"I got work to do," Bo said to the other players, whose jaws had dropped. He ran out to the outfield to shag some fly balls.

May 23, 1989: Bo locked into a fastball battle with Nolan Ryan. Up to that point, they had met six times, and Bo had struck out six times. This time, Nolan kept pumping 100-mph fastballs and Bo kept fouling them off, a real clash of the titans. Ryan was not going to try a curveball — this was man-to-man. He threw one last fastball. Bo connected. Bo hit the ball 461 feet, the longest-ever homer at Arlington Stadium.

"They better get a new tape measure," Bo said.

July 11, 1989: All-Star Game in Anaheim. Bo Jackson led off with a monstrous 448-foot home run to straightaway center field — it cleared two fences out there.

"Unbelievable," Hall of Famer Tony Gwynn would say.

"I got a piece of it," Bo would say.

The next inning, he beat out a double-play grounder by running to first in 3.81 seconds — one of the fastest times ever clocked for a right-handed hitter. He stole second base (becoming only the second player to hit a homer and steal a base in an All-Star Game, with Willie Mays). He scored the game-winning run. He was selected MVP.

July 11, 1990: Bo ran up the outfield wall. Literally. He chased down a fly ball and caught it about four steps in front of the fence. He put his right foot on the wall, then his left, then his right — until he was seven feet off the ground and sideways. For a guy who didn't want to be seen as a superhero, he sure kept doing superhero things.

"What do you think of Bo Jackson?" a reporter asked, well, Bo Jackson.

"I've known this guy for years," Bo said of Bo. "And nothing he does fazes me."

There are so many more. One coach says he saw Bo Jackson swing a bat so hard, he actually broke it even though he missed the ball. Once, he ran over catcher Rick Dempsey. Dempsey broke his thumb but said: "I held him to fewer yards than Brian Bosworth." That goes back to a Monday night game.

We don't even have time for all the legendary football stories.

There was the time when Bo faced Roger Clemens, who had struck him out four straight times. "I'm going to get him this time," Bo said. He smashed a home run over the left-field fence.

And there was "The Throw." That deserves its own section. On June 5, 1989, the Royals were playing at Seattle. It was the tenth inning, score was tied 3–3, Harold Reynolds was on first base when Scott Bradley rifled a double to left field. Reynolds was running on the pitch, so it was obvious he would score the winning run. He rounded third, headed for home, and prepared to have his teammates mob him when he saw his teammate Darnell Coles pumping his arms, the baseball signal for "SLIDE!"

Reynolds thought: *Slide? Are you kidding me?*

So, he was about to launch into what he called "a courtesy slide" when he saw that Kansas City catcher Bob Boone had the ball. Boone tagged him. In the clubhouse afterward, Reynolds would watch the play again and again and again, and never figure out exactly what happened.

What happened was this . . . Bo Jackson had gotten the ball and made a flatfooted throw of 300 feet in the air. It was a perfect strike. It was so impossible, so ridiculous, so absurd that no umpire was on the spot to make the call. Home-plate umpire Larry Young finally came to his senses and made a fist — Reynolds was out.

"Now I've seen it all," Scott Bradley would say.

"This is not a normal guy," George Brett would say.

"That was just a supernatural, unbelievable play," Seattle manager Jim Lefebvre would say.

"I just caught the ball, turned, and threw," Bo grumbled. "End of story . . . It's nothing to brag about. Don't try to make a big issue out of it."

Bo Jackson's baseball career really ended on a football field in Los Angeles — he hurt his hip against the Cincinnati Bengals. He did come back and did a few remarkable things after that, but it was different. He wasn't superhuman anymore.

In four-plus seasons with the Kansas City Royals, Bo Jackson hit only .250. He hit 109 homers and stole 81 bases. He banged 32 homers one season, and stole 27 bases another. He struck out more than 600 times. That was his great flaw. When Bo connected with the ball, he hit .385. He made some great plays in the outfield, but one year he had 12 errors in only 97 games. He played in that one All-Star Game.

The thing is, anyone who ever saw him play will never forget him. Every game was like a Harry Houdini performance — you expected to see something you had never seen before. This story began with that July day in 1990 at Yankee Stadium when Bo Jackson hit three home runs. He got hurt, though, and missed more than a month.

He returned on August 11 to face Seattle but was so unsure about his health that he did not even take batting practice. Then he said, "I can play." He came up in the second inning. The pitcher was Randy Johnson. First pitch, Bo crushed a long fly ball to center field. The ball splashed in the waterfall to the left of the scoreboard. The Royals estimated the homer flew 450 feet.

"I'm not trying to brag," Jackson said. "But I actually saw the threads on the ball right before I hit it."

For once, Bo Jackson had impressed himself. And that might have been his greatest feat of all.

Bo Knows Best

FROM ESPN.COM

FROM BEHIND THE WHEEL of an obscenely muscled Dodge pickup, Vincent Edward "Bo" Jackson is reminiscing about the time he took down a 300-pound bear from point-blank range with a .45-caliber pistol. This was a decade ago in Alaska, a few years after Bo retired from organized sports and a few days before the Princess of Wales died in a car crash, and if you're wondering whether Bo was scared, *hell no,* Bo was not scared. Not even when that bear got so close Bo and his hunting companion could see the hairs bolt upright like pine needles on the back of its neck.

"I wasn't scared," Bo says. "I wasn't scared because I knew I could outrun my white buddy. You've got to *think* about these things, man."

The way Bo tells it, he waited as long as he could, then he fired a slug into that bear's skull. The bear kept coming. His buddy yelled, "Shoot him again!" and Bo shot him again, firing another bullet directly into the bear's noggin. Bo 2, Bear 0. And then Bo skinned that bear on the spot and dragged the seventy-pound hide the half-mile back to camp. Of course he did.

"Bring yo' little ass on," Bo is saying. He is no longer speaking of the bear, nor to the reporter cowering in the passenger's seat, nor to the photographer in the backseat who is endeavoring not to vomit, but to a small vehicle of foreign descent that has mustered the nerve to pass him on the right on a four-lane road in suburban Chicago. Bo lives not far from here, in a pristine house in a gated community, with a long driveway where he sometimes unpacks his bow and arrows, sits in a metal folding chair, and fires at a deer-shaped target set under a tree in his yard.

At the moment, Bo is on his way to a store called DGY Motor-sports, where he is going to pay the balance on a four-wheeled rec-reational vehicle he plans to use exclusively to plow the snow from his driveway. Ever since a snowplow broke the lights that surround his driveway, Bo prefers to plow his own snow. It is one of those lit-tle things that, as he approaches his forty-fifth birthday Friday, give him a disproportionate amount of pleasure. The others include (not necessarily in order) golfing, cooking, hunting, motorcycle riding, and doting on his wife and three children: two sons who are already in college, and a daughter who will graduate from high school in the spring.

It is a modest life, but in many ways Bo Jackson is a modest man, one who was never particularly impressed by his own achievements. He is still intimidating, thick all over, his head shaved, his stare so pointed at times that it seems as if it could melt glass. But he is also shockingly *normal*, considering that two decades ago, he was the most famous athlete in America.

Yet there are times when Bo Jackson does not come across as the least bit modest. Some who are familiar with him say Bo him-self has been known to embellish his past. In fact, his entire pub-lic persona was built upon a perception of omnipotence, upon a polyglottal athletic knowledge that became the basis for the most overused sports marketing catchphrase in history: Bo Knows. That even Bo Jackson has often referred to himself as "Bo Jackson," in the third person, as if his body were inhabited by some other-worldly force that took over when he donned a uniform, has led many to assume that both Bo Jackson and "Bo Jackson" were raving egomaniacs.

"That's what the marketing world [wanted] you to believe," Bo says. He speaks slowly and deliberately, a cadence he adopted to neutralize perhaps the most well-documented childhood stutter in athletic history, a stutter that actually becomes more prominent in one-on-one situations than when he is speaking to groups.

Bo is perceptive enough to see through his own mythology; the true reason he referred to himself in the third person, according to those who knew him as a young man, is that his stutter made it dif-ficult for him to say "I." And yet it also became a convenient de-vice. That "Bo Jackson" was manufactured for public consumption, and a young man in his midtwenties who grew up in rural Ala-bama needed some way to separate himself from his own celebrity.

(Soon, other athletes would emulate his example.) That "Bo Jackson" vanishes when he is at home, whether he's with his wife (the only human in the world who refers to him as "Vince") or his children (who refer to him as "Dad") or his childhood friends back in Bessemer, Alabama (who, Bo jokes, often refer to him as "a — — hole"). Back home, many used to mock him for his stutter until Bo — who grew up with an iron-fisted mother and an absentee father — discovered all he needed to erase that dark place he came from was to find some way to run hard and fast.

These days, the real-life Bo Jackson, the Bo Jackson who cooks spaghetti and washes his own dishes and watches reality TV, doesn't even see a need to run around the block anymore. Why bother when a man can play golf instead? Why bother when there is nothing left to prove to anyone?

"But I also know, if I was healthy, with good hips right now, I'd be the fastest forty-five-year-old in the country, or in the world," Bo says. "That much I know. That much . . . I know."

The Myth of Bo

Of course, we will *never* know, and this is where every discussion of Bo Jackson most often begins and ends. All we have are stories that, with two decades of wear, have already begun to feel like tall tales: of Bo scaling an outfield wall in pursuit of a fly ball until he is hovering sideways, seven feet off the ground; of Bo leaving a dent in the chest of an all-pro safety named Mike Harden; of Bo leading off the 1989 Major League Baseball All-Star Game with a home run, and then making the Pro Bowl after the 1990 NFL season.

And those are just the ones we actually have on videotape.

"We had an outdoor party at a lake after we won the county championship," says Terry Brasseale, Bo's baseball coach at McAdory High School. "Bo's just out there in water up to his waist. All of a sudden, he jumps up, does a back flip out of the water, and lands on his feet. I said to my girlfriend, 'Did you see that?'"

For those of us who came of age in the 1980s, watching Bo take on both professional baseball and professional football at the same time, the myth and the man long ago became tangled. *Bo hits a six-hundred-foot home run! Bo tramples Ronnie Lott! Bo snaps a Louisville Slugger over his knee! Bo snaps a Louisville Slugger over his head! Bo hits a batting-practice home run left-handed! Bo parts a major body of water! Bo cures lymphoma!*

There have always been stories like this, passed on in a telephone game from one generation to the next — about Babe Ruth, about Josh Gibson, about Red Grange, about Marion Motley and Jim Brown and Mickey Mantle — and they seemed apocryphal, almost silly, in their exaggeration. The difference, of course, was that we actually *saw* Bo part the Red Sea on our televisions. We saw it with our own eyes; even those moments that weren't televised were documented and sometimes photographed. In 1986, in a minor league ballpark in Charlotte, North Carolina, a young journalist named Joe Posnanski watched Jackson hit his first professional home run, and then realized Jackson had broken his bat. "Bo's destiny," Posnanski would write in the *Kansas City Star,* more than twenty years later, "was to become a comic book hero."

And so it was: within the span of a decade, his superpowers bloomed and wilted. He won the Heisman Trophy at Auburn, chose to play baseball instead of football, then decided he would play both football and baseball, even as every sports columnist in the country and most opposing players (and some of his own teammates) declared him an egomaniac with a death wish. He was just beginning to blossom as a baseball player, and the scouts called him the greatest raw prospect since Mantle and Mays, an almost unfathomable combination of speed and power and arm strength; although he struck out in prolific numbers, he also hit some colossal home runs and made some extraordinary plays in the outfield.

His myth fully crystallized on a Monday night, on the last day of November 1987, when Bo was a rookie running back for the Los Angeles Raiders, a two-sport athlete sharing time in the backfield with a Hall of Famer named Marcus Allen. Bo took a handoff and Bo parted the entire Seattle defense and then Bo — How does one even *describe* this method of propulsion? Glided? Propelled? Teleported? — ninety-one yards down the sideline, and then Bo kept on running until he disappeared into a tunnel in the bowels of Seattle's Kingdome. The *sound* of Bo running past him, former Seahawks receiver Steve Largent said, was like nothing he had ever heard before.

For a moment, Bo was gone, out of the picture entirely, prompting ABC analyst Dan Dierdorf to proclaim to a TV audience that Bo "might not stop until Tacoma." When Bo emerged from that tunnel, and when he lowered his shoulder and toppled a cocky young linebacker named Brian Bosworth on a short touchdown run later that evening, and finished the night with 221 yards, nothing was ever the same. Bo was on his way to becoming an icon, both physically and commercially, a man who could do anything he wanted on any field of play, a man who made a fortune for embodying that Nike catchphrase concocted by a copywriter in Portland, Oregon: *Bo Knows.*

With those two words, Bo Jackson helped usher sports into the modern age.

The Selling of Bo

It was a silly idea in the first place, this two-word mantra, proper noun followed by verb, and like most silly ideas, it came to Jim Riswold in the middle of the night. But then, this was a silly business, and it was Riswold's sense of irony that had led him here in the first place. Already, in 1986, working out of a rambunctious and offbeat Portland advertising firm called Wieden + Kennedy, working for a burgeoning empire known as Nike, Riswold had brought together Michael Jordan and Spike Lee for a shoe campaign that, according to author David Halberstam, created "a figure who had the power and force and charisma of a major movie star."

Jordan was already on his way to becoming an icon in 1987 when Bo Jackson plowed over Brian Bosworth on that Monday night in Seattle. At the same time, Nike was looking to market its new shoe, called a cross-trainer. The company's first choice, Riswold says, was Howie Long. Riswold suggested there was a far better candidate on the same Raiders roster.

"I'm always surprised by how big something as inconsequential as an advertisement can become," Riswold says. "People like their sports heroes, and Bo was something new. A new shiny toy. That was the best example of how big these things can become."

The year before, in 1986, Bo had been picked first in the NFL draft by Tampa Bay. For reasons that are still not entirely clear — a perception of racism within the Buccaneers organization, a sense of loyalty to Kansas City scout Ken Gonzales, Bo's utter abhorrence for the conventions of football practice, Bo's determination to accomplish what others said he couldn't — he chose to sign with the Royals instead. Already, he was a maverick, and once he came back to football in 1987, on his own terms, Riswold and his colleagues began toying with Bo's image. Bo willingly played along. This was the '80s, after all, a decade suffused with vanity and objectivism, and this was a nation presided over by Ronald Reagan, a man of relentless optimism, damn the long-term consequences. The country was "in a mood for the resurrection of old myths," historian Haynes Johnson once wrote. So why not, in keeping with the times, shape Bo as a modern-day Paul Bunyan?

Beau Brummell. Bo Derek. Bo Schembechler. Bo Diddley. *What an unusual name Bo has*, Riswold thought, and he began brainstorming ideas with Nike executives until that pronoun-verb combination came to him in his sleep that night.

"His career was pretty short, and it was injury-plagued, but by the time all those things changed, he was a marketing star," sports marketing executive Nova Lanktree says. "People were just very fond of him. He overcame his stuttering problem. Everything about his profile was suited to [his becoming a cultural phenomenon]."

That first iconic television ad, culminating with Bo playing a horrific guitar riff and Diddley delivering the line, "Bo, you don't know Diddley," aired during the All-Star Game in 1989, the game that Jackson led off with a home run (he was later named MVP). Riswold was watching in a bar in Portland, with several Nike colleagues. When the spot came on, the entire bar fell silent.

"I think God is a Nike fan," Riswold muttered.

It was absurd what happened next, the way the catchphrase caught fire, the way Bo's profile grew and mutated, until, for a short period, he was the most culturally recognizable athlete in the world, above even Jordan himself. The ads grew more self-referential as Bo got bigger and bigger. The '80s ended, and the '90s commenced, and Bo injured his hip, but Nike was invested in Bo by then, and America was invested in Bo as the manifestation of its outsized dreams. Riswold began writing subversive ads that pierced the myth of Bo, and the myth of Nike (these days, Riswold says, Nike would never permit such self-effacement), not to mention the commercialism and the hype and the excess of the nation itself. In one of the last great ads, from the summer of 1991, Bo cuts off a song-and-dance routine, declaring, "I'm an athlete, not an actor."

Then, in the midst of a workout, as the music cues once more, Bo breaks through the fourth wall, crying out to the Nike logo, "You know I don't have time for this," before George Foreman, huckster and infomercial pitchman, takes his place.

By then, of course, it was too late. The monster Riswold had helped to create — sports as cult of personality — was slouching out of its cage, to be reborn over and over again.

"All the athletes today grew up with these commercials, and they want them," Riswold says. "But the world is more cynical, and with good reason. It has been done before. And the Michaels and Bos of the world don't come around that often."

Hidden Bo

The woman in the produce aisle would like to know if Bo is doing autographs this afternoon. Normally, Bo figures, the woman wouldn't have bothered to ask — he's almost certain he has seen her in here before, and he probably has since he comes to this same supermarket at least once a week, where today his list includes such sundries as pasta and sausage and bananas and Diet Pepsi. But since Bo is being trailed by a reporter and a photographer, since his private sphere is already being intruded upon anyway, he figures he will make an exception.

Bo has never quite accepted the phenomenon of celebrity. His private time is his private time, and he does not always take kindly to those who intrude. Approach him at a restaurant while he is eating dinner with his family, and Bo might rebuff you with prejudice. He has worked hard to achieve normalcy. He has lived in the same house for sixteen years, ever since he signed with the White Sox after a hip injury derailed his football career in a 1991 playoff game against Cincinnati, and the neighbors have gotten accustomed to him, even if most of them, northerners through and through, don't comprehend his hunting fetish. The people in the community know his family; unlike Michael Jordan, Bo's old colleague at Nike, whose star ascended long after Bo's commercial potential was tapped, he is not compelled to live a life apart from the remainder of society. This extended even to his family. Bo's daughter, Morgan, was a high school track phenomenon until she decided to quit to focus on academics (and cheerleading) her senior year. Neither of his sons played college sports. His wife, Linda, is a counseling psychologist at a local hospital, the name of which she does not want revealed here, in part, Bo says, because some of her colleagues do not know she is Bo Jackson's spouse.

There are many people, strangers and idolaters, who have no idea Bo Jackson lives in this part of the country. Part of him would prefer to keep it that way. He does not hide — if you want to find Bo, you can find Bo, and he makes occasional public appearances, such as last weekend at the Iron Bowl game between Alabama and Auburn — but he does not keep himself on display either. He says he has cut off associates who have given out his cell-phone number without permission. He was perfectly willing to allow a photographer into his house, but refused to allow the photographer to shoot any photos of his family, or even to shoot photos of the photos of his family. His wife, Bo says, has not granted an interview for as long as he can remember. He was invited at one point to be on *Dancing with the Stars*, he says, but he declined.

Bo is part owner of a food company called N'Genuity, which provides food — mostly meat, all products Bo has approved personally, some of which bear his name, such as the Bo Burger — to the military and to casinos, and has provided him with a strong post-retirement income. Recently, he partnered with another former baseball player, John Cangelosi, to break ground for a sports dome that will provide a place for young ballplayers to practice during Chicago's frigid winters, and he has a financial interest in a local bank as well.

"People around here, they know me," Bo says. "People that live here see me all the time. I'm quiet. I lay low. I think a lot of people get caught up in this celebrity world to where they have to be treated in a certain way, spoken to in a certain way, and they have to carry themselves in a certain way. And if they don't get their way, their world turns upside down. With me, I'll stop and help somebody change a car tire."

And then Bo makes one of several statements that might be a joke. Or, perhaps, a warning.

"If you're my enemy," he says, "and you're by the side of the road with a flat tire, and it's twenty below zero, I'm going to stop and throw a gallon of water on you and keep going."

Young and Reckless Bo

Bo gets back home to Alabama a few times every year, but he does not have any great yearning to go back there for good, or to retire down South. For every fond memory he has of Bessemer, there is a pain that lingers, because Bo Jackson grew up fatherless. His dad, A. D. Adams, lived across town, and used to work in the steel mills, but Adams had a new wife and a new family, and rarely made an appearance except to leave a few dollars on the table. Bo inherited his father's enormous frame and his greatest burden (his stutter), and he combated his own insecurities by utilizing that musculature he'd been given, by lashing out at anyone who stood in his way. He was a bully of the purest sort, "the John Gotti of my neighborhood," he says, a character straight out of Mark Twain. He once clubbed one of his cousins — a *female* cousin — with a baseball bat. Although his mother, Florence Bond, who worked as a housekeeper at a local Ramada Inn, tried every trick she knew to tame him, whipping him with switches and extension cords, Bo would not be tamed.

Bo — his nickname is a truncation of the term "Bo'Hog," for a wild boar — gained a reputation for throwing rocks with uncanny accuracy, mostly at other human beings. He pummeled his classmates on a regular basis. When he was a teenager, in the summer of 1976, he and his friends began throwing rocks at pigs on their way to a local swimming hole, killing several of them. They got caught in the act by a farmer who had hired the local barber to keep watch, and Florence Bond told the barber who caught them that she was ready to send her son to reform school.

The barber asked Bo for the names of his co-conspirators. The way Bo tells it in his autobiography, *Bo Knows Bo*, he suddenly saw where his life was headed, and he spilled his guts. In truth, the transformation was probably more gradual, but it seems to have begun here. He worked all summer mowing lawns to pay back the money, and then, scared straight, he began playing organized sports, endeavoring to find his niche. In baseball, he volunteered to be a catcher. He wrestled at heavyweight ("slippery as a wet catfish," one of his coaches called him), and he ran track. Later, though his mom didn't want him playing football, Bo joined the football team. When she found out he'd done it anyway, she locked him out of the house, and left him out there all night long; Bo curled up in a parked car and went to sleep.

Somewhere, possibly lost by Bo's coauthor on *Bo Knows Bo*, Dick Schaap, there is a videotape of Bo's greatest hits, a videotape that includes a sequence of Bo playing lead blocker for McAdory's other halfback: he knocks down a defensive lineman, knocks down a linebacker, waves for his teammate to follow him, knocks down a cornerback, and escorts his teammate into the end zone.

All that was a long time ago, and most of the people of Bessemer remember Bo fondly, as people often do when one of their own crosses the threshold of celebrity. Some of them have been known to embellish stories about Bo, stories that don't even need embellishing. Given time, of course, even with the video evidence, it seems likely it will become increasingly difficult to separate fact from fiction, and those who remember a healthy Bo will remember the equivalent of his Nintendo Tecmo Super Bowl replicant, the most potent video-game running back in history, utterly unstoppable to the point of being ridiculous.

Sometimes Brasseale tells the story of when Bo hit two towering homers in his first two at bats in the county championship game, and then in his third at bat, with the left fielder backed up to the fence, he hit a high fly ball to shallow left. *If he hustles*, Brasseale thought, *he could get a double out of this*. Soon enough, the ball dropped, and Bo was rounding third.

He scored standing up.

"I tell that to other coaches," Brasseale says, "and they say there ain't no way."

Unforgiving Bo

A few years ago, Bo made up with his father, and goes to visit him often now that A. D. is old and in ill health. But there is something holding Bo back from a complete reconciliation with his past. Whenever his high school asks him for a donation, Bo declines. All in good time, he says.

"Most of the guys I hung out with are still there," Bo says. "I call them institutionalized country. That's all they know. I'm not saying I'm better than I am, but it's not for me."

It is not easy to let go of everything. Bo's entire athletic career was based upon channeling that seething childhood anger into a purpose; his high school teammates, he wrote in *Bo Knows Bo*, didn't make it in college athletics because "they had better lives at home than I did. It was as simple as that." He played games because that was his gift, because he liked to run — he once called himself "half-human, half-deer" — but he also hated to work at it. Imagine if Bo had actually *worked* at it. Imagine if he had actually cared about something like making the Hall of Fame, in either sport. "Worst practice player I've seen in my life," Brasseale says. "He just got bored real easily."

Mostly, Bo strived to fashion an existence for himself, and for his own family, out of his gift. He used sports, he says, to become a businessman, which might be a little bit of Bo rationalizing the sudden end to his career. But there is truth to it as well. Bo's primary goal as an adult was to exist in direct opposition to his own father. It is nothing Bo hasn't thought out before; his wife is a psychologist, after all.

That anger remains, buried beneath the surface. Mostly, he takes it out on the deer he kills and butchers, on the golf balls he hacks at day after day. Brasseale says Bo told him he would like to make a run at the senior tour when he turns fifty. "You doubt me?" Bo said, when Brasseale laughed.

You want to see that anger bubble and boil? Go up to Bo and put your arm around him. He hates that — strangers touching him, strangers who want to arm-wrestle, strangers who think they know him because they saw an advertisement twenty years ago. At one point, to demonstrate, he took my wrist in his hand and twisted, ever so gently.

It was enough.

"You've really got to get under my skin to get me to snap," he says. "But if I snap, God help you."

Bo in Control

These days, Bo Jackson spends a great deal of his idle time in a room in his basement he calls "the hole." It is about six feet wide and ten feet long, and it is adorned with hunting gear and pieces and parts, much of it unopened and hanging on hooks. In that way, it looks like a scaled-down version of the storeroom at the Bass Pro

Shop where Bo shops for arrowheads and other equipment. Bo approaches his arrows the way an artist approaches a composition: he paints them and pieces them together with meticulous precision, with tiny brushes and a jeweler's touch. An old television rests on a work table, and Bo can put his feet up and watch the Golf Channel or Animal Planet (he says he only loosely follows the sports he once played), and he can work on his secret project, which is not really a secret project at all, but simply involves adding lacquer to his most recent cache of arrows.

But Bo has a fanciful sense of humor, and so he tells me he's building a time machine down here, because he would like to go back and win the lottery jackpot, ignoring the fact he has great gobs of cash on hand, and ignoring the obvious conclusion that would leap into most people's minds — the fact that if he built a time machine, he could go back to January 13, 1991, to that divisional playoff game against the Bengals, when Bo took a pitch and ran right and then, instead of cutting out of bounds, cut back one last time before he was taken down from behind by a linebacker named Kevin Walker, fighting like hell all the way. In the midst of the push and pull, Bo's hip was yanked out of its socket. Bo's doctors told him if it were anyone else, his leg would have snapped like a dry twig — the irony being that a broken leg would have healed within months. Even after surgery, the hip would never be the same (though it is perfectly functional today, since Bo no longer runs).

". . . the gods of sports decided to punish Bo because he came too close to them, had reached the brink of being a god himself," Schaap speculated in a postscript to *Bo Knows Bo.*

Bo has always said, and maintains today, he didn't realize the severity of his injury at the time. Perhaps he just *assumed*, with the body he'd been given, that no mortal could rend it. But there is something horrible and wrenching in Bo's expression in the aftermath of that game, captured in a series of photos of Bo sitting on the bench afterward with his two young sons — photos he keeps, unframed, on the floor behind a filing cabinet in his office, near an autographed picture of Chuck Yeager, the uber-test pilot who is Bo's only hero. Bo's expression in the pictures reflects an emotion he is either unwilling or unable to recognize.

"Sports has never been the main focus in my life," Bo insists, staring at those photos. "Dreams of the Hall of Fame never entered my mind when I was playing. The thoughts I had in my mind were of being a businessman. When I did those Nike commercials, I was broadening my horizon, so when the day came, I could get my foot in a lot of doors that you probably couldn't."

Maybe Bo could have avoided this hit, and maybe he could have avoided all of these *What if?* questions, if he'd listened to the skeptics and made up his mind and chosen one path or the other. As the myth grew, as Nike depended upon Bo to be ambidextrous, that choice came with more weight; still, Jackson says he had all but decided that 1991 would be his last season playing football. By then, he was an athlete *and* an actor — he would later play a prison guard in *The Chamber,* a surprisingly strong performance in an otherwise mediocre John Grisham adaptation. (He caught some of it on cable this morning, in fact.)

Safe within his kitchen, Bo has just prepared lunch for his guests, and now he is washing the dishes. He does them by hand. He didn't have a dishwasher when he was a kid; he doesn't see the need for it now. He lives on his own terms: he has been obsessed with flying since watching the planes take off and land from the community airport near his home in Bessemer. The bird feeder in his backyard is almost always filled to the top, so the birds will never think Bo has abandoned them.

"I know how to feed guys like you with a long-handled spoon," Bo says, before driving me back to my hotel. "I never let you get too close. I tell you what I want you to know, and I tell you what you want to hear."

In the obscenely muscled pickup, with the hunting equipment and a nauseated photographer squeezed into the back seat, Bo flips a wave at the guard, passes through the gates, and then pokes his nose out into the world. He has been telling stories about his past for several hours now, and although he doesn't seem to mind — he appears to relish the way he has been able to condense his experiences into parables — he ran away from that Bo Jackson long ago, ran unwittingly out of a sour childhood and into a peculiar life as a demigod, as a myth, as the last comic book hero we will ever see. And then he didn't stop running until he found himself a place behind those gates.

When his wife calls, Bo tells her he'll be home soon enough. He's not staying out here any longer than he has to.

MICHAEL LEWIS

The Kick Is Up and It's . . .
a Career Killer

FROM THE NEW YORK TIMES PLAY MAGAZINE

MY FIRST EXPOSURE to the precarious social status of the professional field-goal kicker came unexpectedly, at a game between the Detroit Lions and the New Orleans Saints on November 8, 1970. There were just two seconds left, and the Saints were losing, which wasn't unusual. The unusual thing was that the game was still close: 17–16. The Saints had the ball, and a field goal would win it — except the ball was in the *Saints'* half of the field, on the forty-three-yard line. And the record distance the ball would have to travel — sixty-three yards — was only the first of the kicker's problems. He was kicking from a dirt surface churned up like a World War I battlefield. The ball would need to cut through the thick, humid New Orleans air and into the closed end of Tulane Stadium, where the wind swirled unpredictably. On top of all that, the kicker lacked the most basic requirement for his job: a foot.

His name was Tom Dempsey, and he was born without fingers on his right hand or toes on his right foot. The gnarled stub of his arm jutted from his jersey with an effect, to my nine-year-old mind, so grotesque that even from a great distance my first instinct was to look away. The foot, however, wasn't repellent — less a malformed appendage than the business end of a useful tool. Other professional football teams had kickers. We had a sledgehammer, or the head of a 1-wood, attached to the end of a 260-pound cripple.

Stump! Stump! Stump!

From this distance, the chant that usually accompanied Dempsey's field-goal attempts sounds like an entire stadium full of Americans having fun at the expense of the handicapped. But nobody thought of it that way. Even one of Dempsey's coaches called him Stumpy, and he claimed not to mind in the slightest.

Stump! Stump! Stump!

But on this afternoon in 1970 there was hardly a peep. The bleachers were empty. The Saints had been around for only three years, but already their fans expected them to lose. They still showed up in huge numbers, full of enthusiasm, and hollered at the top of their lungs right till the moment when they saw, once again, that the cause was lost, whereupon they fled. Just a few hours earlier, Tulane Stadium held more than sixty thousand supposedly committed fanatics, but as the Saints called a time-out and Dempsey trotted onto the field, I could have thrown a baseball in any direction from our seats under the overhang at the forty-yard line and hit no one but my father and his pal Charles, with whom we went to every Saints home game. Charles's beak-like face — he suffered from anorexia nervosa — was never anything but grim; he seldom actually cheered. Entire sections below us had been vacated, so my father and Charles allowed me to pull us a few rows down, to what struck me as better seats. Along the way, Charles insisted, with total certainty, that Tom Dempsey had no chance of making a sixty-three-yard field goal. He tried, and failed, to distract my father with some boring business topic. Like me, my dad harbored a secret hope.

We weren't the only ones moving closer to the action: everyone who hadn't left was rapidly upgrading to a better view. Somewhere in the stadium another boy about my age, Mike Whitsell, was sitting with his father, Dave, who, as it happened, used to play for the Saints. His dad retired at the end of the 1969 season, and in his final year he was Tom Dempsey's holder. When he saw Dempsey walking onto the field to attempt a sixty-three-yard field goal, he turned to his son and said: "Stumpy can make this! I've seen him make this in practice!" Then he hopped out of his seat and down the rows of benches and over the short fence onto the field — where he raced to a spot right behind the refs at the goal posts. Mike knew his dad adored Dempsey, with reason. When they had him over to the house once, Mike's little brother, age three, stared for about three seconds at Dempsey's truncated hand and foot, before asking, in a loud voice, "What happened to your feet and your hands?" Dempsey pulled him up onto his lap and said: "Well, when I was standing in line in heaven to get hands and feet, I was last in line. And by the time I got to the front they only had one and a half pairs left." The little boy, completely satisfied with the explanation, said, "Okay!" and ran off and jumped into the swimming pool.

Now Dave Whitsell was running out to be a part of one last kick by Tom Dempsey. The ball was snapped, Dempsey took his steps, and his stump collided with the ball. To me, from my place in the stands, which was closer to the field than I had ever been, the longest field goal ever kicked in the National Football League looked like a wobbly line drive. But just as Mike Whitsell saw his dad hollering at the refs to get their arms up because the kick was good, I heard my father shout:

"Holy shit!"

It was the first time I ever heard my father swear.

The kick, fluttering its way just over the crossbar, was easily the most exciting thing that had ever happened to the Saints, and it would remain the most exciting thing that happened to the Saints for the next three decades. Tom Dempsey had performed a miracle.

And yet what should have been a simple story of football heroism quickly became something else. Immediately, football authorities outside New Orleans, led by Tex Schramm, the president and general manager of the Dallas Cowboys, complained publicly and loudly that Tom Dempsey had cheated: his misshapen foot, in effect, offered him an unfair advantage. A rumor spread that he had fitted his shoe with a steel plate. The most famous player on the Detroit Lions, Alex Karras, was quoted saying that the whole situation was so preposterous he didn't even bother to rush the kicker. The classic playground defense: *He didn't beat us — we didn't try*. The longest field goal ever made in pro football wasn't heroic; it was more like a circus stunt. Even in New Orleans, where you might have thought the kicker would be nothing but feted, a joke circulated at his expense: *Tom Dempsey: made it by half a foot; let's give him a hand*.

From this experience there are several lessons to be drawn. First, you should never leave any game before it's over, because you never know what's going to happen. Second, grown-ups watching

sports say a lot of stuff with total certainty when they really don't
know what they're talking about. And finally, it is extremely difficult for a field-goal kicker to be a hero. He can perform a miracle,
but the world will always find some way to shove him back in his
place.

It was this last lesson that I carried with me when I went to Indianapolis to spend time with the kicker for the Colts, Adam Vinatieri.
In the thirty-seven years since Tom Dempsey's miraculous field
goal, kickers had become more and more accurate. They are
thought — possibly wrongly, but nevertheless people say so — to
be more and more important to the fate of their teams. Like other
professional football players, they quickly become millionaires,
though at an average salary of $1.5 million a year they remain
among the lowest-paid regulars on the field, after punters. And yet
their general social standing has, if anything, declined.

Item: Scott Norwood. At the end of Super Bowl XXV, in 1991,
Norwood, who up to that moment has enjoyed a wonderful six-year
career, misses a forty-seven-yard field goal for the Buffalo Bills.
The Bills lose to the New York Giants, 20–19. Norwood retires after
one more season and eventually becomes a real estate agent who
spends part of his day selling houses and another part avoiding
phone calls from sports journalists seeking either to mine his tragedy for pathos or to get even with him on behalf of the city of Buffalo. A decade after his missed kick, he tells a reporter that he
dreads the weeks leading up to the Super Bowl, when his failure is
invariably revisited on national television. "A great, great, great
kicker was Scott Norwood," Jason Elam, the kicker for the Denver
Broncos, says. "And he'll only be remembered for the one that he
missed." It's the first of many reminders of the terms of trade between NFL field-goal kickers and everyone else. "People are quick
to blame the kicker," an executive with a National Football Conference team says. "If he makes the kick, the coach made a good decision. If he missed the kick, it's his fault. There's virtually no upside,
because every kick you're expected to make."

Item: Gary Anderson. In 1998, Anderson, with the Minnesota Vikings, completes the first perfect regular season in NFL kicking history. He attempts fifty-nine extra points and thirty-five field goals
and, incredibly, makes them all. His excellence extends into the

postseason, when he drills eight extra points and his first four field goals. But then, in the closing minutes of the NFC Championship game against the Atlanta Falcons, he misses a thirty-eight-yard field goal by inches that would have put the Vikings ahead by ten points and effectively ended the game. The Falcons get the ball back, score a touchdown, and go on to win in overtime. The missed kick winds up being not only the single kick that anyone remembers from a great season, but also the one that most football fans remember from Gary Anderson's twenty-two-year career. The man spends 600 million seconds kicking brilliantly in the NFL and winds up being defined by a couple seconds of catastrophe.

Item: Mike Vanderjagt. In 2003, Vanderjagt, of the Indianapolis Colts, becomes the only place kicker ever to follow a perfect regular season with a perfect postseason. (By this point he has already acquired what for a kicker — and only for a kicker — seem to be unseemly airs. After the previous season, on a Canadian cable sports channel, he dares to express faint doubts about the Colts' quarterback, Peyton Manning. Manning responds with ruthless efficiency, calling Vanderjagt "our idiot kicker who got liquored up and ran his mouth off.") By the end of 2005, eight years into his career, Vanderjagt has established himself as the most accurate field-goal kicker in the history of the NFL — a distinction he still holds — by making an astonishing 88 percent of his attempts. Then, late in a 2006 playoff game against the Pittsburgh Steelers, he lines up a forty-six-yard field goal that could tie the game and send it into overtime. Before the kick, according to Football Outsiders, the best website for football statistics, Vanderjagt made twelve of the fifteen kicks that either tied or won a game in its last minute (or in overtime) — a success rate well above the NFL average. Afterward, he is twelve for sixteen. And he doesn't merely miss; he misses so badly that it is easy to assume total psychological collapse. "It wasn't a Scott Norwood deal where you wondered if he might make it," a member of the Colts' staff tells me. "You knew it was wrong."

Of course it was wrong. This is what kickers do to define themselves: choke under pressure. After the Cowboys acquire Vanderjagt the next season to solve their own kicking problems, their coach, Bill Parcells, makes it clear from the start that he considers him damaged goods. He wonders out loud if anyone could ever recover his manhood after missing such a kick. No one asks whether this is the best way to encourage a kicker's performance; no one wonders if it is perhaps even a bit cruel. Even before the season ends, Vanderjagt has himself a new life story: less than a year after being hailed as the most accurate kicker ever to play the game, and being regarded as an extremely valuable commodity, he is working out by himself on an island off the coast of Florida, wondering if a team might offer him a job. "Next to the quarterback, a coach's confidence wavers so much with who the kicker is," the executive with the NFC team says. "If a linebacker or a running back or a wide receiver has a bad game it's 'Keep him in there. He'll be fine.' If a coach loses just a little bit of confidence in a kicker, you're making a change."

There are many, many more examples of perverse treatment of professional kickers: kickers brought into camp with high expectations and cut after their first NFL game (Justin Medlock, with the Kansas City Chiefs earlier this year), kickers whose exalted reputation collapsed after a single high-profile bad kick in a not terribly meaningful game (Neil Rackers of the Arizona Cardinals on *Monday Night Football* last season against the Chicago Bears), and too many kickers to name who have been quickly dismissed as inherently weak-minded. A kicker in the NFL can be one of two things: the bland technocrat who does what he's assigned to do but who, even when he's exceptionally good, must accept that the coach and the team will be credited for the victory. Or he can be the little choke artist who is very nearly entirely responsible for the loss. For a kicker in the NFL, as the NFC executive put it, there is no upside.

Which brings me to the reason I sought out Adam Vinatieri: he is the exception. Obviously many kickers managed to get to the end of their careers as something other than a goat. But no one else has used the position to become a hero. Vinatieri discovered the upside. He's the highest-paid kicker in the game, making $2.4 million a year, but he's much more than that. He has kicked his way through some kind of glass ceiling; he has shattered the emotional barrier between football hero and kicker. He's like the first woman in outer space, or the first black man on Wall Street.

In the fourth game of the 2007 season, at home against Denver, Adam Vinatieri started the game by kicking off. He then trailed his teammates down the field by fifteen yards and failed to make contact with anyone. After the kickoff, he ran to the sideline, removed his helmet, and found his big practice net. He dragged it, along with five footballs and a ball holder made of white metal, to his favorite spot, alongside the thirty-yard line. The whole procedure took three minutes, and while the game raged on he looked less like a player than a man staking out his campsite. Once he was finished, he strolled a few yards to chat with his holder, Hunter Smith. Then he went looking for his baseball cap, which he donned. Then he walked a few yards more and blew several big pink bubbles. A football game, even for an ordinary player, is mostly a lot of waiting around. For a kicker it is virtually nothing but waiting around. "I'm on the field at most about sixty seconds," he says. "I've got to figure out what to do with the rest of the time." When he was younger he simply kicked the ball into the net throughout the entire game, but he's now thirty-four years old, and his muscles ache if he kicks too much.

Nearly four minutes had elapsed from the game clock when the Colts' offense took the field for the first time. Seeing this, Vinatieri persuaded the TV crew to remove the coiled wire it dumped on his campsite while he was chatting with Smith. As a matter of principle, he substituted his helmet for his baseball cap. "A lot of guys practice in their baseball caps," he says. "For me, whenever I'm working, I put my helmet on." Helmeted, he kicked five balls into the net and then had a drink. But the Colts were stopped, and forced to punt, so his preparation was for naught. Seven minutes of game time had now passed — and roughly thirty minutes of real time — and he could have spent them more usefully reading a book. "It's a real problem," he says. "Once, with New England" — where he was the Patriots' kicker — "I kicked off to start the game and never set foot on the field again."

Hunter Smith and Justin Snow, the long snapper, returned from punting, and Vinatieri joined them on the bench, as far away from the rest of the team as they could be while still remaining within the area designated for players. If Vinatieri stands, his back can tighten up, so instead he sat and watched the game on the JumboTron. When the Colts got the ball back, he would repeat his routine — though not exactly. He insists he's not superstitious, but that's not quite true: he's superstitious about superstition. Every now and then he'll notice, after making a big kick, that he was wearing a certain pair of socks. He'll make sure not to wear the same socks the next time out. "I never want to feel like I have a crutch," he says. Superstition is mental weakness. And mental weakness leads to choking. And choking leads to . . . well, it would be a sign of weakness to even think about what it leads to.

On this night, nothing led to anything. The Colts won easily, 38–20, and Vinatieri was called upon only to make five extra points and one meaningless field goal, then kick the ball back to the Broncos. We agreed to meet the next day in the Colts' training facility.

The Indianapolis Colts' locker room is a giant rectangle lined with cubbies and teeming with large, thick-necked men. Big as it is, it fails to hold the entire team. Off the main room, on the other side of a wall, is a row of three more lockers, those of Vinatieri, Hunter Smith, and Justin Snow. Over the wall is Mordor; here, in the shire, is where the halflings live. Their lockers are made of the same blond wood, but they are more likely to exhibit signs of a life outside football: pictures of the wife and kids, books. Vinatieri's locker holds several Costco-size boxes of Dentyne Blast, five T-shirts on hangers, a vat of multivitamins, and two books: *Secrets of the Millionaire Mind* and a Christian work called *Wild at Heart*. NFL people will tell you that field-goal kickers tend to take God seriously.

One funny thing about football players is how different they look in their uniforms. When he's in his helmet and pads and the camera is on, Vinatieri is so transformed that I cannot recall his face. In street clothes he might pass for an actor or a lawyer or maybe even a high school history teacher who still jogs every day around the school track. He is willing to talk about himself and his achievements — the two kicks that won Super Bowls, the improbable forty-five-yard field goal against the Oakland Raiders in a driving blizzard that sent the Patriots into overtime (and victory, and into the AFC Championship game) — but it's pretty clearly not his favorite thing to do. He is tactically modest and instinctively honest, and he has thought too much about what he does, and how, for his modesty to be anything but false. So he is often torn between his instinct to speak the truth and his wish not to brag. More so than most football players, he starts sentences about himself with "I don't want to say this" and "Don't quote me on this, but —"

Over several weeks of pestering, however, I eventually get from him what I take to be an honest interpretation of his career. In his view, he is no better, physically, than a lot of other kickers both in and out of the NFL. Every year for the past twelve seasons he has found himself in a training camp with a handful of kickers, many of whom have stronger legs than he does. What sets him apart, he is certain, is his character, though he never uses that word. A combination of innate traits and learned skills has rendered him extremely well suited to handle the pressure of the position. "Kicking at this level," he says more than once, "is all about how you handle pressure. We're on an island; everyone is watching us. It's not like some play where only the coaches who can see the film can tell who screwed up. The difference between kickers is, can you do it when the lights are on?"

Ask NFL players and coaches what role in sports is most like being a field-goal kicker and they usually mention golf. That's a fair description of the job — long periods of waiting around punctuated by short, precise swings at a ball — but it doesn't begin to capture its social dimension. When a golfer fails, he fails no one but himself. He doesn't expect to be ridiculed, or to be forced to move to some distant rural place, with an unlisted phone number. Vinatieri suggests a better analogy: the baseball closer. But this is still not quite right: the closer who fails has a chance to redeem himself early and often, doing well tomorrow precisely what he failed to do today. If he has some psychological defect that prevents him from doing the job at all, he isn't drummed out of his profession. He's merely moved to another job in the bullpen. "No one has more pressure on him than a kicker," Vinatieri says, and it's hard to disagree.

Still, I confess my doubts to him. Fans wish to believe that, whatever the sport, a handful of professional athletes respond extraordinarily well under pressure. In baseball, for instance, fans insist on believing that there is such a thing as a great clutch hitter. And while it is impossible to prove that clutch hitting does not exist, it is easy to show that if it exists it is hard to find. There is no evidence in the statistics. The player most commonly cited as a clutch hitter, Derek Jeter, hits just as well in low-stakes situations as he does in high-stakes ones; or, to put it the other way, he hits just as poorly in putatively high-pressure situations as he does in low-pressure ones.

A better explanation for clutch hitting is the fan's tendency to superimpose his own weaknesses upon the players. Fanthropomorphism. It's true that many people wilt under pressure; those people never make it to the major leagues. It seems at least plausible that any kicker who collapses under pressure would have been weeded out long before he ever got to the National Football League.

"I think that's 90 percent true and 10 percent false," Vinatieri says. He's not upset that I've suggested he couldn't possibly be special. He's not even irritated. He's just saying exactly what he thinks.

"What's the 10 percent that's false?" I ask.

"Guys fail to control their heart rates," he says. "They hurry. You see a guy moving a little fast. I don't want to say there's two types of people. But I think there are. There are people who like to be in these situations and people who don't. Kickers come into camp every year and you say, 'Jeez, this kid, he's better than me.' Then he gets on the field and the coaches are watching. They may have a nice leg, but they're inconsistent."

If you want others to believe that you are good under pressure, you must first persuade yourself, and obviously he has. But what's odd about Vinatieri's narrative of his career is that he had no evidence for this special talent until he got to the pros. In college, at South Dakota State, he made only slightly more than half of his field-goal attempts, and he missed game winners. Of being good in the clutch, he admits, "I think I might have thought that way about myself, but my stats didn't show it in college." His ability to rise to every occasion failed to manifest itself until 1996, when, as a kicker in the World League of American Football, he received an invitation to training camp from the New England Patriots, then coached by Bill Parcells, the nemesis of field-goal kickers everywhere. "You want to talk about pressure," Vinatieri says. "Every single day of that training camp was about creating pressure for me to respond to. I'd go to kick and Parcells would be doing the ground whammy." That is, Parcells would find the exact spot Vinatieri had groomed for his kick and walk back and forth across it. Then he'd say, casually, "Oh, were you setting up here?" Just before every kick, Parcells positioned himself between the sun and the ball, to throw a shadow over the proceedings.

Vinatieri was signed as a kickoff specialist, but before the third game of the preseason Parcells took Vinatieri aside and said, "I want to see if you got what it takes, or you pack up your [expletive] and go home." That game, he made three field goals, and afterward the team released the veteran kicker Matt Bahr. In the first game of the regular season, in Miami, Vinatieri made one field goal; the next week, against Buffalo, he missed three out of four field-goal attempts in a 17–10 loss. The third week, he missed an extra point. ("At this point he's screaming his brains off at me," Vinatieri says of his coach.) Parcells told the press: "Kicking is a results-oriented business."

The next week, against Jacksonville, he made five field goals, including a game winner. But as far as Vinatieri is concerned, what set him on his path, what showed that he might be different from other kickers, happened at the end of the season, against the Dallas Cowboys. The Patriots were up, 6–0, with less than six minutes left in the first quarter. Vinatieri kicked off. Herschel Walker took the ball, found a seam, and bolted down the sidelines. He got all the way down inside the thirty-yard line and looked like he was going to score when Vinatieri nabbed him from behind. He didn't shove him out of bounds either, or get lucky with the old wussy-kicker try; he tackled him hard to the ground. In high school, Vinatieri was a linebacker, and it showed. Right through the slow-motion replay the announcers remained incredulous.

"Vinatieri didn't even have an angle!" Marv Albert shouted.

"The kicker ran him down, Marv!" the color man hollered. "Closing speed! I never thought I'd use that word for a kicker!"

After the game, Parcells sought out Vinatieri in the locker room. "He says to me: 'You're more than a field-goal kicker to this team now. You'll see — the way the guys will treat you will be different now.' And he was right. All of a sudden I wasn't that snot-nose kicker who no one wanted to talk to."

Thus the first step in the rise of this kicker: he proved he could run and hit just like a real football player. He was not an ordinary hobbit. He was Frodo Baggins.

In an office at the Colts' training facility, Vinatieri explained what he actually does for a living. (It isn't tackling: "Ideally, at the end of the year I have zero tackles," he said.) He marked the spot on the carpet, one inch by one inch, then took two deliberate steps back, then two to the side. In a game, he never takes his eyes off that spot.

He doesn't watch the center, he said; he watches Hunter Smith, his holder. "His finger is on the spot. When his hand comes up, it's the key to move." The skill of the holder and the long snapper is one reason he chose to come to Indianapolis — as opposed to, say, joining Bill Parcells in Dallas. Dallas was having trouble with its kickers — Vinatieri suspected that this indicated problems with the process. Indianapolis, on the other hand, was a field goal–kicking machine. "Look, Mike was making 88 percent of his kicks," Vinatieri said, referring to Vanderjagt. "He's a very good kicker. But he's not doing that if they have a crappy holder and snapper."

It was the first hint that anyone but Vinatieri himself should be held responsible for his failure — and that he needs to surround himself with the right people in order to succeed — but when I tried to follow this admission to its logical conclusion, he cut me off. "Don't even ask," he said. "If I miss a kick, it's always my fault. You're never going to get me to say anything else." He resumed the instruction. "The bottom line," he said, "is getting your feet shoulder width." His plant foot, the one that doesn't kick the ball, provides the aim. "It should be aimed in the middle of the upright," he said. "It's like a good golf swing — most of the time you're lined right, you'll hit it in the right spot."

After he gets the position right, most of what Vinatieri thinks about is what he shouldn't do. He shouldn't entertain any thoughts of failure, up to and including the possibly liberating thought that, on a very long kick, no one will blame him for a miss. He shouldn't swing his arms. He shouldn't allow his body to rock back and forth: he starts with his weight forward so his body is stuck in place. "I try to get rid of all the external factors, and keep it as simple as I can," he said. He sees Hunter Smith's hands shift and he moves: step, step, kick. Even after the kick, he keeps his eye on the spot. "Let the crowd tell you it's good," he said. "But most of the time you know if it's good when you hit it."

From snap to kick is a shockingly brief moment. "The goal," he said, "is to be between 1.3 and 1.5 seconds." He's never slow, but every so often he finds himself working too quickly. In practice, a few days ago, he felt it and looked at his holder, Hunter Smith, and said, "That was a little quick." The stopwatch had them at 1.25 seconds.

Theoretically, Vinatieri hits every kick exactly the same way. An extra point in a preseason game is to be treated no differently from a forty-five-yard field goal to win the Super Bowl. He didn't put it quite this way to me — he wouldn't like the way it sounds, I suspect — but everything he does is designed to eliminate himself from the kick. He controls his body out of a suspicion that he cannot control his mind. In his approach to his job, he is not merely making it as unlikely as possible that he will choke, but also as unlikely as possible that he will be forced to view himself as having choked. (How can you choke when you never change what you do?) The end result is a near-perfect self-certainty, which in turn reassures himself, his fans, his teammates, and his coaches — to a greater degree than that of any field-goal kicker in National Football League history.

But what evidence, apart from his three famous field goals, does Vinatieri have that he is actually right about himself? He doesn't pay very close attention to his statistics, he says, and I believe him, because he isn't the sort of person who lies (though he does, on occasion, decline to tell the truth). "I know approximately what they are," he told me, "but they're in the past, so they really don't matter." Since he doesn't know, I asked him to guess: of his clutch field-goal attempts, how many has he made?

"I saw an article somewhere where it said I had made nineteen of them," he said.

But how many had he missed?

"I know I boinked one against Kansas City," he said. "In 2003, I think . . . So nineteen out of twenty, or maybe twenty-one."

The actual number is twenty out of twenty-five with the game on the line and a minute or less on the clock (or in overtime). Adam Vinatieri, in other words, is about as likely to make a clutch kick as he is to make an ordinary kick. And he is not all that more likely to make the clutch kick than the ordinarily good NFL kicker. There are virtual unknowns who have a better clutch record: former Bears kicker Paul Edinger went nine for nine, for instance. There are kickers famous for choking who were roughly as accurate in clutch situations as Vinatieri. (See Mike Vanderjagt.) As Aaron Schatz at Football Outsiders, who calculated the figures for me, says: "The sample sizes are too small to make a lot out of them. It's not really an analysis of clutch ability as it is an analysis of clutch history. And what separates Vinatieri is that he has almost half again as many attempts as any other kicker. That, and his clutch kicks are so memorable."

In judging Adam Vinatieri as the greatest clutch kicker of all time — and thus exempting him from the scorn and suspicion heaped upon his breed — football culture misses what's most extraordinary about him: not his ability to kick under pressure, but his talent for coping with the crazy world that kickers inhabit. He pretends to accept the lie that he bears complete responsibility for what happens to his kicks while shrewdly letting it be known that those around him can mess things up; he arranges his kicking routine to prevent his mind from playing any role at all; he even genuinely forgets the clutch kicks that he has missed. Adam Vinatieri is obviously a gifted kicker, but he's even more talented at adapting to his environment. Still, he remains at risk. He has made two kicks that won Super Bowls and a third — the so-called Kick in the Snow, a forty-five-yarder against the Oakland Raiders, which sent the game into overtime — that is perhaps the most legendary of all. ("I still laugh about that kick because it was such a low-percentage kick," he said. "My main thought was 'Don't fall down.'") On these three kicks — a few seconds of playing time — rests the reputation of the most famous clutch field-goal kicker in pro football history. If he misses even one of them, he becomes just another kicker; if he misses all three, he ends up taking early retirement, perhaps envying Scott Norwood for how well football treated him.

Of course, he didn't miss them. He has been spared. And while he seems like the sort of person with the strength of mind to preserve his sense of self no matter what others think, he nonetheless lives in perpetual danger of having his character reappraised in light of the last big kick. When asked how he imagines his career will end, he couldn't find the answer. "That's a hard thing to think about," he said. My NFC executive, who happens to think the world of Vinatieri, says: "Adam Vinatieri's career isn't going to be over until somebody loses confidence in him. And the only way someone is going to lose confidence in him is if he misses a clutch field goal." The only question is: What happens then? Will his miss be forgotten in time, or will it be the sort of kick — say, a chip shot to lose the Super Bowl — that causes everyone to rethink his miracle Kick in the Snow? In theory, they can never take away from him those kicks he made. But, in practice, they do.

His game against Denver was accident-free. But the game just two weeks before that, against Tennessee, offered an example of just how effortlessly the perception of Adam Vinatieri might change. His first extra-point attempt was blocked. He made his first three field-goal attempts, but the third came out a bit low and, once again, a Tennessee player got a hand on it. "All of a sudden I'm thinking too much," he said. "I'm thinking, 'You got to go a little faster.'" He went a little faster — and missed an easy thirty-six-yard field-goal attempt that would have put the game pretty well out of reach. "You get a field goal or an extra point and somebody gets a hand on it, it gets in your head," the color commentator Dan Dierdorf told millions of television viewers. "Even if that head is on Adam Vinatieri's shoulders." The camera zoomed in on Vinatieri as he walked off the field, wearing the dazed expression of the loser. "I wish I could have that one back," he says now. "It left my foot and I thought, 'Oh, give it back to me.'"

Meghan Crosby tends bar in a New Orleans restaurant called Zeke's, and on one of its walls there is a shrine to the kick her father made thirty-seven years ago. Between framed football jerseys is a black-and-white photograph of the split second after the ball has left his foot. Apart from Dempsey and his holder, Joe Scarpati, it shows a grimacing member of the Detroit Lions, Alex Karras, stretching and diving to block the kick. He doesn't look like he's not trying.

Her father joined me for lunch at Zeke's recently. His hair has gone gray, but apart from that he didn't look much different from his photo in the old Saints program. As he talked over lunch, he hid his hand in various ways — behind a napkin, under the table. But his foot he talked about easily and without prompting. As he warmed to his subject — the Kick — he recalled that under orders from Pete Rozelle, then the NFL commissioner, Tex Schramm phoned him to apologize for saying he had an unfair advantage. "But he didn't really apologize," Dempsey said. "He still thought I had an unfair advantage. I guess if not having any toes is an unfair advantage, I have an advantage." Then there was the matter of the shoe. "Everyone said I had steel in it," he said. "But they X-rayed it. It was just a thin piece of leather." He thought his shoe — created at the insistence of the former San Diego Chargers coach Sid Gillman, for whom Dempsey tried out — may have helped his accuracy but had no effect on his distance. He knew he had that sort of distance the first time he kicked a football, at Palomar College, in southern California. His coach decided that his current kicker didn't have enough leg to kick off, so he asked everyone on the team to line up and kick a ball off a tee as far as he could. Dempsey didn't think he'd have sufficient control of his shoe, so he took it off and, with his bare foot, kicked the ball out of the end zone. Thus began his career.

His father had consciously raised him to live a useful lie: that it didn't matter one bit that he lacked a hand and a foot. Dempsey suspects that he was born right-handed, but he's not really sure, because his right hand was never usable. He taught himself how to throw left-handed, and even played baseball. But his body was better suited to football, and much of what he did to play it — lifting weights, for example — built great strength in his legs. That strength paid off the year he became Palomar's field-goal kicker and, in his stocking feet, nailed a sixty-five-yarder against Compton City College. At least he thought he nailed it; the refs called it wide. ("Their excuse was it was too high for them to see," he said.) But the Compton City College coach thought it was good too, and wrote a letter to Vince Lombardi, the coach of the Green Bay Packers, saying he had seen this kid with no foot make a sixty-five-yard field goal. Sight unseen, Lombardi hired Tom Dempsey and put him on a farm team. After a brief time with the taxi squad in San Diego, Dempsey found himself playing for the Saints. That same year, at the end of a game against the Detroit Lions, and with the ball a long way from the goal posts, he overheard his offensive coordinator say, "Tell Stumpy to get ready." And improbable as it seemed to everyone else, he trotted out onto the field without too much concern about the distance.

Thirty-seven years later, a great deal has obviously changed. It's considered bad form even in the bleachers to jeer at physical deformities. (They now mock what they take to be deformities of spirit or character.) Dave Whitsell is dead, as is my father's friend Charles. Tulane Stadium has been razed, and the spot from which Tom Dempsey launched his field goal is a grassy patch below sea level.

And yet some things haven't changed. Tom Dempsey's record stands, for instance. In thirty-seven years it has been tied — by Jason Elam of the Denver Broncos, who was kicking a mile above sea level — but never broken. Field-goal kickers are still defined by the tiniest sliver of their professional career. "I made a lot of big kicks, but all anyone wants to talk about is that one," Dempsey said. And, finally, there is still some faint resistance to the notion that a kicker could ever really do anything great. Brett Favre can throw ten more game-ending interceptions and fans will still cherish his moments of glory. Reggie Bush may fumble away a championship and still end up being known for the best things he ever does. Even offensive linemen whose names no one remembers are permitted to end their days basking in the reflected glory of having been on the field. Kickers alone are required to make their own cases.

Every so often someone still comes up to Tom Dempsey to put his achievement into perspective. Not long ago, a total stranger approached him wanting to talk about the Kick. "And he said to me," Dempsey recalled, "'You're really nothing but a one-kick kicker.' And I thought: 'Yeah, but I kicked it once. What the hell did you do?'"

PAUL SOLOTAROFF

Casualties of the NFL

FROM MEN'S JOURNAL

HE CAME OFF THE SNAP and started upfield, the linebacker dead
in his sights. Brian DeMarco — six-foot-seven and ripped at 320
pounds; the rare pulling guard who could run like hell and bench-
press 500 — led his tailback, Corey Dillon, into the hole. DeMarco,
with a full head of steam, was set to bury the linebacker, put a helmet between his numbers, and plant him, when someone tripped
Dillon from behind. Dillon fell crosswise on the back of DeMarco's
legs, pinning his knees to the turf. In slo-mo DeMarco was falling
forward himself when the linebacker lowered his helmet and drove
through DeMarco, knocking his chest downfield as his hips went
upfield, practically cleaving him in two.

"I heard the pop in my back as I was going down and just felt this
pain like I'd never felt before," says DeMarco, who had recently
signed with the Cincinnati Bengals after four solid years with the
Jacksonville Jaguars. "I'm at the bottom of the pile under a thousand pounds of guys, and I'm thinking, *I'm never getting up. I'll never
walk again.*"

In the grand scheme of things, he'd been hit harder: shots that
broke ribs and left them slapped on sideways; head-to-head colli-
sions that knocked him senseless and smashed the orbital bone
around his eyes; blows that sheared knees and turned elbows inside
out. None of those, however, had managed to shove his spine forward on his pelvis and shave off bits of vertebrae like ice chips.
Here was terror: DeMarco couldn't work his legs, and the pain between his hips sawed him in half.

They got him to the sideline, where the trainer and his staff laid

DeMarco on the bench and tested his legs. He wasn't, in fact, para-lyzed, though he couldn't sit up. And so the doctor stepped in and did what doctors have done since the banzai days of Vince Lombardi. He produced a four-inch needle, hiked the player's jersey up, and injected him several times with lidocaine. The numbness set in, DeMarco got to his feet, and, minutes after breaking off bits of spine, reentered the game. He was twenty-seven; in a few months he would be out of the sport, a young man with an old man's body.

Eight years later, and a thousand miles away, a woman gets out of a car. She has driven from the airport through the kiln of southeastern Texas to a suburb of Austin that isn't really a suburb; it is more like the rubble of an ugly spacecraft that has crashed in the middle of nowhere and been repurposed. The houses thrown up here are flimsy and dour and the residents mostly evacuees of Hurricane Katrina. The woman rings the doorbell and fans herself; the heat, even in May, is wearing spurs. She waits and waits; at long last, footsteps.

Invited in by his wife Autumn, she finds the man she came to see sprawled on a couch, unable to stand. Although the house is cool, he is sweating profusely and can't find a position, seated or prone, that doesn't cause him grotesque pain. Every so often his huge body jerks in spasms of head-to-toe agony. The fits, when they come, turn him as white as the walls and send un-self-conscious tears down his cheeks. It's DeMarco at thirty-five: dirt-poor, broken, and in a headfirst spiral, taking his wife and children down with him.

The visitor, Jennifer Smith, takes a look around and can scarcely believe her eyes. "There was no food in the house, and I mean none — not a box of mac and cheese or a can of tuna," she says. "Brian and Autumn hadn't eaten in a couple of days and between them had seventy-five cents. Total."

Smith, who runs a charity called Gridiron Greats that gives money and care to ex-football players whose injuries have left them in dire straits, has flown in on short notice. She's come with $2,500 in cash from a private donor and the authority from her board to cut a check for thousands more when the banks reopen on Monday. But before she can take this family to the nearest Wal-Mart for the fill-the-pantry shopping they sorely need, she first has to get a 320-pound cripple off his sweat-soaked couch and into her car.

*

It is one of the master stories of the American century: a working-man's game of make-believe warfare becomes the richest, most ravishing pageant on earth, a carnival of beauty and gore. The players, like the sport, transform before us, turn massive and mobile to make panoramic violence on our behalf, then get up, walk it off, and go again. The big get faster and the fast get bigger, staging goal-line hurdles and blindside hits the likes of which no one has seen before and won't again, till *SportsCenter* airs at six, showing the plays and their end zone celebrations until they're etched in the dura of our skulls. Forty years ago football's TV rights sold for $9 million a year to CBS; last year the networks paid out a combined $3.7 billion, or more than $100 million per team. Thirty years ago it cost $16 million to buy a franchise in Tampa Bay. By 2004 Robert McNair was paying $700 million to found the Houston Texans; for bidders who hope to place a new team in Los Angeles the asking price could top $1 billion.

But the men on the field who generate those billions are real; they bleed; they break; their brains cloud. The nature of their injuries, particularly the mind-dimming concussion, has dominated the off-the-field news of late. Postmortem exams of Andre Waters (suicide at forty-four), Terry Long (suicide at forty-five), Justin Strzelczyk (car crash at thirty-six), and Mike Webster (heart attack at fifty) showed staggering brain damage in men so young and affirmed that football is no longer a contact sport but real-life *Mortal Kombat* in cleats. Stunningly no one in the sport has stepped up to address the scope and depth of the injuries — not the teams, not the owners, and certainly not the one organization charged with looking after the athletes, the NFL Players Association (NFLPA). In a game expected to take in $7 billion this year and that exceeds all others in causing bodily harm, fewer than 3 percent of the men who played in the league succeed in getting disability benefits. Worse, the players union turns away ailing vets despite a pension fund with $1 billion in assets.

The great Earl Campbell is fifty-two and relies on a walker to get around. Al Toon, the best receiver in the history of the New York Jets, ended his career after his ninth concussion, in 1992; the Jets' next-best receiver, the oft-concussed Wayne Chrebet, left equally ravaged after the 2005 season and is still debilitated by headaches. Three of the best centers ever — Jim Ringo, Mick Tinglehoff, and Webster — were all beset with severe dementia as young men.

Twenty years ago, when linemen weighed 280, it was common for them to play on into their thirties. Now offensive tackles average 320, and a typical career lasts three and a half seasons, or just half a season more than the minimum to qualify for a pension. Nor does playing longer secure one's finances during old age. Full pension payouts start at fifty-five, which is around the time the average former player dies, two decades sooner than nonplayers.

But bigger-faster-stronger only begins to tell the story when it comes to short careers and early deaths. The NFL offseason has become a misnomer, with mini-camps, workouts, and OTAs (organized team activities) that the league hilariously calls "voluntary." The regular season has sixteen games, but the postseason now has four rounds of games for those hardy enough to survive. Helmets have improved, but players are taught — still — to lead with their heads.

"If I got my hat between your numbers, I'd take you anywhere I wanted," says Daryl Johnston, the Fox TV analyst and ex-fullback for the Dallas Cowboys, who opened huge holes for Emmitt Smith during Dallas's glory years in the '90s and played in two Pro Bowls. Adds Johnston, who retired with a broken neck after eleven brutal seasons in the league, "Strap a helmet on, run headfirst into a wall, then do it again thirty-five times. That's what I did every Sunday afternoon."

Then there is the matter of the game's mentality, a form of mass psychosis passed down through the decades by coaches and players alike. "You can't make the club from the tub" is its motto, a summation of the imperative to play through pain, get back on the field with all manner of debilities, lest your teammates taunt you and your coaches replace you the very first chance they get. In the only major league sport without guaranteed deals, the majority of players are essentially cows at market — large, anonymous slabs of beef to whom too few in management feel financial loyalty or, for that matter, human concern.

"When I broke my neck doing what I was trained to do, the league and union told me to get lost," says Johnston, who filed for disability and says he was curtly turned down by the retirement board. "The second I couldn't play I was dead meat to them. It was 'So long, see you later, and don't call us.'"

Mike Ditka, the embodiment of old-school toughness as a player and then as the coach of the Chicago Bears, says it was just as bad back in the day. "I took cortisone injections three times a week and had four hip replacements after I quit the game, but that's football, and we chose to play hurt. We paid the price and thought the game would pay us back, but the league and union sold us out. In every sport, you've got your adversaries. I never thought we'd have to fight our own."

Ditka, who earned a pittance by today's standards as a player and whose sizable wealth was amassed off the field, has taken it upon himself to redress the plight of ailing vets, many of whom he played with and against. He's joined forces with Gridiron Greats founder Jerry Kramer and a board of directors that includes several Hall of Famers (Gale Sayers, Harry Carson, Joe DeLamielleure, and others) to raise a hue and cry against the Players Association for its abandonment of ex-players.

"It's criminal," says Ditka at an upstairs table in his huge, clamorous steak house in Chicago. "There's so much money in this goddamn game, and no one gives a shit about these guys. Bill Forrester's attached to a feeding tube, Joe Perry has to choose between eating and pain pills, and here's this Upshaw, with his $6.7 million salary, saying there's no dough left to help them out. That's greed talking, and nothing else."

He is speaking, or more like it, shouting about Gene Upshaw, the long-serving chief of the players union, who's become the white-hot focus of some veterans' rage. "The NFL is the worst-represented league, on the players' side, in pro sports," said Joe Montana in a 2006 newspaper survey of Hall of Famers. DeLamielleure, the anchor of the Buffalo Bills line that blocked for O. J. Simpson, turns red as a fire ant when asked about Upshaw. "I won't stop until that bastard's gone or in jail. He's a disgrace to every player, past and current."

Upshaw, who refused to speak for this article and elected to leave the country when Congress staged a hearing on the union's treatment of injured vets in late June, has responded to his critics with schoolyard taunts, calling Ditka too "dumb" to understand the issue and threatening to break DeLamielleure's neck.

This is odd behavior for one of the highest-paid officials in the history of organized labor, and, in any case, these attacks duck the issue at hand: the needs of broke and battered ex-players. An exhaustive investigation — including interviews with dozens of injured vets, evaluations of their medical charts and reports from doctors selected by the league, and conversations with critics of the Players Association in the medical and legal community — reveals a pattern of conduct by the NFLPA that denies former players the money they need and to which their injuries should entitle them. What emerges is a picture of a labor union that has turned its back on the men who built it, and officials who use their power not to advocate for their brethren but to protect the assets of the thirty-two owners with whom they once did battle.

Because they are always going backward in pass protection, and because, for many years, they weren't allowed to use their hands to block, there's a notion that offensive linemen are passive creatures who stand around waiting to get hit. Brian DeMarco has one word for this: bullshit. "Those draw plays and sweeps where we're coming down the line and have ten yards to pick up speed? Man, I've crushed guys so bad they were carried off twitching. A couple of them were never the same again."

DeMarco was a monster in the free-weight room, loading the bar out till it bowed on his shoulders, doing squats with nine hundred pounds. He'd been like that since boyhood, a five-footer in first grade whose father, a former lineman himself, taught him to play the game of football with a mean streak. He was first to every practice and practically lived at the stadium during the offseason, training six, seven hours a day. A good thing too, because the coach who drafted him was a tireless old-school bully.

"That first training camp under Coach [Tom] Coughlin was the most abusive, hellacious thing I've ever been through," DeMarco says. "An unbelievable heat wave, 110 on the field, and we're doing full-speed hitting twice a day for eight weeks. I saw grown men give up and walk off in tears, good players who signed with other teams."

Coughlin, a bellicose, red-faced screamer who coached the Jacksonville Jaguars from their inception in '95 till his firing eight years later (he's currently on shaky ground as the coach of the New York Giants), is a product of the Bill Parcells coaching tree, a man who, like Parcells and Bill Belichick, had little or no tolerance for "softness."

"Tom told us straight up that injuries were bullshit and he wasn't gonna stand for 'em," says DeMarco. "He said, 'You sit out a game and I'll fucking waive you. I don't want cowards on my team.' No matter how bad you were, you were gonna play, which is why four of the five guys who started on that line are now severely messed up in their thirties."

He ticks off names and medical conditions: Tony Boselli, left tackle, washed out at twenty-nine after a string of surgeries to his shoulder, knee, and ankle; Leon Searcy, right tackle, badly hobbled by leg woes and waived out of the league at thirty-two; Jeff Novak, left guard, retired at thirty-one after playing on a leg that bled like rotting meat, and which the then–team doctor so grossly mis-handled that a jury awarded Novak $5 million when he sued the physician, Dr. Steve Lucie. "Lucie was no more than a yes-man for Coughlin, but it was the trainers who really put the wood to us," says DeMarco. "They handed out these big, long packets of Vicodin and shitloads of muscle relaxers like Soma and Flexerall and were always hassling you with 'You playing? You're playing, right?' — and that wasn't just on game day. That was Wednesday practice." (The Jacksonville Jaguars declined to comment for this article; the Bengals told *Men's Journal*: "The rules regarding injury treat-ment procedures are based on the government regulations and the NFL's collective bargaining agreement. The Bengals, to the best of the team's knowledge, are in complete compliance in these areas regarding Brian DeMarco.")

DeMarco is half-sitting and half-lying on a couch in a house kept dim during the day. Even lamp light can crease his eyes and trigger the cluster migraines that send him back to bed in the middle of the afternoon. Since May, when he stopped taking pain meds cold turkey, he has lived in the kind of crackling, bone-on-bone agony that might best be called electric. Ask him where it hurts and he lets out a breath: "Man, ask me where it doesn't; that's quicker." Just now, there are sharp stabs under his ribs, the residue of the kind of bad-luck spill that linemen take all the time. In a game in '97 he knocked down Tony Siragusa, the Pro Bowl nose tackle of the Baltimore Ravens. Siragusa was on his back, one leg planted in the turf, when DeMarco was slammed sideways by someone behind him and landed on Siragusa's upturned knee. Three ribs shattered and two dislodged from the cartilage that bound them in place. DeMarco was carried off to the sideline by teammates, barely able to breathe for the pain. Trainers laid him out on a metal bench and had staffers huddle around him so that no one would see what happened next.

"The doctor took this needle, filled it up with lido[caine], and put a towel in my mouth saying, 'This'll burn,'" says DeMarco. "He stuck that four-inch needle up under my rib cage — six big shots from my rib cage to spine, and suddenly I couldn't feel a damn thing. They wrapped up my ribs, which were sticking out sideways, and sent me back in on the same series." Many of DeMarco's stories begin and end this way: a savage blow that rips tendon or bone and a hasty in-game visit with the team doctor, who numbs him up with long needles before he's sent back into the game. "Anytime a crowd's gathered around on the sideline," he says, "they're doing something they don't want you to see."

Dave Pear, the ex–Pro Bowl nose guard, agrees. After three stellar seasons with Tampa Bay in the late '70s, he was playing his third game for the Oakland Raiders when he was hit and felt "lightning" down his spine. "I came over to the sideline and the team doctor — his nickname was Needles — sends me back in the game. He says I had a broken neck, and I was in agony the rest of the season; but he said I was a hypochondriac and there was nothing wrong with me, and shot me up with whatever he said I needed."

Pear, who's fifty-four now, has had seven operations on his upper and lower spine. He hasn't known a moment without grinding pain since that game against Seattle in '79. He somehow played on through the Super Bowl in 1980, getting handfuls of Percodan from the Raiders' staff and doing further damage to the discs in his neck till he was properly diagnosed in 1981 by an independent physician. (The Raiders declined to comment, except to say that Pear's back surgery was not performed by a team physician, he played only after completing a physical, and he was released due to personnel issues, not injuries.) Like DeMarco, Pear's spine is busy with rods and screws that creakily bolt the whole mess together. He hasn't worked in years and barely earned a living when he did, driving around in a series of lowly sales jobs that left him doubled over in his van. Pear had two young children that he couldn't chase after and a wife who had to do the bulk of the parenting while holding down a full-time job, and in 1995 he applied once more for NFL disability. The first time he did so, in 1983, Pear was approved by the physician the league sent him to, and he waited for a check. Instead he was told by Dee Becker, a union claims rep, that he'd brought too much "information" to the examining room (i.e., X-rays and case files from his surgeon) and was disqualified for "influencing" the doctor. "I said, 'You must be kidding,' and she said, 'Nope, that's how we do it. Flat out, you're not going to get it.'"

Pear, whose neck and back pain had become intolerable, applied in '95 for a new class of claims — permanent and degenerative conditions. As before, he had a slam-dunk medical case: three fused discs, a host of neural damage, and a sheaf of reports from spine experts. The league's appointed doctor found him "markedly incapacitated," but again Pear learned he'd been denied. "I called Dee Becker at the players union and said, 'What do you have to be to be called "disabled"?' And she says, 'Unless you're in a wheelchair like Darryl Stingley, you won't get the benefit.'"

In despair, Pear took his pension early and gets $600 a month from the NFL for his six years of backbreaking service. His drugs alone cost him twice that much, and he survives, albeit barely, on his spouse's salary and a modicum of Social Security. He has, however, managed to keep a roof over his head, which is more than Mike Mosley can say.

Mosley, a blazingly fast returner and flanker for the Buffalo Bills in the '80s, ripped his right knee making a cut on turf and went down in a heap, untouched. The doctor who attended to him botched the treatment so badly that Mosley, who ran a 4.28 in the 40, could barely stop and start on a two-move pattern. "He 'fixed' the cartilage, which was fine, and left the ligament, which was torn, and I ran on it and frayed it completely," says Mosley, now forty-nine, in the thick-as-gravy accent of small-town central Texas. "I went from being the return champ in 1982 to being unable to bend my knee by '84. Then the leg withered, and that was it. I was home on my front porch at twenty-six."

Mosley, a golden boy in high school and college — he was the wishbone quarterback at Texas A&M, where boosters threw cash and cars at him and the girls lined up to ride shotgun — fell fast and hard once football was done, lapsing into deep depression. He tried to get a job, but his knee kept buckling, and he had additional problems with his shins and back. In 1998 he filed for disability and, to his shock and relief, was approved. The $9,000 a month allowed him to buy a small house and win custody of his five-year-old daughter Kendall, and though medical expenses ate up most of the rest, he was able to fashion a life again. And then in '04, without a word of warning, the pension board cut him off. He appealed to the union, but it soon stopped taking his calls. In short order he lost his house and truck, and he and his daughter were forced to move in with his seventy-five-year-old mother. She is in very frail health, has run through her savings, and must feed three people on her Social Security check of $319 a month. Mosley, a man of forty-nine, hides in his room, surrounded by football trophies. The look he wears when you flush him out is that of a dying quail.

"There's nothing left," he says. "They took it all from me, and never even gave a reason. If you talk to Upshaw — and I tried like hell to — could you ask him how he lives with himself?"

The billion-dollar question, of course, is why. Why have the pleas of DeMarco, Mosley, et al., been met with indifference, even hostility? Why has ex–Pro Bowler Conrad Dobler been denied five times for disability, despite thirteen operations on one leg? Why is Willie Wood, the gallant Green Bay safety, unable to pay for his assisted living facility? Why is Mercury Morris, the fleet tailback who fractured his neck as a Miami Dolphin, still fighting in appeals court to overturn the pension board's decision, twenty years later? Why did Johnny Unitas, the onetime face of the NFL, die embittered by the league's callous treatment of his teammates?

Since no one at the union's D.C. office responded to multiple e-mails and phone calls, the best one can do is sift the facts. Begin with the pension fund, which the players union won after a bitter fight with owners in the '60s. It has grown, like the game, from a shoestring concern to an instrument of vaulting wealth and continues to take in more — tens of millions more — than it pays out in benefits each year. Team owners paid $67.9 million in 2005 to cover the monthly checks for retirees, and the plan, called the Bert Bell/Pete Rozelle NFL Player Retirement Plan, earns millions more a year in additional interest on its vast investment holdings. From early on a supplement of the plan provided disability funds for injured ex-players. The checks were mostly modest and not easily gotten, particularly if you said your suffering was football-related. Nonetheless, some veterans won, and eked by on sums equal to what they'd get as pensioners.

But all that changed in 1993, with the landmark bargaining agreement between players and owners that made partners of the long-term enemies. The Groom Law Group, a K Street, Washington, outfit, was hired first to write the collective bargaining agreement and later to represent the NFL retirement plan. To the existing bureaucracy — a six-man board of trustees, made up of three reps from owners and players apiece — a screening committee was added with the power to approve or reject claims. Confusing new rules and categories were added, and retired players were reduced to one kind of claim, football degenerative injuries. But unless they could prove that their health woes were caused by football, they stood no chance of ever collecting the $9,000 a month. And most of those who won claims had to win them over and over again, as the board sent them to doctors every second year to recertify their debilities. "That's the trick they pulled on me," says Mosley. "They shopped and shopped till they found a quack doctor who would cross me off the list."

The union says it pays out $20 million a year to 317 disabled ex-players and that many of them get the maximum benefit of $18,600 a month. But tax forms for 2006, the most recent year available, show that only 121 players receive disability, for a total of roughly $9.2 million.

Then there is Upshaw's oft-repeated assertion that the money to pay these claims comes from active players. That's misleading. Every cent of the fund is put in by the owners, although in 2006 active players reduced their annual salaries by an average of $56,000 to contribute to the fund.

"Gene lies and lies, telling the young guys today that they'll have nothing to retire on if he pays us," says Bernard Parrish, the former cornerback for the Cleveland Browns, who's a spry seventy-one and comfortably fixed, having earned a handsome living building hotels. "It's divide and conquer, and it distracts them from his real job, which is guarding the owners' money."

Because disability claims are protected by privacy laws, the union doesn't disclose who is turned down or why. But the case of Mike Webster, which played out in court, afforded a rare look at its mindset. Webster, the seemingly immortal Steelers center who made the

All-Century team and was the four-time captain of a Super Bowl champion team, retired in 1990 after seventeen seasons and immediately presented signs of dementia. As offensive line coach for the Kansas City Chiefs, he slept on a bench in the locker room and couldn't recall where he lived. He gave whatever money he had to total strangers, wound up bedding in his truck, and frequently zapped himself with a Taser gun to quell the pain in his back.

"He was drifting for years when I got him to doctors who diagnosed severe TBI [traumatic brain injury]," says Bob Fitzsimmons, a West Virginia lawyer who worked, pro bono, for seven years to bring the case to closure. "The union hired an investigator to try to discredit Mike, brought their own doctor in who agreed with my doctors, and they still denied us three or four times and kept trying to spend him dry. Finally we got to trial and won a huge judgment in district court. But even after the union lost again on appeal, Upshaw told reporters that if the board voted that day, they'd still go against Mike, six to nothing."

Upshaw's confidence in the board is hard to fathom, given that three of its reps are, like Upshaw himself, supposed to put players' interests first. But Upshaw's appointees are all compromised in one way or another. One, Tom Condon, is Upshaw's agent, who negotiated his salary as the head of the union, a sum that wildly exceeds what union chiefs make in other sports. (Upshaw: $6.7 million a year; Billy Hunter: $2.1 million in basketball; Donald Fehr: $1 million in baseball.) A second is Jeff Van Note, a broadcaster for the Atlanta Falcons, whose salary is paid by team owner Arthur Blank. The third is Dave Duerson, who pled guilty to beating his wife and throwing her out a hotel door and into a wall.

If that seems a shabby way to staff a pension board, it is very much in keeping with Upshaw's style. From his bellicose beginnings as a union chief in 1983, Upshaw, the Hall of Fame guard for the Oakland Raiders, has been dogged by allegations of fiscal mismanagement. As reported by the *Boston Globe* in 1990, the sloppy bookkeeping included a loan of $100,000 made by the union to Upshaw that prompted a Department of Labor investigation in 1988 (it's illegal for a union to lend any official more than $2,000), but that was later chalked up to back pay, deferred salary, or an advance on his severance.

But the greater outrage, by far, is what he hasn't accomplished.

He failed to win guaranteed contracts in bargaining, failed to get his players long-term health insurance, and failed to get as big a percentage of total revenues as union chiefs have in other sports. Baseball, which took in $5.1 billion in revenues in 2006, provides ten-year veterans a maximum annual pension of $180,000; football, by contrast, which grossed $6 billion last season, pays ten-year vets only about $50,000 a year. On a yearly basis, according to figures provided by union critic Parrish, baseball pensions average three times the NFLPA's (roughly $36,000 to a sub-poverty $12,000). Some of the greatest men who ever played the game receive pensions of a couple of hundred dollars a month.

"It's a colossal failure of leadership by Upshaw, who simply refuses to admit he made mistakes," says Cy Smith, who was co-counsel in the Webster case. "He failed to account for the violence of the game by getting insurance and disability, and is afraid to go back to the owners now and say, 'Guess what? I fucked up.'" Jerry Kramer, the Pro Bowl guard who founded Gridiron Greats, adds, "You could almost understand this in 1967, when the TV deal with networks paid $9 million. But the sport grew like crazy and the billions rolled in, while the attitude at the union never changed. It's still 'delay, deny, and hope they die,' which is thinking that I can't fathom."

When you talk to ex-players like Kramer and Ditka, what you come away struck by is their acceptance of pain as the wages of a job well done. Hips that don't work, knees that have stopped bending: it is all part and parcel of the warrior life, something to be borne with equanimity and a certain brand of crusty pride. It is a very different thing, though, with the rash of brain trauma that has overtaken the sport. That is spoken of with dread and sorrow, even by the martial Ditka.

"I know way too many guys it's happened to — Larry Morris, Jim Ringo, Harden Hill, John Mackey — I could go on and on," Ditka says. "It just tears you apart to see 'em like that, and then have the league claim it didn't come from football. Why aren't we doing more to help these guys? Why is it all on their wives and families, and how many more are out there?"

Brent Boyd, a former guard for the Minnesota Vikings, has some thoughts on these matters, though he can't always string them together. When you've been hit in the head as much as he has, moments of clarity are hard to come by, and words and memories can elude him. He can't, for instance, tease apart the blows that hurt him from the ones that left him merely dazed. But that first whack — no, he doesn't remember that either, though he does recall his terror on waking up. "I'm laid out, wondering why I can't see, or get up, and then I'm on the sidelines screaming, 'I'm blind! I'm blind!' Well, coach comes over and asks if I can see out of one eye, and he sends me right back in."

This last story is related not in rancor but fondness; Boyd loved his offensive line coach, a guy named John Michaels, and worshiped the man they both worked for in Minnesota, the god-of-thunder head coach Bud Grant. Even as a rookie Boyd was a mainstay on a line that included two Hall of Famers, and the only way a lineman left a game, he says, was if they carried him off in a box. And so he played through the haze and smoke in his head and managed to slog on till the final gun. With all the concussions, major and minor, that followed over the course of seven years, this got to be something of a habit with him, and he discovered he was actually adept at it.

"We had a drill with the Vikings where they mimicked concussions, though guys called them 'dingers' then and laughed about them, like you'd had a few too many at a party," says Boyd. "They'd lie you face-down on the Astroturf, spin you around twelve times, then roll a ball out in the other direction and tell you to go get the fumble. Well, sooner or later you'd learn to get that ball when your legs wouldn't go in that direction."

Boyd, a soft-bellied, wheat-haired man whose manner suggests an affable dentist, is fifty now and has reason to regret his nonchalance on closed-head wounds. After wandering, post-football, through his thirties and midforties in a dizzy, dog-tired stupor, he saw a neurologist who peered inside his skull and found irreparable blunt-force trauma. The lesions are in his brain's vestibular region and have left him with the equivalent of an incurable migraine, in constant, vise-grip pain that can't be quelled. He has bouts of vertigo that knock him off his pegs two or three times a day, exhaustion that fells him after a couple of hours upright, and nausea and cold sweats that come from nowhere and render him a dripping mess. His life, or what passes for one, is a crawl of appointments with doctors and physical therapists, and the counter in his kitchen is lousy with drugs that don't seem to do him much good.

It has been like this for Boyd since 1986, his last year in the game. A third-round draft pick from UCLA, where he graduated with honors in 1980 and hatched long-range plans to become a lawyer, he learned all the positions on the offensive line and became the second rookie ever to start a game for Grant, whose disdain for playing kids was loudly known. But in his second season Boyd tore a ligament in his knee and, after major reconstruction, began taking an anti-inflammatory that compounded his on-and-off headaches. Between the side effects of the drug and his frequent concussions, he found it harder and harder to manage his symptoms, and in 1986 the Vikings cut him midseason, after he'd played for half a year on a broken leg. Exhausted, he retired at thirty, having earned about a half-million dollars over seven years.

For the next two decades Boyd sputtered and stalled like a Yugo in the breakdown lane. He got a job selling insurance, but couldn't remember appointments and often had to stop en route somewhere and nap for an hour in his car. He and his first wife divorced, and Boyd, with his small son Anders in tow, free-fell down the economic ladder. By the summer of '99 he was officially homeless, having sent Anders off to live with his mother while he slept in a car borrowed from his pastor.

In the spring of 1999, though, he got in to see a psychiatrist who asked him, for the first time ever, if he'd had a concussion. An exhaustive three-day assessment was done by a neurologist, using SPECT scans and MRIs. It located the lesions in the brain's vestibular region and ruled emphatically that the damage there was causing his multiple symptoms. Boyd applied for disability, using the report to back his claim. He says a union liaison named Miki Yaras-Davis scoffed at him on the phone, saying that the owners "would never approve a claim for concussions," adding that "they wouldn't open this can of worms because the problem was too widespread."

Nevertheless Boyd was sent to a physician picked out by the NFL. Dr. J. Sterling Ford echoed Boyd's doctor and approved him for disability. The appeals board deemed Ford "equivocal," however, and sent Boyd to a psychiatrist for a second opinion. He too found on Boyd's behalf, and Boyd, who by now had enlisted the help of a lawyer friend, the powerful baseball agent Barry Axelrod, demanded the board obey its own findings. After hemming and hawing, it gave him the minimum of $18,000 a year. But Boyd insisted on his due, and the board shipped him to Baltimore for yet a third opinion, this one from a neurophysiologist named Barry Gordon. The tests there were conducted by a grad student, not Gordon, who popped in only to tap Boyd's kneecaps and shine a light in his eyes. Gordon wrote a report noting Boyd's records were "incomplete," despite his substantial history of doctors' visits. He was out of appeals.

Boyd, who hasn't worked since 1999 and is all but housebound by his symptoms, lives in Nevada with his second wife Gina and Anders, who is now nineteen. They are crowded into a nine-hundred-square-foot cottage with leaks they can't afford to fix. In a flush month they get out to see a first-run movie, though Boyd rarely has the energy to do so and can't easily follow what he's watching. "If I'm like this at fifty," he worries, "what's sixty going to be like? Is that when the union finally cuts us a check, to have someone come in and change my diaper?"

This is a reference to a rare benevolence from the league — the so-called 88 Plan. Named (or numbered) for the great John Mackey, the Baltimore Colts tight end who was afflicted in his fifties with severe dementia, it provides a sum of money for the care of ex-players beset by Alzheimer's or comparable brain conditions. There's a catch, naturally: survivors of athletes on the 88 Plan don't receive any disability from the NFLPA, and payments don't kick in till the patient has been deemed unfit to care for himself. If Boyd ever does get the money he's owed, he may not be intact enough to know it. In the meantime he seethes over his treatment by the union and shakes his head at the shameful way the league has addressed brain trauma.

"Every reputable expert says that blows to the head'll cause damage if they happen enough," Boyd says. "But the NFL happens to have the only neurologists who say that the jury's still out."

In 1994 the NFL established the Mild Traumatic Brain Injury Committee, with Dr. Elliot Pellman as its chair. If the league has little trouble finding experts to discount the link between concussions and early-onset dementia, Pellman may be why. His specialty is rheumatology, not brain trauma and neurology, and his committee reports, including one that backed the practice of sending players with concussions back into games, have been widely scorned by neurologists. In 2005 the *New York Times* reported that he'd misstated his bona fides for more than a decade. Two years later he stepped down as chairman.

This summer, unable to ignore the startling news — Andre Waters's suicide in November 2006 and the release of forensic exams that showed he had the brain of an eighty-year-old Alzheimer's patient — the league staged a "concussion summit" in Chicago. At the conference, whose stated aim was to share knowledge of brain trauma, brain scans of Justin Strzelczyk done by Dr. Bennet Omalu, a neuropathologist at the University of Pittsburgh School of Medicine, showed that Strzelczyk, like Waters, Long, and Webster, had the brain of a much older man, or a severely punch-drunk boxer. The NFL committee's doctors downplayed this as exceptional and sneered at their credentialed critics, dismissing their work as "soft science."

"They'll go to their graves denying that concussions hurt guys, and in Upshaw they've got the perfect stooge," Boyd says, adding that the summit was nothing more than PR. "Gene'll do and say anything the owners want, as long as he gets his money."

Jennifer Smith spent a week with the DeMarcos, getting their rent paid and utilities settled, then persuading a wealthy friend of Gridiron Greats to buy the family a used truck. All told, the fund has given them more than $20,000, though it can't extend itself much further.

"We're a new nonprofit with a tiny staff, and there are a lot of guys out there who need our help," says Smith, a vibrant blonde in her early forties who quit TV and film producing to run the fund. It raises money primarily through its online auction of football memorabilia (gridirongreats.org), and has so far taken in about $400,000 in the seven months since opening its doors. "What Brian needs — what all our guys need — is for the league and union to honor their obligations. We're a Band-Aid at best."

Smith put DeMarco in touch with Cy Smith (no relation), the lawyer who helped win almost $2 million for the children of the late Mike Webster. DeMarco will file — again — for his disability benefits, this time with Smith over his shoulder. "I can't tell you how grateful we are," DeMarco says. "If Jennifer hadn't stepped in when she did, we'd've been out in the street with our two kids. We're nowhere near safe yet, but —" he stops himself short, perilously close to tears "— at least we're part of the way there."

Before Smith left town she enacted one last mercy. On a smoldering June day she piled the DeMarcos into a truck and took them to a pawn shop in north Austin. She'd called ahead, and owner Mark Ekrut had the goods in question ready for their arrival.

Out of a plastic bag came a weathered pigskin that had been signed by every member of the Jacksonville Jaguars, a keepsake given to DeMarco by his teammates from the Jags' inaugural season. Smith had redeemed the ball to auction online; all proceeds will go to the DeMarcos for living expenses.

DeMarco, who'd been hovering near tears all morning, clasped it to his chest and broke down. In a near-empty store on a Thursday morning, his sobs echoed off the hocked golf clubs and band saws and dusty Jesus crosses in the case. "Thank you," he croaked to Ekrut, who'd advanced him $1,000 and never put his treasures up for sale. "Forget it," said Ekrut. "I knew you'd come back. You're a good man who fell on hard times."

DeMarco thanked him again, then thanked and hugged Smith, laughing, crying, and wincing all at once. Taking up his football, he started for the door, a long, slow haul on one good leg.

RICK TELANDER

Atkins a Study in Pride and Pain

FROM THE CHICAGO SUN-TIMES

KNOXVILLE, TENN. — I drive slowly past the small red-brick house on the narrow, winding road in the hills outside town.

I pull into a driveway a quarter-mile farther on. A dog barks somewhere. It's a few days before Christmas.

The dog stops. Silence.

I turn the car around, drive past the house again.

I don't know.

The house has its curtains drawn. There are two old cars in the carport, one of them very old, I'm guessing thirty, forty years. Fins. Rusty.

There's a wooden wheelchair ramp that looks weathered and un-used leading to the front door. A NO SMOKING sign in the front-door window. Two tiny American flags on the wall next to the carport.

No lights on. No decorations.

Doug Atkins, seventy-six, the legendary Hall of Fame defensive end for the Bears, lives here.

"I don't want to see anybody," he had told me during one of our phone conversations. People had their minds made up about a lot of stuff, he said. Predetermined. The country was going to hell. No middle class. Only rich and poor.

I didn't need to ask which side he fell on.

"I'm doing okay," he had said. "I cracked my hip awhile back. Never got well since then. I can walk with a cane, but it's getting rough. I got sick, and I've been poisoned from some of the medicine they gave me — lead poisoning. They don't put out the truth about medicines. So many crooks in the country nowadays — politicians, oil companies, pharmaceutical companies, lobbyists. A lot of people are worse off than I am. But I don't need to see any reporters."

Paying the Price

Everybody knows that football is a rough game, that the NFL is the roughness polished bright and turned into performance art, the brutality into religion, the cracking bones into the percussive soundtrack that suits our times.

But not many know the toll the game takes when the players themselves, the artists, have left the stage.

A shocking number of the men, starting sometimes well before middle age, begin to limp, then hobble, then stop moving much at all.

Dementia, mood disorders, osteoarthritis, surgery, more surgery, pain — the wheel of football repercussion spins and spins.

And often, the longer a man played — meaning the better player he was — the worse his debilitation.

Doug Atkins played seventeen years in the NFL, the best twelve for the Bears.

In that time, the long-legged, hickory-tough six-foot-eight, 260-pounder did things that hadn't been done before on the gridiron. A scholarship basketball player at Tennessee as well as an All-America football player, Atkins sometimes jumped *over* blockers like a hurdler vaulting rolling logs.

He went out for track at Tennessee and won the Southeastern Conference high jump, clearing 6–6. In the NFL, he went to eight Pro Bowls from 1958 to 1966.

"I didn't know what I was doing in the high jump," he said on the phone. "In high school one time, I scissored 6–1½."

All that talent came together on the football field like a rainbow palette.

George Halas, Atkins's coach with the Bears and the man who helped found the NFL, said of the giant from Humboldt, Tennessee, "There never was a better defensive end."

But now there's the embarrassment the game has exacted.

Mike Ditka hosts a golf tournament each year wherein Ditka and sponsors earmark money for Hall of Famers in need.

Sometimes it's a payout for surgical procedures or medicine.

Sometimes it's a wheelchair ramp.

One time it was for a tombstone.

"It's pitiful," says Ditka, tearing into the NFL's stingy pension plan for old-timers, the NFL players union, and all PR aspects of the league. "Rip 'em all. I don't care."

The league's frugal pension plan is complicated, but it's simplified nicely by the fact that the veterans die at a swift pace.

There's a new pension agreement being put into place, but as of last year, NFL players who had reached age fifty-five might typically get between $200 and $425 a month.

Enough for aspirin, for sure.

While the current Bears swagger down the road to success and the NFL wallows in money, the old men who helped build the brand suffer in silence, often lame, often nearly destitute, their pride too great to allow pity.

Battle Scars

Atkins had mesmerized me when I had asked him, please, just for me, to detail his injuries.

The groin pull that tore muscle off the bone, leaving a "hole" in his abdomen. "My fault," he said.

The big toe injury. The broken collarbone. The leg that snapped at the bottom of a pile. ("I got to the sideline, and it didn't feel right.")

The biceps that tore in half, Atkins's arm hanging limply.

"It's just a show muscle," he said, explaining why he never got it fixed.

"I see these old football players," says Dr. Victoria Brander, the head of Northwestern University's Arthritis Institute, "and every joint is ruined — their toes, ankles, knees, hips, fingers, elbows, shoulders. The supporting structure in the joints is gone. Their spines are collapsed. I see one former star who is bent like a *C*.

"But they are noble. They played their game because they believed in something. They were warriors. They never complain."

I have gone past Atkins's house four times now. I take a deep breath.

I dial his number on my cell phone.

His wife answers and gives him the phone. I just happen to be in the area, I say. Would he mind if I stopped by, maybe for a minute or two, on the way to the airport?

"Damn it, why do you all keep bothering me?" Atkins yells into the receiver. "I told you I was sick!"

And then the line is dead.

"These guys don't need much," Ditka will say later in barely controlled fury. "Your best players? Ever? Why can't the league give them enough to live out their lives in dignity? Is that so f — — ing hard?"

I drive on, feeling terrible, feeling cruel. I never should have imposed on Doug Atkins. On his pride.

In the midst of our bounty, I feel lost.

TOMMY CRAGGS

Hammering on Hank

FROM SLATE.COM

THIS BASEBALL SEASON, it fell to the sporting press to drag a reluctant Hank Aaron once more into public view, the occasion being Barry Bonds's slow-motion pursuit of a stationary number. Now, anytime an old baseball personage hobbles back into frame, he is invariably described in awed, petrifying language better suited to, say, the Archbishop of Canterbury. The treatment of Aaron hasn't been any different. A spin through the sports pages over the past few months reveals that he is a man of "cool dignity," "quiet dignity," "innate dignity," "immense dignity," "eternal dignity," "unfettered dignity," "unimpeachable dignity," the very "picture of dignity" who "brought so much dignity to baseball" and who, "having exuded dignity his entire life," continues to this day "exud[ing] class and dignity." Aaron, proclaimed the inevitable George Will, who perhaps learned about dignity from selling his to Conrad Black, was "The Dignified Slugger from Mobile."

No one would quibble with the sentiment, unctuous and condescending though it may be. Aaron's forbearance was indeed remarkable; in many ways, he holds up better in history's eyes than the peer to whom he is often compared, Jackie Robinson — himself a "pillar of dignity" — whose outspokenness regrettably extended to the odd HUAC hearing and Nixon campaign stop.

No, what's unfortunate about Aaron's latest turn in the public eye is that he has been reduced to a sportswriter's cheap trope. The great slugger's dignity is of interest only insofar as it can be picked up by the likes of George Will and swung in the general direction of Barry Bonds. (As of Friday morning, Bonds stands just two home runs shy of Aaron's 755.) "As Barry Bonds continues his gimpy, joyless pursuit of such glory as he is eligible for," Will wrote, "consider the odyssey of Mobile's greatest native son." Or as a *Cincinnati Post* headline pronounced: "Safe to Say Bonds No Aaron." Of course, with Aaron, it has always been thus. It is the singular curse of his career: to be treated like a sandwich board for the prevailing attitudes of the day.

It was uglier a half-century ago. Aaron hit the majors in 1954, after a stint in the Negro Leagues and a year with the Milwaukee Braves' affiliate in the South Atlantic League, which he helped integrate. As baseball historian Jules Tygiel points out, his timing was impeccable — Aaron was one of the first black ballplayers whose career unfolded more or less naturally, without segregation or war chipping away at his prime.

Once in the bigs, he quickly became, as a comically obtuse 1958 *New York Times Magazine* profile put it, "a symbol of a new era of slugging," a savage of preternatural talent. (The headline: "The Panther at the Plate.") "Aaron brings to baseball an atavistic . . . single-mindedness," William Barry Furlong wrote, going on to describe the "somniferous-looking" Aaron's "insouciance" and "indolence" and taking care to twice point out his "shuffling" gait. No mention was made of Aaron's thorough preparation, before which even Ted Williams salaamed. The *Times* was far from the only offender. Even Aaron's first manager, Charlie Grimm, went in for this nonsense. He liked to call Aaron "Stepin Fetchit."

Some of this was surely a product of Aaron's shy and unadorned personality at the time, which offered the media little but a bare armature on which to shape whatever they wished. He didn't have Willie Mays's élan; his hat didn't whip off whenever he rounded second. He drove a Chevy Caprice. "Grace in a gray flannel suit," one writer called him.

Likewise, Aaron's performance over twenty-three seasons — consistently very good, occasionally great, always a notch or two below Mays's — lacked the dizzying peaks that give a career the flavor of personality. He never hit more than 47 home runs in a year, never hit better than .355, never had an on-base percentage higher than .410.

Because he was so outwardly bland in personality and performance, Aaron seemed to take on character only in relation to things people felt strongly about: Willie Mays, Babe Ruth, civil rights. On his own he was, and remains, an abstraction, someone whom writers could only explicate with banalities like "dignified." Our perception of Aaron today stems almost entirely from his pursuit of Ruth's 714 home runs, in 1973 and 1974, during which time he faced down an assortment of death threats and hate mail. By then, Aaron had shed his reticence and begun to speak out against baseball's glacial progress on matters of race. Still, very much his own man, he seemed to dismiss some of the loftier interpretations attached to his home-run chase. "The most basic motivation," he wrote in his autobiography, *I Had a Hammer*, with Lonnie Wheeler, "was the pure ambition to break such an important and long-standing barrier. Along with that would come the recognition that I thought was long overdue me: I would be out of the shadows."

No matter. Aaron was fashioned into something of a civil rights martyr anyway. "He hammered out home runs in the name of social progress," Wheeler recently wrote in the *Cincinnati Post*. And Tom Stanton, in the optimistically titled *Hank Aaron and the Home Run That Changed America*, dropped what has to be the most unlikely Hank Aaron analogy on record: "[P]erhaps it's *The Exorcist*, the period's biggest movie, that provides a better metaphor for Hank Aaron's trial . . . Hank Aaron lured America's ugly demons into the light, revealing them to those who imagined them a thing of the past, and in doing so helped exorcise some of them. His ordeal provided a vivid, personal lesson for a generation of children: racism is wrong."

Small wonder that, upon eclipsing Ruth, the exorcist told the crowd, "I'd just like to thank God it's over."

Now here is Aaron, once again, this time in the midst of the galloping national hysteria over anabolic steroids. In Aaron, we have our cardboard hero, propped up in the corner to stand in exquisite counterpoint to Bonds. He is not the only one dragooned into this particular mess — "Ryan Howard, No Asterisk," went one preseason headline — but it is most certainly Aaron who is shouldering the psychic load. Even the flatness of his career, strangely, now earns him praise.

"[N]ot one of Aaron's single-season home run totals is among the 68 highest of all time, yet he pounded more in his career than any other player in history — and without suspicion of chemical enhancement," wrote Tom Verducci in this week's *Sports Illustrated* cover story, blithely sidestepping the very real possibility that Aaron popped amphetamines like Chiclets along with, you know, *everyone else in baseball.* To even consider that would, of course, call into question a rather large piece of the argument in favor of baseball's current war on steroids — maintain the sanctity of the record books! ferret out the cheats! — something sportswriters evidently have little interest in doing. Instead, they summon a hero from the past to redress the supposed sins of the present. "I guess," Reggie Jackson told Verducci, "you can call him the people's home run king."

Our national celebration of Aaron is, fundamentally, childish stuff. This is baseball telling fairy tales to itself, pretending the bad things away, using a Hall of Famer as a rhetorical bludgeon and in doing so diminishing the very man it pretends to exalt. There is a word for that. Undignified.

THOMAS BOSWELL

The Rocket's Descent

FROM THE WASHINGTON POST

NOW, ROGER CLEMENS joins Barry Bonds in baseball's version of hell. It's a slow burn that lasts a lifetime, then, after death, lingers as long as the game is played and tongues can wag. In baseball, a man's triumphs and his sins are immortal. The pursuit of one often leads to the other. And those misdeeds are seldom as dark as their endless punishment.

Shoeless Joe Jackson, an illiterate outfielder who hit like a demon in the 1919 World Series, but neglected to blow the whistle on his crooked teammates, died with his good name as black as their Sox. Pete Rose, who bet on his team, but never against it, finally confessed. It could be good for his soul, and buys him dinner at my house any night, but may never get him into Cooperstown. Now, they have company: two giants of our time, just as humbled, though no less tarnished.

Yesterday, the only man with seven Cy Young Awards came crashing down the mountain of baseball's gods and ended in a heap beside the only man with seven Most Valuable Player Awards. What a sport. Half the players of the last twenty years may have cheated, but who gets nailed? The greatest slugger since Babe Ruth and the greatest power pitcher since Walter Johnson.

Clemens and Bonds now stand before us like twin symbols of the Steroid Age: cheats, liars, ego monsters who were not satisfied with mere greatness and wealth but, as they aged, had to pass everyone in the record book, break every mark, and do it with outsize bodies, unrecognizable from their youth, that practically screamed, "Catch me if you can." The whole sport whispered as both walked by. Now, everyone can speak aloud. Not because their guilt has been admitted or proven beyond any doubt, mind you. That would be too clean and easy for us, for baseball.

But the Rocket and Barry stand convicted in the court of public opinion, in Bonds's case by his flaxseed-oil defense and now, in this thunderclap Clemens catastrophe, by the direct I-injected-him-many-times-in-the-buttocks testimony of his own personal trainer. Clemens denied all charges vehemently. In a statement, he claimed that he is being slandered by "the uncorroborated allegations of a troubled man threatened with federal criminal prosecution."

Yet those nine pages of Mitchell report "slander" have been placed in the public's hand by baseball itself in 311 pages, plus attachments, blessed by the commissioner. Pete Rose had ten times the chance against the Dowd report that Clemens has against the august Mitchell. What a public-relations mismatch: a tobacco-chewing, hot-tempered Texas right-hander against a former federal judge and Senate majority leader who helped bring peace to Northern Ireland. This time, the Rocket's out of gas and the bullpen is empty.

For more than a year, the Mitchell commission on performance-enhancing drugs appeared to be a harmless fishing expedition that might land a few guppies. After all, what can you expect to catch with five-pound test line, a defiant players' union, and no subpoena power? Yet, apparently by dumb luck, a baseball drug peddler got caught, then rolled over on an insignificant scoundrel who happened to be Clemens's trainer. In a blink, baseball's blindfolded Ahabs found a whale in their seine. What's this? It feels like, it might be, oh my God, it's Clemens, hooked and gaffed, whether we want him or not.

"Bud, this is George. We're going to need a bigger boat."

Mitchell's opus was intended as many things. It was, of course, a severe front-to-back slam at the union for its twenty years of intransigence on drug testing. The charge is absolutely correct. Still, how self-serving can Commissioner Bud Selig be? He appoints Mitchell, closely affiliated with management in general and specifically with the Red Sox, to spend twenty-one months finding out who's guilty when he already knows that Don Fehr will get handcuffed in the last chapter.

And, of course, owners, midlevel baseball employees, and even Selig get taken to ritual task. Oh, everybody should have acted faster, been smarter, seen the signs. But, gosh, how were we to know? Just because our players showed up for spring training like they'd spent the winter inhaling helium. Just because scouts in their reports and general managers discussing trades evaluated how much weight to give the "juice" factor.

Finally, naturally, because Congress knows a vote-grabber in an election year, the report serves as baseball's proactive shield against further embarrassing visits to Capitol Hill. I'm shocked, *shocked*, to discover that both Mitchell and Selig — who, just two hours later, endorsed every recommendation in the report — are passionately in favor of tougher "best-practices" drug testing. What a stunner. Why, right off the bat, Bud said there would be no more twenty-four-hour warnings to clubs that a random drug test would be held the next day. You mean there were warnings for "random" tests? And MLB could have changed it unilaterally, but it took the Mitchell report before they did it? What impressive self-motivation.

However, the report's predictable functions — a punch in the nose to the union, a slap in the face to MLB, a predictable recitation of the usual (already revealed) steroid suspects, and a T-bone steak to placate congressional watchdogs — were all obliterated by the discovery nobody expected. In the end, the Mitchell report will forever be the Clemens indictment.

Clemens plummeted from icon to fallen idol in a matter of hours. Even if he is innocent, as his lawyer claims, the damage is done. The report devotes nine scathing pages to him, far more than any other player. This is baseball's own officially commissioned history of its most tainted period. And who is its protagonist? Clemens.

How can that ever be undone? If Mark McGwire got only 25 percent of the Hall of Fame vote a year ago because he refused to answer questions before Congress — and, coupled with Jose Canseco's accusations, looked ashamed and guilty — then how does Clemens get elected when his own trainer and longtime friend says he injected him more than a dozen times?

Baseball and its fans may require a few days to digest the pairing of Bonds and Clemens, one player so prickly and against the grain, the other the ultimate good ol' boy. But the match is fitting because it makes us face the core of baseball's drug problem. At one end of the cheating spectrum, performance-enhancing drugs provided a last hope for marginal players clinging to a big league job. Their dilemma may touch us. We understand. Perhaps we sympathize. At the other extreme, among the greatest players, we harden our hearts. They had it all and threw it away for more money, more glory, and more years in the spotlight.

That harsh judgment is true, but only by half. The fiercer the competitor, the greater the pride, the bigger the talent — in other words, the more qualities a man possesses that we claim to admire in a champion — the greater his fury will be at the thought of being beaten, outstripped, surpassed by another man. And the greater the chance that he will defy the rules, risk his health, and "do what it takes" to win.

How like a superman to be above the law. How close to invulnerability to disregard your own health. How easy to confuse self-sacrifice for your team for a deeper and governing selfishness. How easy to mistake the sins of ego for the virtues of sport.

Such men would almost be heroic, if they weren't so tragic.

T. J. SIMERS

Family Carries On After Tragic Day at Rose Bowl

FROM THE LOS ANGELES TIMES

IT'S FRIDAY, four days after the fact, and the three women in Ron Zavala's life are laughing. Lisa, twenty, has been having a problem with the company computer, which proves she's Ron's kid, all right.

Patrice, twenty-four, known as the cell-phone queen in the family, gets the ringer on Dad's phone working, which means everyone in the small Glendora office at Purrfect Auto Service is now listening to the USC fight song.

"Obviously, we haven't turned the service off," wife Sandy says. "I guess I'm just waiting for him to call."

There were only a couple of moments remaining Monday in the Rose Bowl, the Zavala family whooping it up because, for longtime USC season-ticket holders, there's nothing like a Trojans victory.

Ron bought a huge motor home in the summer so the family could really tailgate. They had gone together to Arizona for a game, and it's still a family joke.

Ron took the motor home to the Rose Bowl days before the game, and the family spent the weekend tailgating. They got dressed up for New Year's Eve, went into Pasadena for dinner, and as Patrice says, "We haven't had that much fun in a long time."

They returned to the Rose Bowl to party into the night, and Ron joined the girls' boyfriends the next morning to play football. "The way he was throwing the ball, I'm surprised he didn't throw his arm out," Sandy says.

When it came time to go into the stadium, it wasn't soon enough for Ron. Ron's idea of showing up for a noon start is to be on hand by eight. He's always been that way — just eager to watch his USC football.

"You miss a kickoff and he's flaming," Sandy says. "So we go into the Rose Bowl, but he knows we're going to be late and he's complaining. Now the tunnel is clogged with people and they're stopping us from getting to our seats. And I'm praying to God, please don't let them kick off."

They make it in time, Ron, Sandy, Lisa, and boyfriend Brady sitting behind the goal post at the Michigan end, while Patrice and boyfriend Noah sit three sections away because the family could not secure six seats together.

Lisa has a new camera, a Christmas gift from Dad, and she realizes the game is ending and she hasn't taken any pictures. Lisa is Daddy's little girl, working with him at the auto store every day, and so she asks someone to take their picture together.

Ten minutes later, just before the game ends, Ron falls on top of his daughter. He doesn't say a word, doesn't do anything, just collapses.

Some people laugh, knowing it's been a long day of drinking for some. Lisa figures right away her diabetic father needs some food. Sandy asks him if he's okay, and as soon as they prop him up, Ron falls the other way toward Brady.

"The whole section goes quiet, and it's obvious it's not some old drunken fool who has fallen down," Sandy says. "I'm standing there about to lose my cool because they're trying to find a pulse and can't, ninety thousand people and I'm yelling they can't find a doctor. Then this man looks at me, he's got a Michigan sweatshirt on, and he says, 'I'm a doctor.'

"The paramedics and firemen arrive, they're trying to revive Ron and the doctor in the Michigan sweatshirt steps back and says, 'I did all I can. I'm an obstetrician.'"

It's hard not to laugh the way Sandy tells the story, and she appreciates that. "I had exactly the same reaction," she says. "He probably thought I was insane, but ninety thousand people and I get an obstetrician. If I had asked for a lawyer, I would have been swarmed."

The paramedics work on Ron. Three sections over, Patrice notices the commotion and figures Lisa's boyfriend has probably gotten into a fight. Everyone else just stands and watches. Sandy says, "But God bless those paramedics the way they worked. They never stopped. Never."

The game ends, the USC celebration on the field starts, and officials close a tunnel so Ron, medics, and his wife can get to an ambulance.

"I'm still thinking he will come around," she says, although five attempts to shock him fail to get any movement. "I'm such a Pollyanna, I think once we get to the hospital magically things are going to get better. But two seconds after we're there . . . [it's over]. I'm expecting an adrenaline shot to the heart, a glucose shot, and I'm thinking, *What's the matter with these people, you don't have any needles?*

"This man just turned fifty-three. He's at a football game, he loves USC, he's having the best weekend ever with his family, he's feeling fine, and he drops dead."

She's told it's sudden cardiac arrest, and it's sudden, all right. "If someone told me I would be going to the Rose Bowl and coming home a widow, I would never have believed it."

Sandy and Patrice return from White's Funeral Home in Azusa, dropping off the clothes Ron will be wearing for Monday's viewing.

They are going to have Ron dressed in the USC shirt he bought at the Rose Bowl — under his white shirt and suit. Sandy is also putting one of his favorite USC hats in the casket along with a copy of Tuesday's sports section on the Rose Bowl.

"I thought that was a nice headline," she says, holding up the paper, which reads, "Trojans Come to Pass."

Each of the pallbearers, once they leave church, will be wearing USC baseball caps. The plan is also to have nothing but cardinal and gold flowers.

Neighbor Mike Kurkierewicz, who has had a standing UCLA-USC six-pack wager for years with Ron, calls the USC athletic department and USC makes plans to send flowers to the funeral home.

"If they sent Matt Leinart, that'd be really cool too," Sandy cracks.

She also reminds herself, because Ron didn't get the chance to get around to it, "I owe Mike a six-pack."

A customer here and there interrupts the conversation, Lisa still fighting the computer and Sandy trying to remember what to charge for some brake repair.

Each one takes a turn over the next couple of hours wiping away tears, shifting comfortably back and forth between the memory of what has just happened and so many funny stories to tell.

"I come from an Irish family, so we think everything is funny, but the girls and I have had our pity parties too," Sandy says. "I know Monday and Tuesday [the day of the funeral] are going to be tough, but I've got five families to support — my own and the four employees who work for me. If I worked for someone else, maybe I could go home and pull the blanket over my head . . ."

Brady, the boyfriend, interrupts: "He was the funnest guy I've been around. I wouldn't say hanging around with a fifty-three-year-old man is very much fun, but it was like hanging around with my twenty-one-year-old buddy."

It helps explain the picture on the wall of the guy wearing the goofy hat.

"He was my best friend," Sandy says, while suddenly sounding perturbed. "Yeah, I'm quite angry — angry at him for leaving me.

"Why did you leave me?" she says, one of her daughters handing her a tissue. "We still had stuff to do. He was going to get a physical — if you didn't want to see the doctor, all you had to do was say so. But he just checked out on me."

She sits up and smiles. "This girl here [Lisa] was weeping for two days straight but had a little moment of clarity," Sandy says. "She looked at me and said, 'Dad didn't just walk to the light, he went running to the light.'"

It's been four days, and so many details to take care of before next week, while still running the auto shop.

"Every so often it just overwhelms," Sandy says. "You know, I got up in the middle of the night and found myself checking to see if the toilet seat was up. We've all fallen in, thanks to him. Oh God, I just can't believe it, but then as badly as I feel, I still reflect on the more positive things because I had twenty-seven years of good stuff and just one real crappy day."

*

If a man's family is a reflection of how he lives, he really does get the last word here, of course, although Sandy asks for one favor.

"If there's any way you could — could you set the record straight?" she says. "The Pasadena newspaper said a sixty-year-old man died at the Rose Bowl.

"He's not sixty, and he has a name. And Ron was a great father, a great husband, and a wonderful boss."

Getting a Second Wind

FROM SPORTS ILLUSTRATED

ONE DAY five years ago bubbly, gorgeous soccer goalie Korinne Shroyer came home from eighth grade, found her father's revolver in his closet, and fired a bullet into her skull.

This is about the lives she saved doing it.

Out of a million kids you'd pick Korinne last to commit suicide. She was a popular kid in her class in Lynchburg, Virginia. But then she started feeling sad for no reason. Her parents took her to a therapist, who recommended Paxil. But one worry with Paxil is that it can give teenagers suicidal thoughts when they first start taking it. Korinne made it through ten days.

That bullet tore a hole in her father, Kevin, that you could drive an eighteen-wheeler through. Korinne was Kevin's best friend, the kid who would Rollerblade with him as he ran for hours, the kid who'd come with him to Orioles games and chat with him until his ears hurt. "I used to run all the time," says Kevin Shroyer, forty-six. "I loved it because it gave me time to think. But [after the suicide], thinking was the last thing I wanted to do."

Kevin, an investigator in the public defender's office, and his wife, Kristie, a hair stylist, were able to think one clear and brave and terrifying thought during the six days Korinne survived after the shooting. They decided to send out her organs like gifts.

Her green eyes would go in one direction, her glad heart another, her kidneys still another. Her liver and her pancreas went somewhere else, and her two good lungs — the ones that played the saxophone — went to a Gainesville, Georgia, man named Len Geiger, who was so close to dying that he was practically pricing caskets.

A runner and swimmer and nonsmoker, Geiger suddenly found one day that he only had enough breath for walking or talking, not both. Turns out he had genetic emphysema, also known as Alpha-1, and a lung transplant was his only hope for survival.

He was on his fifth year on the waiting list and "life wasn't worth living," he says, when Korinne pulled the trigger. Geiger received those two young lungs six days later in an operation at the University of Virginia Medical Center.

And that's where this story gets good.

Geiger, now forty-eight, went from 15 percent lung function to way above average for his age. He got his second wind and his second life. He was so grateful, he wrote Korinne's parents to say thank you. And that letter changed everybody's lives.

Korinne's parents wrote back, and Geiger asked to meet, and next thing you knew Geiger was at a bittersweet gathering that became soaked with every kind of tears.

The Shroyers and their other daughter, Kolby, now sixteen, gave Geiger a photo album of the girl whose life was now inside him. "She starts out as this beautiful baby," Geiger says. "Then she's a little girl in a Halloween costume. Then a gorgeous teenager. And then the pictures just stop. It was the saddest thing I've ever experienced."

Hours later the group was parting when Kristie said, "Len? Can I ask you a favor?" She walked over and stood before him.

"Anything," Geiger said.

"Can I put my hands on your chest for just a second?"

And she stood there, crying, as she felt her dead daughter breathe.

Kevin started to run again. And someone had a great idea. Why didn't he and Len run together? So they did. They ran an 8-K together, step for step, next to each other. One man's overflowing joy coming straight from the other's bottomless sorrow.

That whole run, Kevin never shut up. It was so unlike him that, at the end, Geiger asked him, "Why?"

"I had to," Kevin admitted, "because every time there was silence, I could hear Korinne breathing."

Next they ran a half-marathon, then a full one. By then, though, the steroids that Geiger had taken for years just to stay alive had damaged most of his joints, and he was running on two artificial hips. The best he could do was race-walk. At the seventeen-mile mark his hips were screaming. But he refused to quit.

It took them six hours and twenty-five minutes — with Shroyer matching him step by agonizing step — but they finished, hands clasped together, the three of them.

Kevin and Kristie aren't whole yet, but they're getting on with their lives. Geiger, meanwhile, is relishing his. He met a woman, Christina, married her, and they named their first baby after Korinne — Ava Corinne. Sometimes he stares at her, awed. "I know that without Korinne, I'm not here today and neither is Ava Corinne."

Sometimes life just takes your breath away, doesn't it?

DAN JENKINS

Golf in Geezerdom

FROM GOLF DIGEST

WHEN I WAS A LAD IN MY TWENTIES, as carefree and debonair as any other underpaid newspaperman, I happened to be a golfer who could flirt with par fairly often, and I was adventurous enough in those days to play any known or unknown thief who showed up at Goat Hills for whatever amount he fancied. Then I'd break the shaft on at least two clubs in my bag if I didn't shoot close to 70 and swoop all the cheese. But now, fifty years later, I don't even want to hit a green — it'll mean bending over to mark the ball.

I can live with the quick hook, the one that dives into the Rough of No Return. I can live with the diseased slice that soars into Sherwood Forest, where Friar Tuck can have it with my compliments. I haven't looked for a golf ball since mulligans were free, which was a law I passed in 1995.

But this stooping-over-to-mark-the-ball thing. Every time I'm forced to do it today, I tend to stagger a few steps and mumble, "Paging Mister Ritis . . . Mister Arth Ritis."

Mr. Arth Ritis is the title of one of the medical books I'm working on. Some of the others are titled: *Gall Your Own Bladder, Something's Leaking Behind the Retina, Get High with Your Blood Sugar, The Ulcer That Couldn't Bleed Straight, The Hearing Aid That Didn't Speak English, Whose Cataract Is It, Anyway?, The Hip and I,* and *Bypass Bubba and the Chest of Doom.*

Let me make something clear before I go on. I do love the game, but I've never played golf for the joy of it. I've always played it to compete — and bet. But now that I can't compete as I once did, thanks basically to age and the fact that today's modern, magical, nuclear-advanced equipment seems to laugh at me more than it helps me, I play golf only at gunpoint.

This means I no longer play gambling golf, client golf, charity golf, pro-am golf, friendship golf, or family golf, and it goes without saying that I don't play geezer golf. It means I play golf only if it's not too hot or too cold outside, if there's absolutely no hint of wind, and if some pal or relative comes to town with a lifelong ambition to play Colonial — okay, fine, I take him out to Colonial.

But I start hating myself for agreeing to it the minute I'm struggling to put on the golf shoes. Putting on the golf shoes has become almost as pathetically exhausting as marking the ball.

Of course, after the shoe ordeal, when I'm out on the course, I'm in my pocket half the time. Even from the whites. Plus I'm instantly paranoid about whether the cart has enough juice to get me all the way to 18 and back indoors where I belong.

Really a fun time. But I don't know that it was ever fun, even in my youth. It was a competition, a challenge, a test. But fun? Fun was a car date with a cheerleader.

Nowadays, I run into these golf lovers in my age group everywhere I go. Fellows who have come late to the game — the worst kind of sicko golf nut, in my opinion. They play twice a week without fail, and some play seven days a week — particularly if there's the barest threat at home of having to go to the mall or Costco with the missus. And invariably these people want to tell you about the 96 they shot the other day, their personal best, and how it should have been an 87.

They hit dribblers and pop-ups with equal regularity. They hit blazing, half-topped line drives that have been careening off bulkheads, rock walls, and condo patio furniture for years.

They achieve great distance on their short putts but very poor distance on their long putts. This is true even though they study them from all four sides and plumb-bob the line into a two-lane farm road and methodically take fourteen practice strokes before they pull the trigger.

You might know similar people. They play in the same group every day, have the same tee time every day, and they've never lost a ball. *"Naw, it's here somewhere. I saw it skip across the water, hit that tree trunk over there, and bounce off the fence post. I think it rolled into this ditch. Help me move these rocks, Floyd."*

Worse, they play by the rules. They find improving your lie in the fairway comparable to armed robbery. Tee it up slightly ahead of the markers, they'll call a priest for you. Boundary stakes and ground under repair are their favorite vacation spots. They also have a tendency to squat in a sharp-eyed position, poised to pounce on anyone who plays a shot out of turn.

One of these golf-nut friends was my houseguest not long ago. An old pal from Houston. He plays only five days a week with his wife, then two days a week with somebody who can break 124. If that doesn't qualify him to be buried someday in a suit of Tiff 328, consider that he knows all about equipment, river sand, lateral hazards, Arron Oberholser, and he even watches the senior slugs on TV.

The first morning after his arrival, over coffee and the papers, and after knowing I'd set him up to go hit balls somewhere, he said, "You sure you don't want to play today? It's beautiful outside."

"I've never been more certain of anything in my life," I said.

"What will you do today?"

"You mean aside from sitting around?"

He said, "You really don't like to stop and smell the flowers, do you?"

I said, "If I wanted to smell the flowers, I'd buy myself a corsage."

The Prime Golf Years

It wasn't always like that. Growing up in Fort Worth — the town that gave you Ben Hogan, the ice-cream drumstick, and the washateria — I played golf almost every day of my life from the age of eight to the age of thirty.

In the beginning I'd be taken at least once a week to play a round with an aunt, uncle, or cousin on a real golf course, to Goat Hills, maybe, or Katy Lake, a tricky nine-hole public layout with sand greens, the course where Hogan started learning the game as a kid. But when I wasn't doing that, I'd play on the six-hole course I designed, built, and maintained in the neighborhood where I was being raised by loving grandparents while my mom and dad spent several years trying to decide whether they liked marriage or divorce the best.

The course was laid out on the lawns of my grandparents' home, and on their yard next door, and across the street in my aunt and uncle's yard, and on their side lawn and garden.

It was easy to obtain permission to design and build this course, seeing as how the entire neighborhood knew I was starring in the human family drama, "Only Child, Spoiled Rotten."

The greens were Bermuda, roughly five feet in circumference, carved out by a hand-pushed lawn mower, watered by garden hose, and closely cropped by scissors. The cups were Campbell's vegetable soup cans sunk into the ground, and the flagsticks were just that. Sticks. With discarded dishcloths attached and fluttering in the enchanting breezes of Fort Worth's south side of town.

The fifth and sixth holes were as tough as any eight-, nine-, or ten-year-old ever went up against. They required a shot across the street, over to the fifth, back to the sixth. But it wasn't enough to have to negotiate the row of full-grown sycamores along the sidewalks and the telephone wires stretching above the treetops. There were Mrs. Rose's flower beds and Mrs. Tarlton's shrubs to worry about, and I can tell you that those ladies were not golf lovers, boy.

Hogan, Byron Nelson, and Sam Snead played a good many three-man National Opens on this course, me hitting a ball for each one. Being brought up a huge fan of Ben and Byron — the hometown heroes — I have to confess that the time Snead captured one of my majors with an accidental chip-in on the last hole, I suffered a heartbreak that could only be compared with the day I found out that dogs were colorblind.

So much for junior golf. Well, junior golf back in the day when juniors had to be more creative than today's robots.

High school golf, college golf, and the decade that followed all come back to me now as one big raucous, goofy gangsome. The years when you learned how to bet, and how not to get out-bet. Guys going for their rent, their gasoline money, their lungs, their kidneys. Winners telling jokes, losers thinking up get-even games.

Cod Yrac Ffocelddim.

That about sums up those times for me. That's Doc Cary Middlecoff spelled backward, and correctly pronounced "Cod E-rack Fockledim" by those in our elegant gangsome.

Moron Tom, one of our leading intellectuals, started it. He had a talent for pronouncing names backward, and he always wanted

Cod Yrac Ffocelddim when we'd bet real whip-out on the weekly PGA Tour results.

I speak of a PGA Tour on which the events were known by such exotic names as the Los Angeles Open, the Western Open, the Motor City Open, the St. Petersburg Open — you get the idea.

Not a Deutsche Bank Acupuncture Cell Phone Snickers Bar Invitational in the bunch.

When we weren't betting on the tour results, we might well be betting on what color shirt Weldon the Oath would be wearing when he showed up at the course later in the day.

Because Weldon the Oath quit the game in anger just about every time he played, you could bet on something else where he was concerned. You could bet on whether he'd show up at all. Weldon, No Weldon.

As for betting on the tour, I always wanted Matnab Neb Nagoh, Bantam Ben Hogan, but he rarely played back then — the accident, you see — so I was often left to choose between Dyoll Murgnam or Nek Irutnev while others would ride along with someone like Mas Daens, or those up-and-comers, Dlonra Remlap and Wod Dlawretsnif.

Yeah, it was silly, but you have to understand how bored we were.

Soon enough, we all tended to speak in the shorthand of Moron Tom, who spoke in a combination of rhymes and old West Texas sayings, be it on the golf course or in the greasy lunch room where we'd sit around after golf and play gin, poker, fan-tan, crazy eights, whatever. Anything to win or lose more for the day's efforts.

I can still hear Moron Tom in a poker game announcing a "cramped cottage" — full house — and laying down what he called "threckings and twoquins." Three kings and two queens.

Standing over a putt out on the course, he'd say, "Think I can't, Cary Grant?" Then if he sank it, he'd stride toward the cup, saying, "There he is in all his might, the big raccoon'll walk tonight."

Quitting Golf, Part 1

The first time I quit golf, it wasn't because of aches, pains, illness, or surgery. It was because of New York City.

I quickly discovered that trying to go play golf while living in

Manhattan was about as easy as trying to grab a taxi while standing out in front of Saks Fifth Avenue in the freezing rain on the last shopping day before Christmas.

It involved finding a place to rent a car, renting the car from someone who spoke in an unknown tongue, driving back to the apartment to collect the golf clubs, fighting traffic to get to Westchester, Long Island, Jersey, wherever you were going, getting lost two or three times, finally arriving at the country club, finding out that nobody at the club had been told to expect you, and then having some assistant manager follow you around and stare at you like you were there to steal the silverware.

So I quit playing for ten or fifteen years. But it wasn't like a total divorce. I was always around golf, watching it, listening to it, covering it. For a while I'd still be conned into playing three or four times a year, and for a while I could still break 80 from the blues on just about any course I played, thanks to muscle memory.

Then one day I couldn't break 80 from anywhere, or 90, or even 95. It was all gone. Power, timing, pride. Hello, Rust City. But no big deal, I thought. I was still around the sport, and I had cocktails, the reliable Winstons, typing for food, and memories of occasional birdies on 9 and 18 when some thief pressed to get even.

It wasn't until I was living part-time in Florida and Texas, and had seen so many old friends give up whiskey for golf, that I started trying to play again.

If you haven't picked up any golf clubs for a number of years, you have no idea how heavy they are. For weeks, my driver felt like I was trying to swing six feet of sewage pipe.

Then something else happened. Once I got used to it and was advancing the ball forward somewhat regularly, I noticed that all the other recreational golfers were using strange equipment. Drivers with bowling balls for club heads, and big, fat irons with holes dug out of the backs.

I could only watch in awe as seventy-five-year-old midget lepers would out-hit me one hundred yards off the tee. And others would rifle their 4-irons past me by sixty, seventy, eighty yards. More embarrassing, they kept doing it even after I'd bought the same equipment.

I considered blaming it on the sudden inconveniences of a bleeding ulcer first, and then on an attack of pericarditis, a heart thing, but I didn't really feel bad. In fact, I argued with my wife that I wasn't sick all the way to the hospital.

"What is pericarditis?" I asked the doctor. "It sounds like a Notre Dame linebacker."

"It's not a heart attack," he said. "It's an inflammation of the sac surrounding the heart. We'll treat it."

"Fine," I said. "Can I go now?"

Roughly a year later, if I remember correctly, after I'd worked my way up to a prodigious 215 off the tee, I was forced to give up distance forever.

I don't know that you can realistically say the three angioplasties and the ultimate bypass were responsible any more than you can say it was the three packs of cigarettes a day for forty-five years.

What I clearly remember is the cardiologist saying, "Here's why I think we need to go ahead with the bypass: you've never had a heart attack, but if you ever do, it'll be the only one you ever have."

Maybe you can guess what my immediate response was. This comes close: "Can we do it today?"

So they cut me open a couple of weeks later and eventually located my heart tucked in there between the enchiladas and the chicken-fried steaks. It was supposed to have been a quadruple bypass, but I birdied one — it wound up being a triple.

Happily, I never heard the noise the thing made when it cut open my chest, and I never had any recovery pain. And in five weeks I was back out on the golf course, once again challenging for pie plates in member-guests and various geezer events.

Frankly, the gallbladder removal a year or so later hampered my grip, timing, and distance more than the ticker deal, but in one way it turned out to be more thrilling than the bypass.

During my recovery in the hospital on that occasion, all I ever wanted was a grape Popsicle, but it would take from six to eight hours to get it because the nurses couldn't manage to tear themselves away from their soap operas and Krispy Kremes.

But the real fun started when I was sent home. I turned the color of French's mustard and began to hurt like a run-over dog. What had happened was, the surgeon had forgotten one of the things he had explained he was going to do when we had our little pre-op meeting. He forgot to make sure he didn't leave something inside of me. I think it was a Titleist.

After I requested a different surgeon to come to the rescue, I returned to the color of a human being, and I even forgave the first guy. Figured he'd only been in a hurry to close me up because he had an early tee time.

The Rules of Enjoyment

It wouldn't be right if the dental implants, the hearing aids, and the cataract surgery didn't come in for their share of the credit for helping me develop a set of rules that would enable most sensible people to play enjoyable golf a while longer in their lives:

- Mulligans are free.
- Roll it over everywhere, especially in the rough.
- Take relief from behind any tree or other obstacle.
- One free throw in every fairway.
- Lift and toss from all bunkers.
- It's not out-of-bounds if you say so.
- Red tees if the hole seems longer than it was last week.
- If it's your honest opinion that a putt should have gone in the cup instead of lipping out, by all means consider you sank it.
- Never keep score entirely.

Two years ago, however, before all of these rules were set in place, I played what my two grown sons and a close friend still describe as my career round. We played from the whites at Colonial, and naturally it was on a day that wasn't too hot or too cold and there was no hint of wind.

I might add that it was before the cataract operation and before I'd paid four hundred million dollars for the new hearing aids that worked.

Everything I did seemed to go right that day, although I hardly saw any of it. A lot of the conversation went like this:

"Where'd my drive go?" I would ask.

One of my kids: "It's in the fairway."

Me: "You're kidding!"

Then I'd hit an approach shot somewhere.

I'd ask, "Where'd I wind up?"

My friend: "It's on the green."

Me: "It's where?"

My friend: "*IT'S ON THE DAMN GREEN!*"

Me: "Really?"

It was somewhere on the back nine that my oldest son, Marty, a pretty good player, said in utter disgust, "Can you believe this? He can't hear and he can't see, but he's on the green and I'm in the river!"

They say I broke 80 that day. I said I'd take their word for it — and might even play again sometime.

One thing I know for sure. Going back ten or twelve years, I'd never have swung another golf club if I hadn't taken the advice of my cardiologist.

The two best things I could now do for my heart, he said, were one, stop getting so hot at three-putts, and two, stop cussing traffic. I've done it. Life is good in the declining years.

MARK LUCIUS

Joining the Club

FROM THE GREAT RIVER REVIEW

> Don't think you really win until you live up to that high thing within
> you that makes you do your best, no matter what.
> — Patty Berg

> I would never join a club that would have me as a member.
> — Groucho Marx

It Happens Every Spring was the title of an old baseball movie I loved
as a kid. But baseball was no longer happening for me in April
1966. After thirteen opening days in Milwaukee, the Braves were
playing their first in Atlanta. I'd spent the winter trying to convince
myself I could still be a fan. But even at fourteen, I knew a weak
story when I told one.

Then, on Easter Sunday, something astounding occurred. Golf
appeared on our family TV, and I did not turn it off. Until that moment, my zeal for sports viewing had known but a single boundary.
I'd grown up watching most anything with a winner and loser, but
golf had always been a channel-changer, *par excellence.*

That afternoon I sat for hours and watched, in blurry black and
white, something called "The Masters." Inexplicably, golf took on a
new drama, and a world of possibilities opened before me. Travel!
Achievement! Fame! Wealth!

A few weeks later my mother heard some news about a local
country club that was a recent transplant to the area. Urban sprawl
had squeezed the venerable North Shore Country Club out of
nearby Bayside, and the club found wider fairways in our more rural suburb of Mequon. Now North Shore was "looking for caddies."

I showed up there in a drizzle and got hired. But this was no Biblical parable. Many were called; all were chosen. A week later I was out on my first job, carrying for a Mr. O'Leary, his face fixed in a permanent scowl, more hair in his eyebrows than on his head. Mr. O'Leary rarely took a caddie, and on the few occasions he did, as penance, was assigned the likes of me. "It's his first time," Romy Erdmann, the stocky young head pro, cautioned O'Leary. Nothing more needed to be said.

Mr. O'Leary and I spent two hours together in a light rain, a two-man parade, me a constant five paces behind, taking care to hop the same puddles he did, doing a reasonable impression of a bewildered pack horse. I caught up to him on about the fourth hole and, trying to establish rapport, said brightly, "Well, it certainly is muddy today." This elicited an even darker O'Leary scowl and drilled into me one of the first and most important rules of caddying: you can rarely go wrong by just shutting the fuck up.

Dearth of the Cool

I spent that summer quietly learning more rules. At first I struggled to keep up, keep my eye on the ball, keep the clubs clean. Gradually, I learned the proper way to hand Mr. Member his driver (grip first), when to give him his putter (the instant his ball settled on the green), where to keep my shadow when he putted (anywhere but in his line), and why I needed to hold the flag as I tended the pin (to keep it from flapping in the wind, like a dying fish).

But I was missing something, and I knew it. All summer I tiptoed around those velvety greens like I'd crashed a party. While it's easy now to ascribe my discomfort to inexperience, my adolescent brain registered the problem as far worse. I was appalled to find that even success at a summer job depended on the pursuit of the *cool*. And I neither felt nor looked like a cool caddie.

A cool caddie never strained when lifting even the heaviest golf bag. A new caddie picking up a bag looked to be trying to lever a loose load of bricks onto his shoulder. He'd fidget, grimace, sweat. But the cool caddie whisked that same bag from ground to shoulder in one fluid motion. No stopping, no stooping. It was an act of such grace and dexterity that I was reminded of Roy Rogers leaping onto Trigger with a running start.

Members asked for cool caddies by name. "Is Bobby here?" a member inquired, looking past staff member Dennis Fox through the rack room to the sorry group of unassigned caddies peering back through the doorway at the other end.

"Sorry, sir," Fox replied, "but he's been out for an hour."

"Ah, that's okay, I'll take a cart," said the member, trudging off, spikes clattering on the stone path.

Cool caddies made top dollar, which in 1966 meant five bucks. Even. Not the flat rate of $3.25 or $4 or even $4.75. When someone asked what you'd earned, there was one right answer. "A fin, of course." It was an immutable rule of caddying; a mere quarter helped define the chasm between uncool and cool. And on the rare occasion when the cool caddie didn't get five dollars, we all knew it was only because he'd had the misfortune of winding up with a "cheap prick." Which was another thing: vulgarity seemed to come naturally to cool caddies. I had to work at it. The cool caddie sounded like he'd been cursing since birth. If it was Thursday, I sounded like I'd been cursing since Wednesday.

At the end of each round, golfers evaluated their caddies by filling out report cards and dropping them into a small box screwed to the wall just outside the pro shop. Every few weeks you'd find out where you stood in "caddie points." But sometimes you'd get a more immediate report.

One midsummer's day I was waiting with another caddie at the "turn," the break in each round between the ninth and tenth holes. Our golfers had stopped to buy us Cokes, and now walked up with the head pro himself, Romy Erdmann.

Squat and broad-shouldered, Romy didn't fit anyone's stereotype of a classic golf pro. But he was the only nonmember who showed up at the club in a Cadillac, and he'd earned that bright yellow convertible by keeping a close watch on his members' wishes.

On this July afternoon, Mr. Erdmann sidled up to where I was standing and slipped a club out of my golfer's bag. He held the club like a rifle, staring down the shaft as if aiming it at the group holing out on the eighteenth green.

"How do you like these?" Romy inquired of my golfer, who had acquired the new set a few days earlier in Romy's pro shop.

"Not sure yet," my golfer replied. "You sure didn't put enough pars in 'em."

Romy chuckled and set the club head on the ground. He took a lazy swing at an imaginary ball. "How're these boys doing?" he asked suddenly, nodding in our direction.

The other golfer, silent until now, could not have answered more quickly. He reeled off a rhapsody of his caddie's fine qualities: smart as a whip, strong as an ox, a veritable Old Faithful of caddies. "Bruce," he concluded, "is a helluva young man."

There was a long and awkward pause as we waited for my golfer's verdict. "Mark's a good caddie too," he said, finally, rationing out words like new Titleists. "Always asking me if he can clean my ball — whether it needs it or not." Then he looked at Romy and laughed, and Romy laughed, and the other golfer laughed, and even Bruce couldn't suppress a smile. I smiled too, but my ears burned from more than the sun. Cool caddying seemed a distant mirage.

I may have felt ambivalence about caddying but none about golf itself. I paid $20 for a mismatched set of used clubs and began golfing each Monday morning, on "caddie days," when the club opened the course to employees. Golf also gave me a new fantasy life to help pass the winter. There were rules to learn, books to read, heroes to worship, and a history to memorize. I returned to the club in spring 1967 six inches taller with a shade more confidence. But my brave feelings could still vanish quicker than Romy Erdmann's smile.

Answered Prayers

Dennis Fox was king of the rack room, but on this Tuesday morning he burst out of there like a fullback, carrying a small table under one arm and a folding chair under the other. He took a shortcut across the cart path and hurried down the grassy descent that led to the caddie shack. A few caddies ran up alongside him, but they had to hustle to match his giant strides.

All country clubs have guys like Dennis Fox, who work ungodly long hours for scant pay and about as much respect. Though he wasn't mean, Fox could be menacing. He was strong enough to hold a golf bag in front of him with one hand, as if he were carrying a coffeepot. He could turn a simple gesture, like setting that bag in front of you, into an act of intimidation. He'd drop the bag like a rock, and the collision between bag and asphalt produced one of the most violent sounds one could make at a country club.

On this bright June morning, Fox planted his table on a patch of grass in the shade of the caddie shack. He unfolded his chair, removed a piece of notebook paper from the back pocket of his Levi's, and sat. He stared out at a motley crew of forty to fifty teenage boys wearing sawed-off blue jeans and sneakers. They were eating the breakfast of caddies: Fritos, Mounds bars, Pepsi or Mountain Dew.

"Listen up," Fox called. A few kids kept snapping the wet towels caddies carried to clean clubs. Fox raised his voice, which he did well. "Look," he boomed, "this is serious business. It's hard for me to believe, but you guys are caddying in a golf tournament."

In its second year in Mequon, North Shore was hosting a professional women's golf tournament — the Sixth Annual Milwaukee Jaycees Open.

Golf history would be made that week, though not in Mequon. A thousand miles to the east, at the storied Baltusrol course, Jack Nicklaus would win the 1967 U.S. Open for men with a record-shattering performance. Of the total purse of $175,000, he'd get $30,000. Back in Mequon, the world's best women golfers would carve up what the *Milwaukee Journal* called a "prize melon" of $16,500. The winner's slice would be $2,250.

"All right," Fox continued, "we need to pick some caddies. First up . . . Patty Berg."

The raucous laughter was quickly stilled. For the longest time we all listened to the whoosh of the sprinkler on the putting green. *Pfft. Pfft. Pfft.*

It was no surprise that no one raised a hand. Though past her prime, Patty Berg was still the closest thing to a legend in women's golf. But caddies knew just one thing about her. We didn't want to carry her clubs.

Rumors had begun circulating for days.

Patty Berg hated caddies. She chewed out caddies. She chewed up caddies. Mostly, she fired caddies — three in a week at a recent tournament; we had it on good authority.

Little of this, maybe none of it, was based on firsthand knowledge. Though she'd played Milwaukee many times before, it had always been at other courses. But to newly minted adolescents, experience will never beat a rumor that begets a story that becomes a fact. Patty Berg roamed and stalked the fairways like a mad fire-breathing monster, leaving twisted clubs and crumpled caddies in her wake. You could look it up, somewhere.

And with such a strong field, who needed that? $16,500 may have been chicken feed to the men, but it was one of the more lucrative purses on the women's tour. Big names were coming: Betsy Rawls, Marlene Hagge, Kathy Whitworth, and Mickey Wright.

"Nobody?" Fox pretended to look incredulous. "Honor caddies?"

The "honor" caddies stood around looking bored. They knew they could hold out until the right one came along. Younger. Prettier. Someone with a chance to win. Someone who wouldn't kill them.

I was standing on the fringe of the group, watching my friend Dale Neeck make one of his Red Skelton faces that he knew would always make me laugh. You'd think I'd remember who started it, but I'm not sure I knew even then. Probably it was meant as a joke. But suddenly, I heard a familiar name.

"Lucius!"

I shrank in denial at the sound. But the notion was so preposterous I felt little fear at first. There was even a hint of flattery. Me? Starting quarterback? Patty Berg's caddie?

Then another voice, a smirk, from someone standing up front, on the white crushed gravel that edged the caddie shack. "Yeah, Lucius. Let him do it."

A chorus began, "Lucius, Lucius." It hardly resembled rolling thunder, but it was enough to give me the feeling that I was, by then, sunk. My cheeks reddened like they'd been slapped, and I stood as if impaled by a flagstick. I made the mistake of looking up at Dennis Fox, who sat grinning behind the rickety card table. His eyes beckoned. I trudged toward him, walking to the gallows.

"Lucius, Lucius!"

Dennis Fox always looked to me like Eddie Mathews of the Milwaukee Braves. He had dark hair on top of a thin but strong face, and a five o'clock shadow even at eight in the morning. But up close, he looked more thoughtful than I'd seen, and his voice was softer than I'd heard. He spoke gently, almost fatherly.

"Well," he looked straight at me. "Do you think you can do it?" More than one ass was on the line.

"Sure," I lied.

Dennis Fox looked down at his list. Next to "Berg, Patty," he wrote "Lucius, M."

Fox's space was filled. The crowd's prayers, answered. My week, altered.

Sunshine on My Shoulders

I passed the next few hours in monkish deliberation, pacing back and forth, wearing out the path from rack room to caddie shack. Neither brought much refuge.

Someone was passing around a list of current LPGA money leaders, and I searched in vain for the name of Berg. Then it hit me — maybe she wouldn't show up! About noon I began bargaining with God. Okay, Lord, it doesn't have to be an accident. Maybe just a cold or the flu. Even a sprained wrist would do it.

My perverse thoughts provided a measure of comfort. Pros kept arriving, the parking lot filling up with late-model automobiles. But still no Patty Berg. I threw myself down on some cool grass in the shade of the pro shop. A familiar voice cut short my reverie.

"Lucius," snarled Dennis Fox, "she's here. Get your ass out to the parking lot."

I loped my ass to her car as fast as I dared. With others watching, I didn't want to seem too eager.

Patty Berg emerged stiffly from the driver's side of a long blue car. I was surprised to see her all dressed up, in white blouse, dark skirt, earrings, and heels.

She was wider and shorter than I expected. If I was close to six feet tall, she was nearer to five. She turned and advanced, rather sternly I thought, to the back of the car where I stood.

Patty Berg looked like a grandma, and a pixie. That was it, a pixie grandma with curly red hair going gray, freckles, and bright blue eyes.

"So," she said in a low voice, "you got the bad duty."

If I said anything at all, I don't recall it.

Patricia Jane Berg grew up in Minneapolis, where she won the Ladies City Championship in 1934 at age sixteen. The next year she won the Minnesota State Amateur, and the U.S. Women's Amateur three years later. That year, 1938, she entered thirteen tournaments and won ten. The Associated Press named her "Woman Athlete of the Year." She would eventually earn that distinction three times — in three different decades.

Berg's father was a wealthy grain merchant who encouraged a certain sensitivity to a time when most people were lucky to be working, much less golfing. Herman Berg financed his daughter's amateur career on the condition that she "contribute something to society."

He booked Patty and a small group of other Twin Cities athletes to play weekend exhibitions for charity in Minnesota, Iowa, and Wisconsin. At each stop, they'd golf with the local pro, put on short clinics, and perform dramatic readings of popular poems. "Casey at the Bat" was a particular favorite. Maybe there was no joy in Mudville, but by available accounts, the folks in Duluth were charmed.

After winning twenty-nine tournaments in seven years as an amateur, Berg did something in 1940 that few respectable women of the day dared to do. She turned professional. At the time, only a handful of women were so employed. Just three tournaments allowed entry to these "proettes." It was, someone noted, an occupation demanding "thick-skinned immunity to public disapproval."

"Golf was considered a dignified game," recalled Betty Hicks, who turned pro in 1941 after winning the U.S. Women's Amateur. "But it was frowned upon to be too competitive. I hit the ball too hard and practiced too much for the local women."

Prizes reflected status. When Berg won her first professional tournament, the 1940 Women's Western Open, she received a $100 war bond. It was a modest step up from the previous year's first prize of a silver bowl.

Berg was a queen without a kingdom. So she created her own. While still a student at the University of Minnesota, in July 1940 she signed a "lucrative contract" with the Wilson Sporting Goods Company — joining an "advisory staff" that included two guys named Sarazen and Snead. Wilson introduced Patty Berg golf clubs, which in time became one of the most popular women's models in the country. And this "rollicking extrovert" began conducting the first of a reported ten thousand clinics and exhibitions that many credited with dramatically reshaping the role of women in sports. "For fifty years," goes a typical acknowledgment, "Patty Berg strutted across the world's practice tees in her crazy collection of hats, a natural comedian . . . who loved crowds."

A skilled athlete, she was also — perhaps preeminently — an entertainer with an act. She mixed jokes, personality, and trick shots with a novel concept: a woman who made a living playing golf.

So when Patty Berg opened her car trunk for me in June 1967, I found myself peering into what passed as a satellite office stuffed with boxes of balls and shoes and assorted other golf gear. But the focal point was an enormous red-and-white golf bag with PATTY BERG and WILSON emblazoned on the side. As caddies, we made a distinction between a regular golf bag and the "pro" bag — any oversized, ostentatious model that had claimed the lives of several herds of cattle. Patty Berg's bag was a choice cut. But when I reached for it, before I could touch it, she halted me with a pair of single-word commands.

"Wait! Careful!"

She hefted the bag herself and began a step-by-step commentary on the proper way to lift, hold, and set a golf bag upright without scratching its smooth leather or banging a club on the trunk lid.

Then, having poured on vinegar, she ladled a bit of honey. She gently lifted her driver halfway out of the bag. It was swathed in a woolen head cover, a knitted replica of some kind of animal — a cat, perhaps. Pulling the club close in a mock embrace, she leaned forward and pretended to apply several soothing smooches. "Don't eeeever," she exclaimed, her face a mask of magnified horror, "hurt my baby."

Miss Berg's sketch produced the desired effect. From that moment on, I treated her bag more carefully than if it had been my three-year-old sister.

When she pulled a suit bag from her car and slammed the trunk lid, I cautiously shouldered the bag and hurried behind her to the clubhouse door. "Wait for me at the practice green," she ordered, and without looking back disappeared into the coolness of the women's locker room.

I envied her — such a clean getaway! I had nowhere similar to hide. Instead I walked through a gauntlet of curiosity to the edge of the putting green. I stood there holding the bag, sun beating down like a spotlight, and in my fevered imagination all who passed — Erdmann, Fox, Dick Wallace, the young assistant pro, pool men, lady pros, and caddies — were scrutinizing me. *Well, buddy, show us what you got.*

A would-be athlete, I had often dreamt of such a moment: everyone watching me. But in my fantasies they were cheering, not smiling ironic smiles, not casting looks of thinly disguised pity, and certainly not studying me like they could see every bead of the sweat I felt bubbling on the back of my neck.

Duty, Honor, Country Club

The Patty Berg who walked out of the locker room thirty minutes later looked more like the woman I'd brooded about. Now she wore clothing stern as her face. Not for her were the bright, colorful shorts or slacks favored by the younger set. She dressed as she had a generation earlier: dark skirt hiding her knees, nylons thick as tights, shoes sturdy as Buster Brown's. She'd shown up dressed for business. Now, after donning sports clothes, she looked even more like she meant it.

We started on the putting green, where her instructions again revealed a woman who favored the imperative. "Stand there. No . . . there!" She moved about mixing with her competitors, and I noticed something else. She walked funny. Oddly, she walked funny but moved fast: in a pigeon-toed limp, her rounded shoulders hunched forward, a woman who wanted to get there faster than she could.

I attributed her gait to advancing age. After all, she was nearing fifty. What I didn't know was that Berg had been walking that distinctive walk for most of her professional career.

Like most sports, golf excels at turning tragedy into legend. Though new to golf lore, I'd memorized details of certain historic events. For example: the 1949 auto accident that nearly claimed the life of Ben Hogan. I knew, because I'd read about it, that Hogan's doctors said he'd never walk again. I'd even seen it happen, on late-night TV, in *Follow the Sun*, the 1951 Hogan "biopic" that starred Glenn Ford. In both reel and real life, Hogan proved his doctors wrong and returned in 1950 to win his first tournament, post-rehabilitation.

Until I started writing about her, I never knew that the woman who limped alongside me in 1967 also had overcome a serious car wreck. She just never became grist for Hollywood. Berg was hurt December 8, 1941, the day after the "date which will live in infamy." Berg and a fellow woman pro, Helen Dettweiler, were en route from Texas to Tennessee, where they were due to raise money for British war relief. Dettweiler was driving the car when it was struck broadside.

Barely a year into her professional career, Berg's left knee was torn open, broken in three places. Six months into her convalescence, doctors discovered that the knee had to be reset. In all, she rehabilitated for a year and a half. She spent the last six months working out at a camp for prizefighters in Mobile, Alabama.

She would never regain full strength or movement of her leg. But in 1943 she returned to golf anyway and quickly won two more tournaments. Then, because there was a war on, she joined the Marine Corps Reserves, emerging from Cadet School as First Lieutenant Patricia Berg.

If I'd known some of that at the time, it might have helped me understand how she approached our association. Lieutenant Berg clearly had high expectations of all who would assist her. But, apparently, she also believed that even someone like me, who wore his inexperience like a frown, could be trained.

Our first practice session moved to the driving range. A dozen or so other women pros were set up there, all using the yellow-and-black-striped range balls provided by the club. Their caddies stood watching them hit.

I'd been to the range with members many times. But this was a different trip. "Watch where I hit this 5-iron," she said.

She pulled a Wilson Staff from her shag bag, dropped it to the ground, hit it out onto the open range.

"Now, run out there, set the bag down, and pick up any balls that don't land in it."

"Okay." I had started speaking by then.

I still recall the particular loneliness I felt as I stood out in the middle of that field and gazed back at a long line of golfers and caddies. I can see them outlined against the sky, fixed in my memory like soldiers in a film by John Ford.

But this was a silent movie. I could see Miss Berg, but I could not hear her. I watched her swing, and my eyes scanned the sky for the white speck. But no matter how intently I focused, I instantly lost its flight. I tensed a bit, for after all, I was the target. Then, suddenly, I spied the ball dropping like a rock just a moment before I heard it split the air around me. I did not have to walk far to pick it up.

Measuring Up

"What does she have you doing tomorrow?" asked my father that night, slowly carving my second helping of roast beef.

"She wants me to measure the course."

"Don't they know how long it is?" asked Lynn, oldest of my three sisters, a month shy of thirteen. She wasn't usually a smart-ass but may have been feeling left out. I'm sure I was playing the you-don't-know-how-tough-it-is role to the hilt.

"Of course they know how long it is," I shot back in that special didactic tone reserved for older brothers. "But she wants me to measure the distances to the green from all kinds of . . . kinds of . . ."

Pride goeth before the fall. My mother came to my rescue. "Landmarks?"

"Yeah, you know, sand traps, sprinkler heads," I said. "Stuff like that. She wants me to help her figure out which clubs to use."

Good luck.

We'd finished that first day with a nine-hole practice round. Berg would ask how far she needed to hit a particular shot, and I couldn't tell her. Oddly enough, neither could anyone else. At the time, North Shore didn't supply even its members with course yardages. Thus my assignment: to pace off all eighteen holes.

For a change, I looked forward to it. This seemed like something I could do — walk and count. I'd also be working by myself, at my own pace. I didn't realize the problems my own pace might present.

A little after dawn the next morning, I stood in the middle of the ninth green ready to walk my first hole in reverse. (A squadron of lawn mowers was still attacking the back nine.) At that hour, the course seemed lonelier than usual. A thin tissue of fog hung in the heavy air. The greens, uncut and dew-covered, looked more like grays.

I squinted back through the fog toward the ninth tee and started out; striding, counting, my sneakers making squishing sounds. The course was still waterlogged from three inches of rain the previous weekend.

Reached the front of the green and kept striding, counting, squishing down the fairway.

I stopped at the first sprinkler head, mercifully not pumping water. I'd sketched a crude map of the hole in a small green notebook. Now I used a golf pencil to record my first measurement. I resumed striding and counting, sneakers starting to soak through.

Striding, counting, now fretting.

I'd measured my stride the night before in my backyard. On the familiar turf of my backyard fantasy golf course, it had seemed easy. I felt confident I knew the pace of a yard.

But out here now the sun was rising and my heart sinking, as my confidence ebbed away with the fog. I began adjusting each soggy stride to make up for the previous one. This one shorter, that one longer. None felt right.

By the time I reached an oak tree that separated the ninth fairway from the old farmhouse (home of George Duga, the groundskeeper), my conscience was coming hard at me. It felt like God and Patty Berg, not necessarily in that order, were glaring over my shoulder as I jotted down "147" in my notebook.

One hundred forty-seven steps, sure. After all, I could walk and I could count. But I was also good at multiplication. And now it occurred to me how little room I had for error. Just a couple of inches off on each stride, over a distance of, say, 147 yards, could mean an error of as much as 10 yards. And that would be the difference between a 5-iron and a 6, between an ugly shot in the bunker and one sitting tight to the flagstick.

For the next few holes I mixed striding and counting with fretting and feeling guilty.

But a funny thing happened on my long trail back to the caddie shack. The more holes I walked, the better I felt. I met up with members of the grounds crew; they were raking traps and cutting grass, their leathery backs baking in the sun. We nodded to each other, exchanging silent looks of what I took to be respect. A few caddies even walked over to watch me finish my final hole at mid-morning. By then I was hamming it up a bit, marching around like a seasoned surveyor.

I don't exactly know why, but for this caddie on that morning, the simple act of walking the golf course, of scrawling down highly approximate measurements on hastily drawn maps, of striding where no caddie had strode before — seemed like an achievement unto itself. The numbers I put down may not all have been accurate, but in my mind they added up to something. And while I never fully shook off my secret feelings of guilt, neither did I share with anyone my fear that my measurements were anything but ruler-perfect.

Maybe it was as simple as knowing that I had something nobody else had. It was my word against the world's. And for the moment, it seemed that my word had the advantage.

Of course it didn't take long — about two holes, I think — for Miss Berg to begin questioning the validity of my word. That's not to say she thought all my measurements wrong, only that not all of them seemed right. And sometimes, I think for both of us, it was hard to tell. In golf, as in war, hitting a target in the 1960s was a more mysterious venture.

But now when she asked for a distance, I could give her a number. And if she sometimes responded with skepticism, she seemed to hold a modicum of respect for the green notebook that became my constant companion.

She turned her attention to further expanding my vision of the possible. Later that same Wednesday afternoon we were finishing a practice round, walking up the same ninth fairway where I'd started my day twelve hours earlier.

"You should think about what you want to get out of this week," she said.

"Ma'am?" Her question, framed as an instruction, rattled me. I wanted to get out of this week, period.

"Have you thought about what could happen here?"

I'd thought about little else for a day and a half, but I still wasn't sure what she was getting at.

"Yeah, I have thought about it."

"I hope so," she answered, and moved closer to me as we reached the spot in the fairway where her ball lay. I caught a faint hint of perspiration in the breeze. It was all mixed up inside her perfume, but there nonetheless.

She started telling me stories about caddies — and tournaments — past. Not distant ones either. She talked about a tournament from the previous year, when she'd finished well and paid her caddie a great deal of money.

She reached for an iron. But even as she lined up her next shot, she kept lecturing, looking straight at me.

I think it was that moment when a more practiced observer would have realized something. Though she was five years removed from her last victory, though just two days earlier she had told the *Milwaukee Journal* that it was "somebody else's turn," though no one around believed she had any chance, Patty Berg at age forty-nine passionately believed she could win this tournament.

Instead I must have stared back with an expression mixing blankness with befuddlement. She stopped, raised her club high, and pointed out at the great green expanse of North Shore's rolling acres — Moses signaling the Promised Land.

"There is something you have to understand," she said. "This isn't just golf. This is business."

The Lady Is a Golfer

She must have found it excruciating to see the great business boom after World War II — to watch it and not really be part of it. The boom lifted many pro sports, but it took a while before women's golf hopped aboard for the ride.

There was an encouraging development. When Berg was honorably discharged from the service in 1945, she joined a new golf tour for women professionals. The previous year, a small group led by teaching pro Hope Seignious had introduced the Women's Professional Golf Association. Seignious and her father, a cotton broker, put up much of the financing for the WPGA.

Seignious and company managed to add a few new tournaments, doubling the total from three or so to six or so a year. But with more Hope than money, the WPGA failed to lure many new women to cross the bridge from amateur to professional. The typical women's tournament drew far more local amateurs than traveling pros, and the new tour stalled after a few years.

Berg had no visible role in starting the WPGA, but she was in the thick of it as both player and administrator. She won a dozen more tournaments in the four years it survived, and one of those victories was historic — the first U.S. Women's Open, played in 1946 at the Spokane Country Club.

But perhaps Berg's greatest contribution to the WPGA came in 1948 when, as president, she helped put it out of its misery. She helped kill it not out of malice or spite but, it seems, out of impatience, frustration, almost a sense of duty. "I thought we just had to get going," she was quoted as saying.

Getting going meant bringing in the head of Wilson Sporting Goods, L. B. Icely, with his money and connections. One of those on Icely's payroll was Fred Corcoran, a promoter with his own celebrated associations. Corcoran's friends and clients ranged from entertainers to athletes, from the famous to the really famous — Ben Hogan, Joe Louis, Ted Williams, and Bing Crosby. A decade earlier, Corcoran had helped organize the men's Professional Golf Association (PGA). Now Icely pressed Corcoran into service as director of another new women's tour.

Corcoran gave the new tour a new identity, as the women of the WPGA became the ladies of the LPGA. "He thought the name change would give us a little publicity," said Berg, "and that's what happened."

It was more complicated than that, and several books have tried to unravel the tale of how women's golf finally "got going." All cite Berg's enormous influence.

She was not the best female golfer. That status belonged to Babe Zaharias, the 1932 Olympic track champion who turned to golf and became a household name based on her dashing style on (and off) the course. Zaharias was Berg's chief rival and, surprisingly, one of her best friends.

"Babe was the greatest woman athlete I've ever known and a great friend," Berg recalled. "She brought a power to the game that I had not seen before."

Plenty of the new tour's other "ladies" were more glamorous.

When Hollywood came calling in the late 1940s and early '50s, Berg was noticeably absent from such films as *Pat and Mike*, in which Katherine Hepburn and Spencer Tracy were joined by Zaharias, Hicks, and Dettweiler. But Berg juggled multiple roles and sundry demands for years. Behind the scenes, from 1948 to '52, she was the first LPGA president. As a competitor, though she played only part-time, she racked up forty-two LPGA tour victories between 1949 and 1962, which raised her combined win total, amateur and pro, to eighty-four.

Maybe most important, she was the freckled public face of the LPGA, chatting up reporters, mugging for the crowd, and circling the globe for more than fifty years as an "ambassador" of golf.

"She carried the name of Wilson and the LPGA into every corner of the golfing world," said fellow LPGA Hall of Famer Betsy Rawls. Berg, said Rawls, "did more to promote golf than any person in the history of the game."

World War Three

I'm sure Miss Berg noticed when the tournament started Friday morning, but I did not detect a difference in her demeanor. I suppose she could hardly be more serious than she'd been in practice. As she told people, Patty Berg kept a written record of every golf shot she ever hit. In her eyes, there was no such thing as an insignificant swing.

Her mood kept swinging too, which kept my nerves a-jangling. But I began to find some comfort in her familiar patterns. One was how she approached each shot. I knew her routine by heart; how she'd stand behind the ball, left hand gripping the club, club head resting on the turf, club tip pointing like a blunt arrow down the path the ball would travel. She'd stare at her target for a moment, two, three, as if in silent prayer, then with her right hand brush the brim of her cap as she moved swiftly to the left of the ball, took her solid stance, and unleashed a rhythmic, clocklike swing. She'd take off after the ball like a runner breaking from the blocks, sometimes shooting a fiery glance my way when she saw, or maybe didn't want to believe, the result.

In particular I recall her focus — if you will, her look. It's a look

I've seen many times since, in athletes I've admired and bosses I've worked for, a look of concentration, absorption, engagement. It's a look that says the only way you matter to me right now is in how you can help me drop this putt, block this kick, sink this jump shot, close this sale, write this speech, reach that finish line. The sports world calls it "game face," but I've come to think of it as the look of work. If I had a mirror in my office, I might see it a hundred times some days, and other days not at all.

But there are those who must bring that look every day. And so I endured more than one scene like the moment in the first round when we arrived at the ninth hole. The ninth was the very hole on which I'd begun my mapping assignment two days earlier, the same fairway where she'd delivered a pep talk on the opportunities knocking at my door. Now she hit a strong, straight drive, and we walked up the graceful slope of the hill to her ball.

How far? she asked.

I checked my green notebook, glanced at George Duga's oak tree, surveyed the distance between me and tree, and tree and green, lowered my eyes to the notebook, looked back up at Miss Berg. All the time I was thinking — this was the first hole I meas- ured; no chance in hell is it gonna be right.

One hundred sixty-one yards, I said.

Jaw set, lips pursed, eyes steely with suspicion, she chose a club for 161 yards. Uphill, the distance called for a 5-iron. The sound of club striking ball told me she'd nailed it. Immediately she began striding to the green, a Marine on a mission. Her hip and knee may have been ailing, but I had to hustle to keep up.

She turned to me without breaking stride. "If that ball isn't right on the pin," she seethed, "we are going to have World Wars One, Two, and Three, right here, right now." I could envision her rolling through the desert in a tank — and not just because June 1967 had already seen the Arab-Israeli "Six-Day War."

We hurried to the green, where my eyes nervously swept every square inch. Alas, there was no white Wilson Staff to greet us. So our death march continued ten yards beyond the green, where we found the ball cowering in a clump of crabgrass. She reached for her wedge in stony silence, and I learned that looks really can kill.

My ego was still, shall we say, developing, so it was hard not to take it personally. Eventually, I grew more accustomed to her temperament. She would assume, as a lawyer might say, "ahead of the evidence," erupting even before she was certain I had screwed up. But even when she was right, the World War turned out to be just another Cold War. And as a passive-aggressive fifteen-year-old intro-vert, I was used to those. I rode it out. In golf, there's always a next hole.

Eventually, I became protective of her. One afternoon, on the way to a concession stand, we passed the caddie shack. A few off-duty caddies, close enough so we could hear them but not close enough so they felt threatened, began calling out — "Hey, Mark, how's it going? Having fun?"

Their teasing seemed to bother her even more than me. "What in the world is wrong with those boys? What is their problem?" If she understood the true target of their mockery, she never let on.

I was silent for a long moment. "Ah, they're just goofin' around," I said finally. "They're always like that." Which was true.

As for the tournament, I wish I could say that I helped her turn back the clock and contend. But she was out of it almost from the start. She shot 76 in the first round, eight shots behind leader and eventual winner, twenty-five-year-old Susie Maxwell of Oklahoma City. Maxwell's score of 68 that day was the only sub-70 round of the tournament.

On Saturday the wind shifted, and the weather turned from hot and humid to cool and wet. The conditions sent many scores soar-ing, so Berg's 75, like Wagner's music, was better than it sounds.

On Sunday another 76 left her knotted in a five-way tie for twelfth place. Because her best finish in ten LPGA tournaments in 1967 was a tie for ninth, you could say a twelfth-place finish wasn't bad. It just wasn't golf as she'd known it.

I'm sure that final Sunday was more ordinary than how I recall it. But I think of it now as a swirling kaleidoscope — a sound here, a color there, here a scene, there a feeling, and everywhere the chilly wind. While Berg and the others tried to play golf, the weather played havoc with my senses. The wind muffled even the occasional bursts of applause, of which there weren't many to begin with be-cause it's hard to play golf in the wind. And the sun beamed down with the brightness of the solstice, just two days before the longest day of the year. What that gave us was a clear look at a strange sum-mer sight: women wrapped in sweaters and jackets and slacks, gri-

macing as they tried to swing around all that clothing and somehow lift golf balls from the mud.

Reaching the Green

All week, when I looked forward to the end of the tournament, I
felt that my big reward would be that it was, in fact, the end of the
tournament. That Sunday, since I hadn't been fired, I began thinking about getting paid.

I didn't know what to expect, though I'd been teased by her generosity of the previous day. She'd bought me a hot dog and Coke,
paid the dollar-and-a-half check with a $5 bill, and handed me the
change — an amount a "cheap prick" might give you for eighteen
holes.

My mind started rolling around some numbers. Six days times
five bucks a day; well, that didn't seem to be enough from Patty
Berg. What about six days times ten bucks a day? Naw, she wasn't
going to give me $60. I pushed those thoughts into that corner of
my brain where I forced most pleasurable fantasies — notions that
could only bring bad luck.

She went to the locker room to change. I cleaned her clubs for
the last time, using a wooden tee to scrape mud from the grooves of
each iron. Then I stood, waiting, trying not to wonder.

She came around the corner of the pro shop and waved for me
to sit down next to her on a bench. My left hand held her golf bag
upright, balanced at my side. She stretched out her stubby legs in
front of her and from somewhere produced a checkbook.

While she wrote in silence, I watched the victory ceremony taking place about a hundred yards away on the eighteenth green. I
tried to look past her as she wrote and wondered if she could hear
the pounding of my heart. Now my ears were pounding too, so
pounding was about all I was hearing. They didn't have a microphone at the ceremony anyway, so I just watched as a Jaycee in a
sport coat handed a check to Susie Maxwell, her face creased with
the easy smile of the winner.

After Berg paid me, I slung her red-and-white bag over my shoulder, and together we walked to that long blue car. As we walked, she
gave me some advice. The details are fuzzy, but the general subject
was my future in the world. This was her last chance to improve me.

She asked for my address. I wrote it down. Then I thanked her again, and she got into her car by leaning back onto the front seat, then swiveling her legs stiffly inside. I closed the door, and behind the window, freckles and curls under glass, Patty Berg in an instant was transformed back into the pixie grandma I'd first seen six days earlier.

I climbed into the backseat of my parents' Country Squire station wagon. Dad was sitting in the driver's seat, quiet, staring ahead. "Are we ready?" he asked. As he turned the key, Mom turned back, broad smile, said how much fun it was to meet Patty Berg, which they'd done right after the round. She had told them I was a fine young man.

I don't know what else Mom said to me because inside I was screaming, for a change, with something resembling joy. Who knows if Mom could see that? Who knows if Dad looked at me in the rearview mirror? And if he did, did my face give me away?

"The goal when I was a teenager," said songwriter Randy Newman, "was to be without affect, to have a mask-like face." He was born a few years before me, but I know exactly what he meant; this was an essential element of cool. But I could contain myself no longer. I dangled the check over the plastic seat and presented it to my mother. She took it and inspected it and looked back at me with a different kind of smile.

"Why, Mark," she said after a long moment, "this is a check for one hundred dollars."

Print the Legend

And then the thing I'd feared most was the thing that boosted me to a higher level in the caddie hierarchy. People began talking about me.

You couldn't keep secrets from other caddies, least of all about what you'd been paid. I once saw two caddies roll another — not to steal his money but simply to discover how much he'd earned for a round. He didn't give it up easy: they had to pry open his fist until the stash tumbled out: four crumpled dollar bills and a quarter that rung hollowly as it hit the asphalt parking lot. Rarely, in Mequon, did so little mean so much to so many.

Not that I wanted to hide my good fortune. My father even made

a Xerox copy of my check before he deposited it. Caddie gossip being what it was, it was soon an established "fact" that only one caddie, the guy who caddied for Susie Maxwell, made more than me
that week. And he didn't matter because he was the only stranger
among us, a caddie from a different club.

It goes without saying that she could have paid me much less and
still made a point. Her twelfth-place tie netted her $322 that week,
and she handed me almost a third of it. For me there was a kind of
vindication, my own little *Rocky*-like moment of reflected glory. The
honor caddies stopped joking about me, and before long, I was
one of them. The next year I would caddy in a new tournament at
North Shore, the first Greater Milwaukee Open for men.

But I soon discovered that Berg had given me more than a hundred bucks and some keepsakes. Few things in my life have so illuminated the power of myth. It's even clearer today, as the world of
marketing appropriates myth and calls it branding.

As "The Kid Who Survived Patty Berg," I went from a nobody to a
somebody, at least at North Shore. And if I didn't quite deserve it, I
was treated as if I did, and before long I became, if not a cool caddie, then a valued one.

A week after the tournament, I was polishing some clubs following a round. I turned to see Mr. Warner walking up to me. He was a
tall, horse-faced man, usually seen grinning, with a large hank of
gray hair that leapt straight up before gravity finally forced it sideways. His wife had played with Patty Berg in the pro-am before the
tournament. I'd caddied for Mr. Warner before and found him to
be a square guy. But his smile had never been this broad.

"Hey, I've got a match next Thursday."

I stared back, suspicious.

"I'd like you to caddy for me."

A match was a big deal even if the golfer wasn't.

"Sure. Thank you." I never could shake the habit of thanking
people for the privilege of working for them.

"Okay," he said. "Be here at noon. And bring that notebook, the
one with all the magic yardages. I need every advantage I can get."

My green notebook, which arguably contained some of the least
reliable measurements since Vespucci plotted the new continent,
had become my talisman.

Caddying was more fun after that. When I think back to that

time, my thoughts tend not to run to my (admittedly modest) achievements at Homestead High School. I think about caddying, of turning a role of servant into one of adviser, confidant, even coach.

The members I favored played for money, but that didn't seem to be the point. While many joined country clubs for business or show, those guys seemed to play for the sheer competitive thrill of it all. Often they'd finish eighteen holes and just keep playing, because they couldn't stop. The sun would start to go down, and the breeze would come up to cool the sweat on my neck. Twilight is still my favorite time to be on a golf course.

To be a regular caddie in those regular groups was to be part of a team, in a way I never quite felt with my peers: running cross country, playing drums in the high school band, or as a member of the debate team. Too often my native insecurities took over.

Hanging out with adults at play, I came to feel I belonged in the world of work.

Berg Redux

In August 1988, I read in the *Milwaukee Journal* sports section that Patty Berg would be giving a clinic at the Missing Links Driving Range in Mequon. By then I was living in Milwaukee and decided to make the short fifteen-mile trip. My friend and golfing buddy, Virgil, went with me.

Before I went, I pawed through the files on Patty Berg that I kept and still keep in a cabinet in my attic. Tucked away between old clippings of the Beatles and Braves, my Berg file includes mementos of my week in the sun: newspaper clippings, tournament programs, and some things she gave me.

I found one of the golf gloves she wore that week, robin's-egg blue, pressed flat and brittle as an old flower. I carefully tried it on and was surprised to discover that such a short woman apparently had such long fingers.

I found some of the Christmas cards she sent to me. I was on her list for a few years, solving the mystery of why she wanted my address.

I found the black-and-white publicity photo she autographed for me. It shows a middle-aged Berg in a half-crouch. There's a golf ball in the foreground to make it look like she's lining up a putt, but she's actually smiling for the camera with a slightly forced gap-toothed grin. She looks uncomfortable.

Her message to me, written in indelible ink, had not faded.

> To Mark
> My very best
> wishes to you
> always
> Sincerely,
> Patty Berg
> 1967

The clinic had started by the time we arrived, and it took us a while to find the center of attention, the little woman in the big crowd. Big is a relative term, but I'd guess well over a hundred people had come out to see this seventy-year-old woman hit a few shots, crack old jokes, and praise Wilson equipment, which in the new age of Pings seemed as much an anachronism as, well, Patty Berg.

Her jokes hadn't been written that morning, but her verbal timing and swing tempo were intact. Some of her golf tips took the form of simple "Casey at the Bat" rhymes. "Swing it high," she shouted, then swung the club, "and let it fly."

She'd had a malignant tumor removed successfully in 1971, and a hip replaced in 1980. Yet her swing was sweet as I remembered it, and each shot looked and sounded like a line-drive single to left. The audience responded with genuine laughter and applause, seeming almost surprised that she was more than a relic.

Afterward, she sat down on a chair they'd brought for her, and many of us lined up for her autograph. When it was my turn, I presented her with the photo she'd autographed for me in 1967, and started to explain.

"I caddied for you many years ago in a tournament over at North Shore," I began, "and . . ."

My voice trailed off as she stared hard at me with the steely blue eyes I remembered so well. She looked down at the photo, as if she could not believe I'd handed this to her, and looked back up at me.

"What do you want me to do with this?" she asked, rather sternly I thought.

Her reaction hadn't really surprised me, and I smiled. "I was hoping you would sign it again."

And she did. Slowly, methodically, her pen cut into the old photo, and when her first attempt left a sketchy signature, she traced it again to make it bolder.

Patty Berg

1988

She handed it back to me without another word.

On the drive home, Virgil, for whom interpersonal relationships tower above all else, told me that, on balance, he hadn't really thought much of Patty Berg. I told him I could certainly see his point. I tried, without much success, to explain why she mattered to me. And I thought, not for the first time, that some day I would try to write about my memories of a woman who demanded so much and received so little — and a young man who expected so little and received so much.

Bibliography

Barkow, Al, et al. *20th Century Golf Chronicles.* Lincolnwood, Illinois: Publications International, Ltd., 1993.

Glenn, Rhonda. *The Illustrated History of Women's Golf.* Dallas, Texas: Taylor Publishing Company, 1991.

Hahn, James and Lynn. *Patty! The Sports Career of Patricia Berg.* Mankato, Minnesota: Crestwood House, 1981.

Kahn, Liz. *The LPGA: The Unauthorized Version.* Menlo Park, California: Group Fore Productions, Inc., 1996.

Void, Mona. *Different Strokes.* Holbrook, Massachusetts: Adams Media Corporation, 2001.

ELI SASLOW

The Old Ba' Game

FROM THE WASHINGTON POST

KIRKWALL, SCOTLAND — William Thomson's family had played this sport for centuries, so he understood that he needed to choose between two strategies for the annual Christmas Day ba' game.

The scrawny seventeen-year-old could fight for the ball in the center of the riotous scrum, where more than three hundred men would function as a human juicer, turning his face red, then purple. He would be scratched, punched, kneed, and bitten. His ribs might break. He could pass out unconscious.

Or, Thomson could follow convention for players his size and stay near the edge of the scrum, pushing the pile. This would work well unless the ball popped out and the mob changed direction. Cars, gravestones, houses, strollers, hotel lobbies — all had been kicked, shoved, or trampled in pursuit of the ball during previous games. Anticipating such a stampede, business and home owners in town had nailed wooden planks across their doors and windows. "If you're on the edge of the scrum and it turns on you," one veteran player said, "then you might as well be dead."

This, Thomson decided, was his safest option.

He never considered not participating. The men in the Thomson family — like the men in most families here — have played this game since at least the mid-1600s. It is one of the oldest and most physical sports, and it's almost certainly the most simple. Half of the men in Kirkwall, called Doonies, try to push a small ball into the sea using any means necessary. The other half, called Uppies, work to push the ball to a wall one mile across town. The ba', which refers to both the game and the ball with which it is played, can last anywhere from four minutes to nine hours in freezing temperatures and hurricane-force winds.

The ba' is played nowhere else. It has persisted in Kirkwall because its basic tenets are congruent with life on these Orkney Islands in northern Scotland. If you're tough enough to survive in this old Viking territory, in a frostbitten town of around six thousand bordered by whitecapped seas, then you don't worry about relaxing on Christmas and New Year's Day. You put on steel-toe boots and a rugby shirt and walk downtown to the almost nine-hundred-year-old St. Magnus Cathedral, ready for hell.

The Uppies and Doonies squeezed into a tight pack last Tuesday afternoon in front of the cathedral, where they waited for a former player, standing in front of a cross, to throw the ba' into the middle of the scrum. Thomson, a Doonie, stood on the edge as planned. He had wrapped duct tape around the bottom of his frayed jeans to ensure that nobody could rip them off. He had hastily patched two holes in the back of his rugby shirt, mending relics from one of last year's games.

The ba' flew over Thomson's head and disappeared into the chaos behind him. A few Uppies circled behind Thomson for a better angle to push the scrum into a side alley. Doonies circled behind those Uppies and tried to pull them away. Before Thomson realized what had happened, he was in the center of the pack, his arms trapped at his side.

For almost thirty minutes, the scrum deadlocked in the fifteen-foot-wide alley. Two hundred Uppies grunted and pushed in one direction; 115 Doonies held their ground. Thick steam rose from the pack, and Thomson couldn't find fresh air. He called out for space, but the screaming mob drowned his request. His eyes rolled backward and his head fell on his shoulder. A nearby Doonie slapped him across the cheek and poured water on his face, desperate to wake him. Thirty seconds passed before two spectators climbed down from the alley wall and stepped on the heads and shoulders of ba' players to reach Thomson. They pulled his limp body from the pile and carried him one hundred yards away.

Once he awoke, Thomson asked his girlfriend what had happened. His ribs ached, but he felt otherwise okay. A few friends stopped by to check on him, and one offered a flask of whiskey.

"Thanks," Thomson said. "I need this to get my nerves back."

He took a swig and handed back the flask. Then he lifted himself up over a wall and dropped back into the riot.

Three days before the Christmas ba', Ian Smith diagrammed game strategies while sitting next to a coal fire in his house overlooking the town. At sixty, Smith is one of the oldest men still participating in the ba'. He has played for forty-five years, never missing the twice-annual game despite heart surgery, a hip replacement, nine broken ribs, and two knee surgeries. A butcher and a lifelong Orcadian — he refuses to call himself Scottish — Smith identifies first and foremost as a Doonie.

When the ba' game was first played in Kirkwall, teams were divided by whether a player was born closer to the ocean (a Doonie) or the wall (an Uppie). A hospital opened in Kirkwall about fifty years ago and became the location for all births, so now family history determines the teams. Newcomers to the island usually move into recent housing developments near the wall and declare themselves Uppies, which has created an imbalance. With almost twice as many men, the Uppies have won fifteen of the last sixteen ba's.

Smith promised friends he would hold off on retirement until after the next Doonie win, a vow that further stretches the conventions of good sense with each passing year. Arthritis has begun to seize his already weathered hands, making it impossible for him to clench them into fists. Because Smith believes his body has started to shrink, he grumbles when asked his height. "I'm five-feet-and-who-gives-a-damn," he said. "Mind your own bloody business."

For this year's Christmas ba' (after a week of recuperation, the game also is played on New Year's Day), Smith had solicited help from his two sons in hopes of finally pushing the ba' into the ocean. Kevin, twenty-seven, had traveled from Edinburgh to play in the game, his first trip home in a year. Sean, twenty-five, had agreed to participate in the ba' for the first time since he lost consciousness in the middle of a 2003 scrum. The brothers had decided to play mainly because they wanted to cash in on their father's retirement promise before a ba' left him seriously disabled.

"What they don't know is that even if the ba' goes down, I'll probably keep playing," Smith said. "What's life in the Orkneys without a ba'?"

Librarians have traced the Kirkwall ba' back to the 1650s, but several local legends place its origins even earlier. Many Uppies believe the ba' is the descendant of a game played by Vikings here in the ninth century. Smith and most Orcadians swear the ba' began in the 1400s, when a Kirkwall leader beheaded a neighboring tyrant and residents kicked and shoved his skull across town.

Ba' players have preserved the game by steadfastly refusing to modernize it. There is no set of written rules, no official organization, no record-keeping of any kind. Even the four-pound, black-and-brown-striped ba's still are made specifically for each game by a rotation of local craftsmen. To survive the scrum, a ba' must withstand the equivalent pressure of a two-ton weight. The craftsmen stuff Portuguese cork into London leather and spend three days stitching the ba' together with fifty yards of eight-cord flax.

Neither Uppies nor Doonies wear uniforms or distinguishing marks of any kind. Players are supposed to recognize their teammates because their fathers played together, and their grandfathers before that. If anyone should get confused about who's who in the midst of the three-hundred-person tangle of arms, legs, and faces, he's wise to keep it to himself. Leaders on both teams said confusing an Uppie with a Doonie often warrants banishment from the next ba' game.

Since local newspapers began writing about the ba' in the late 1800s, the historical record indicates the game has existed predominantly in isolation and in peace. A ten-person crew of voluntary paramedics and an unwritten code of sportsmanship have limited ba'-related fatalities to one, in 1903. There always has been a boys' ba' for children fifteen and younger at 10:30 A.M. on Christmas and New Year's Day, followed by a men's ba' at 1:00 P.M. An experimental attempt to start a women's ba' in the 1940s lasted only two years because of meager participation.

Once every decade or so, an uppity mainlander from Scotland moves across the eight-mile Pentland Firth and throws a fit about liability, brutality, and pointlessness. But the Uppies and Doonies ignore the protests and show up at St. Magnus Cathedral to continue playing, because that in itself is the point.

Smith obsesses over each game for three months in advance, and he continued to contemplate strategy at his house until almost 10:00 P.M. His two sons returned home from the pub and sat down on a couch opposite their father. Sean, the family baby who weighs only 135 pounds, rubbed his forehead against his palm. He'd been wanting to confess something, he said, and the night's quaff had fortified his confidence.

"You know, da'," he said, "still not quite sure I'm playing this year."

"Hell you're not!" Kevin said, punching his brother in the shoulder. "What, you scared? Come on!"

"Naw, I'm too small," Sean said. "I could get killed in there."

"Ahh, it's not about size, never has been," Smith said. "If I taught you boys one thing about the ba', it's that nothing matters but heart and effort. Don't make a damn difference if you're seven foot tall or four foot. You're a Smith, so you'll play. And you'll play Doonie."

The sun — or something vaguely like it — filtered through a thick sea fog and rose over Kirkwall at nine on Christmas morning, illuminating the epicenter of this seventy-island archipelago that sits closer to the Arctic Circle than to London. It would set again in less than seven hours, leaving the town's residents in the eerie darkness that accompanies their extreme geographic isolation.

The day's ba' forecast called for temperatures in the high thirties and "a bit of a breeze," a term Orcadians use for all gusts under 100 mph. A "bit of a breeze" translates: Yes, you might have to tack sideways to make progress while walking up the sidewalk. Yes, the halogen streetlights probably would shake and rattle in their foundations. Yes, the whistling gales might lift mist off the sea and spray it across the islands, bathing the Orkneys in salty foam.

Kirkwall, though, had been built in the likeness of a fortress, capable of withstanding a bit of a breeze and more. The brown and gray walls of its single-story buildings were constructed with stone and covered with roofs of poured concrete. Streets curve radically like corkscrews to block the wind. On the day of the ba', wooden planks three inches thick cover each door and window, a precaution mandated by the town council before every ba'. The adornments made Kirkwall look particularly sinister, less like a town than a collection of war bunkers hunched against the sea.

An hour before the beginning of the ba', the streets remained still and silent, as they had since the end of October. Most residents here are fishermen and livestock farmers whose work goes dark during the winter. From early December until the end of February, these islands enter into a hibernation. Residents stay at home or, if they're feeling brave, trudge to one of the well-lit local pubs to escape the darkness.

The harsh winters prevent trees and most other plants from growing on the islands, but Kirkwall continues to lure newcomers by offering a rare portal into history. The town has shunned chain restaurants, stoplights, and stop signs. Crime is rare, and the unemployment rate is lower than 1 percent. Many of the islands' greatest relics — five-thousand-year-old burial grounds, Viking graffiti marks — remain unlocked and unguarded. A half-dozen sunken battleships from World War I and World War II fill the harbor, casting shadows across the water when the tide ebbs.

Past and present smudge together in Kirkwall, and never more so than on this Christmas Day. As the giant clock on St. Magnus Cathedral neared 1:00 P.M., hundreds of spectators gathered along the cobblestone main street. Two hundred Uppies strutted down the street from the north; 115 Doonies approached from the south. They met in front of the church and glared at each other like opposing street gangs. Then the church bell chimed to signal 1:00 P.M., and the ba' descended into the pack.

The ba' traveled less than one hundred yards in the game's first hour, with Uppies and Doonies pushing in opposite directions to create a near standstill. The only significant movement came once every five minutes or so, when spectators climbed over the pile and pulled unconscious players — first William Thomson, then a half-dozen others — out to safety. Participants stopped moving altogether for thirty seconds early in the game to allow paramedics to strap one man onto a stretcher.

Players always have expected to return home with bite marks, gashes, bruised hands, and black eyes, but the rate of serious injuries has doubled in recent games. Kirkwall's population has grown by more than one thousand in the last decade, and the size of the ba' scrum — and the pressure at its center — has correspondingly metastasized. New players unfamiliar with the game's tradition of picking up fallen athletes are now just as likely to trample them, veterans said.

"Some of these young boys take 'by any means necessary' a bit too far," Smith said. "Used to be we'd beat each other for a while but never throw that final punch. Now, they'd kill you if they had to. We've got too many players and too many people crowding around to watch. It's almost too big."

Instead of trying to push the expanded scrum toward a goal with sheer force, Uppie and Doonie leaders now rely on strategy and trickery to move the ba'. As the deadlock continued on Christmas, Smith climbed a wall for an aerial view of the action. He spotted the ba' in the center of the scrum, held by two Doonies. With a succession of winks and hand movements, Smith instructed the Doonies to surreptitiously hand the ba' backward, from one teammate to the next, in the opposite direction of their goal. When the ba' finally reached the last Doonie, the player sprinted off. He made it four blocks toward the water before a dozen Uppies caught him.

Spectators — and most players — almost never know who holds the ba', and that mystery increases the frenzy. It's not unusual for a lesser player to participate in five or six ba's without ever seeing the namesake of the game, much less touching it. The ba' spends considerable time hidden under players' shirts, and participants rarely throw or kick it. Rather, the team in possession typically hands the ba' around discreetly, like a stolen jewel.

As the sun faded on Christmas, three Uppies left the scrum and climbed onto the slanted roof of an Indian restaurant. Two of them grabbed the third Uppie's ankles and dangled him from the roof, so that he was suspended upside down over the scrum. A teammate on the ground handed up the ba', and the Uppie pulled himself back onto the roof.

"Ba's up there, boys," Smith yelled, pointing frantically at the roof. "Come on! Get him."

A pack of Doonies hurriedly climbed above the Indian restaurant, where one player's foot broke through the shingled roof. He pulled himself back onto solid ground, caught up to the ba' holder, and tackled him. Two Doonies kicked the ba' loose and threw it back into the scrum, but an Uppie caught the ba' and eventually sprinted away amid the chaos. He made it within a few blocks of the Uppie goal before the rest of the pack caught up.

Fifteen minutes later, at about 5:00 P.M., two hundred Uppies shoved the remainder of the way to their goal and pressed the ba' against the wall for victory. As dictated by tradition, a handful of experienced Uppies stood at the wall and continued to fight over the ba', a process that determines the game's individual winner. Ian Gorn, thirty-six, eventually emerged with the ba', and teammates hoisted him onto their shoulders. They carried him in the direction of a local pub, where Gorn gulped down a beer. Then he walked to his downtown apartment, where, as the ba's individual winner, it was his responsibility to host an immediate, all-night party for all three hundred sweat-soaked ba' participants.

Gorn hugged his wife as he walked in his front door and grabbed another beer from the hundreds stacked on his dining room table, donated to the winner by a local grocery store. He set the ba' down for display on a counter in his living room. His two sons, ages seven and twelve, reached up to grab it. Then they fell onto the floor in a tussle for possession.

Behind the Bamboo Curtain

FROM ESPN.COM

WE LEAVE THE CAPITAL on Highway 108 early in the morning, ahead of the sludge of commuter traffic, which grows by a thousand new cars a day. The blacktop beneath the green Jeep knocks us around; we're taking the back road west, ignoring the modern, smooth expressways.

More than 2,500 kilometers separate us from our destination: Chengdu, the dominant city in China's Wild, Wild West. A driver, interpreter, and I are setting out to look at a sprawling, complex country through the prism of the 2008 Olympics. In front of us is a week of white-knuckle mountain roads, countless oxen, a Rolls-Royce, homes made of mud, skyscrapers made of steel, a dreary coal-town wedding, a forest of smokestacks, a quilt of rice paddies, hundreds of villages and cities filled with people, each with a story to tell about the hopes and dreams of the real China and what, if anything, the Summer Games can do to make those dreams come true.

Behind us lies Beijing. With just a year until the opening ceremony — and all the metaphors of rebirth that go along with it — the construction in the city is breathtaking. New roads keep up with all those new cars, enough that lifelong Beijingers often get lost, sometimes finding themselves at the end of an uncompleted freeway. Entire ancient neighborhoods are bulldozed by day. At night, sparks rain down the sides of buildings, welders working around the clock, replacing the old with the new. Everywhere you look, there are bundles of steel and towers of wood and stacks of bricks, stretching to the horizon like soldiers, raising the obvious question: where does all of this stuff come from?

The nerve center for the Games is a marble-floored skyscraper not far from the two main Olympic stadiums, and not far from the start of Highway 108. The sunlight makes the Beijing Organizing Committee of the Olympic Games headquarters glow, as though it's generating its own energy, which, in a way, it is. It's drawing a road map for places like Chengdu, and all the villages and boom-towns in between. It's saying: this is what the new China should look like.

"We are building a harmonious society," BOCOG spokesman Weide Sun says. "You have only seen half the story in Beijing. But when you travel to the western part of China, you're going to see there are many, many areas that have difficulty even finding clean water. There are still lots of challenges for China. The goal is to build a well-to-do society, and the Olympic Games will be a mile-stone event for that."

Those are the stakes, as defined by the government itself. The Olympics are clearly more than a sporting event, and next August will be a historic moment for China, symbolizing the strides of the past decade and pointing the way for a century to come. But will the Games help bridge this growing gap between the new and the old, using sports to give people common ground? Or will the growth represented by the Olympics split the country in two, haves on one side, have-nots on the other? The answers to these ques-tions will determine the future of the world's fastest-growing eco-nomic superpower, and they lie in front of us, covered in soot, growing in emerald green fields. That's where China's Olympic spirit lives, beyond Beijing's sea of merchandise stands and the jun-gle of cranes.

It's out along Highway 108.

Road Diary, Entry 1: Following the Signs Driving Between Beijing and San Lou

A few hours down the road, I see a sign painted in blue and white on a long brick wall. It's one of the more popular propaganda slo-gans that fill rural China. The fears of government officials are writ large out in the sticks — the more worried they are about some-thing, the more frequently it shows up on signs.

This one reads: NEW SOCIALIST COUNTRYSIDE.

With China growing so fast, with the images beamed down to television sets filled with sudden wealth and modern conveniences, the government is trying to assure the 900 million subsistence peasants in China's interior that they haven't been forgotten. Not everyone is buying. Again, check the signs. In one small town our first day on the road, graffiti covers a wall in the middle of a village. On it, we see the first whispers of anger over the development initiated by the 2008 Games.

IT'S NOT WORTH IT, one writes.

THE WRONG PEOPLE BENEFITED, says another. TEN THOUSAND PEOPLE SUFFERED.

It's not the signs we see that are most telling, though; it's the ones we don't, namely, not a single official sign for the Olympics in rural China along 108 so far. Indeed, in the next week, we will see exactly one sign for the Games that is not in a city. But the cities, they are full of signs, thousands of them, each one connected to an advertisement. The Olympics, it seems, are mostly about selling things, about a consumer revolution. The peasants don't have the money to buy these trappings of modern life.

We drive through the mountains. Around a corner, there's one final sign of the day.

It reads: STOP.

Two hours' wait, we're told. They are actually building a new portion of Highway 108 in front of us. Traffic idles until the blacktop cools.

While we watch them build our road, a young peasant named Sun Bin approaches us. He's sixteen years old, with a round belly and face. We're taking a picture and, amidst the babble of Mandarin, he says, "Go," in English. I turn around.

He grins and invites us to his village.

San Lou Village, 439 Kilometers from Beijing

A football field long and a few blocks wide, San Lou squats alongside Highway 108, the town's only real street. Small homes dot the roadside, thin ribbons of smoke float from chimneys. Supper's on. Night's falling. Mountains rise behind the villagers, throwing shadows across the narrow lanes.

Sun walks through the town, soon arriving at his house. It's made of mud, and he shares it with his grandparents. The two-room hut is dark. Against one wall is the large, wood-heated kang — a traditional bed made of bricks or clay. They all sleep here. Nearby, a calendar lets them know that today is not a good day to bury the dead. It's not a good day for much of anything.

Sun says the village has no natural resources to sell to the cities, nothing that can make it a part of the new China, not even as a place to be exploited and then forgotten. The village lives in a different century. The average family makes less than $200 a year. Folks are more concerned with water than the GNP.

"There used to be a big river and we'd swim in the river," Sun says. "Now there's no river anymore."

The mountain stream that fed the village dried up too. The faucets sit parched and rusted. The villagers can't afford a pump to run water from the local well to each house. Sun and his grandparents have a tiny television; every night they see so many things they cannot afford. Simple things. Things like pork.

"We feel sorry for ourselves," he says. "We see wealthy people eating fish and meat, but we only have corn and potatoes. Of course we feel bad and feel jealous."

The television also brings breathless accounts of the coming Olympic Games. Sun had never heard of the Olympics until Beijing's bid was successful. Now, he has a vague notion of what will actually happen in a year's time. He is certain of one thing: it will not benefit him. Like so many things in a country he recognizes less each day, the Olympics live in the city. Meat, fish, games — these are things for people with money.

"This is a very poor village and if people get by, that's a good day," he says. "Nobody cares about the Olympics."

The peasants only eat what they grow. Sun's grandparents, in their seventies, still work in the fields. His grandmother is a short woman, with white hair and a sturdy frame. She has lived her entire life in this tiny place. When things seem hopeless, she remembers when the Japanese occupied the area in the 1930s and '40s. That was worse.

"When I was young," she says, "I had to go to other villages to beg for food. Some rich people would have extra food and throw it into the plate for dogs, and we'd pick it up."

People still go to other, wealthier places looking for a way to live. Life can't be sustained much longer in rural towns like San Lou.

"If people have money," Sun says, "they will move to the city. People without money, they stay."

He stands up in the darkened space that serves as living room and bedroom. He wants to walk through town. Outside, the last few rays of sunshine light the narrow alleys. Flies move in bunches like paparazzi. First, he points to the town well. It's by the big cement roller that can turn rice to flour. Without this supply of water, San Lou would likely dry up and blow away. The village's entire future is down that hole. History suggests it won't last long. But Sun still holds on to hope.

"This well will never dry up," he says, at once both defiant and naive.

He keeps walking, stopping in a small courtyard by a walnut tree with flags hanging from the branches. This is sacred ground.

"Magic tree," he says quietly.

The villagers believe the spirit who lives in this tree will give them a peaceful life. And when a day seems especially hard, or they feel especially left behind, the villagers of San Lou come and stand beneath these broad branches and ask for help. As Sun looks up, a small girl throws something at the tree. He wheels around and glares. It is foolish to anger the gods.

Road Diary, Entry 2: Midnight in the Apocalypse

Driving between San Lou and Xin Zhou Nighttime on Highway 108, we're bound for a gold mine deep in Shanxi Province. To my left is Singing Songs, our driver, the son of a People's Liberation Army soldier, a veteran of Tiananmen Square who, in the flush of this new China, changed his name from Forever Revolution. Behind me is my interpreter, whom I call Austin, because she has a master's degree from the University of Texas.

Trucks line up for a kilometer, then two, then three, most carrying coal to power the cities. Some are loaded with bricks and steel. Where does all this stuff come from? It comes from here.

The scene is something out of *Mad Max*; this must be what America was like 150 years ago. I have a front-row seat to an industrial revolution. The highway is torn beyond repair by the overloaded eighteen-wheelers. In some places, Highway 108 is nothing but a mud hole. There isn't a road, per se, just a space with no buildings. Where there is road, clouds of coal dust float and dance a foot above it. The grime sticks to everything. Trucks stretch for twenty kilometers, then forty. Then sixty kilometers of trucks, lined up, two wide in some places, bumper-to-bumper.

The drivers pull into oncoming traffic without hesitation; this stretch of highway isn't notorious as one of the most dangerous roads in the world for nothing. Soon the traffic grinds to a halt in both directions. With the headlights blinding us, Singing Songs tries to slip past two parked trucks blocking the road. There is barely enough room for our Jeep. We are in the mountains, on a curve, with no guardrail. He climbs out to look at the sheer cliff, then back in the Jeep to make his way forward. Half the right-side tires are hanging off the road. Somehow, we make it. That dance repeats itself a half-dozen times. We move kilometer by slow kilometer into the belly of the beast.

Black-smeared faces poke out into the glare of headlights, then disappear back into the shadows. Men sleep beneath parked trucks. Others squat in the swirling clouds of coal dust to slurp down noodles, to nurse a warm beer. Their eyes are wide in the halogen glow. They are thin, with hollow cheeks and hacking coughs. Finally, worn out, we sleep for a few hours in a ragged roadside motel. The next morning, we wake to find the trucks still backed up, stretched in both directions as far as we can see.

Xin Zhou Gold Mine, 529 Kilometers from Beijing

This area is off-limits to the public and, especially, to foreigners. Only a local contact and some luck can get you past the guards. It's a Chinese government gold mine, and narrow-gauge railroad tracks take men down and bring rocks up. A decrepit dormitory is home to many miners and their families, some for longer than a decade. They congregate in the fly-infested courtyard, washing clothes with powdered soap, drinking tea.

An old man named Yan, with thin fingers and a thinner physique, speaks for the group. They are all excited about the start of

the Olympics. The government is shutting down this mine for
three weeks during the Games. The miners will get a vacation.

So you can watch on television?

The old man and the other miners laugh.

No, he explains, shaking his head. This is such dangerous work,
the state doesn't want to risk a catastrophic accident resulting in
bad press. Mining in China — for gold, coal, iron, and anything
else that can be forcibly extracted from the earth — can be fatal. A
miner a day dies in these parts.

Payouts to the families of killed miners are factored into budgets, and those payments keep the salaries of the workers low.
Competition for jobs — a dangerous job is better than no job —
drives those salaries even lower. When Yan first came here fifteen
years ago, he made about $1,300 a month. Now, it takes him three
months to earn that much, working twelve hours a day, seven days a
week. He is being left behind. And not just left behind by the far-off
fantasy world of Beijing. Left behind in this courtyard.

Not ten paces away, a miner named Liu listens. He once worked
for the government gold mine. Then, in 1995, he decided to mine
for himself. "There is more freedom if I work for myself," he says.

Private business has spurred growth in the town. Liu bought a
television set made by Changhong, an Olympic sponsor. He bought
a Volkswagen Santana, which he doesn't really know how to drive.
He built a new house, with a big courtyard for animals and some
vegetables. His family isn't rich, but they aren't just subsisting anymore.

"The road condition is better," he says. "The houses are better. In
general, life is better. Ten years ago, people still lived in the yellow-
earth mud houses."

Right now, he says, there's a ban on private gold mines. But national bans don't mean much out in the provinces, where the whim
of local power brokers carries more weight than any edict handed
down from Beijing. "If I'm caught, I'm not afraid," Liu says. "I'm
well connected, and I know everybody in the village."

From afar, Liu has been following the Beijing 2008 campaign.
He isn't that interested, but, as a businessman, he has respect. "The
Olympics have nothing to do with my life," he says. "What they are
doing is just to make some money."

Squatting a few feet away, Yan, the old man, says the Olympics are Beijing's business, though he does hope to have one connection, which is one more than the peasants of San Lou. Maybe, he says, they will use the gold he helps blast out of the earth to make the medals. He knows the highest honor an athlete can receive is a gold medal, and his gold, he wants you to know, is 100 percent pure.

Soon, it's time to go. Behind the dormitory, workers push tons of rock. Above the mine face — where darkness is broken only by a swaying, naked bulb — five red flags hang limp, twisted around their poles, all of them turned pinkish-white by the sun and the rain and the smoke. They are flags of warning.

Yan continues sipping his tea, lighting another cheap cigarette. He has twenty days off after six straight months in the mine; he'd lost so much weight the bosses were worried. He looks ancient, with the hard years underground wrapped around him like a bundle of yesterday's news.

Before leaving, we ask how old he is.

"Fifty-three," he says.

Road Diary, Entry 3: Descent into Hell Driving Between Xin Zhou and Linfen

There is a tunnel ahead.

Coal dust and smog block out the sun. It's morning but it feels like dusk. Kilometer by kilometer, we close on Linfen, the most polluted city in the world. Smokestacks line the road like telephone poles. The white road markers are stained black. The red bricks are stained black. The faces of the people we pass are stained black.

The tunnel gets closer.

We pass a cement factory. Then a brick factory, one of many we've seen in the past hour, some of them known to be manned by children kidnapped and forced into grueling labor. Every so often, an impromptu Delta Force of angry fathers rescue their children. The hours are long and hellish here in the place hope forgot. Austin, the interpreter, calls her husband in Beijing. "It's horrible," she tells him. "It's a disaster zone. Everything is black. I don't want to get out of the car. It's shocking."

We pass a wedding procession, a train of black Audis covered in red ribbons and balloons. This should be a joyous day. But the air is black and the future is bleak. "I feel sorry for those newlyweds," Austin says.

Finally, we're inside. The tunnel seems to be about a kilometer or two long, straight as an arrow. The air is so thick with pollution and coal dust that we can't see. Headlights don't help much. We hear a truck rushing toward us before we can pick it out of the blackness. Singing Songs slows. We are driving toward the most polluted city in the world, and there is no light at the end of the tunnel.

Linfen, 1,070 Kilometers from Beijing

The three twenty-somethings eating lunch upstairs at the New Hunan are like young men anywhere. They play video games by the hour, which their wives tolerate. Barely. The guys met online. They make grand plans for getting matching tattoos of the god of death. They love speed metal. One of them runs the city's pickup basketball league; another is the star player.

And, like young men everywhere, there is one thing coveted above all others.

"I want to own a Hummer," Zhao Kaihong says.

This is Linfen. Home to at least one Rolls-Royce and two Bentleys. Most polluted city in the world. Coal boomtown, like Pittsburgh in the glory days of U.S. Steel. One day, the big-spending mine owners will be China's Rockefellers and Vanderbilts and Mellons. They will have plazas and universities and arenas named in their honor. Presently, they are newly wealthy barons who buy sports cars they rarely take outside. The three young men and their peers breathlessly track their every move.

Dreams are close enough to touch. The Rockefellers-to-be roll down the street in Porsche SUVs, wearing the same trendy clothes, because when one coal mine millionaire gets something, the rest simply must get it too. That's how the black Audi A6 fell from favor overnight. Someone bought an A8.

"The coal mine owners," says Liu Xinyu, the league director, a skinny young man with glasses, "they find a villa they like and pay for everything in cash."

Zhao, the league's best player who goes by the screen name Cocofish, nods.

"In Linfen, when the coal mine owners want to buy something, they don't just buy one or two apartments," Cocofish says. "They buy the whole building. Then, as a gift, they give it to the local officials."

All this consumption makes the young men hungry for their piece of the Chinese dream. So many things are happening so quickly now that inertia feels like a million miles an hour in reverse. They want all those goods advertised with the Beijing 2008 logo alongside. They want them ten minutes ago. The Olympic Games sell hope, progress, and a future, all of which they desperately wish to buy.

If progress is on one side of the scale, destruction is on the other, and all three see the price paid for a shot at wealth. It's a steep one. As Cocofish says, coal is the best and worst thing to happen to their city. Twenty years ago, the air was good. Industrialization changed that. The third guy at the table, a local business reporter named Duan Jun, gets nosebleeds from the pollution. Cocofish had to move back to Linfen to take care of his mother; she, like so many, is suffering from lung disease. "Everybody in Linfen has chronic throat infection," he says.

But there is hope. The air is slowly improving. Some experts even think Linfen has given up its long-held title, having to settle now for a top-five spot in the rankings of most polluted cities, which means it's still worse than any place most Americans have ever been. Severe national government crackdowns have closed some of the worst polluters. A new, wildly popular mayor cracked down even further. The guys can now play basketball outdoors. And, since they're young professionals, there's even better news: they can wear white shirts again. A year ago, because of pollution, a white collar wouldn't be white by lunchtime.

In this new Linfen, they play PS3 (good) and debate China's chances in the Olympic basketball tournament (bad). They go five-on-five, full court, first team to make six buckets. They wait for next August. They dream impossible dreams. They believe those dreams can come true.

"My big plan," Cocofish says. "First, a Hummer. Second, an apartment."

*Road Diary, Entry 4: Morning Breaks Triumphant Driving
Between Linfen and Zhouzhi County*

We roll the windows down. Clean air whistles in. This is the China
I'd imagined. The old China. Fluorescent green rice paddies, laid
out in steps, halfway up the side of a mountain. Men in conical
straw hats. Entire villages pick the crops. We're following the harvest west, first grain, then rice. Families separate the grain from the
chaff along the roadside by throwing shovelfuls into the air and letting gravity do the work. The road is smooth, undamaged by coal
truck tires. "This looks like a proper countryside," Austin says. "Water. Fields. Everything looks clear. Mountains."

We are headed for a small village not on the maps, looking for a
brave peasant who fought the developers. We stop and ask for directions countless times. Finally, we are close.

"Next bridge," someone tells us.

We cross. The road narrows. It turns to gravel. We park outside a
house. The sign tells us we're in the right place, but the door is
locked. So we wait. The air smells fresh, like a Utah trout stream. A
noise catches our attention . . . it's a bird chirping. We haven't
heard a bird chirp in days.

Down the road, someone approaches, getting larger and larger
until it's clear he's headed straight for us.

We've found our man.

Zhouzhi County, 1,656 Kilometers from Beijing

Duan Zhiqiang sits down in his living room on a small wooden
stool. He lights a cigarette, rolls up his pant legs, and begins telling
how corrupt local officials tried to sell the villagers' farmland to developers, who were going to turn it into a golf course, of all things.

"What are we going to do?" the peasants asked.

"You can be caddies," the developers replied.

Land grabs are common. In every province, local citizens protest
and, in some cases, riot when their land is taken. What happened
here was typical. The developers offered the local government
$5,600 per person for the land. The government was going to pay

out $1,100 a person, pocketing the rest, leaving the villagers without enough money to move and without enough land to feed themselves. It is happening everywhere, as "progress" creeps in from the cities.

"We are in a battle," Duan says.

The golf course was a bridge too far. A golf course? Duan wasn't having it. He grew up here. Lived all his fifty-two years here. His brother, a Communist Party official, lives next door — in a much nicer house. Duan himself had been a teacher and a farming team leader, a respected man in town. So he did some research, found the Chinese laws forbidding stealing land from peasants. He copied them and passed them around to villagers.

This royally ticked off local officials. He was jailed for forty-eight hours until the other production team leaders wrote impassioned letters on his behalf.

He continued the fight. Village cell phones were tapped. Meetings were secretly recorded. Allies were bought off. When the local pressure got too great, he went north and hid in the city of Xi'an for six months. His wife often fainted because of the stress. Police monitored his house almost every day.

"My family was not very happy about what I did," he says.

His biggest fear was dying. Those who stand up to developers sometimes simply disappear. A stern television warning echoed in his ears the whole time: "Anybody who hurts the county's development will be severely punished." He imagined his family never finding his body.

"In this region, a lot of people die in the name of development," he says, though such claims are hard to prove or disprove. "If the local government wants to develop and you are against them, they hire some gangsters, and they beat you to death and use cement to bury you."

Finally, after writing letters to the Xinhua news agency — the Communist Party wire service that serves as de facto voice of a nation — a story appeared praising Duan's actions in defending his village. He had done what once would have been impossible: taken on local strongmen and won. It came at a price. His family likely will never get over the stress. The developers had already destroyed the crops in hopes of starting construction.

At least the village has peace. For the moment. But there are other developers out there, marching from Beijing and Chengdu. One day, they will arrive. The peasants are fighting a war they will eventually lose. It's a war against the developers' taking their land, a war against irrelevance, a war against progress. A war, the astute among them realize, against many of the things these Olympic Games symbolize.

"The countryside won't benefit from the Olympics at all," Duan says. "You can just tell."

In this little hamlet, where birds chirp and sons farm the land their fathers farmed, the Olympics are just another reminder that China is leaving them behind. "I think we were forgotten," he says. "We are forgotten. I think we are forgotten by the government and forgotten by the policy. I'm very worried."

Road Diary, Entry 5: In the Shadow of Progress

Driving between Zhouzhi County and Mianyang we're in the mountains again, but this time it isn't post-apocalyptic. Little groups of clay-shingled houses, with their sweeping rooflines, huddle together in the elbows of valleys. Trickles of smoke waft from chimneys. Beekeepers check on their boxes by the side of the road. It's like driving through the *Crouching Tiger, Hidden Dragon* movie set.

In the forests above us, pandas eat the tops of the bamboo. We enter another tunnel. This time, there's light at the end. And rich greens and browns. And blue sky. As we drive, I wonder what the future holds for this place. Will development come this far? Will this one day be a maze of smokestacks and coal trucks?

"Is this what Shanxi used to look like?" I ask Singing Songs and Austin.

"I guess so," Austin says. "I guess before the coal."

She tells me, forty years ago, songwriters wrote about the beauty of Shanxi — home to Linfen and the mines. I look out the window, at these little pieces of old China, these wonderful anachronisms. Progress is coming. A recent World Wildlife Federation report about this area warns: "Economic development continues to creep up the valleys. One piece of prime panda habitat outside the reserve is about to be split in two by a ten-kilometer-long reservoir behind the planned Fujiang hydroelectric dam. The dam will power

Mianyang, a city recently earmarked as China's very own Silicon Valley, and the provincial capital, Chengdu."

Our destination, almost the last of the trip, is Mianyang, with its sparkling clean streets and electronics factories. We drive along the narrow road, which disappears into the mountains behind us, getting smaller and smaller, the crenellated guardrails making it seem like a long section of the Great Wall, winding, twisting, snaking, stretching further and further into the past.

Mianyang, 2,404 Kilometers from Beijing

Maybe it's the streets clean enough to eat off, or the cops who issue tickets for dirty cars, or the kilometer-long Chonghang factory — the folks who made the entrepreneurial gold miner's television. Could be the local celebration they had when Mianyang was named one of the cities that the Olympic torch will pass through on its journey from Athens to Beijing. Maybe it's the downtown lined with billboards from each official Beijing 2008 sponsor, the streets canopied by lush trees. Or maybe the fact the city changed the name of the local sports academy to the Olympic Sport School.

Whichever clue works. It's not hard to figure out the people in this bustling tech-town are jacked about next summer's Games and the rising China they represent. It's what they're talking about in the trendy cafés.

"China hosting the Olympics is an opportunity for China to show the world its strength," says Mr. Li, the deputy secretary of the local Communist Party. "And the torch passing through Mianyang makes the people very proud. It's proof of the country's power."

He's sitting at his desk on the second floor of the sports school. His office has hardwood floors — a seldom-seen luxury. Talking to a foreigner about something as important as the Olympics freaks him out: he spills tea all over the floor trying to pour some for his guests, and his leg taps a mile a minute beneath the heavy wooden desk. Giving out his first name makes him uneasy.

In the classrooms down the hall, students finish up their work before practice starts for the day. They are training the next generation of Olympians here. Two signs in the lobby watch over the athletes. The first tells them their task: CARRY ON THE OLYMPIC

SPORTS SPIRIT. The second lays out the goals for this entire community. It lists the ten steps to becoming a "civilized city."

- Advance education
- Speed up development of industry
- Industrialize agriculture
- Build tourism
- Push forward state-owned enterprise reform
- Improve standards of construction
- Protect the environment
- Alleviate poverty
- Try to be in first group of national civilized city
- Make sure social order is stable

To the deputy secretary, the awarding of the torch is proof the city has been developing properly. It's a nod from Beijing. "Being a torch city will make more people know about the city," Li says. "More businesspeople and experts will pay attention to Mianyang."

The four o'clock bell rings and the students bound down the stairs to the practice fields. Two girls stop to primp in front of a mirror. A group of guys goes straight to the basketball court. Others gather on the track. The deputy secretary goes down to watch, sucking on a cigarette. Chinese pop music plays on the speakers.

One girl runs past him, breathing hard, pigtails bouncing. She's digging deep, catching up with the pack. Halfway down the backstretch, she pulls ahead. Then she doubles her lead, then triples it, really huffing and puffing, grabbing her throat. The deputy secretary takes another drag, watching her run, ignoring the pain, head up, eyes bright. Out on the road, trucks loaded with electronics rumble past.

Road Diary, Entry 6: The Shibboleth Driving Between Mianyang and Chengdu

The last stretch of road brings a bit of everything: crops and smokestacks, bicycles and coal trucks, bland suburbs and picturesque villages. I ask Singing Songs whether he'd ever go back to the factory where he once worked. He shakes his head.

"Why?" I ask him.

"Because," he says, pointing out at the road winding in front and behind us, a road that can take you not just across a country but back in time.

"Freedom."

We've driven the equivalent of New York to Dallas, and the numbers next to Chengdu are getting smaller on the signs. This city is like the Denver of China: metropolitan, artsy, modern, all the things that Beijing wants the western cities to be. Soon, the Olympic advertisements start again. That's how we know we're close to an urban area. The sixteen-year-old peasant from San Lou was right: the 2008 Games live in the cities.

In two days, a provincial party official will say, earnestly and with a straight face, "All of China is excited about the Olympics." But, after a week out on Highway 108, it's clear this isn't true. New China is excited. Old China isn't. This simple question — Are you excited about the Olympics? — is actually a much more complicated one in disguise, one that gets to the heart of modern China. It's many questions, really. Are you moving forward or being left behind? Do you have something to offer? Are you the future or the past? Are you a have or a have-not?

These thoughts fade away as the skyline grows larger. We follow the signs to the city center, dominated by a monument to the man who founded the People's Republic, and finally we come to the end of our time on Highway 108. It continues straight, all the way to Kunming, through black soot and green fields. We take a right at the Starbucks, driving past the Bulgari and Cartier boutiques, down toward the statue of Mao.

PATRICK HRUBY

Murder by Cricket

FROM ESPN.COM

THE BODY IS GONE, long since removed, stuffed into a black zip-up bag, chilled to forty degrees. Lifeless and embalmed.

Yet still the detective is taking pictures.

Actually, he's not taking pictures. He's telling another guy to take pictures, which makes sense, since the other guy is holding a big black camera and the detective is holding a small black notebook. The detective wears dark pants, a dark tie, and a white, short-sleeved button-down; he sports a close-cropped, drill sergeant haircut and a tattoo on his right forearm. He says he's from Scotland Yard. Won't say anything else. He studies the room like a cheat sheet, gives orders with an authoritative English accent — the unmistakable voice of a long-abandoned empire — making quick, fastidious notes in his ledger. Shoot over here. Stand under the CCTV cameras. Get this angle. Hovering nearby are five other men, watching intently, all wearing tucked-in short-sleeved shirts of their own. I assume they're detectives as well; pistol handles peek out from their waistbands, little periscopes of deadly intent, and as far as I know, the hotel isn't hosting a handgun convention.

While all of this is going on — the pointing and bulb-flashing and stone-faced milling about — I'm taking pictures of the detectives, trying to act inconspicuous, pretending I'm genuinely interested in the cricket paraphernalia dotting the room, the bronze statue of West Indies legend George Headley and the oil painting of a demonic-looking Sri Lanka bowler and the multicolored national flags of former British colonies hanging from the ceiling like superhero capes on a laundry line. Only I think the detectives see through me because they keep moving out of my digital camera's frame, subtly but unmistakably, and I realize I would make a lousy CIA agent and an even worse paparazzo.

Nobody else in the lobby pays us much mind.

Nobody else pays much mind because the whole irredeemably postmodern scene — a guy taking pictures of a guy taking pictures — isn't unusual. Not anymore. Not here at the Jamaica Pegasus in downtown Kingston, not after everything that has happened, not with the sports talk radio hosts broadcasting live from the plush brown leather love seats and the tabloid reporters bivouacked around the poolside bar and the three uniformed police officers guarding the elevator exit on the twelfth floor, where they're up and out of their borrowed ballroom chairs before the polished metal doors even finish sliding open, ready and eager to detain you for questioning, even though you're just looking for the gym. No. The capacity for shock has long since left the building.

These are the facts: On March 18, Pakistan cricket coach Bob Woolmer, a genial Englishman, was found unconscious, likely already dead, in this very hotel, behind the cream-colored door of Room 374. A chambermaid discovered his naked body, slumped on the bathroom floor, between the toilet and the tub, blood and vomit spattered against the white tile walls. Hands and feet turned blue. Woolmer, fifty-eight, was taken to a hospital and pronounced dead of undetermined causes; four days later, police changed the cause of death to asphyxia as a result of manual strangulation. Murder. Murder in the Pegasus, where the cops held a news conference, and another half-dozen after that, transforming this otherwise sleepy, marble-tiled waiting area into the epicenter of an international newsquake, concentric rings of breathless rumor and half-substantiated speculation, all radiating out from the biggest and most awful story to hit international cricket since . . . well, ever.

And yes, just to be clear: we're talking about cricket.

Cricket, the sport of afternoon tea and sliced cucumbers and pristine white outfits. And now, a bona-fide murder mystery, where investigators have no named suspects, no clear motive, and no certain cause of death. A murder mystery in which all of the above has created a factual and narrative vacuum, filled by a raft of increasingly crazy yet strangely plausible theories, spouted and dismissed and exhumed by fans and reporters and local taxi drivers alike, a deranged yet irresistible game of Clue. *A crazy fan in the bathroom with a towel. The Indian mafia with exotic poison. Pakistani Intelligence in league with al-Qaida, financed by Chinese offshore accounts.*

Who killed Bob Woolmer? Such is the macabre riddle hanging over the Cricket World Cup, a sixteen-nation tournament taking place throughout the Caribbean that concludes Saturday with the final in Barbados. How does a cricket coach end up dead in the first place? Such was the question consuming me. After all, I wouldn't be surprised by a boxer dying of a massive brain hemorrhage, or a football player breaking his neck in a violent tackle, or Stephen Jackson getting shot at a strip club. But death by cricket? This was new, and terrible, and potentially very scary, because if cricket isn't safe, what is?

Cricket, spiritual cousin to lawn bowling. Gentility with bats. An unhurried sporting pursuit in which the escapist pleasure lasts not ninety minutes or two halves or four quarters, but for days and days of blissful remove called a Test match, which really seems to be a test of one's socioeconomic ability to take an extended intercontinental vacation. Cricket, that enduring Victorian hand-me-down, resolutely fair and mannered, of which noted cricket author and West Indian nationalist/Marxist historian C. L. R. James once wrote, "The British tradition soaked deep into me was that when you entered the sporting arena, you left behind you the sordid compromises of everyday existence."

Cricket. A harmless country game. Only here is Woolmer's body, stashed in the basement of a Kingston funeral home for weeks, awaiting repatriation to his wife and two sons in South Africa — a process delayed by both a postponed coroner's inquest and one of the largest and most complex investigations in the history of Jamaican law enforcement, an investigation waiting on the results of toxicology tests that have yet to be completed. According to Jamaican authorities, Woolmer may finally head home by the end of the week.

But the mystery surrounding him isn't going anywhere.

And though four Scotland Yard detectives and an Interpol pathologist and the Pakistani detective who headed up the Daniel Pearl case are now on hand to jump-start a whodunit unfolding at the rate of a melting glacier, only one thing seems clear: if Woolmer had been something other than a cricket coach —

worked as a BASE jumper, perhaps — he probably would still be breathing.

How could this be? I wanted to know. I needed to know. I had made an entire career out of following games, the better to avoid real life; now, real life was intruding in the most horrific way possible, the most unexpected way possible, in the form of very real, sordid death. One that compelled me to catch a flight to Antigua, and then Jamaica, in order to poke my nose into a strange and unfamiliar world.

A world — and a sport — that can kill.

They Don't Call Them "Fanatics" for Nothing

A deranged fan. A deranged fan did it. Distraught, inconsolable, enraged that Pakistan has just crashed out of the tournament by losing to Ireland — the international cricket equivalent, I'm told, of the Seattle Seahawks falling to a slightly above-average high school football team — and in the mood for vengeance.

Justice.

It wouldn't be hard. Just go to the Pegasus. Wait for the team bus to return from nearby Sabina Park Stadium, where the Irish fans are probably still making merry at the party stand, dancing and grinning and getting sloshed — it is St. Patrick's Day, after all — and where a Pakistan side ranked number four in the world has just laid an egg the size of Humpty Dumpty, losing to an Irish side largely composed of part-time players. Let the dazed Pakistani pros and their deflated coach slouch into the lobby, mingle with fans and officials, soak themselves in a warm bath of commiserative nods and get-'em-next-times. Be still. Watch. See Woolmer head upstairs, early, around 7:30, leaving behind the self-described worst day of his coaching career, apparently making good on a postgame news conference promise to sleep on his future as Pakistan's skipper.

Now stop. Wait. Bide your time. Let it get late, quiet, calm. Slip into the elevator, hit the plastic button for the twelfth floor. Walk down the hall. Knock on Woolmer's door. Show him a jersey, a hat, a program. Ask for an autograph.

Grab his throat.

So goes one of the murder scenarios, one I initially dismissed as preposterous, in a bad Wesley Snipes/Robert De Niro flick sort of way. But then . . . well, then I start reading the papers.

Dateline, India: Following a loss to Sri Lanka, a cricket fan in Bilihar dies of a heart attack.

Dateline, Pakistan: A senior politician calls for the national cricket program to undergo "major surgery." Sans anesthetic.

Dateline, India: A loss to Bangladesh prompts a seventeen-year-old fan in the Samastipur district to die of shock, while irate fans attack the home of star Mahendra Dhoni.

Suddenly, the Cameron Crazies seem like dilettantes. Surfing the Web, I come across the story of Mahadeb Swarnakar, twenty-eight, a cricket fan from Shaktinagar, a village sixty kilometers north of Calcutta. Swarnakar wanted to watch the India–Sri Lanka match on a neighbor's color television; his wife wanted him to watch at home, on a black-and-white set. They fought. He hanged himself.

His wife tried to do the same, only the rope broke.

Here's the truly batty part: nobody I meet finds any of the above disturbing. Or even particularly noteworthy. They don't even find it ironic, never mind that the official World Cup theme song is titled "The Game of Love and Unity." Woolmer's murder? Horrible, terrible, yes yes. A very great tragedy, of course. Absolutely *not cricket*. But the obsessive passion that may have led to his murder? Cricket all the way.

In my hotel's lobby bar, I share a drink with Ashish Panjabi and Deveinder Singh, a pair of middle-aged cricket fans, mild-mannered as can be. Until we talk World Cup. Panjabi gives me an earful — about spoiled, uninspired players, money-grubbing corporate sponsors, cynicism and corruption. He's simultaneously salient and unhinged; he ought to be drowning out the Sri Lankan equivalent of Woody Paige on a Southeast Asian version of "Around the Horn." The whole time, he's only drinking water, not buzzed in the slightest.

Singh sits and smiles, nodding intently. I ask Panjabi a simple question: why would anyone hang themselves over cricket?

"Cricket is a religion," he says. "You're born and bred into it. For your whole life."

I can't relate. Not in the slightest. I mean, sure, I love college basketball as much as anyone, and probably detest Duke more than most. Yet even in my pettiest, most spiteful moments — read: anytime one of those annoying armed-for-life AmEx ads comes on — I've never wanted to literally whack Coach K, leaving him vomit-drenched and blue on a bathroom floor.

On the other hand, Woolmer's still dead, and a fan might be to blame. So I go to a game.

New Zealand versus Bangladesh. Second round. The gleaming new Sir Vivian Richards Stadium in Antigua, halfway between the airport and the capital city of St. John's, beneath a hazy, sun-splashed sky, buffeted by a steady tropical breeze. Twenty minutes from anywhere, just like every place else on the island.

Women on the grass in tank tops. Shirtless men in slathered-on sunscreen. Concession stands selling vodka and champagne. The smell of coconut oil. I see Aussies in Milwaukee Bucks caps — a nod to Andrew Bogut, I suppose — and West Indies kids dressed like extras in a rap video. On the north stand concourse, the tournament mascot — some sort of neon-orange ferret — poses with fans for pictures.

I turn my attention to the field, the better to see what I've been missing. Answer: not much. Cricket is languid. Much like baseball, but on Quaaludes. Everything takes an eternity, especially the at bats, which play out like Paul O'Neill working the count in hell's softball league. I fixate on a New Zealand fielder, a guy named Bond. Black shirt, black pants, black hat, black wraparound shades. He's dressed to fight high-tech vampires. Standing in the equivalent of deep left field, he's basically removed from the action; during the twenty minutes I watch him, not a single ball comes his way.

Still, he fidgets. Swings his arms. Claps his hands. Crouches on every bowled ball, staring intently at the batter, alert as a fire alarm. Ready to move. And here, I realize, is the sport in a nutshell: a game of perpetual focus, not wham-bam fireworks, a game akin to a candle in an empty wine bottle, perfectly attuned to slow-burn obsession.

Thwack! Swinging from a one-legged crouch, a Bangladeshi bats-man uppercuts a six, the equivalent of a home run. The ball arcs over the left-field fence, a crazy quilt of sponsor signs, landing in the party stand area, near the in-stadium swimming pool. The crowd erupts — only not for Bangladesh.

In-dee-ya!
Clap-clap-clap!
In-dee-ya!
Clap-clap-clap!

Turns out the place is full of India fans from Dubai, England, and New Jersey, great big groups of partisans, clad in the national team's distinctive baby blue jerseys. They all bought tickets months ago, assuming India would reach the tournament's second round; when the squad bombed out — a failure as stunning as Pakistan's — they decided to come anyway, in part because the $100 game tickets are nonrefundable, in part because, well, they're still playing cricket, and cricket is a hell of a drug.

It's also a national identity. Under British rule, cricket was the one arena where the subjugated natives could be equal — even ass-kickingly superior — to their imperial overlords; throughout the West Indies, the sport helped inspire national independence movements.

Today, cricket remains intensely political. When India and Pakistan meet, the games recall Clausewitz's definition of politics: "war by other means." In both nations, government officials manage the national team: in India the dropping of the last national team captain was debated in Parliament; in Pakistan, the entire cricket apparatus serves at the pleasure of chief patron President Pervez Musharraf. (Not surprisingly, fans hate this. Imagine Nancy Pelosi sticking Jason Kapono on the USA Basketball roster, to curry votes with UCLA alumni.) A few years ago in England, conservative pol Norman Tebit famously suggested Asian immigrants be subjected to a loyalty "cricket test" — as in, do they root for England and if not, give 'em the boot.

The game of love and unity, indeed.

Later that evening, I catch an Irish newscast. The subject is Woolmer. The footage is old, recorded just hours after Pakistan's loss sent pubs across the planet into delirium. Only I don't see any joy. I see the good people of Pakistan, born and bred into cricket, take to the streets, burning effigies — a practice usually reserved for the Great Yankee Satan himself, George W. Bush — screaming and chanting, Woolmer murdabad! Woolmer murdabad!

Death to Bob Woolmer.

A Long History of Corruption — and Worse

A match fixer. A match fixer did it. A bookie from Dubai. A gangster from Karachi. Somebody somewhere who lost a bundle. Somebody somewhere with even more to lose. Emerging from a safe house, armed with ever-shifting cell-phone numbers, materializing from the shadows of the vast subcontinental sports gambling syndicates like a crocodile from a muddy swamp. Reptilian. Single-minded. Because Woolmer, see, he must have known. Known about the payoffs, the pregame calls to the players, the subtle little fixes that no one ever sees, the suspicious movements in the Mumbai betting markets a month before the Ireland-Pakistan game. The endemic corruption that has long bedeviled the sport. Must have known too much, must have been ready to talk, perhaps in one of his forthcoming books, perhaps with a quiet, behind-the-scenes phone call. And even if he didn't know, he could've known, and if you step back and do the math, the mere possibility is more than enough.

Enough for Woolmer to be silenced.

Silenced like Hanif "Cadbury" Kodvavi, once Pakistan's top bookie, linked to disgraced cricket star Salim Malik, found dead in Johannesburg in 1999, reportedly shot sixty-seven times — and, for good measure, hacked into pieces. Or silenced like former South African captain Hansie Cronje, cricket's fallen angel, the God-fearing, born-again Christian who took money from bookmakers, confessed to a judge, earned a lifetime ban, triggered an ocean-spanning slew of scandals and investigations, and died in a mysterious 2002 plane crash.

Cronje, who once played for Woolmer.

Again, it wouldn't be hard. Sip some tea at the Pegasus café, right next to the hotel lobby. Nibble on a croissant. Let Woolmer head upstairs, order room service, a last meal of lasagna. Let him open his laptop, e-mail his wife, Gill, around 3:00 A.M., vent his depression and disbelief at the Ireland loss. Let him send a second message to Pakistani cricket board chairman Nasim Ashraf, announcing his immediate resignation as coach, his intention to return home to Cape Town, where he plans to open a cricket academy.

Make your move. Room 374. Tap the door. Talk your way inside. Grab a towel. Wrap it around Woolmer's throat.

Make sure he never speaks again.

In the shaded yellow seats of Viv Richards Stadium's north stand, K. Phillip Kutty, a friendly Indian man with soft, rounded features, asks me what I know about Woolmer's murder.

I give him an honest answer: not bloody much.

"The people behind it, it's the mafia," he says, eyebrows lowering like a garage door. "It's 100 percent a preplanned murder. Any other excuse for it is bulls ——. It's the mafia, the millions in money pouring in."

Kutty turns his head, points over his right shoulder. A pudgy man in a tan T-shirt and a gray baseball cap, part of Kutty's group, sits one row back and four seats down. He's wearing headphones, which appear to be plugged into some sort of PDA. He watches the game intently, making careful notes on a flip pad.

"That guy," Kutty says, "he's betting in England right now."

Three things to know about cricket gambling: First, it's huge. Dubai bookmakers took in a reported $25 million on a World Cup match between India and Sri Lanka, and some experts estimate that as much as $1 billion can be bet globally on a single game. Second, much, if not most, of that wagering is illegal, because India and Pakistan forbid gambling for religious and moral reasons. So organized crime controls all the action, sometimes violently so. Third, cricket punters (the English term for bettors) can wager on just about anything: the winning team, run totals, starting lineups, even if the first ball bowled will be wide. Would you put money on Steve Nash's first assist coming on a two-handed chest pass? No? Then don't even think about betting on cricket.

All of this makes the sport pathologically vulnerable to fixing. Getting most of the players on a team to throw a game, à la the Black Sox, is hard; getting a single player to bowl one ball wide or pass inside lineup information is fairly trivial. Between 1999 and 2001, cricket was rocked by a series of fixing scandals. By the time the International Cricket Council's newly formed anticorruption unit released a comprehensive report at the end of 2001 — a seventy-seven-page document containing allegations of kidnapping, murder, and fixing dating back to the 1970s — Pakistan had banned Malik for life, India had done the same to former team captain Mohammad Azharuddin and fellow star Ajay Sharma, Cronje had given South Africa a black eye, and Australian stars Shane Warne and Mark Waugh were found to have accepted money from an Indian bookie in exchange for inside information during a 1994 tour of Sri Lanka.

In 2003, former London police commissioner Paul Condon — author of the ICC report and the first head of the anticorruption unit — declared cricket to be virtually free of match fixing. Shortly thereafter, Kenyan captain Maurice Odumbe was suspended five years for taking money from Indian bookie Jagdish Sodha, a man previously accused of trying to bribe English players to underperform.

Unsurprisingly, Condon's most recent speech on the topic struck a different chord. Speaking in the British House of Lords just weeks before Woolmer's death, Condon warned against endemic fixing and corruption, links to the mafia and terrorism, then dubbed the problem a "spreading cancer."

Had the cancer metastasized? James Fitzgerald, an ICC spokesman and former Irish cricket journalist, agreed to speak on the condition we not discuss the Woolmer investigation. Fitzgerald was surprisingly candid, in a way that only someone who won't discuss specifics can be. The vast sums bet on cricket? Potentially problematic, no question. But also a sign of the sport's relative health. "It indicates interest," he said. "It indicates that a large percentage of people have faith in cricket."

Fitzgerald has a point: there's a lot of fiscal faith in cricket these days, and not just on the part of punters. Thanks to a fortuitous confluence of fan passion, television, and the booming economies of Southeast Asia, cricket is enjoying a financial Big Bang. To wit: Sky Sports and ESPN recently partnered to pay a reported $1.1 billion for ICC broadcast rights for the next eight years, and an ICC that reportedly had a $150,000 deficit in 1992 is expected to earn a $239 million profit on the current World Cup.

The sport's nouveau riche reality is visible on the sponsor signs ringing the Viv Richards Stadium outfield: Visa, LG, Johnnie Walker. It's evident at the ticket and concession stands, where a shaded seat goes for $100 and a bottle of Gatorade costs $8. It even pops up along the narrow, winding island road that leads from downtown St. John's to the stadium, where Pepsi billboards proclaiming WE

LOVE WEST INDIES CRICKET — only featuring India star Sachin
Tendulkar — share space with handmade signs promoting a local
"Gals Garn Wild" show taking place right . . . after . . . the game!

Maybe this is the way of modern sports: stoke fan passion and dis-
posable income like particles in a nuclear reactor, generating a
chain reaction of light, heat, and revenue. All the while, hope the
whole thing doesn't go Three Mile Island.

Andrew Miller, who writes for the website Cricinfo, tells me
about Cronje, and how Woolmer — then South Africa's coach —
defended his captain to the last. Even though Cronje planned his
fixes in the team dressing room, right in front of the teenage atten-
dants, and later said it was all so easy it bored him.

"We all have a gut feeling fixing goes on," Miller says. "Trying to
stamp it out is like trying to stamp out breathing. Think about it:
you're only a sportsman for ten years. You come from a poor country, a poor family, from a place not rooted in the traditions of
cricket. I can almost understand."

Pakistan captain Inzamam-ul-Haq and assistant coach Mushtaq
Ahmed were both fined as a result of the same match-fixing investigation that brought down Malik. West Indies star Marlon Samuels
was allowed to play in the World Cup despite links to an Indian
bookmaker. Woolmer's friends and family insist that he knew nothing, that his forthcoming books — one a coaching manual, the
other autobiographical — contain no bombshells. Could he really
have been naive? About Cronje and all the rest? Miller fidgets in his
seat.

"Not to speak ill of the dead — I knew Bob and he was a very
nice man — but he must have known more," he says. "At least more
than he let on."

A Very Trusting Man

Unless he didn't. Unless his love of cricket left him blind to the
sport's larger sins. True story: When the English national team
toured Pakistan in 2005, Woolmer noticed that a player he once
coached in English domestic cricket, Ian Bell, had a small flaw
in his batting grip. Bell wasn't expected to play against Woolmer's
Pakistan squad, so the coach told his former pupil about the
problem.

Injuries subsequently forced Bell into the English lineup. He finished as the team's leading scorer.

"That's the kind of man Bob was," says Vic Marks, a former English national team player and a cricket writer with the British newspaper *The Observer.* "A very trusting man. In South Africa, he was in the same locker room as Cronje, and he was as stunned by everything as everyone else. That leads you to think there was a naiveté there. Otherwise, you start to get conspiratorial."

Marks played against Woolmer in English cricket; as a journalist, he came to know the man behind the competitor. During Pakistan's tour of England last summer, he met Woolmer in Canterbury for a short chat that mushroomed into a two-hour discussion of cricket and life.

"He was so good at the intimate details of the game," Marks says. "Maybe he didn't always see the bigger picture."

Born in India to English parents — his father put a bat and ball in his crib — Woolmer learned the game playing for Kent, in a rhododendron-strewn setting Marks likens to the Garden of Eden. Woolmer's mentor was Colin Cowdrey, a former ICC president and England captain, widely considered one of the game's great sportsmen. By 1976, Woolmer had established himself as a talented, well-liked, almost archetypal English player, a Cricketer of the Year, and leading candidate for a future national team captaincy.

That never happened. In 1977, Woolmer became the youngest of six English players to join World Series Cricket, a rival to traditional international Test matches, sponsored by an Australian tycoon during a fight over television rights. The seeming cash grab — very *not cricket* — made Woolmer a near-pariah. He further sullied his professional reputation four years later, playing in a controversial apartheid-era tour of South Africa, which was under sanctions. Woolmer insisted before an English cricket board that he was doing it to promote interracial harmony. He never played for England again. In 1984, he retired from the sport with a back injury, then immigrated to South Africa to coach high schoolers in Cape Town's poor, black townships.

Woolmer returned to England three years later, coaching at Kent and then at Warwickshire, where he pioneered the use of a seldom-used reverse sweep shot that has since become a cricket staple. Subsequently appointed coach of the South African national team, Woolmer introduced laptop computers and detailed statistical analy-

sis to the sport — think "Moneyball" — and during the 1999 World
Cup outfitted Cronje with a radio earpiece, a practice that has
since been banned.

Woolmer was successful in both places — South Africa fell just
short of the '99 World Cup final — but also presided over con-
troversy: rumors of widespread recreational drug use dogged the
Warwickshire locker room, and the Cronje affair was a huge blow
to international cricket. His tenure in Pakistan, where he lived
alone in a small Lahore apartment, was marked by more of the
same: Woolmer pushed the nation's cricket board to begin drug-
testing, a move that resulted in two of his best bowlers being
banned for steroid use; over Woolmer's objection, the team refused to take the field after being accused of ball-tampering during
a game against England last year, earning an unprecedented international forfeit (Pakistan was later cleared of the charge); unconfirmed reports suggest Woolmer had a hard time relating to a religious faction within the squad, led by Inzamam, that practiced a
conservative form of Islam.

A trusting man. With a talent for pissing people off.

"To take on Pakistan is a real challenge as a coach," Marks says.
"You have lots of talent, but it is all enmeshed in politics. And on a
personal level, it was a huge sacrifice. But again, Bob showed his
unconventional streak."

Marks can't shake the feeling that Woolmer's death is somehow
entwined with the sport he loved, a sport gone quietly mad, in
which one of Woolmer's favorite phrases on the golf course — "the
ball's in the lake; nobody died" — no longer applies.

"It's such a horrid thing," Marks says with a sigh. "And to seem
that it happened as the result of cricket, as opposed to a personal issue — that's remarkably alarming, isn't it? It causes you to question
your own game. It's not so daft to say that if Pakistan had beaten
Ireland, he would still be alive."

"Not so daft." I write this down.

No Possibilities Ruled Out

There's another possibility: Woolmer wasn't murdered. His death
was simply a tragic accident. Police say his body showed no obvious

outward signs of violence, no telltale red bruises on his neck. His room showed "very little" of the same. No signs of forced entry. His passport and credit cards were found in a drawer. The laptop he forlornly packed into a bag at the end of the Ireland game wasn't taken. Pakistani player Danish Kaneria was staying in an adjacent room. West Indies captain Brian Lara was sleeping across the hall. Both men say they heard nothing — no shouting, no screaming, no wheezing.

Not a sound.

Woolmer suffered from type 2 diabetes, was under tremendous stress. Unconfirmed reports claim that he had been drinking Scotch, that an empty bottle was found in his room. Perhaps he had a seizure, a blackout, lost his footing, fell into the sink or bathtub, and fatally injured his neck. Perhaps Woolmer perished after the chambermaid discovered him, when his body was moved and a house doctor and nurse attempted to resuscitate him, when at least six Pakistani players reportedly entered his room, all before he was placed in a diplomatic car and taken to the hospital where doctors pronounced him dead. Perhaps the autopsy, initially inconclusive, was botched. Garfield Blake, president of the Jamaican Association of Clinical Pathologists, says that to go from "inconclusive" to "strangulation" is odd, that the two diagnoses are "poles apart."

Or maybe this is all foolish tail-chasing. Maybe Woolmer really was murdered, only he wasn't just strangled. Maybe he was poisoned first. That's the rumor the day before I arrive in Kingston, with a British tabloid claiming police received an anonymous phone tip that Woolmer was murdered with aconite, a nasty little substance that causes nausea, vomiting, diarrhea, loss of power in the limbs, a slow shutdown of one's internal organs, and, finally, death by asphyxiation. Investigators refuse specific comment. But they acknowledge that they've received information about possible poisons.

"I'm sure they have," a British reporter says, voice dripping with sarcastic contempt. "And the call probably came from the reporter who wrote the story."

In two weeks, British papers will report that Woolmer was possibly murdered with snake venom, and that police have identified an unnamed suspect from hotel camera security footage. The cops neither confirm nor deny both stories. But for now, there's only one way to clear everything up: talk to Deputy Commissioner Mark Shields, the forty-eight-year-old former Scotland Yard cop heading up the investigation. Only Shields isn't talking. Not anymore. Turns out I'm late to the party. One week earlier, before I arrived, Shields gave news briefings in the Pegasus lobby, formal and informal, sometimes more than once a day. He confirmed that Woolmer's body showed no visible signs of life when it was found. That the lack of marks on his neck was "not unusual," given the "circumstances surrounding" Woolmer's death. (Prompting speculation that Woolmer was strangled with towels, which reportedly were found near his body.) Shields said that while police believe Woolmer may have known his killer — he was found naked, after all — no motives or scenarios have been ruled out entirely, not even a random stranger coming in off the street to kill Woolmer on a homicidal whim.

Shields also confirmed that police are digitizing and analyzing almost a day's worth of hotel security camera footage, that detectives had looked to question three Pakistani fans linked to the team — two from the United States — in order to clear them from the investigation, that statements, fingerprints, and DNA samples were taken from every member of the Pakistani squad, that three members of the team had been questioned a second time before being allowed to leave Jamaica, and that two Pakistani diplomats from Washington, D.C., had been given a tour of the crime scene.

And now? Not a word. Shields's lips are sealed. He's ticked off at the media, and with good reason: while I was in Antigua, the *Sunday Mail* ran a piece dubbing Shields a "sexy man in a sexy job" and detailing his rather active social life, which apparently includes a twenty-four-year-old fashion designer girlfriend and invitations to all the best cocktail parties. The evening after Woolmer died, the story said, Shields was spotted at a soccer match. In a follow-up report, the paper claimed that Shields planned to take an Easter vacation to London to visit his two sons, a trip Shields subsequently canceled.

"He wasn't too happy with that," says another English reporter.

The assembled English press isn't too happy with the *Mail* either: the paper urinated in the pool for everyone else. Is Shields, tall and handsome, less a dogged Jim Rockford than a male Charlie's Angel? I can't say; I never managed to contact him. But I do find it slightly disconcerting that he has a Yahoo! e-mail address on his business card. And I'm told the locals have a nickname for him: Disco Cop.

My first morning in Kingston, I eat breakfast with a local reporter. He describes the political pressure on the Woolmer investigation as intense, almost disruptive: governments around the Caribbean have largely staked their continuing viability on a successful World Cup; cost overruns, unexpectedly low turnout, and Woolmer's death have given opposition parties plenty of campaign ammunition. And locals hate nothing more than "murder in paradise" stories.

Then there's the media mini-invasion, Omaha Beach with expense reports, by turns irritating and comical. One British paper sent four different writers—four!—all looking to scoop their rivals. And, of course, each other.

"Watching them try to avoid each other all week was ridiculous," the reporter says between gulps of fruit juice. "They can't get scoops because there's nothing to scoop. So they've all been here with nothing to do. It's like going to church and not putting money in the tin for these guys."

Chuckling, he asks whether I've seen today's edition of the *Sun*, probably the most shameless Fleet Street tab. I shake my head.

"They've got pictures of Woolmer's room."

We're sitting next to a window in the Kingston Hilton, just down the street from the Pegasus. Through the glass, you can see the building's twelfth floor; I wonder aloud whether a photographer rappelled down the side. The reporter laughs, but I later discover I'm half-correct: the *Sun* photogs rented a room a few floors above Woolmer's, then used a rope to lower a camera rigged with a ten-second timer.

"It's terrible, isn't it?" marvels Barry Wigmore, a Florida-based reporter with the *Daily Mail.* "But in a way, you have to admire them."

Barry is right: it is terrible, and you do have to admire them. Because here, writ small, is the full and total awfulness of human ingenuity, the same twisted imaginative power that allows disco cops to solve murders from the scantiest of clues while letting the rest of us play along in the media and at home, one *CSI*-shaming theory at a time. I think back to an Indian cricket fan I met in Antigua, a doctor who once lived in Colorado.

"It's the JonBenet Ramsey case of the Caribbean," he told me. "A lot of finger-pointing. But you'll never know."

Which, in turn, means one thing: somebody somewhere is already writing a book about this. And probably shopping the TV movie rights.

He Lived — and Died — for Cricket

They hold a memorial service. Actually, they hold two memorial services. Neither one with Woolmer's body.

The first takes place in a Pakistani cathedral, led by an archbishop, two weeks after Woolmer's death. Players and cricket officials fill the pews. I watch the footage on BBC News: a framed picture of the former coach, smiling, clad in a white team polo shirt, flanked by burning candles. Tears. A moment of silence. The laying of wreaths, one on behalf of President Musharraf. Everything solemn and dignified. Heartfelt. Nothing like a few days earlier, when Pakistani players returning from Jamaica are greeted at Karachi Airport by jeering fans, some screaming, "Go to hell!"

A second service. This time in South Africa, attended by Woolmer's friends and family, teary-eyed and still in shock. But also proud. They remember a generous man, a gentle soul, a hero who helped the national team emerge from the shame and poison of apartheid, from two decades of international sanctions, who coached mixed-race boys' teams before almost anyone else would. A man who shook hands with the Queen of England but also worked with children in Cape Town's most downtrodden townships. Allan Donald, a former South Africa player and close friend, reads a statement on behalf of Woolmer's widow Gill and sons Dale and Russell, thanking an entire world of well-wishers for their condolences. Another friend wonders if cricket has now lost its moral compass. Nasim Ashraf, the chairman of the Pakistan Cricket Board, announces that an indoor cricket center in Lahore will be named after the coach.

Woolmer, he says, lived cricket. Loved cricket. Died for cricket.

I write this down too.

A Mind-Numbing Conspiracy Theory

Who killed Bob Woolmer? Here's the only conclusion I can draw
with any degree of certainty: hang around cricket long enough —
like, say, a week — and you'll end up through the looking glass.
Way through the looking glass. Oliver-Stone-on-the-Kennedy-assas-
sination territory.

I talk to a Guy. A Guy who knows stuff. A Guy in the information acquisition business. I can't tell you more. Sorry. We meet
in the lobby of the Pegasus, at night. I suggest we get a drink.
He walks me past the hotel gym, past the poolside bar, past the
chatty barkeeps and the tabloid writers downing Red Stripes. We
sit at the far end of the pool, on white plastic chairs, in near darkness.

This is what he tells me:

He says Jamaica's ruling political party is gunning for an unprecedented fifth consecutive term, that the current prime minister is
widely liked but considered a bit dumb, the current government is
counting on the World Cup to help it win the upcoming elections,
a sound strategy in a sports-mad nation where high school track
meets are shown on prime-time television.

He says Woolmer's murder has shot this all to hell, though,
and that the failure to catch his killer, or killers, has added to a
growing, widespread discontent with the tournament and the people in charge.

He says Woolmer was definitely murdered. Of this, he has no
doubt.

He says he saw a picture of Woolmer's body, there was a mark on
Woolmer's neck, on the right side, just below the jaw line, that suggests physical trauma.

He says he's spoken to someone in international intelligence,
someone well placed, and that ever since the United States cut off
much of al-Qaida's funding after the September 11 attacks, the ter-
rorist group has used illegal sports gambling in India and Pakistan
as a major source of revenue.

He says al-Qaida has ties to Dawood Ibrahim, the Al Capone of
India, a man accused of masterminding a 1993 bombing that killed
257 people in Mumbai, a man with ties to the bookmaker alleg-

edly linked to Samuels, a man rumored to have lost millions on the Ireland-Pakistan match.

He says al-Qaida also has ties to Pakistan's Inter-Services Intelligence Agency, the former — and some say current — patron of Afghanistan's Taliban.

He says the ISI is intertwined in both the Pakistani government and Pakistani cricket, and that one of the members of the Pakistani cricket team's traveling party is actually an ISI operative.

He says that al-Qaida may have put a lot of money on the Pakistani team, and may have been disappointed in its poor performance. Murderously so.

He says that Woolmer may have found himself between a rock and a hard place, because despite what his friends and family have said, the coach knew about larger-scale corruption and was going to blow the whistle.

He says Woolmer found out that three international umpires were being paid off, and that the ISI had set up offshore banking accounts for them.

He says the bank accounts were financed with Chinese money. I ask why. He doesn't elaborate.

He says he believes the ISI is involved in Woolmer's murder. He says someone in the Pakistan team party knows what happened, and during Pakistan's final World Cup game — against Zimbabwe, after Woolmer's death — a member of the team party was spotted with his feet up, drinking champagne, and the champagne-sipper in question is probably ISI. He says all of the above is why Pakistan dispatched two diplomats to Jamaica.

While mouthing the word "diplomats," he makes air quotes with his hands.

He says the Jamaican police have no suspects and no motive, and yet a coroner's inquest has been scheduled. He says this is a way to drag things out.

He says he does not believe the Jamaican police will solve the case.

He says after Woolmer, the real victim in the case is Jamaica, because this is the World Cup, not a shooting in downtown Kingston, and that the country led newscasts around the planet for two days.

He says the best thing for Jamaicans is for Woolmer's body to leave the country.

He says all this, a jigsaw puzzle without a box, and then he says he has to leave. I close my notebook. My fingers hurt. We shake hands. He heads inside. I turn around, take a last look at the pool, the bar, the half-empty bottles of beer. I want to ask him whether any of this head-spinning madness can possibly be true, whether he grasps the implications of everything said and unsaid, the bigger picture beyond the boundaries of this strange and unfamiliar sport: cricket is daft because the world is daft, and the truly daft thing about it is that it takes a dead man to notice.

But he's already gone.

Who Killed Bob Woolmer?

The detective is gone. The lobby is quiet. No police, no photographers. A few people are watching an England–Sri Lanka game, shown on four televisions scattered around the room. The Brits are totally out of it. I'm sitting on a plush, cream-colored recliner, typing notes into my laptop; across from me sits a man with tree-trunk forearms, arms crossed, facing a television, snoring lightly.

I put on some headphones, zone out. When I open my eyes, I notice that the room is filling up. A group of young Jamaican guys — none older than twenty-five, tops — plops down on the couch next to me. They're watching the game. So are two British writers, who have moved closer to the big-screen TV at the center of the lobby.

England, it seems, is making a comeback.

I don't completely understand how cricket works. Doesn't matter. I take off my headphones. England needs twelve runs to win. They have six balls left. The game is being played in Antigua. On the television screen, I see British fans jumping up and down in the stadium pool; in the stands, Sri Lankan fans are leaning forward in their seats, chins on palms, wide-eyed and nervous. An England batter strokes a hit. The Jamaican guys are clapping, whooping it up. *Big shot! Big shot!* Perversely enough, they're rooting for Sri Lanka. The British journalists are clapping too.

Thwack! The run chase is on. Seven runs needed from four balls. *Thwack!* Five from three. Four from two. One of the British writers stands up, places his hands atop his head. It's too much to bear. Mr. Tree-Trunk Forearms is wide awake, sitting up straight as a flagpole. The lobby is full.

Last ball. This is it. The Sri Lankan bowler races toward the wicket, lets the ball go. One hop. The batter swings and misses completely, the ball shattering the little white thingamajig resting atop the three wooden stumps behind him. It's the equivalent of a strikeout. Game over. The Jamaican guys erupt in cheers. The British journalists look heartsick. On the screen, one of the party pool kids buries his face in his hands, sobbing. A beautiful young Sri Lankan girl shakes her hips, dancing around her seat, waving a national flag like a shipwrecked sailor swinging an orange-smoke rescue flare.

Who killed Bob Woolmer? The truth is that no one really knows, and maybe no one will ever know, and the only people who might know aren't saying. Yet take a picture: right here, right now, none of that matters. For a moment, what matters is the moment, the joy in the lobby and despair in the stadium pool, the fleeting sense of complete and total remove — from toxicology reports and match-fixing, coroner's inquests and potentially deadly towels, from the sins of cricket and life itself, the horror of Room 374 and the dark secrets lurking within. All of it a waking nightmare, half-forgotten but lingering, a crime scene photograph stuffed into the junk drawer of our collective dread, yellowing and sinister. The blood and the vomit. The last, silent gasps of a man left to die on the altar of a country game. The sordid compromises of everyday existence we call sport.

TIM NEVILLE

Go, Speed Flier, Go

FROM SKIING

THE THING THAT CHANGES EVERYTHING unfurls with a crisp crackling sound and François Bon is pleased. He will not die skiing today. The wing he spent so many months designing and testing inflates overhead as soon as his skis pick up speed. It is shiny, curved, and puffy, like a paraglider's, but the Frenchman does not fly — not yet. He drives his skis deeper into the snow.

It is May 2006, high on Mont Blanc in France, and a helicopter pilot is circling overhead to film the descent. Things aren't going well. Bon is carving turns so quickly down the mountain's northerly faces that the pilot assigned to follow him curses wildly. Alarm bells and warning lights fill the cockpit. "*Big shit!*" the pilot shouts in French. The air at fourteen thousand feet is too thin for such fast maneuvers and the pilot is struggling to keep a good angle for the cameraman. The lensman has filmed Bon dozens of times and never barfed once — *but this!* The scene unfolding outside the bubbled glass is so big, so new, that the pilot is caught off-guard. "*Foocker!*" he shouts. "*Foock! Foock! Foock!*"

Bon is calm, just a man and his soul patch hurtling by. Thirteen thousand feet. Twelve. Eleven-five. He slices snowfields so quickly that contrails burn off his bases, and he pulls on the wing's controls to help steer and sits back in his harness to keep his balance. The slope is dotted with bone-breaking rock fields that end in one-thousand-foot cliffs, but such obstacles are of little concern. The wing floats overhead like a strong and benevolent hand, ready to pick him up, and over, anything.

Speed riding, speed flying: people call it both, though the French just call it speed. Either way, it's redefining what it means for a skier to go big. Sure, free-skiers will always find the most perilous lines, and ski-BASE jumpers throw double gainers off two-thousand-foot cliffs. But a speed flier can carve virgin slopes locked between rocks, skip over glacial ice, huck a one-thousand-foot wall, and carve again. And if you're François Bon, you can fly.

There he goes, a hissing blur of baffled nylon. Seracs appear on the glacier — too dangerous to ski. The foil sighs and scoops the wind, plucking him gingerly from the surface. Up and up he goes, soaring into the sky.

Bon feels sorry for the little people scraping groomers in lousy 2-D. He feels sorry for those who aren't French. To get good at speed flying, say, to the point where you can descend 12,467 vertical feet of Mont Blanc in eight minutes (and then ski the Eiger in two minutes, forty-three seconds), it helps to live in France, where dying is a personal problem.

It was here, after all, among the litigationless folds of *les Alpes françaises* that someone first dared to sink axes into ice, expanding the reach of ski mountaineering to places it'd never been. French skiers were among the first to tackle lines so big, impossible even, that the rest of us watched on tenterhooks and called it "extreme." Who else could invent a sport like parkour, the acrobatic art of leaping between rooftops and running up walls? Here in America, it took years for resorts to allow snowboarding — and we invented it. As for speed flying, maybe tort reform will someday make it okay to do at ski areas in North America. In the meantime, there's France. Here you can ride the lifts with parachute packs, take a lesson, and let it fly all day long. The only rules are, don't hit anyone and always wear a helmet.

It's now March 2007, five years after Bon's maiden voyage, and the slopes of Les Arcs, just south of Mont Blanc, are filled with skiers tugging on Marlboros, Gauloises, and hand-rolled Drum. It's a stunning blue-sky day, and a small crowd of spectators — Brits, Romanians, a Euro in a tight blue suit — gathers among a billowing copse of brightly colored flags stuck in the snow. This is the finish line for a speed-flying course above.

"Let's give some voice to all the speed fliers!" an announcer booms into a mike, and everyone claps and hoots.

Twenty-six of the world's top pilots have come here for the 2007

Gin Speed-Flying Pro, all of them handpicked by Bon. Over the next two days they'll race GS, downhill, and big-mountain courses as part of an event that Bon hopes will give the emerging sport some exposure. So far it seems to be working. A small American team is here making a film while a camera crew from Paris prepares for live interviews. "This competition should be *tup*," one of the Parisians tells me excitedly. "Absolutely *tup*."

French rap kicks in and a pregnant lady in oversize sunglasses (not smoking) walks around with free cans of Red Bull. Though there have been a few speed-flying competitions and demos in Valfrejus and Tignes, never before have so many of the best fliers converged on one spot. The purse isn't huge, $5,000 and some free skis. But today is the sport's first definitive attempt to name a champ.

The idea, in general, is to be the fastest pilot to weave around a series of flags scattered down thirty-five- to forty-five-degree slopes that tumble off Les Arcs' toothy ridges. Contestants must round the gates no more than six feet off the ground or suffer a thirty-second penalty. For the big-mountain event, fliers have to touch down in three zones marked by flags, but otherwise it's do-as-you-please on a three-thousand-vertical-foot face with gullies and spines and a one-hundred-foot cliff. "Generally it's faster to ski because to go up you have to brake," Bon tells me. "But you can go faster over the terrain if flying it makes it shorter, so it really is a blend."

For three hours in the morning and three in the afternoon, flier after flier comes whipping by. Two-thirds of the field is French, but there are three Americans competing. At first the action boggles the mind — each flier coming by so fast that it's hard to tell who's who by anything other than wing color. The best guys pick the cleanest lines, point it across the flats, and control their speed and altitude with hard banking turns. Antoine Montant, a paragliding acrobat in the summer, locks his skis into an angry arc ripping by a gate. Amandine Boivin, the lone female contestant, pops off a ridge and soars hundreds of feet down to the finish line. When the Americans zip by, the wind whistling around their skis releases an eerie, unfamiliar moan.

"Everyone who sees this says, 'Holy shit, how can I do that?'" says Carson Klein, a speed flier from Utah. "I feel safer doing this than I do just skiing."

Though each run is spectacular and fast and indeed a blend of carving and flight, few of the competitors are truly magnificent skiers. While most can hold their own, others could very well die getting down these inbounds steeps without a wing. Loic Jean-Albert, a favorite for the podium, grew up as a skydiver on Reunion Island, in the Indian Ocean, and just strapped on skis "more or less for this event." Two seasons ago, Klein was a snowboarder. At one point he asks how to do a kick turn.

"You don't need to be a great skier so much as a great pilot," explains Matt Gerdes, an American competitor living in France. "But you do need to be a confident skier."

Five years ago, Bon says, only five people were dabbling in what would become speed flying, and they were all friends. In the winters, Bon, who grew up among the chalets and apartment buildings of Bourg-Saint-Maurice, skied with the Les Arcs ski patrol. But he found his calling in the summer, when he could paraglide for hours, soaring like a hawk on the updrafts, flipping and spinning.

"It got to the point where I was chasing summer," Bon says. "But I love skiing. I wanted to get back to these mountains and the snow. In winter, there are no thermals. We got thinking. The goal would be to not fly so much, but to ski more, to have that perfect moment when the two could touch.

"Speed flying contributes to the collective consciousness," Bon says. He's tan and lithe, a handsome, athletic type with straight teeth and a hoop earring. He's one of the few people on the planet to call speed flying a full-time job, by designing and testing wings for a Korean paragliding company named Gin. His skills and connections are shaping the sport.

"The French are all about exploring *les possibilités*," says Hal Thomson, a global marketing executive for Salomon Sports based an hour away in Annecy, France. "It's like in soccer. The Germans methodically kick, pass, score. The French curve the ball this way, pass it over there, head it back, have everyone touch it, and then shoot. For them, emotion, style, and art always win."

So in the French way, Bon and his friends decided to strap on skis, unfurl skydiving wings into the snow, and simply point their tips downhill to see what would happen. They promptly realized someone was going to get seriously hurt.

"It was shit," Bon says. "It was hard to get the canopy to inflate and the turning was too radical."

Since then, largely thanks to Bon and companies like Gin, wings have become far more stable and easier to control, even for beginners. Generous estimates say there are about 3,000 people who speed-fly, with about 2,900 of them in Europe. Roughly ten companies make speed-flying wings, which cost between $1,200 and $2,000.

Still, Bon believes the sport has a future since it draws from both the skiing and paragliding pools — not to mention its considerable YouTube appeal. "What skier doesn't want to fly?" he says. "And what flier doesn't like to go close to the ground?"

Figuring out the best glide ratios — how well a wing floats versus drops — is an ongoing process. Create a fat, floaty wing and you're paragliding, not skiing. Use a skydiver's chute and it'll drop you so fast that steering is nearly impossible. One company called Bio Air Technologies makes a wing called the Boozz, which is French slang for "cow shit." "Cow shit doesn't fly," says Étienne Perret, who helps design them. "It just sort of falls."

The crowd is considerably larger on day two of the competition, when fliers hop a cable car to the top of the Aiguille Rouge, a 10,584-foot pyramid of reddish rock and the start of today's big-mountain event. As a DJ cranks out a remix of "Brick House," spectators gather at a lift station to ogle the final day of action.

So far Bon sits in third place with yesterday's winner, twenty-nine-year-old Loïc Jean-Albert, in first. The amphitheater that Bon chose for today's competition looks dangerous: forty degrees to sheer in spots as it plummets more than three thousand vertical feet. Most fliers will drop it in about a minute. Along the way they'll navigate down a gully, pop over a rocky section, and launch themselves off a one-hundred-foot cliff. Just getting to the starting gate is scary enough. Fliers clip their harnesses to a safety rope fixed along a knife-edge ridge and inch their way out into the sky.

"This is really more about getting a group of friends together than competing," Bon says. But it's about putting on a good show for the crowds and cameras too. A helicopter circles overhead with a filmmaker dangling from the door. "We asked for the best pilots they have," Bon adds.

A few moments later a small swatch of color appears up high. "They're off!" the announcer booms, and a sea of five hundred mostly smoking heads look up. Fliers slip down the chute with arms pumping wildly on their wings' controls. Spindrift comes swirling down the gully. Mike Steen, one of the Americans, dumps altitude by flinging himself nearly horizontal, his green, black, and yellow wing whistling. His skis touch exactly where he needs them to before he launches off a cliff in a tuck much to the crowd's delight. Others throw huge back-scratchers or cross their tips midflight for style. Bon's run is steady and fast, but others are faster. His standing slips to fourth.

There are a few tense moments. Patrick Lachat, a Swiss flier, comes down hard after a long flight and explodes on touchdown, sending one ski twanging into the rocks. One French competitor, Frederic Fugen, comes up short on a jump over a cat track and tweaks his back hard enough to take himself out of the race. During a skydiving demo halfway through the day, Jean-Albert leaps into the blue wearing a wing suit that allows him to fly down the mountain's contours so close to the ground you swear he'll splat. He throws his chute just feet from the ground and hits a blue run so hard I wonder if his brains have turned to *boozz*. "It was a bit extreme," he says later.

"Speed flying seems safe compared to that," Klein says. "Anyone can learn it."

"I know some people think this will be the next big thing, but no, it won't," Steen counters. "Joe Schmo isn't going to just go rent a wing and cruise the 'Bird. You need to know what you're doing." Even then it's still dangerous. An experienced Swiss speed flier died near Verbier in December 2006 when he smacked into a rock.

But today such thoughts of doom fade behind the jovial mood. The music's pumping, there's more Red Bull to drink, and (somewhere in this crowd) hash to smoke. Jean-Albert claims the championship and a check for $2,800. David Eyraud takes $1,400 for second, and Vincent Reffet $700 for third. Bon stays at fourth. Gael Amman, a Swiss pilot, is the only top-five finisher who isn't French.

It doesn't seem to matter who won, though. The moment the competition is over the already boisterous French seem giddy. Dozens of them hurry through the orange light to find a wide slope off to the side that few people ski. Others follow and soon the

French are rallying everyone into a mass speed-flying start. "Come on!" one of them says. "We are so many!" Their enthusiasm for the idea would seem silly if it weren't so infectious.

The air fills with the rustle of crinkling wings inflating in the warm winter sun. As the fliers take off, the quiet slope is suddenly a collage of puffy blues, reds, and greens. They look like fighter pilots, whipping around rocks, carving turns, and smoothing out the fall line's imperfections with graceful swoops and arcs. They hit the cat track far below, passing skiers who seem so limited, so stuck in their own gravity.

ALEC WILKINSON

No Obstacles

FROM THE NEW YORKER

PARKOUR, A MADE-UP WORD, cousin to the French *parcours*, which means "route," is a quasi commando system of leaps, vaults, rolls, and landings designed to help a person avoid or surmount whatever lies in his path — a vocabulary, that is, to be employed in finding one's way among obstacles. Parkour goes over walls, not around them; it takes the stair rail, not the stairs. Spread mainly by videos on the Internet, it has been embraced in Europe and the United States by thrill seekers and martial-arts adepts, who regard it as part extreme sport — its founder would like to see it included in the Olympics — and part grueling meditative pursuit. Movies like its daredevil qualities. A bracing parkour chase begins *Casino Royale*, the recent James Bond movie. It includes jumps from the boom of one tower crane to that of another, but parkour's customary obstacles are walls, stairwells, fences, railings, and gaps between roofs — it is an urban rather than a pastoral pursuit. The movements are performed at a dead run. The more efficient and fluid the path they define, and the more difficult and harrowing the terrain they cross, the more elegant the performance is considered by the discipline's practitioners.

Parkour was created in Lisses, a medium prosperous suburb of Paris, in the early 1990s, by a reserved and restless teenage boy named David Belle. His father, Raymond, who died in 1999, was an acrobat and a hero fireman. In 1969, he appeared in newspaper photographs hanging from a cable attached to a helicopter above Notre Dame. The night before, someone had hung a Vietcong flag on the cathedral's tower. Raymond was lowered like a spider on a thread, and he grabbed the flag. David Belle is now thirty-three. He has an older brother, Jeff, who is also a fireman; they have the same father but different mothers. (A third brother died a few years ago, of an overdose.) David was raised by his mother's father. On the few occasions when he tried to live with Raymond, their temperaments clashed. David's grandfather told him stories about Raymond that revolved around his exploits — "Spider-Man stories and Tarzan stories," David says — and left him wishing to emulate him. He wanted to be Spider-Man when he grew up.

The parkour scene in *Casino Royale* is performed by a childhood friend of Belle's named Sébastien Foucan, who has developed a parallel pursuit to parkour, called free-running. Belle appears in two kinds of films, movies that show him performing parkour for its own sake, and movies and commercials in which he appears as an actor performing parkour. All of the films have the kind of vaudeville improbability of a video game. He leaps gaps between rooftops that it doesn't seem possible to cross. Or he jumps from a rooftop to one that is so much lower that he gets smaller and smaller, descending like a spike about to be driven into the ground. If parkour has a shrine, it is the climbing wall in Lisses, called the Dame du Lac, where Belle played as a teenager. The wall is about seventy-five feet high, and the films I like best show him fearlessly racing up and down it as if it had stairs. All are so steeped in risk that there are none I can watch without anxiety.

A young man who practices parkour is called a *traceur*, a woman is a *traceuse*. A *traceur*, Jeff Belle says, is someone "who traces David's footsteps, the way David traced our father's." Enthusiasts also say that a *traceur* is someone who goes fast. The video of Belle that *traceurs* seem to find most compelling, judging from how often they mention it, is one in which he crashes into a cement wall. I have found it on YouTube, using "David Belle fall" as the search term. Belle is attempting to leap over a double-wide ramp that leads to an underground parking garage. The ramp is enclosed by cinderblock walls, about three feet high. Belle arrives at a run from the left. He lowers his hands but they appear to miss the first wall entirely; he seems to be looking at where he means to land. Incredibly, while aloft, he turns, so that his shoulder, not his head, strikes the opposite wall. Ten feet beneath him, at the bottom of the ramp, a cameraman is lying on his back in order to shoot from below.

Belle manages not to land on him. His first gesture is to see if the cameraman is all right. Then he begins walking briskly up the ramp. Toward the top, he turns and can be seen to be grinning.

Parkour has no explicit glossary, but *traceurs* typically describe the fundamental maneuvers as the cat leap, the precision jump, the roll, and the wall run. There is also the tic-tac, in which a nearly horizontal *traceur* takes at least one step and sometimes several steps along a wall and launches himself from it; and the underbar, in which a *traceur* dives feet first through a gap between fence rails, like a letter going through a slot, then grabs the upper rail as his shoulders pass under it. In addition, there are several vaults, including the lazy vault, the reverse vault, the turn vault, the speed vault, the dash vault, and the kong or monkey vault, in which a *traceur* runs straight at a wall or a railing, plants his hands on top, and brings his feet through his hands. All these moves link to one another, so that a *traceur* might say that he went cat to cat, or that he tic-tacked a wall or konged it, then did a roll and a wall leap. The intention is to become so adept that the movements recede in one's awareness and can be performed without reflection. Jazz musicians occasionally say that a novice needs to learn all about his instrument, then he needs to learn all about music, then he needs to forget everything and learn how to play, which is a paradigm that also fits parkour, especially because both activities at their most proficient are improvised. A jazz musician wants to be comfortable in any key. Similarly, a *traceur* wants to be sufficiently fluent so that he can cross any terrain in flight without compromise.

Parkour's most prominent disciple in America is Mark Toorock, who lives in Washington, D.C., and runs a website called American Parkour. Toorock is thirty-six. In 2002, a brokerage firm where he worked as a computer technician sent him to London. "Some guys in my office were talking about this 'nutter' who was jumping across rooftops in an ad on TV — David Belle," Toorock says. "I started looking for him on the Internet, and I found a French forum where he was mentioned. Back then, there weren't any parkour sites. I made an attempt to speak to the people in the forum, but they were less than interested in talking to anyone who spoke English, and they weren't polite about it. I found out later that they didn't really want parkour spread. It was theirs, or so they felt. It's a very narrowly defined discipline, and they didn't want it misunder-stood."

A few weeks later, Toorock discovered a British website called Ur-ban Freeflow, which had just started up. Toorock arranged to meet some of the people involved in a park, and they went around climb-ing walls and jumping over benches. After two years, Toorock was transferred back to the United States and ended up in Washington, where he began his website.

Toorock is a little old for parkour. He says that he concentrates on "stuff close to the ground, on speed and efficiency." At his apart-ment, he showed me a photograph of a parkour artifact — a sign posted in a park in Bethesda, Maryland, that reads, NO SKATE-BOARDS, BICYCLES, ROLLERBLADES, PARKOUR TYPE EXERCISES OR SIMILAR ACTIVITIES. "The only one in the world," he said. "So far as we know."

In 2005, Toorock organized a team of American *traceurs* — ten men and two women, who call themselves the Tribe — and when I asked him who among them was the most adept he said Ryan Ford, who is a sophomore at the University of Colorado at Boulder. Ford is five-feet-nine, and he weighs 145 pounds. His face is round, and his eyes are slightly slanted. He has Sioux and Navajo blood, and bristly dark-brown hair. Everyone in the Tribe has a nickname. Ford's is Demon, but, being earnest and unassuming, he's not very comfortable with it. He lives in an apartment in a rambling house with two roommates. We sat in the living room. Ford said that he discovered parkour on the Internet toward the end of his junior year in high school, in Golden, Colorado. He wanted to learn how to run up to a wall, plant his foot on it, and do a back flip. Looking for instructions, he found images of David Belle, among others. In the fall, he quit the football team, on which he was a wide receiver, to pursue parkour.

"I was always climbing rocks and trees, so parkour was already kind of in me," he said. "Pretty much everyone you talk to will tell you that parkour was always part of them." His parents were un-happy with it, though. "To them, it just looked like I was jumping off stuff recklessly for no reason," he said. "But I kept saying, 'It's not pointless, there's a whole philosophy to it.'"

I asked how he had learned.

"A key factor in parkour is gradualism," he said. "You can't find the highest thing to jump from in order to practice your rolls. You get down on the ground first and practice your rolls, then maybe you find something three feet high to launch yourself from. When you can do something correctly a hundred times out of a hundred, you increase your task. Maybe. If you feel confident. People wonder how David Belle can leap between buildings and fall thirty feet. He started low and built up the difficulty."

It was a warm day, and the windows were open. We heard a dog bark, and a woman tell it to stop. "Parkour is about repetition and practice," Ford went on. "To say that no one in the U.S. has reached David Belle's level doesn't mean that there aren't extremely skilled people doing parkour; it means that he's trained for years, and no one here has. When I see a skilled *traceur*, I admire the dedication and the mental strength. There are some people who just have superior physical ability, but there are no secret techniques in parkour. A lot of the things *traceurs* do aren't necessarily impressive physically anyway. From a *traceur*'s point of view, the task is often mental. Some people can master fear. Other people might have more determination and, in the end, accomplish more things. I see myself fueled more by determination than by the ease of putting fear in the back of my mind. I overthink, and I don't have the craziness some people do, but I have the determination."

"How often do you practice?"

"I try to do something every day," he said. Then he frowned. "One thing we say is we do parkour, but a lot of the time we aren't; we're practicing for parkour. True parkour is hardly ever done. If I'm practicing a vault and I turn around and do it again, that's not parkour, because it's continuing a circle — it's not making a path. The videos on the Internet are spliced together, so that's not really parkour either.

"My fantasy is to be walking late at night on the street in New York City and have some guys try to rob me, and I use parkour to get away from them, but I've never had to use parkour, so in a way I could say I've never really done parkour. I practice parkour not because I think I'm going to have to use it but because I see it as making me stronger physically and mentally, just the way people don't go into martial arts because they plan to fight someone — they keep fit or get discipline. Everyone's different, but the philosophy of parkour that drives me is that progression of ability, being better than I was the day before. There's a quote by Bruce Lee that's my motto: 'There are no limits. There are plateaus, but you must not stay there, you must go beyond them. A man must constantly exceed his level.' If you're not better than you were the day before, then what are you doing — what's the point?"

The next morning, I drove to Denver with Ford; his girlfriend, Kathryn Keller, who is brown-haired and petite and was a gymnast in high school but had to give it up when she hurt her back; and a tall, skinny high school boy with freckles and a turban named Sat, whose full name is Sat Santokh Khalsa. Sat's American mother and father had converted to Sikhism, and when Sat was nine they sent him to a Sikh boarding school in India, called Miri Piri Academy. He had gone there for six years — he was now fifteen — and had just started Boulder High School. When he came home from India at the end of the school year, a friend had shown him a parkour video, and then he found Mark Toorock's website.

We drove downtown, to a small park called Skyline Park, outside a Westin hotel. Ford had invited several other *traceurs* to join us, and when we arrived one of them, a Russian named Nikita, was sitting beside a fountain that had been drained. Nikita was twenty. He had shaved his blond hair, and he had a small face, avid eyes, thin lips, and a sharp nose. He was six-feet-two and weighed 160 pounds. He looked like a big spider. He said that he was from Belarus. "I grew up in a village," he said. "It was just five houses." In New York, where his father now lived, he had trained for two years to be an ultimate fighter. "We paid money to a manager to arrange the fights, and he left," he said. "After that, my trainer went into the movies." He shrugged off a backpack. "Two more days, and it will be one month I have done parkour."

The fountain in Skyline Park is a collection of reddish-brown concrete forms, squares and rectangles, stacked like children's blocks. It is about twenty feet tall. "We call this the Cat Fountain," Ford said, "because there's a lot of cat leaps here." There is a fountain in a park nearby, designed by the same architect, which is called Precision Fountain, Ford said, "because it has a lot of precision jumps." The Cat Fountain was set into the plaza, so that from the pavement to the blocks there was a gap several feet wide and a few feet deep, which would be filled by water in warmer weather.

Making a run toward the gap, Sat made a cat leap to one of the blocks. He was so slight that it seemed as if he had been lifted into the air by a wire. Once he had grabbed the block, his feet slid against it as he pulled himself up. "The slips are part of the technique," Ford said. "It's controlled. When you first start, you rely more on the equipment to hold you in place, your sneakers, then you learn to use your strength."

Warming up, Nikita twisted from side to side, like a screw. Ford did a handstand but had difficulty maintaining it. "My handstands are not so good," he said. "I fall over, since I got hurt."

"What happened?"

"Separated my shoulder," he said.

"Where'd you do that?"

Ford walked about ten paces. "Right here," he said. "Kong vault over this eight-foot gap. I should have landed in that flower bed, but I clipped a foot and fell into the gap and hit the wall. At first, I thought I broke my collarbone. I also cut my head. I drove home using one arm."

Keller said, "He left a message on my answering machine: 'I got hurt pretty bad, so just call me back.'"

While we stood looking at the wall and the flower bed, another *traceur*, a high school boy named Dan Mancini, came walking across the plaza. He was tall and thin, with brown hair, and wore a T-shirt and jeans. Ford clasped his hands above his head and stretched, then said, "Shall we hit some stuff on the fountain?" When Ford talks about people naturally gifted for parkour, one of the people he means is Nikita. We watched him pace off a ten-foot gap from the border to the fountain, then approach it at a run. The first time, he landed short of the wall, and the second time he cleared the gap but couldn't hold on to the wall and dropped to the bottom of the fountain.

"I did that once," Ford said. "Never again."

Nikita said that he wanted to try one more time.

"You should," Ford said. "I'll film it."

"You shouldn't tell me," Nikita said.

Ford got a video camera from his knapsack. He stood on a block beside the one Nikita was attempting to surmount and filmed Nikita as he came rushing forward, leaped into the air, and struck the block feet first, like a hawk, then grabbed the edge and pulled himself to the top. He stood on top of the block, jiggling his hands, and said, "Scary vault."

They grew tired of the fountain shortly and began hoisting themselves onto a railing a few feet above the ground and walking along it on all fours: a maneuver called a cat balance or a cat walk. The railing framed three sides of a rectangle. The longest section was about thirty feet. "Cat walking is very tiring," Ford said. "Your legs start to burn." Nikita went up one side of the railing and made the turn and passed us. "Your legs burning yet?" Ford asked. Nikita shook his head. He turned the second corner. "Now burning," he said.

After Nikita got off the railing, he paced out a cat leap from the plaza, over a gap of about eight feet, to a block in the fountain.

"The last guy who did that hit his face," Ford said.

"Bit through his lip," one of the others said.

Nikita soared over the gap and held on to the block, and the others shook their heads. Ford said, "You guys want to move? I got another cat leap for you."

We crossed the street to a ramp that led to an underground garage. The boys leaned over the walls on either side of the ramp and looked down soberly. At the deep end, the drop to the pavement was about fifteen feet, and the distance across about twelve.

"This is the smallest parking-garage ramp in Denver," one of them said.

"Yeah, we scouted it," another said.

"Those French guys do it at the deepest part."

"Yeah, but in France the cars are smaller, so it's as deep but not as wide."

They walked to the head of the ramp in a little pack. A few of them climbed up on the wall around the ramp and made tentative standing jumps to the pavement, landing at the far wall and grabbing the edge of it with their fingers, but no one wanted to try it for real. Embedded in the wall were pieces of gravel, making it rough to the touch. Nikita stood on a rail several inches above the wall, wobbling, as if on a branch. Through a window of the hotel, about ten floors up, a man watched him. Nikita bent his knees, thrust his arms forward, and leaped, his path making a little arc in the air. His fingers grasped the wall, but he landed hard and banged his shin. He lifted his pants leg to see if he'd cut himself. Then he said, "Let's get out of here," and everyone followed him across the street. His hands were scraped and bleeding. On a Velcro strap around his chest he had a zippered wallet from which he took some tape and wrapped his fingers.

After crossing several streets, we came to an apartment building and a concrete parking garage that was four floors tall. Between the levels, running nearly the length of each wall, were broad openings like slits. Each was about a foot tall. Using them, the boys began climbing. One said, "Is this, like, the Asian place where the lady yelled at us to get out?"

A door at the top of a flight of stairs in the apartment building opened and a small, black-haired woman stepped out. "What are you doing climbing here?" she yelled. "Are you supposed to be up there? Get off. The stairs are for going up and down." She glared at them, and one by one they sheepishly climbed down. We took the stairs to the roof, which was connected to a walkway leading to a row of stores, all of them closed — it was Sunday. By one of the stores were two sulky girls and a boy dressed in black clothes.

"Are you guys some kind of youth group?" one of the girls asked.

"No, this is just us using the buildings to keep fit," someone said.

"Oh, I understand," the girl said. "That's cool."

"She does *not* understand," Kathryn said.

"Oh, my God," the other girl said. "It's like Spider-Man."

I turned and saw Nikita climbing a drainpipe to the roof of one of the stores. While I was writing "Spider-Man" in my notebook, his shadow as he leaped from one roof to another passed over the page.

Jeff Belle has an office in Paris, where he handles fire department business. To speak with him, I brought a translator, Susan Chace, an American novelist who lives in Paris. Belle, who is forty-five, is small and wiry. He has a round face, a sharp chin, dark eyes, and black, cropped hair with flecks of gray. He was wearing a fireman's uniform, a dark-blue garment like a jumpsuit. The legs ended just above the tops of his black combat boots. Over the uniform, he wore a long coat that had POMPIER DE PARIS written on the back. We met at his office, then he took us to an empty, low-ceilinged room with a bar and an espresso machine and some tables stacked on top of each other. On the wall were photographs of firefighters.

Jeff said that David was a restless boy. "He was always exercising in front of the TV," he said. "He still takes whatever's next to him, maybe a big book, and starts lifting it. He can't sit still. He lives with it." The brothers did not see much of each other until David, at fourteen, moved to Lisses to live with his mother. Then Jeff, who was already a fireman, began to look after him. He would show him how to climb ropes and perform gymnastic maneuvers, and David would go off and do it his own way. Now and then, David would go to the climbing wall in Lisses with his father and show him things he had taught himself, and Raymond, thinking that he was being encouraging, would say, "I could do that when I was nine."

Through Jeff, David was exposed to the methods of Georges Hébert, a French sports theorist, whose motto was "Be strong to be useful." Hébert believed that modern conveniences such as elevators were debilitating. He thought that Africans he had met while traveling were healthier and stronger than Europeans, and that the proportions of the bodies he saw in Greek and Roman statues were ideal. The philosophies and the exercises he developed, which are part of a French fireman's training, were also meant to cultivate courage and discipline. Inspired by Hébert, a Swiss architect developed an obstacle course called a *parcours*. "David took Hébert's ideas and said, 'I will adapt it to what I need,'" Jeff said. "Instead of stopping at a reasonable point, he just kept going."

David was briefly a fireman recruit, until he hurt his wrist. While he was recuperating, he started thinking things over and saw that the life of a fireman had too many rules, and not enough action, and he decided to join the Marines, but he didn't find the same values among them, the "traditional values." He left the Marines and went to India, where he stayed for six months. When he came back to Paris, he was twenty-four, and he didn't know what to do with himself.

"He came to see me at my house," Jeff said, "and he told me he didn't know where his life was going. He was only interested in parkour. You could be a super policeman or a firefighter using it, but you can't earn your living, because there's no championship. I said, 'Maybe if we film what you're doing.'"

It was 1997, and Jeff was involved in planning an annual ceremony in which recruits perform firefighting drills. He decided that David should put on a show. He told him to get a group together, so that he wouldn't look insignificant by himself. David collected two of his cousins and some other kids from the neighborhood, including Sébastien Foucan, with whom he ran around doing parkour. Jeff choreographed a routine for them. They dressed as ninjas and called themselves the Yamakasi. "It means 'strong spirit' in the language of Zaire," Jeff said, "but it sounded Asian." During the show, David climbed a tower and did a handstand at the top. He also scaled a fireman's ladder and did a back flip from it. After the demonstration, David began getting invitations to perform.

Jeff is proud of David, but worries about him. "This was a kid who refused any kind of system, who just wanted to live his life," he said. "If he's surrounded by the right people, he can do what he wants. Ordinary life really upsets him, though, because this world the rest of us live in is not where he finds his pleasure. He's easily disturbed by ordinary things. But he's also asking, 'Why am I doing this parkour?' All his family who did this physical stuff were doing it for a reason, but he's asking, 'Why am I doing this, what does it mean?'" Jeff added, "He's simple in his purposes. He doesn't like talking very much. He's someone who is looking for his way." I asked what sort of routines David observed in his training. Jeff shook his head. "He's still eating Big Macs and drinking Coke," Jeff said. "He likes chicken sandwiches. He trains when it comes to him. He's usually sleeping in the morning. He's really a night guy."

We arranged to meet with David the following day, in Lisses, where he was staying with his mother. When David is in France, he lives either with her or with Jeff. "He doesn't really have a lot of money," Jeff said, "although people think that he does." He added that David was very easy to live with. "We don't know about the inside of his head, but outside he's very neat. His room is always in perfect shape."

The next day, I took a taxi with Susan Chace to Lisses, about half an hour south of Paris. When we were under way, the driver asked why we were going there. Chace said, "To see David Belle." The driver nodded. Chace asked if he knew who Belle was, and the driver said, "Of course. *Il est unique.*" We left the highway and, following Jeff's directions, went around a rotary and came to a collection of low, flat-roofed, two-story buildings, like shoeboxes, painted light brown. We stopped in front of Belle's building. Chace knocked, the

door opened, and the driver said, "That's him!" Belle had his chin
tucked slightly, like a man looking out from under the brim of a
hat. He had dark hair cut short like a pelt and a thin, asymmetrical
face, with a sharp chin and a hook nose. He was wearing a red
fleece top and jeans. As I paid the driver, Jeff Belle drove up behind
us. We went into the apartment. The kitchen was by the door, and
there was a living room beyond it with a circular stairway leading
up. In the living room was David's girlfriend, Dorine Sane. David
had his fleece top zipped to his chin — he had a sore throat — and
he seemed subdued. He had just come back from three weeks in
the Czech Republic, where he was making *Babylon AD*, which stars
Vin Diesel, and is based on a French science fiction novel. David
plays the head of an Internet gang that does parkour, and he choreographed scenes for ten actors.

Jeff and David spoke for a few moments, and then Chace said
that David was going to rest, while Jeff took us to the Dam du
Lac. Outside, we crossed a parking lot, then took an asphalt path
through a park. Several hundred yards off, the Dam du Lac rose up
against the side of a small lake. It was the color of sandstone and
had the shape of an arch. "David was afraid of it in the beginning,"
Jeff said. "Now he walks on it like it was solid ground." The *lac*
turned out to be made of concrete. As we walked along the edge,
ducks paddled away from us. For some time now, a fence has enclosed the wall, but it was easy to climb around it. The wall was
slightly concave, and the top was intersected by a horizontal slab,
which had roughly the dimensions of a king-size mattress and was
curled up at one edge. Here and there on the face of the wall were
footholds and handholds in the form of slots the size of bricks. On
one side was a rectangular box, open at one end, like a cave, which
is called the cabana. Below, sticking straight out from the wall and
about fifteen feet tall, was a form in the shape, more or less, of a
hammer. Jeff said that the first maneuver David had done was a
back flip from the cabana to the hammer. About twenty feet from
the ground was a sign saying, ESCALADE INTERDITE. On it were
signatures. "The kids climb up and sign their names," Jeff said. "David also went barefoot on it." He pointed at the top. "And at night
sometimes he slept up there."

For a few minutes, my mind screened images of David in videos I
had seen — running up and down the wall, doing a hair-raising

handstand at the top — then we began walking back toward the apartment. We passed a low building with picture windows — a nursery school — and Jeff said that when David and his friends were young "they jumped over the bushes beside it to the roof. That was their first trick." While we were looking at a stairwell that appears as a prop in videos for a series of David's cat leaps, Jeff's cell phone rang, and it was David saying he was ready to talk.

When we got back to the apartment, David sat on a couch with Dorine, and I sat next to them. Jeff made coffee. For the most part, David sat quite still, like a machine at rest. The only part of him in motion was his right hand, which moved from Dorine's hand, to her knee, to her lap, and so on. I asked how he knew whether a movement was too dangerous. "It's just intuitive," he said, shrugging. "My body just knows if I can do something or not. It's sort of an animal thing. In athletics, they have rules — you have to take your distance and stop and jump, everything has a procedure — but I never did it that way. I don't take a risk, though, that I know I can't do. I like life too much."

He said that parkour hadn't changed much, since he started it, but his intention had become more specific. "When I was younger, I was playing, the way kids play at parkour, but now I ask the question 'Is this going to be useful for me to get to the other side?' The movement is simple. I don't do anything special, because I want to get to the other side. What I'm interested in for parkour is the utilitarian thing of getting to the other end, whether as a task or a challenge, but in film they like a little entertainment, so I do that too, but it's not what I'm interested in.

"You always have to get through the first obstacle that says, 'I can't do it,' whether in your mind or for real, and be able to adapt to anything that's put in your path. It's a method for learning how to move in the world. For finding the liberty men used to have."

I asked David why he had gone to India, and he said that he had friends there.

"How did you pass the time?"

"I just kept training," he said. "I was training in the trees." Jeff handed me a scrapbook with a photograph of David leaping from the limb of one tree to another. He was stretched flat out, horizontal to the ground, like Superman.

"I was at a waterfall one day," David went on, "and there were huge trees all around, and in the trees were monkeys. There were fences and barriers around them, so they couldn't get out, but I went around the barriers and played with the monkeys. After that, I watched them all the time, learning how they climbed. All the techniques in parkour are from watching the monkeys."

He then showed us, on a computer, a documentary called *Warriors of the Monkey God*. It was about a tribe of monkeys who live on the rooftops of Jodhpur. The people regard the monkeys as holy. We watched them leaping from rooftop to rooftop and through the trees. The scene that made David smile was one in which numbers of them leaped onto, then off, a piece of corrugated tin that was loosely attached as a roof to some stakes. Their landings made the tin shake. Some of the monkeys were leaping from the ground, turning on their sides in the air, landing on the stakes, and shoving off from them — a tic-tac.

Watching the movie, which was about forty-five minutes long, took only about fifteen minutes, because David kept advancing it to scenes of the monkeys in flight, looking exactly like *traceurs*. When it was finished, he said that after coming home he had just continued perfecting what he had learned from the monkeys. He had plans, he said, to make a movie with them.

I asked about the fall on the Internet, the one that the American *traceurs* always talk about. David gave a little smile. "I was a bit tired," he said. "It was the end of the day. I was just doing stuff with a bunch of kids. I fall all the time — I fall like the monkeys — but it never shows up on film, because they just want the spectacular stuff."

I thought of Nikita with his bleeding hands and said, "You never wear gloves?"

He said that he wanted to be able to feel the surfaces he was grabbing. He held his palms out for me to feel, and they were as hard and slick as linoleum.

I told him that I had been to see people do parkour in Colorado, and that they had imagined themselves as preparing to use it for an escape, and he said, "That's good. If you're really thinking about how to defend yourself, how to be useful, then that's a very different mind-set from just doing things to look good."

Last fall, David said, he had discussions with Sam Raimi, the director of *Spider-Man*, about playing the role of Spider-Man's double, but he decided he wasn't interested. "That was a childhood dream, to be in a Spider-Man costume," he said. "Now I'd rather appear on a poster with my own name, not as a character, saying, 'This is me performing.'" He was planning to tour the world doing parkour, he said. A French film company partly owned by the director Luc Besson paid his expenses to perform last winter in Madagascar, and David had also given exhibitions in Italy, Germany, and Portugal.

He yawned and rubbed his throat, and I took it as a sign that he was at the end of his interest in talking. I thanked him and stood up. We shook hands. He seemed to think for a moment, then he said, "I'm still learning. I'm not sure of anything yet, I'm just trying to be as complete as I can."

I nodded.

"What I do is not really something that can be explained," he said. "It can just be practiced." Then he went to call us a taxi.

SAM SHAW

Run Like Fire Once More

FROM HARPER'S MAGAZINE

THE RUNNERS SLOG past a bivouac of plastic card tables and folding chairs, past electric-green Port-O Lets ripe with disinfectant, past indifferently groomed hedges and the red brick facade of Thomas A. Edison Vocational and Technical High School. At the corner of 168th Street, they cut north to the Grand Central Parkway, the course rising gently as trucks and cars rocket by. The concrete apron is a blinding white line. They pass illegally parked cars, wipers festooned with tickets. Trash has blown into the grass of Joseph Austin Park, named for Mario Cuomo's childhood baseball coach. Here are silent handball and basketball courts, and a playground where sprinklers throw a flume across a midway empty of children. Alone or in twos or threes, the runners pass the hydrants and trash cans of 164th Place, moving southward to Abigail Adams Avenue and thence east a half-block under shade trees to the row of card tables, where women jot notes on clipboards, like a delegation of Green Party poll watchers. At a comfortable pace, you can walk the loop in about ten minutes. The course of the world's longest footrace measures .5488 miles.

I first walked it myself on a balmy day last June, then found a seat at Base Camp among a half-dozen volunteers, bright-eyed European women and men with the lost-boy quality of scoutmasters. A giant digital clock was perched atop a pair of milk crates. Every few minutes one of the racers passed by, and we all applauded.

At 3:00 P.M., amid a crackling of police bullhorns, two thousand mostly black and Hispanic teenagers emptied out of Edison High. They pumped their legs, lampooning the runners' form, sometimes diverting the race into traffic. "The first couple years, the kids threw things at us," a volunteer told me.

Such were the hazards last summer in Jamaica, Queens, at the tenth running of the Self-Transcendence 3,100. The fifteen participants — all but two of them disciples of the Bengali Guru Sri Chinmoy, who has resided in the neighborhood for forty years — hailed from ten countries on three continents. They ran in all weather, seven days a week, from 6:00 A.M. to midnight, or until their bodies compelled them to rest. If they logged fewer than fifty miles on a given day, they risked disqualification. By their own reckoning, the runners climbed eight meters per lap, mounting and descending a spectral Everest every week and a half. They toiled in this fashion for six to eight weeks, however long it took them to complete 5,649 circuits — 3,100 miles — around a single city block.

Before any concerns aesthetic or spiritual, the loop serves the practical function of enabling the Base Camp crew to attend to the physical requirements of runners traveling at all speeds. (By the sixth week of the race, nine hundred miles would separate course record holder Madhupran Wolfgang Schwerk, of Solingen, Germany, from Suprabha Beckjord, in last place.[1]) But in another, more ethereal sense, the Self-Transcendence Race could not exist on any other course. Here was a kind of living koan, a race of invisible miles across a phantom plain wider than the continental United States. For fifty days, breathing miasmal exhaust from the Grand Central Parkway, the runner traversed a wilderness of knapsack-toting teenagers, beat cops, and ladies piloting strollers. Temperatures spiked. Power grids crashed. Cars also crashed — into the chain-link fence around Joe Austin Park or into other cars. There was occasional street crime. One summer a student was knifed in the head. The runner endured. He crossed the finish line changed. It was said to be the most difficult racecourse in the world. Point-to-point racing is gentler on the spirit, and concrete is ten times more punishing than asphalt. Such hurdles were more than necessary evils; they were central to the nature of the race. As one of the disciples told me, grinning and drawing air quotes with his fingers, "It's 'impossible.'"

I fell into step beside Abichal Watkins, a forty-five-year-old Welshman with a keen, appraising squint. After only five days, he looked like a man who had wandered out of the desert with a story to tell. "There are so few things for the mind to dwell on here," Abichal said. "It loses its strength." Relative to most of the racers, Abichal — born Kelvin and rechristened in 1999 by Sri Chinmoy — came to distance running late in life. That tale begins in the mid-1990s, when Chinmoy announced the completion of his millionth "Soul Bird" painting (artworks expressing the "heart's oneness"), and his disciples resolved to match the feat by running, collectively, a million miles. Abichal pledged an even thousand. Within a year, Chinmoy had painted another million Soul Birds, and the running project was scuttled, but Abichal kept it up. In Wales he edits a magazine and a website devoted to multiday ultra marathons. He had finished the Self-Transcendence Race twice before; a third attempt failed when his visa expired 2,700 miles in.

We passed Edison High, progressing counterclockwise up 168th Street toward the Grand Central Parkway. (The runners switch direction every day, not for the sake of novelty but to ensure that the toll of rounding corners is borne equally by both legs.) Abichal does not consider himself an athlete. "The race is a metaphor for life." He gestured, lassoing the whole of Jamaica around us. "People in the neighborhood, we'll see them year after year. They stop by, say hi. They ask, 'How do you do that?'" He laughed. This was the first interview I conducted while power-walking. It was awkward. My pen kept slipping in my hand.

Abichal wore an iPod clipped to his waist, jarring my notion of the Chinmoy disciples as latter-day ascetics. I wondered what he had been listening to. "'Fix You,'" he said, "by Coldplay." For more than a hundred miles, Abichal had been listening to the track on a continuous loop. ("Lights will guide you home," the chorus intones, "and ignite your bones.") He gazed philosophically at his iPod. "There's something special about this song."

As we neared 164th Place, a white town car pulled gently to the curb. With the speed and nonchalance of a dope dealer, a man in the passenger seat reached through the window and deposited something into Abichal's hands. Sri Chinmoy. The sight of him tripped me up. Here was the Guru himself, gold-complected, resplendently bald. Dressed as if for a day at the public pool, in shorts and a cotton shirt, he did not look like a man who had inspired seven thousand followers in sixty countries to forswear alcohol, tobacco, meat, and sex. I wanted to stop, but the race paused for no man, not even an avatar of divine consciousness.

A few paces ahead, Abichal studied the objects he'd received: two strawberries, cupped in his palms like bulbous, red communion wafers. "I don't know why he gave me two," he said. He turned to me, suddenly serious. "I think one of them is for you." Our fables, stretching back to the myth of Persephone and Genesis 3:6, teach circumspection in receiving gifts of fruit. Abichal nodded, and I ate the Guru's strawberry. Within a few weeks, the runners would be hobbled by distance, gorging ice cream and butter to stem the loss of body weight. We passed the giant digital clock, and the women applauded. Two thousand eight hundred and thirty miles to go.

The specter of death has hung over long-distance running since Robert Browning published his *Dramatic Idylls* in 1879. In a flight of lyric fancy widely mistaken for truth, the poem "Pheidippides" describes an ill-starred footman sprinting from Marathon to Athens with news of a surprise Greek victory in an early battle of the Persian Wars.

> So, when Persia was dust, all cried,
>   "To Akropolis!
> Run Pheidippides, one race more! the
>   meed is thy due!
> 'Athens is saved, thank Pan,' go
>   shout!" He flung down his shield
> Ran like fire once more: and the space
>   'twixt the Fennel-field
> And Athens was stubble again, a field
>   which a fire runs through,
> Till in he broke: "Rejoice, we
>   conquer!" Like wine through clay,
> Joy in his blood bursting his heart, he
>   died — the bliss!

Never mind that the story is plainly apocryphal, a pastiche of Herodotus, Plutarch, and Lucian. When Pierre de Coubertin organized the first modern Olympic Games, his friend the philologist Michael Breal urged him to include a distance race in tribute to the doomed runner. Today, in spite of the fact that hundreds of thousands of Americans run marathons,[2] the long-distance athlete in popular culture is typically a Jobian figure, tortured and solitary. Iconic Nike ads of the '90s cast him in grainy black and white, doubled over and unleashing a stream of vomit onto his shoes. The hero of William Goldman's *Marathon Man* gets his teeth drilled by a Nazi. Always, the runner is haunted. His race is a form of flight — from himself, from the mediocrity of society, from a lugubrious backstory.

Browning reimagined Pheidippides at the height of the so-called Golden Age of Pedestrianism. In 1878, the Crimean War veteran, baronet, and amateur sports promoter Sir John Dugdale Astley launched a series of six-day exhibition footraces, held along ellipse tracks before throngs of delirious spectators. The winner crawled away with a cash purse and a small fortune in gate fees, as well as a silver-and-gold belt valued at £100 and bearing the legend LONG DISTANCE CHAMPION OF THE WORLD.

In June 1879, Edward Payson Weston strode 550 miles in six days along a wooden track in London's Agricultural Hall, beating ten-to-one odds to become the first American-born Astley Belt champion and an international sensation. "There were Weston shoes, Weston hats, and Weston coats," rhapsodized *Harper's Weekly*. "Musicians composed Weston marches, and young ladies danced to Weston Waltzes." His "clean-cut and shrewd" face gazed nobly from photographs "in thousands of private dwellings as well as in most public places." The dandyish Rhode Island native was a star, and he behaved like one, preening and sulking, issuing crackpot statements to the press, and hobnobbing with deep pocketed strangers.

That August, Weston sailed from Liverpool to New York City on the steamship *Nevada*, but his triumph was partial and short-lived. The steamer *Harlem*, engaged to intercept the great pedestrian in New York Harbor with six kegs of beer, two cases of wine, and a basket of sandwiches, failed to arrive on schedule, and his admirers greeted him instead in a tugboat. Dressed in a priestly black suit, Weston griped to reporters about a prize watch he had been promised by the mayor of Newark that had never materialized. "If I owned a house in perdition and another in Newark," he said, "I'd rent the Newark house."

At a time when a pound of mutton cost fourteen cents, some seventy-five thousand spectators paid a dollar apiece for admission to

the next Astley Belt match, at Madison Square Garden. Loiterers
choked Twenty-sixth Street. They scaled drainpipes and shinnied
up ropes to the low windows of the theater, where sentries lay in
wait with sharpened sticks. The Englishman Charles Rowell covered 127 miles within the first day and night of the race. His early
lead left scant doubt as to the eventual outcome, but the circus inside the Garden roiled on with a Boschian grandeur. Bands played
"Yankee Doodle," "Tommy Dodd," and "Marching Through Georgia." Rowell sucked on a sponge while his countryman George
Hazael cut a simian figure with his fumbling headlong stride. "The
question is often asked, 'What is that thing?' when Hazael goes
around," a reporter wrote with jingoistic cruelty, "but the ques-
tioner is always awed into silence when told that that is one of the
best runners in England." Ever the showman, Weston burlesqued
the gaits of his rivals, stopping now and then to spritz himself with
eau de toilette from an atomizer he toted around the loop. The
other contestants shuffled more or less suicidally toward the grail
of 450 miles, short of which they would not see a nickel. It was a
scene befitting the venue, raised by P. T. Barnum as a hippodrome
for mock-Roman chariot exhibitions. Rowell took ill in the last days
of the race, but his advantage was overwhelming. Amid a flurry of
rumors that he had been mickeyed with a cluster of poisoned
grapes, he completed his 530th mile and repaired to his tent with
Weston's prize belt and a share of the gate receipts totaling $25,000
— roughly the equivalent of $500,000 today.

The winner of the Self-Transcendence Race would return to his
home country with a plastic trophy and a scrapbook. Each contestant forked over an entry fee of $1,250 — an investment none
would recoup. Self-transcendence, it seemed, was not a lucrative
career. In late June, Kuranga Peele of Neusiedl, Austria, flew home.
In 2004, Peele had finished second, with the seventh-best time in
race history. This year he had logged just over 660 miles. "Kuranga
didn't feel up to it," Abichal explained. "You have to be totally committed, or the mind can get in the way."

As the fourteen remaining contestants sauntered around the
block, it was impossible to tell at any given moment who was winning and who was losing. Madhupran Wolfgang Schwerk, with a
lead of more than a hundred miles two weeks into the race, was

heavily favored. Nobody at the racecourse expressed much surprise — Madhupran held the course record. I shadowed him past the playground with a mixture of admiration and unease. His gait called to mind pistons and crankshafts, the famous efficiency of German engineering. Just looking at him made me thirsty for a Coke. Short of a bunch of poisoned grapes, it was hard to imagine anybody closing the gap. This might have had something to do with Madhupran's support team. He was the only runner to have imported a full-time handler, Helmut Schieke, himself a former trans-America record holder, who hailed Schwerk whenever he finished a lap, often with a plastic cup of diet cola or tea or a slice of honeydew melon. He was also alone in having landed a corporate patron. LANXESS, a German producer of plastics and rubbers, had fronted his airfare, along with his registration fee. In exchange, he arrived each morning dressed in a crisp LANXESS singlet, matching shorts, and sneakers.

Cars passed Base Camp at the requisite school-zone crawl, and the drone of a lawn mower filled me with a strong Pavlovian urge to lie down in a hammock. On the refreshment table an argosy of chips, raisins, granola bars, olives, cookies, ice cream, and butter lay open to would-be saboteurs, but who would tamper with a race whose profits are tallied in the coinage of the soul?

On the corner of 168th Street, a man in a baseball cap was squinting through a hand-held video camera at the pageant of runners drifting southward. "The footage isn't very good," he confessed, wagging his head. His name was Daniel, and he had flown to New York to report on the race for RTL, a German television station. A second German news team was supposed to arrive tomorrow, and Daniel planned to beat them to the story. Suprabha ambled past, talking on a cell phone. "The problem is, they don't really run," Daniel said. "They jog, they stop, they walk. I need *running*. I need sweat streaming down faces."

If the scene on Abigail Adams Avenue disappointed Daniel, the trouble was partly semantic. The Self-Transcendence Race was not, strictly speaking, a sporting event. It was spiritual detox. For two months the athletes paid no bills, ran no errands, conducted no business. They lived in a state of Thoreauvian simplicity. "The mind says it's stupid to go around and around," I was told by a volunteer named Aklanta, one of a squadron of chiropractors at the race-

course. "But it's not stupid on a higher plane." The race revealed
the "true nature" above one's "base nature," he said. "You find out
what your true nature wants. What does it *want?* Not what advertisements on television tell you you want. That's manipulation. I don't
want to be manipulated. You need joy in your life. Otherwise, it's
just stimulation — up and down, nothing constant."

A middle-aged man approached Base Camp. With his white mus-
tache and straw boater, he recalled Edward Payson Weston walking through Confederate Maryland in 1861, disguised, in Weston's
own words, by "Messrs Brooks, Brothers, clothing dealers" as a
"Susquehanna Raftsman on a bender." He stopped on the sidewalk, watching the runners shuffle past with the dazed look of a
man who had just been sprung from jail. And so he had — it was
summer vacation. His furlough would stretch until the last week of
August, when he would return to his post as a laboratory specialist
at Edison High. "Essentially, a test-tube washer. I help to purchase
— or to prevent the purchase of — equipment. Mercury used to be
a thing you played with," he said with nostalgia. "Now it's a deadly
poison."

A credential sticking out of his shirt pocket identified the speaker
as one M. Cogan. He wore his nametag religiously, a precaution
dating to the years he worked at Bellevue Hospital. "Someone had
to die for that," he explained. Europeans in high-performance
sportswear parted around us as he related a long, grim story about
a psychiatric patient in a stolen lab coat butchering a female doctor. "I'm not sure if he raped her before he dissected her or after or
a little of both." On another occasion, he told me, a paraplegic escaped from the prison ward and disappeared across the border
into Mexico. The thought of this wheelchair-bound fugitive thriv-
ing under Latin American skies seemed to cheer him up. "They're
good neighbors," he said of the Self-Transcendence crew. "That's
all I know. Chinmoy seems to attract a nice crowd. But I haven't got
to the point where I want to join." He had first encountered the
group on an afternoon in the 1970s when a bald-headed stranger
reproached him for lighting a cigarette in a local restaurant. The
stranger was Sri Chinmoy. "I guess it's a clean-living cult sort of
thing. Like the Mormon Church." Not long thereafter, noticing
Chinmoy's name in a letter submitted to the *New York Times* by the
composer Leonard Bernstein, Cogan realized the Guru was a famous and important man.

We strolled together past the line of Port-O Lets to the refreshment table, where Cogan stopped and told a spindly German volunteer that he intended to run a race of his own, albeit one of humbler length. He seemed an unlikely candidate for cardiovascular exercise, but in this climate of burgeoning goodwill, with songbirds flicking through the trees and rival German news teams trolling Joe Austin Park, all things seemed possible. Cogan beamed at the disciples, "You've inspired me."

What, exactly, had Leonard Bernstein written to the *Times?* I never found the letter Mike Cogan remembered, but an item in an April 1979 "Notes on People" column described a recently formed "mutual admiration society" comprising the Guru and the flamboyant composer of *West Side Story*:

> Sri Chinmoy, whose followers say he has written 3,000 songs, dropped by Mr. Bernstein's Manhattan apartment a few weeks ago, and brought with him a choral group that sang a new Chinmoy number called, "Leonard Bernstein." It went, in part:

> > Leonard Bernstein, Leonard!
> > Eternity's singing bird!
> > Beauty truth, Truth beauty,
> > Nectar oneness your divinity.

Bernstein had responded in kind, presenting the Guru with an original work for sitar, flute, tabla, bass, and drone. Until recently, all I had known of the Guru I owed to an LP called *Love, Devotion, Surrender*, a 1973 jazz-rock fiasco by Carlos Santana and John McLaughlin, both former Chinmoy disciples.[3]

Born August 27,1931,[4] in East Bengal, India, and orphaned at twelve, the Guru spent his adolescence and early adulthood studying meditation at the Sri Aurobindo Ashram, where he earned the title Fastest Runner twelve years in a row. In 1964 he emigrated to New York and took a job as an assistant in the passport-and-visa section of the Indian Consulate. These were lean years for the Guru. According to his memoirs, he lunched on potato chips or candy bars, often in a telephone booth outside his office, but already he was laying the foundation for his spiritual mission, playing free concerts and lecturing on Hinduism. In the ensuing decades, the Guru's self-transcendence empire fanned across six continents, spurred by a distinctly American flair for public relations.

He has performed original tribute songs for a motley assortment of public figures, including Sting, Jane Goodall, Carl Lewis,
Kofi Annan, and Quincy Jones, whose cryptic endorsement "Sri
Chinmoy is such a brave musician!" appears on posters promoting
the Guru's concerts. Besides Grammy winners and athletes, his disciples include Ashrita Furman, the manager of a Queens health-
food store, who has set 148 Guinness World Records — a meta-
record itself — most recently for backward bowling, egg-and-spoon
racing, and lemon eating. Photographs posted on Chinmoy's
official websites and displayed in the businesses operated by his
disciples show the Guru, whose philanthropic network the One-
ness-Heart-Tears-and-Smiles delivers medical supplies around the
globe, glad-handing a varsity roster of world leaders — Princess Di-
ana, Popes Paul VI and John Paul II, Mikhail Gorbachev, Mother
Teresa. Nelson Mandela once called him an "outstanding soldier of
peace."

In 1996, a district superintendent of the National Park Service
approved a plan to install a brass plaque in the lobby of the Statue
of Liberty that would officially designate the foremost icon of American democracy a Sri Chinmoy Peace Blossom site. Three hundred
or so spectators attended the unveiling on the Guru's sixty-fifth
birthday. Within a month, the Park Service reversed its decision,
and the plaque was removed, but similar plaques identify more
than nine hundred surviving Peace Blossoms around the world, including cultural centers (the Sydney Opera House), natural formations (the Matterhorn, the Great Barrier Reef), airports (Afonso
Pena in Curitiba, Brazil), and political frontiers (the entirety of the
Russia-Norway border). In 1994 the late king of Nepal officially
christened an unclimbed four-mile-high Himalayan peak "Sri
Chinmoy Peace Mountain."

I took to lunching a few blocks from the racecourse at Annam
Brahma restaurant, where footage of Sri Chinmoy's sundry exploits airs continuously on a wall-mounted television. In 1985, he
took up weightlifting; clips of the Guru hoisting all manner of ec-
centric burdens flashed across the screen while I sipped my *lassis*.
With the aid of a special scaffold, he calf-raised people,[5] cars, the
1,495 volumes of his collected poetry and prose.[6] It brought to
mind the omnipotence paradox: could God produce an oeuvre He
couldn't lift? The footage resembled one of those supplemental
tapes certain enterprising high school juniors append to their col-

lege applications. The Guru was a grind *and* a jock. He was the most prolific painter who ever lived. He had read poetry with Joyce Carol Oates and jammed with Carlos Santana. He claimed to have lifted 7,064 pounds and 7,040 pounds with his right and left arms, respectively. Not since Da Vinci had a single man been so well rounded.

Other videos were available for download on the Guru's websites. In one of them, the seventy-four-year-old Chinmoy purports to curl a 256-pound dumbbell. The weight rests on a platform above the Guru's left leg. He knits his face and hums. At the appointed moment, an assistant lowers the platform and the weight sits motionless on Chinmoy's leg. After ten seconds, the assistant replaces the platform, and the Guru smiles beatifically. The footage presented a kind of Rorschach test. Where some found proof of the existence of God, others saw an old man supporting a dumbbell on his knee. I showed the video to friends. "I don't get it," they said. "Did he lift the weight or not?" I kept silent. Here was the pertinent question. Once you answered, there was no turning back. For the moment, I preferred to live in a world of divine strongmen.

In six decades of professional footwork, Edward Payson Weston endured all manner of setbacks and injuries. He sprained ankles and toes. Fevers and stomach cramps dogged him, as well as creditors, who took advantage of his highly publicized walks to have him arrested for unpaid debts. Once he was shot in the leg. Always Weston rallied. On the seventh day of the walk that made his name, a pilgrimage from Boston to Washington, D.C., for Abraham Lincoln's 1861 inauguration, he broke for a predawn restorative of sandwiches. This proved a tactical mistake, saddling the pedestrian with chest pains, which he blamed on mustard. His companions noted:

> He stopped every quarter of a mile and sat down to sleep; was exceedingly irritable, which caused the whole party to have the blues, of the "darkest kind." Mr. Weston concludes to go back half a mile, to a public house and sleep. . . . He returns a few steps, when, suddenly throwing off his blanket, he exclaims: "*No, I won't go back!*" and, wheeling around, strikes into a four-mile gait.

Such theatrics, anticipating James Brown's stage show by a full century, typified Weston's spirit on the road. Some of the same mettle could be found in Jamaica, where ingrown nails on both of Pranab

Vladovic's big toes had become a topic of worried conversation. Slight and boyish, with close-cropped hair, Pranab sat on a massage table considering the problem. His feet looked like they had been dredged out of the East River — chalky white with a thick brownish discharge at the nail beds. "These are the cards you get," he announced with equanimity. A few disciples stood around the massage table while a podiatrist, sober and brusque in a tan nylon jacket and gray nylon pants, frowned at the suppurating digits. The diagnosis was bleak. If he left the nails intact, he explained, the infection might compromise the bone, and the toes would have to be removed. Pranab hugged his knees.

"Can he keep walking?" someone asked.

The question seemed to rattle the doctor. "That's his choice. I wouldn't do it. How much farther till he's done?"

"Two thousand miles." The distance unfurled like a carpet spanning from Queens to Juarez, Mexico. I winced a little at the sound of the figure. "You got no shot," the doctor said.

The race, however, had a physic all its own. "You get scared beforehand," Abichal had told me. "Your body gets scared. It's like stage fright. Like moving into a different realm." For two months, the high school and ball courts and the abutting stretch of parkway became a shrine. Did I know about ley lines? Abichal asked. The theory, as articulated in the 1920s by one Alfred Watkins (no relation), posits a system of arcane pathways linking megaliths, tors, and other craggy points across Britain, and possibly the world. Largely ignored by science, ley lines have enjoyed a colorful life in the hinterlands of paranormalism, championed to various ends by psychics, pagans, dowsers, UFOlogists, dime-store novelists, and a few Nazi cranks who attributed a network of *heilige Linien* or "holy lines" crisscrossing Europe to the ancient Teutons.

"There are rivers, superhighways of energy," Abichal told me, "and there are junctions where they meet." The junctions exert a spiritual tug. Stonehenge, for instance, or Sedona. "Sedona is a big energy vortex." So, too, the racecourse. "I get a good vibe here," he said, indicating a triangle of lawn behind the wrought-iron fencing of the high school. "It's open. It's green. There's some kind of energy vortex on this corner."

The Self-Transcendence runners being mostly European, July 4 went largely unremarked at the racecourse. The fields teemed with

men engaged in various team sports. Flags hung limp in the cooling air as Madhupran and Abichal strolled past, each brandishing a
Popsicle. A couple of Indian families spread blankets on the grassy
margin by the bleachers in Joe Austin Park, and chops on a clam-
shell barbecue threw gusts of meaty smoke into the paths of the
vegetarian runners. At dusk, Sri Chinmoy arrived in a white jeep to
dispense bananas.[7]

By moonlight, Joe Austin Park was a place of desolate beauty.
Traffic thrummed eastward undeterred, blanching the runners in
a wash of halogen beams. On 168th Street, a man watered his lawn
in the dark, while a few stray fireflies winked among the hedges of
Edison High. I was given to understand that miracles sometimes
visited Jamaica. A white woman in a sari told me that Sri Chinmoy
had cured her of lupus. The runners, too, had recovered from injury and illness. "Shin splints that would stop an ordinary runner
for weeks last only days," insisted one of the disciples, another
chiropractor, on loan from Chicago. "The will of the — if you allow me to say — soul conquers the will of the physical." Witness
Pranab, who clipped past me, murmuring into a dictaphone. He
had left the racecourse for two hours to have his toenails removed,
resuming the race at his usual pace as soon as he returned. "Now I
have to soak my toes," he said. "It's a little more work." His date
with the podiatrist's knife had cost him roughly eighteen miles.

Beyond the rooftops of Jamaica, the horizon throbbed with light,
as of a millenarian firestorm engulfing Manhattan. Now and then a
plume of colored sparks crested the tree line, Queens County's re-
joinder to the thirtieth annual Macy's Fireworks Spectacular with
Lionel Richie and the New York Pops. I decided to buy a proper
pair of running shoes.

"Without preparatory training . . . the most fatal injuries may be
committed in attempting pedestrian feats." Such was the counsel of
Beadle's Dime Hand-Book of Pedestrianism, published in 1867. On the
cover of the thirty-two-page tract, a man wearing a sporty hat and
gaiters trots across a sketchily rendered countryside. Mysteriously,
he carries a riding crop. "In a mind upset by literary study," the author urges, "the best plan, if practicable, is to give up the reading
and writing entirely, for a time." Duly warned, I toed the line by the
weathered scoreboard on Joe Austin Way at a minute to six.

Ribbons of peach and pink banded the eastern horizon, giving the sky the look of a novelty cocktail. At dawn, the scene here was somber. The racers sat glumly on folding chairs or stretched against trees. Many of them doctored their feet with balms and tapes. Sri Chinmoy had returned from a trip to the Far East bearing gifts for the runners, ceremonial white bandannas emblazoned with the bloody sun of the Japanese flag. A few tied these souvenirs around their foreheads. They looked a little like bandages on a company of outnumbered and ill-equipped soldiers marching to certain death. One of the race directors called us to attention and we stood together, observing a moment of silence rendered incomplete by traffic sounds. Then we were off.

The pace was leaden. After five hours of stasis the body of the multiday runner locks up like a rusty transmission. Madhupran alone advanced at his usual clip, lunging and working his arms like an animatronic cross-country skier. Within fifteen minutes he had lapped me. Sri Chinmoy visited the course at around 6:20, and his arrival had an immediate restorative effect on the disciples. Wearing a preppy pink-striped shirt, he circled the block three times in a blue Smart car, goosing little fanfares from the horn when he passed a group of racers. It was oddly exhilarating to see the Guru operate a car, particularly one he could have parked in a walk-in closet. The runners bowed their heads, touched their hearts, or waved, quickening their pace. "It's the same as if you like the author of a book and then you meet him in reality," a disciple explained. It was difficult to imagine John Updike inspiring this sort of reverence.

The Guru's drive-by was only the opening act in a morning lineup of music, poetry, and cheerleading. Two female choral groups staked out stretches of Abigail Adams Avenue, clapping and singing. Meanwhile, the sun had broken through the clouds, and commuters were tumbling groggily into cars to ford the Grand Central Parkway. When I'd asked her how she felt about Jamaica, Suprabha had told me, "If you use your imagination, you can feel as if you're running on a beautiful country road. You tune out the traffic, the motorcycles." Helmut, Madhupran's handler, echoed her advice. "This is the hardest race you can find. Very hard concrete. You should have it in your mind like an endless road. Don't see it as it is, a dirty sidewalk. You must have the fantasy to see it another way — you must see flowers, a beautiful forest with trees."

I tried to conjure these pastoral mirages as I ran. Here was the broad green sign directing motorists to Queens' Utopia Parkway. The same brown Honda had been parked outside Edison High for weeks. Eventually the summer school contingent straggled in, glassy-eyed and inured to the sight of nylon-clad wraiths hustling up the block. I wished one of the runners would tell me how to clear my mind of all this urban wrack. After a morning of continuous locomotion, my legs were confused. Each step reverberated up the tibiae, delivering an unhappy shock to my knees. My stomach, too, rebelled. To the aspiring pedestrian, *Beadle's* prescribed a midday smorgasbord of roast beef, mutton, partridge, pheasant, or venison, along with one or two potatoes. No other vegetable was permitted. Short on fresh game, I snacked on nectarines and granola. Even so, I spent a good deal of time locked in the piney, sauna-like seclusion of a Port-O-Let.

At around 1:30, I finished my forty-eighth circuit of the block, and a volunteer informed me that I had surpassed 26.2 miles. "You've run a marathon!" she announced. Was this my first? I admitted it was. She clapped her hands. I had transcended myself! Was I excited? My time of seven hours, twenty-five minutes left room for improvement, I felt. Nonetheless, I traded high-fives with a few of the runners, who received the news variously with bemusement or wide-eyed gravity. Remembering Pheidippides, I took care to hydrate. Self-transcendence aside, I didn't intend to die in a pair of red nylon shorts.

By nightfall, I was circling Edison High in a trance. The sign for Utopia Parkway shone inscrutably in the darkness, beckoning me eastward toward parts unknown. As if afflicted by a kind of anatomical Stockholm syndrome, my legs bore me clockwise of their own accord, and I had the idea I could keep plodding forever. I was wrong. Blisters ruptured on the soles of both my feet, and every step became a slog through molten glass.

I drove home at geriatric speeds, unsure I'd be able to work the brake pedal in case of emergency. On the advice of a disciple, I sat for a long time in a scalding bath of Epsom salt. I had made eighty circuits of the block for a cumulative distance of 43.904 miles — six miles short of the required daily minimum. My base nature wanted aspirin and 10,000 BTUs of air-conditioning. What did my true nature want? I couldn't say.

*

A sense of giddy anticipation attended Madhupran's final push on the morning of July 22. LANXESS had dispatched a coiffed and cheerful stringer, who sat in the van interrogating Helmut on the champion's progress and typing what I assumed was a press release on a laptop.

"If I want to say that his diet consisted of da, da, da — " she prompted.

"Rice, sweet potatoes, coconut milk," Helmut replied. "And he ate every day one honeydew. And dinkel bread. No wheat. So. Now comes my horse. Don't forget my horse."

Near the Port-O Lets, a violinist serenaded an empty swath of sports fields. By Madhupran's penultimate lap, the throng of acolytes, friends, and confused passersby at the racecourse numbered about two hundred. That morning, Sri Chinmoy had written three new compositions in honor of Madhupran's success. Xeroxed sheet music was handed out, and men and women gathered in scrums along Joe Austin Way to rehearse. A blue ribbon bearing the gold-embossed legend SELF-TRANSCENDENCE RACES was strung across the sidewalk opposite a gauntlet of camera-wielding disciples.

Madhupran accelerated through his final quarter-mile shouldering a victory flag fringed with gold tassels, each stride an object lesson in the kinetics of belief. He had knocked more than a day off his own world record. When he crossed the line, Sri Chinmoy led the crowd in a triumphal sing-along. "The champion of champions / Am I," proclaimed the chorus. "In God's limitless pride sky / I fly."

Like his many thousands of poems, the Guru's songs are nothing if not pithy. After the disciples repeated the first song several times, they proceeded to the next. "In the world's longest bravest distance run / Who waves the victory flag? / Madhupran! / Madhupran!" The Guru clapped a metronomic beat against his knee. Whenever the singers fell silent, he beckoned for more. The third song was the longest, and the most popular:

> I am the world's longest distance
> Daring and shattering runner
> My Supreme Lord's
> Sun-power Smile
> And his Moon-Bliss-Love
> Winner

Madhupran crooned along in his operatic baritone, clasping his plastic-sheathed bouquet like a beauty pageant winner. Sri Chinmoy dispensed vanilla creme cookies and individually wrapped Keebler Club & Cheddar Sandwich Crackers, and then he left. The crowd dispersed, and the runners who had quit circling the block to watch Madhupran enter the record books returned to the grind. Some had nine hundred miles ahead of them.

By the vans, an enterprising disciple scavenged for crumbs in an abandoned cardboard box. "They may be dregs," he said, smiling, "but they're the master's dregs." A kindly, heavyset Russian woman sat counting off laps. In the 1980s she had fled the "atheist state" of the Soviet Union for Texas, where she discovered transcendental meditation. Now she gazed mournfully up the block. She felt empty, she said. "It's always like this. You wait and wait for the event. Then in thirty minutes — it's history."

In the last days of July, the tempo of the race changed. Wind jostled the trees, while in the park a woman herded leaves with an electric blower. Endgame had arrived. Sometimes two runners reached 3,100 miles in a day. Each finish triggered music and applause, but the excitement of Madhupran's victory was never quite matched. We sang the Guru's songs again and again, like a touring cast of *Godspell* at the end of a fifty-city run.

The Self-Transcendence Race was supposed to end on August 1, but Sri Chinmoy granted a week's extension so the laggards could finish. The last miles would prove the cruelest. Scattered power outages had afflicted Queens. To conserve energy in the stupefying heat of August, government buildings set their thermostats at a balmy seventy-eight degrees, and the lights of Coney Island's totemic Parachute Jump went dark. So, too, NASDAQ's digital display in Times Square. Summer school was officially pronounced "optional." Mayor Bloomberg declared a heat emergency; later, the city would confirm a heat-related death toll of 140. I worried about the four runners still circling Joe Austin Park.

By day fifty-eight, deep red circles bloomed on Abichal's cheeks. "I think sometimes even the runners ask, 'What am I doing here?'" he confessed. Often he would orbit the block for hours without glimpsing another racer, a phenomenon he called "the dark side of the loop." At night he veered into the fence outside Edison High. He had numb toes and a strange vertiginous feeling, as if the ground were rolling beneath his feet. Sometimes he dreamed about the race. In the dreams somebody chased him around the block, or he was chasing someone else, he couldn't say which. He woke unrefreshed. "I just run all night," he said. "Round and round." The energy on the loop had changed. The race has a force, he explained, a power you feel at every level of your being. "Then when you cut the head off, it's gone."

Rathin Boulton from Australia crossed the finish line on August 7. He held his bouquet while a modest crowd sang and clapped. A few yards away the door of a white sedan hung open. Sri Chinmoy emerged wearing flip-flops, his striped shirt tucked into canary-yellow trunks, and made his halting way to the scoreboard.

Last year, Rathin had run 3,100 miles in fifty-six days, eleven hours. At the Guru's urging, one of the race directors read this figure aloud. Then he repeated Rathin's latest score of fifty-seven days and change. "This is — more?" the Guru asked.

There was nervous laughter from the gallery. Rathin had traveled 3,100 miles around a concrete block in Queens, but he had not transcended himself. The Guru sipped from a juice box while a disciple set up a microphone attached to a small public-address system. "How many years have you been on our path?" Chinmoy asked. "Ten years, Guru," Rathin answered. Chinmoy sat clutching his right knee, head bowed, as neighborhood kids passed by in jeans and baggy shorts. Then, in a warbling voice, he began to sing. *"Rathin, Rathin, Rathin, Rathin."* I had the impression he was composing this number on the spot. Heedless of the roaring planes overhead, the disciples joined in, timidly at first but with mounting conviction, until the Guru produced a box of vanilla cookies and called them to order. It was snack time.

Afterward he indulged in a little postprandial lecturing. I dutifully recorded what I could, but the very first sentence confounded me. "Once upon a time," the Guru said, and a siren drowned him out. Whole paragraphs were lost in the muddle of ambient street noise, giving his remarks a Dadaist quality. I heard the phrases "unimaginable joy" and "peace blossoms." Chinmoy acknowledged a man who had helped him organize a trip to New Zealand, where he had lifted a thousand sheep. His voice was breathy and sweet. "I am playing a flute for a kangaroo. My only audience is a kangaroo." He spoke at length about Lord Krishna, breaking off to quiz his disciples on their mastery of the Bhagavad-Gita. "In which chapter does Lord Krishna show his divine form to humans?" he asked. "Eleven," someone shouted. Wind buffeted the microphone. I made out the words "bodyguards" and "karate chop." Now and then the Guru paused for a bite of creme cookie, and sounds of mastication crackled from the PA. My notes resembled a collection of haikus. Finally, the Guru stood and waved, padded to the white sedan still idling at the curb, and was spirited away.

On the loop, Abichal offered some perspective. The mind likes to grasp things, he told me; this is its nature. But reality cannot be grasped. A true master addresses the heart. To do so, he must short-circuit the student's intellect, a process sometimes calling for "special techniques." He speaks indirectly, in riddles, coaxing the student toward a more receptive state. It made a certain sense, but half the time I'd found the Guru simply inaudible. Abichal nodded. "It's like that for a lot of people," he said.

"Even the disciples."

By the late 1880s, the pedestrian craze had cooled. "The public may occasionally lose its head," the *New York Times* concluded, "but it is unsafe to assume that it will do so more than once or twice in the same direction. It rushed to see Rowell trot over 500 miles of sawdust because long-distance pedestrianism was a new thing." Slave to the god of novelty, the great unwashed had forsaken distance footracing for such au courant conveyances as the bicycle and the roller skate. A century later, the pedestrian has wandered into cultural oblivion, his feats relegated to microfilm archives and a few out-of-print sports chronicles.[8]

Edward Payson Weston clung doggedly to fame well into his senescence, but an accident brought his career to an unceremonious end in 1927. His glory days behind him, the great pedestrian was broke, sharing a Greenwich Village flat, and begging for work in the pages of the *Times*. Eight days after he received a gift of $30,000 from Anne Nichols, author of the popular Broadway comedy *Abie's Irish Rose*, Weston was pasted in the streets of New York by a taxicab. He was eighty-eight years old. For decades he had railed against the evils of the motorcar, an invention for loafers and slobs. Weston spent the balance of his life confined to a wheelchair. The age of pedestrians was dead.

*

I returned the next day to watch Abichal cross the finish line. The heat wave had broken, and he circled the block with a look of resignation. He would finish a week later than he'd hoped. "I feel joy," he said, but I couldn't shake the sense that past races had meant more to Abichal. As we walked against the stream of traffic on the parkway, he told me about a particularly grueling race he'd run a few years back. "I was so looking forward to the end. Dying, dying, dying. Then on the last lap — it all fell away." He made a little magician's flourish with his hand. "What I thought would be the goal just vanished, like a mirage. There was no goal. It didn't exist. I realized that my mind had been playing this trick. It was just another lap, same as all the other laps." This summer, Abichal had not transcended himself in precisely the way he'd imagined, but he would run again.

As we neared the diminished Base Camp with its skeleton crew of volunteers, Abichal's thoughts turned to the future of his sport. There was an upcoming 1,200-K in Germany, the Deutschlandlauf; 2006 would see new six- and seven-day races in France and Greece. A note of hope entered his voice. "They said the marathon was impossible. Now hundreds of thousands run them. Maybe this is it."

At 10:20 P.M., a few disciples gave up tossing a Frisbee to watch Abichal embark on his final lap. Someone had arranged two long files of tea candles leading to the finish line — the lights of Coldplay's "Fix You," come to guide him home. A bicycle horn bleated in the dark, and we called his name as he lumbered eastward bearing the Self-Transcendence banner in one hand and the Red Dragon of Wales in the other. An unexpected knot formed in my throat as Abichal walked gingerly across the line and accepted his flowers. After the usual singing, Abichal sat with a cake in his lap, while friends filed past to shake his hand, and then we stood in silence. Altogether, the turnout was about a quarter the size of Madhupran's. "Speech," somebody called. The brake lights of a passing car flashed, and a mild electrical current passed through the crowd. "Guru," came a whisper behind me. There was a collective turning of heads. "Guru's here?" "Abichal, I think Guru's here." But the car sped down the block. Pink and blue balloons joggled above Abichal's bowed head. His time was fifty-eight days, sixteen hours, twenty-two minutes, three seconds.

*

The next week Abichal met me for lunch at Smile of the Beyond, a vegetarian diner managed by one of the race directors. Suprabha had crossed the finish line the previous Thursday, and now the racecourse was empty. Some of the runners had already returned to the jobs they had left behind in their home countries. Others planned to hang around Jamaica for the Guru's seventy-fifth birthday party at the end of the month. The previous year, he had celebrated with a solo concert performance on seventy-four pianos. It would be difficult to top.

Abichal showed up twenty minutes late, his hair newly trimmed to a boyish wiffle — most likely at Perfection in the Head-World, the disciple-operated barbershop down the street. He looked ten years younger, but he walked on the legs of a senior citizen. It was strange to see Abichal in a restaurant. In the seven weeks I'd known him, I had almost never caught him sitting. Now that the struggle was past, he said, he felt a constant sense of freedom. The race was like a weight he'd been carrying for months. He was relieved: not physically — although his body was recovering — but psychically. He intended to edit a poetry anthology. There was also his magazine and website. In December he would fly to Arizona to run Across the Years, the race that killed a man in 2004. He hadn't decided whether he would return to Jamaica next June. "Have to wait and see," he said. On a television screen in the corner, Sri Chinmoy lifted an airplane.

After lunch, Abichal offered to walk with me to the racecourse. His thoughts followed a meandering path. "For many of us, the mind is limited," he said. "It's useful, we need to use it, but it grasps at bits. Then it uses those bits to form a picture and acts as if the picture is reality." We lingered at the verge of the racecourse. He looked mistily at a trash can heaped with ice cream wrappers and soda cans. "I still feel a connection to this bin. Sometimes it would be full to overflowing. Sometimes somebody would dump a big bag in." Abichal squinted up at the clouds. The light was different now, he said. The race starts just a week before the summer solstice, when the days are at their longest. We fell into a natural orbit around the block. "It's all the same," Abichal said. He pointed out features of the loop like a docent leading a cathedral tour. "Same bins, same cracks in the sidewalk." He nodded at a sapling by the high school. "This oak tree replaced a birch that was here a few years ago. You know what lives where. Blue flowers live at this corner. And a flower called a scarlet pimpernel, and yellow clover. This pine tree lives here. And little red flowers too." Abichal crouched down to show me. Somebody had tossed an empty Newport box in the grass, alongside a foil printed with the words BOMB BAG. The flowers were minuscule, each blossom the size of a Q-Tip. "There's still something here. I can feel my echo. Some trace of the experience." Abichal rounded the corner. "This is where the course flattens out. Now it starts to rise gently. In the past sometimes, I'd get a burst of energy here. You feel that you can run forever."

Notes

1. The fifty-year-old proprietor of the Washington, D.C., gift shop Transcendence-Perfection-Bliss of the Beyond, Beckjord is the only female competitor in the race's history and the only ten-time participant, having returned to Jamaica every June since the inaugural running. She has logged enough miles around Edison High to circle the equator.

2. The ultramarathon (any race exceeding 26.22 miles), which attracts a smaller and more fanatical community of athletes, gained brief notoriety in January 2004 when a member of the Colorado running cult Divine Madness banked 207 miles in the forty-eight-hour race Across the Years and then dropped dead. Further afield, the "Marathon Monks" of Japan's Mount Hiei have practiced spiritual running in a ritual that dates to the eighth century. At the culmination of seven years of training, the aspirant logs two back-to-back marathons per night for three months, carrying a length of rope and a knife so that he can hang or disembowel himself if he fails to complete a run.

3. The music critic Robert Christgau describes its artwork thus: "On the back cover is a photograph of three men. Two of them are dressed in white and have their hands folded — one grinning like Alfred E. Neuman, the other looking like he's about to have a Supreme Court case named after him: solemn, his wrists ready for the cuffs. In between, a man in an orange ski jacket and red pants with one white sock seems to have caught his tongue on his lower lip. He looks like the yoga coach at a fashionable lunatic asylum. Guess which one is Sri Chinmoy."

4. The 3,100-mile distance of the Self-Transcendence Race celebrates Chinmoy's birth year; an earlier incarnation, held in 1996, measured 2,700 miles, in honor of his birthday.

5. Since 1988, when he launched his "Lifting Up the World with a

Oneness-Heart" campaign, Chinmoy has ceremonially hoisted more than seven thousand friends and celebrities, including Jesse Jackson; Cambodian Prime Minister Samdech Hun San; Ravi Shankar; Moorhead Kennedy, held hostage 444 days in Iran; Mickey Thomas, lead vocalist of Jefferson Starship; and the actresses Mercedes Ruehl and Alyssa Milano.

6. A selection of titles from the Chinmoy library attests to the breadth of the Guru's interests: *The Earth-Illumination-Trumpets of Divinity's Home, Part 1; I Play Tennis Every Day; The Ambition-Deer; Einstein: Scientist-Sage, Brother of Atom-Universe; Impurity: The Mad Elephant Mental Asylum; A Soulful Tribute to the Secretary-General: The Pilot Supreme of the United Nations; God Wants to Read This Book; Great Indian Meals: Divinely Delicious and Supremely Nourishing; Gorbachev: The Master-Key of the Universal Heart; Muhammad Ali and Sri Chinmoy Meditate; Come, My Non-English Friends! Let Us Together Climb Up the English Himalayas; The Mushroom and the Umbrella; My Heart's Salutation to Australia; A Mystic Journey in the Weightlifting World, Part 1; Airport Elevation: Questions Answered by Master Sri Chinmoy at the San Juan International Airport, October 29, 1976; I Love Shopping, Part 1; My Ivy League Leaves: Lectures on the Spiritual Life; Niagara Falls Versus Children's Rise; Religion-Jugglery and God-Discovery; The Sailor and the Parrot; War: Man's Abysmal Abyss-Plunge, Part 1; Sleep: Death's Little Sister; Canada Aspires, Canada Receives, Canada Achieves; Yes, I Can! I Certainly Can!!*

7. The offering of sanctified food — called *prasad* — sometimes flummoxed visitors to the racecourse, as in late July, when the Guru made an offering of Granny Smith apples to a pair of emissaries from Russian TV. The reporter accepted with telegenic diplomacy, but the cameraman froze, plying his camera like a rifle trained on a buck. An hour later, both apples lay uneaten on a table cluttered with audiovisual equipment.

8. Notably John Cumming's *Runners and Walkers* and *Ultramarathoning: The Next Challenge* by Tom Osler and Ed Dodd.

MIKE SAGER

Scito Hoc Super Omnia

FROM ESQUIRE

FOUR MILES EAST OF Las Vegas Boulevard, well beyond the glitter of the Strip, the Valley High School gym is cool and humid, redolent of floor wax and old socks. The ball pounds on the polished hardwood, the sound echoes off the familiar glazed concrete blocks that form the inner walls. Sneakers squeak. Voices rise and fall, curses and laughter. There is high tragedy and low comedy, often displayed on the same face split seconds apart. There are no fans, no sportswriters. There is no trash talk, no ego, no dispute. There is nothing but this court, this play, these men, this ball — this peculiar ball, the usual orangey brown, only this one dressed up with the two white rings of international play — as it traces a high arcing parabola through the air, meanwhile rotating sweetly backward, a shot born of the countless other shots that have preceded it, hundreds of thousands of shots, perhaps millions taken and made over years and years of solitary practice in gyms and driveways and playgrounds from Italy to Philadelphia . . .

Kobe Bryant bobs in place on the balls of his feet, holding his pose, frozen for a split second in his red-white-and-blue Zoom Kobe II's, his impossibly long and Pilates-sculpted arm, bark brown and moist and smelling of complimentary hotel lotion, still extended overhead like a kid raising his hand in class. The names of his daughters, Natalia Diamante and Gianna Maria-Onore — which he pronounces with the proper Italian inflections, the *t* in Natalia more of a hardened *th* sound, the *r* rolled in Maria, a bit jarring against the contrast of his usual dialect, a somewhat put-on version of hip-hop (from age six to thirteen, he lived in Italy, where his father was a pro basketball player; later they moved to Wynnewood, an affluent suburb of Philadelphia) — are tattooed on the meat of his forearm, which is now facing the basket, his wrist still holding its perfect gooseneck follow-through, a gesture at once delicate and strong, like something from ballet, and so essential, adding as it does the ball's backward rotation, the so-called shooter's touch, which acts as a damper around the rim, helping to ensure that the nine-and-a-half-inch-diameter ball will fall with greater frequency into the eighteen-inch-diameter hole.

A few years ago, Kobe fractured the fourth metacarpal bone in his right hand. He missed the first fifteen games of the season; he used the opportunity to learn to shoot jump shots with his left, which he has been known to do in games. While it was healing, the ring finger, the one just adjacent to the break, spent a lot of time taped to his pinkie. In the end, Kobe discovered, his four fingers were no longer evenly spaced; now they were separated, two and two. As a result, his touch on the ball was different, his shooting percentage went down. Studying the film, he noticed that his shots were rotating slightly to the right.

To correct the flaw, Kobe went to the gym over the summer and made one hundred thousand shots. That's one hundred thousand *made,* not taken. He doesn't practice taking shots, he explains. He practices making them. If you're clear on the difference between the two ideas, you can start drawing a bead on Kobe Bryant, who may well be one of the most misunderstood figures in sports today. It is a tragic misunderstanding, for his sake and for ours. You can blame it on the press. You can blame it on the way the world revolves around fame and money. You can blame it on Kobe himself.

Having just celebrated his twenty-ninth birthday, Kobe is about to begin his twelfth season in the NBA. Lately, somewhat grudgingly, people are beginning to acknowledge him as the greatest all-around player still active in the game, mentioned as a peer of Wilt Chamberlain, Larry Bird, and Michael Jordan. This year, Kobe will make upwards of $45 million from salary, endorsements, and business ventures. He is constantly in the news, usually on the wrong side of public favor as he continues to play for a once glorious team, the Los Angeles Lakers, that simply doesn't have the manpower right now to will itself into contention. Spending five days with Kobe — a dozen hours, really, spread over five days — is to glimpse the life of a highly skilled craftsman. He sees his work as his art, his calling. Like Jason Bourne and James Bond, two of his cinematic heroes, Kobe sees himself as an über-practitioner: a modern warrior able to solve any problem, able to train his way into dominance. He is the self-styled black mamba, known for its striking ability, aggression, and speed. All those sweaty commercials for Sprite and Nike? Those were his idea. Film my workout, he suggested. That is the essence of me: the guy who guts it out on every rep. Kobe's logo, which you will hear more about in the coming years, is called the Sheath. It is drawn to resemble the sheath of a samurai's sword. The sword is the raw talent, Kobe explains. The sheath is the package it's kept in — everything you go through, your calluses and your baggage, what you learn.

"*Scito hoc super omnia. . . . Tempus neminem non manet. . . . Carpe diem,*" he proclaims in Latin (which he learned in elementary school in Italy) on the home page of his website, KB24.com. "Know this above all else. . . . Fully use every point, moment, and hour that you have. Time waits for no man. . . . Seize the day." He wakes at 5:30 in the morning to work out. He eats five times a day, a special diet, stressing not just the ingredients but the way they're cooked. He studies tape of past, present, and world players with the curiosity of a scientist in the lab. (As a kid, he used to study bubble-gum basketball cards in order to see which moves the players were showcasing and "which of their muscles were firing to make the move happen.") He can look at a random still photo of himself making a particular shot from a game and tell you exactly when and where and what happened. He has spent hours at a time chasing tennis balls along the floor, running the same patterns again and again on an empty court to get his cuts right for the triangle offense, running steps, running suicides, running distance. After his first season as a pro, when he was the Lakers' sixth man, his summer workouts stressed ways to keep himself mentally involved in the game so he could come off the bench ready to contribute. Before Phil Jackson was ever even mentioned as a possible coach, Kobe contacted Tex Winter, the godfather of the triangle offense, to discuss the intricacies of the play — just because he was a student of the game and wanted to learn *everything*. In his first season without Shaq, he added fifteen pounds of muscle to handle the heavier workload he expected. This summer, he lost eighteen pounds, partially due to his need to watch his cholesterol (a family history of diabetes and heart disease) and partially to take some strain off his body in general and his knees in particular, which have been operated on several times, once in Colorado, an ill-fated trip undertaken with life-altering results.

According to his specifications, Kobe's shoes have been designed with a special alloy band inside the arch to cut, he believes, hundredths of a second off his reaction time. For the same reason, he's asked Nike to design a sock-and-shoe system, maybe something like pro soccer players have. That fraction of a second he loses when his foot slides inside the shoe is the time it takes him to blow by a defender, he says. When he ices his knees, he ices the backs as well as the fronts, something that is usually overlooked because it takes longer. He has also asked Nike to design a new kind of warm-up that will wick heat away from his knees and thus enhance recovery time; recovery time, he says with conviction, is the most important element of working out.

With one ball and one rebounder, shooting his usual 80 to 90 percent in practice (with no defender), Kobe can make five hundred shots in about sixty minutes. Last year, as a result of all that practice, all those hundreds of thousands of makes, Kobe scored at least fifty points in four consecutive games and led the league in scoring. Two years ago, he turned in an electrifying eighty-one-point performance at home against Toronto, the second-highest total on record, after seven-footer Wilt Chamberlain's hundred-point game, all of which came from within fifteen feet of the basket. The reaction to Kobe and his achievements has been puzzling, as it has been since the beginning of his career, when he was voted into the All-Star game as a second-year player (he was the sixth man on the Lakers at the time), and then criticized for inciting an electric duel with the reigning king, Michael Jordan. Perhaps no figure in NBA history has been at once more loved and more reviled than Kobe Bryant.

Now, in the gym, the ball arcs perfectly through the rim and ripples the bottom of the net with a distinctive, thrilling swish. The moment is unfrozen; time moves on. Kobe nods his head once, almost imperceptibly, as if to say, *That's what I'm talkin' about,* an expression he uses with exuberance when he's in private, when something catches his fancy, when something he believes is borne out. A picture of Kobe seldom seen: his perfect white teeth bared in the large carefree smile of a young man who loves watermelon and those yummy ice cream Kahlúa drinks he and his wife had the other night for dessert at the restaurant in Las Vegas before seeing the show *Kà*, and who is lately in love with the Harry Potter series, which he read at a breakneck pace, trying to beat out his wife, the first books he's read since twelfth grade, when he became obsessed with the sci-fi thriller *Ender's Game*, about a boy who suffers greatly from isolation and rivalry but ultimately saves the planet.

The doorbell chimes musically. Kobe and his party have arrived, a contained but complex weather system of youthful energy and expensive perfume.

Leading the way is the bodyguard, Rico, a soft-spoken man of unremarkable size, a former LAPD SWAT-team member with a background in martial arts. It is said that Rico (his first name is Cameron; nobody thinks it fits) is trained to hold off a surging crowd long enough for Kobe to get to safety. In a few days, Kobe will be off on a Nike-sponsored tour of Asia, six cities in seven days, where his apparel sells through at almost twice the normal rate and where surging crowds are actually a threat. Worldwide, Kobe apparel outsells that of all other NBA players: the undisputed fact of his statistical dominance seems to outweigh the perceived negatives of his personal history — the aloofness and selfishness of his early career, the Colorado sexual-assault case that was dropped by prosecutors and the civil suit that was settled out of court, his pissing match with America's beloved clown-giant Shaquille O'Neal, his on-again, off-again insistence on being traded from the Lakers.

Jerry Sawyer is Kobe's marketing manager, six-foot-two with Malcolm X–style black-frame glasses and an enviable collection of vintage sneakers. His father managed boxers; one of them was Leon Spinks. Jerry carries two different communications devices in the pockets of his oversized shorts. He's one of the four pillars of Zambezi Ink, Kobe's mixed-media ad agency. Like record labels owned by rappers, Zambezi is Kobe's attempt to harness the means of production. Jerry also does a lot of other things for Kobe, from screening press contacts (like me) to dealing with charitable causes, like the After-School All-Stars, an enrichment program for needy kids

in L.A., which we visited together one day with the predictable up-
roar (snapshot: a large cooking class of middle-school-aged black
and Latina girls learning to make potato salad, wearing hairnets
and plastic gloves and holding knives, screeching at the top of their
lungs). Jerry was also charged with making sure that Kobe's black-
and-white polka-dot polyester sport coat, custom-made for him by
Gucci (as are many of his clothes — he sits at the dining-room table
with his wife and chooses swatches), was pressed and delivered for
this photo shoot, which is finally about to happen in this borrowed
suite in the Wynn Tower on the Strip in Las Vegas, where Kobe is
playing in a summer tournament with the U.S. National Team, attempting to qualify for the Beijing Olympics. The Wynn is booked
solid the entire month with basketball royalty.

Clutching tight to Kobe's hand is the former Vanessa Urbieta
Cornejo Laine, twenty-five, she of the infamous $4 million purple
makeup diamond. Kobe met Vanessa — and her mother, who was
along as chaperone — on the set of a video shoot for his rap album, an experiment in cross-marketing that came and went with
little fanfare. (Note: Try Googling the lyrics of "K.O.B.E.," performed in duet with the model and TV personality Tyra Banks.) At
the time, Vanessa was still a seventeen-year-old high school junior.
Kobe himself was only twenty-one, a four-year veteran of the NBA.
(You will recall, perhaps, that he took the pop singer Brandy to his
own senior prom.) Criticized early in his career for holding himself
separate from his teammates — while they were playing cards, going to clubs, and discussing child-support payments, Kobe was playing pay-per-view Nintendo and ordering room service — Vanessa
seemed more his speed. A sheltered Catholic girl from Orange
County, she was as close to her family as he was to his; after residing
with her own parents for two years, Kobe had only recently started
living on his own. Vanessa had been discovered outside a hip-hop
concert by a music producer and had recently begun booking jobs
as a dancer and an extra. Kobe tells me unabashedly that when he
met her, it was love at first sight. They've been together every possible moment since. The first week, he flooded the administrative office at her high school with flowers for her; he'd pick her up after
the bell in his big black Mercedes, causing a stampede of lookie-
loos.

Vanessa's dark beauty and silken coal-black hair bring to mind the kind of idealized Mexicana frequently seen in tattoos sported by Latino gangbangers. She is known by some as Kobe's Yoko. I have seen her, purring and demure, at Kobe's side in her four-inch heels, her makeup and wardrobe obviously the work of someone with ample time and money on her hands, bringing to mind the image of a tower-kept princess before her mirror, primped to the last eyelash, the last curl, the last bangle. In public, she patiently endures the endless cell-phone pictures taken by all comers, who seem to be lying in wait around every corner, all the time, graciously thanking each and every person who comments on her looks: *You're so very kind*, she will say, her smile royal and Splenda sweet, *thank you so very much*. And I have seen her go *off* — off like a mother bear, like a cornered cat, like a streetwalker on D.C.'s notorious Fourteenth Street strip, zero to sixty in a snap of her manicured fingers, hurling a string of expletives outside the Lakers' dressing room at a fat guy who she perceived had been looking at her daughter in an inappropriate fashion. She might well own the record for the most *motherfuckers* in one sentence.

Kobe calls her "Mamacita." He holds her hand everywhere they go. Sometimes he speaks to her in Spanish. Later this afternoon, when his fruit plate finally arrives, Kobe will ask her: "Quieres un poquito de fruta, Mamacita?" Kobe and Vanessa are teaching their kids Spanish and English. Sometimes, Kobe throws in some Italian too. He'll say *mangia*, for instance, telling them to eat. Natalia, four, known as Nani, will look at him like he's crazy. "You're not saying the *Spanish* word, Daddy," she will chide. Nani, of course, is tall for her age. Kobe's older sister, with whom he is very close, is six-two. Kobe's mother, Pam, as long as we're doing this, is five-ten. His father is six-nine. Joseph Washington "Jellybean" Bryant, a product of Philly and La Salle University, left school early for the NBA through the "hardship draft," after showing financial need. He was nicknamed for his love of sweets. (He named his son after the pampered Japanese beef: Kobe Bean Bryant.) The rap on Joe is that Kobe didn't get his work ethic from Joe's side of the family. Joe was known as a showboat. He played eight years in the NBA, four with his hometown Philadelphia 76ers, who stuck him under the basket in their old-school, East Coast offense. Jellybean thought of himself as more of a Magic Johnson–type player who was being held back from greatness. In Italy, he became the player he dreamed of being, high-scoring (he had two fifty-plus-point games) and beloved; Kobe remembers the fans singing songs about his dad. When Kobe was a toddler, he'd put on his little Sixers uniform and watch his dad on television. Kobe would pretend to play in the game, mimicking his dad's moves, taking time-outs for water when the team did. As Kobe got older, he would end up playing for the same Italian club team as his dad, only in a younger division, wearing the exact same game uniform for real. Frequently, Joe would bring Kobe to his own practices. At age eleven, a team from Bologna tried to buy him from his parents. By thirteen, Kobe was beating his dad's teammates one-on-one. Kobe's daughter is athletic, he can already tell. Nani is playing soccer, a game Kobe still loves. (He picked his USA-team number, 10, because it was the number of his favorite soccer players — Pelé, Maradona, Ronaldinho.) Usually, when he plays games with Nani — the younger, nicknamed Gigi, is only eighteen months — Kobe lets her win. Occasionally, he goes ahead and beats her at something. He's noticed she plays a lot harder the next time around. His daughters' all-time favorite game is something called Tickle Man. As you might expect, it involves Daddy.

This weekend, with the Tickle Man in Vegas playing his own big-boy game and Mamacita here to keep him company, the girls are being watched by Vanessa's mom at their big house in guard-gated Ocean Ridge, near Newport Beach, California. The couple has lived there since their marriage in 2001. It is not publicly known whether it is still decorated, as was earlier reported, with his *Star Wars* memorabilia and her Disneyana. Presumably, it is big, with a lot of kids' stuff everywhere. The Bryants do not employ a nanny.

After much discussion, the photographer, Nigel Parry, an affable Brit known for his stunning black-and-white pictures, has managed to secure this suite for a photo session. Once the date was set, Jerry e-mailed *Esquire*'s photo editor, saying that Kobe needed to have his own stylist for the shoot and that Vanessa Bryant would fill that role. *Esquire* assented, offering Vanessa its standard $250. Jerry countered with a request for "a more typical" rate somewhat higher. After a bit more back-and-forth, a compromise was happily achieved.

Now, upon arriving in the suite and making everyone's acquaintance, Kobe and his crew set about ordering the aforementioned fruit platter. Vanessa — who has asked to be identified as Lady V in the photo credits — dives right in, voicing her concern with Nigel about his choice of black and white for the photos. As it happens, she has picked out a wardrobe of black-and-white clothes — prints on prints, everything from the Gucci to the size-16 lizard-skin shoes — all of it to be dramatically offset by the red paisley on a Neiman Marcus one-hundredth-anniversary tie. "The brown seamless has gotta go too," she tells Nigel, referring to the backdrop that he and his three assistants have so painstakingly raised. She turns and addresses her husband. "Kobe," she demands, "did you know it was going to be black and white?"

For one long moment, the room becomes very still. All eyes are turned toward the big man. At six-six and 207, he dwarfs most of us by nearly a foot. On the court, however, with the rest of his USA teammates, huge specimens like LeBron James and Dwight Howard, he appears small and wiry, almost delicate.

Kobe looks at his wife intently with his exotic, almond-shaped eyes. "I didn't know that," he says. "I did not know that."

"It needs to be color," she says with conviction. "Otherwise, we can't see the *red* in the tie."

"Can you shoot both?" Kobe asks Nigel.

"We can shoot both," Nigel says.

"You do *have* color, right?" Lady V asks, not convinced.

"Ain't no big deal," Kobe says, sweet but preemptively, raising his chin, exposing the large escarpment of his Adam's apple just beneath. "It's all good."

And so it is. With help from Vanessa and Jerry, Kobe gets dressed and into a seated position. Nigel and his assistants go to work, the flash popping, followed by the electric whine of the recharger. Lady V chooses a couch off to the side. I stand next to her, so as to be close.

"That looks really sexy," she says.

"I only have two facial expressions," Kobe muses.

Pop. Whine.

"Smiling Kobe and Intense Kobe."

"Look smack-dead onto me," Nigel says. "Bring your eyes down."

Pop. Whine.

"Not so fierce," says Vanessa.

"Fierce is good," says Nigel. "I like fierce."

"He's fierce in every photo! A little softer."

"She don't want me to be intense all the time," Kobe explains.

"Yeah — it's the same picture in every magazine. And at Nike. I love when he smiles."

"We're changin' it up over at Nike this time around," Kobe says. Yesterday, he had a meeting with Nike designers, his player rep, and his agent, Rob Pelinka, who played college ball with the NCAA Division I–champion Michigan Wolverines — on the same team as the Fab Five. (He was open on the wing at the moment Chris Webber called the fateful illegal time-out, or so the story goes.) At the meeting, they previewed Kobe's new fall line of apparel. Per his suggestion, it had a retro, old-school theme, circa *Yo! MTV Raps.*

"You should see these shirts they made," he tells his wife. "One of 'em looks like it comes with a complimentary *bong!*"

"Yeah?" she says, a little unsure.

"It's got some pink-and-green checkerboard and shit." Big smile.

"That's it," says Nigel. "That's awesome. You *do* have a great smile."

"This is the Kool-Aid smile," Kobe says, adjusting the jelly-bean-sized ruby he is wearing as a solitaire in his left ear.

"*Awwww,*" Vanessa coos. "That's like the pictures we have at home. I love it when he smiles." The look on her face says that she has just been smitten all over again by her man.

"By the way," Kobe says, "they made me a pink tracksuit."

"Oh no, they did *not,*" exclaims Vanessa, her tone straight out of the OC, her head swiveling on her neck.

A deep voice, singing: "Oh yes, they *did.*"

"What *shade* of pink?" she challenges.

"I don't know. Pink. Dusty pink."

"Like mauve? Or like bubble gum?"

"Bubble gum," he declares, enjoying the game. The Nike rep had sold it to him as "a dusty gray-pink." He flashes a huge and untroubled smile.

"That's nice, excellent," Nigel says. *Pop. Whine.* "Now: no smile. Intense."

"Like when you're looking at Nani and Gigi," Vanessa says.

"But I can't help smiling when I look at them."

"Like when you're fixing one of their boo-boos."

"That's right." says Nigel. *Pop. Whine.*

"I forgot to tell you," Vanessa says. "Nani spilled some Kool-Aid on the couch today. She told me when I called. She said, 'Mami, I have to tell you something. Grandma gave me Kool-Aid and I spilt it on your couch.'"

"The white couch?"

"My mom says she got it out 'cause she was quick. My mom was like, 'I *told* her not to' — you know, she's not allowed to take any juice in there. But give her credit. Nani told me herself what she did, thank God. I'm like, 'I appreciate your honesty, Nani. Don't do it again.'"

"I wish they were here, man," Kobe says wistfully. "They'd be running around this whole place. Nani is such a poser," he tells Nigel proudly.

"Yeah?" Nigel asks, a bit distracted. It's easier to take portraits when people aren't talking so much.

"She'll do a million different poses for you," Kobe says.

"That's nice," Nigel says. *Pop. Whine.* "Would you mind taking your jacket off?"

"Nope," Kobe says.

"Nope," Lady V reiterates.

"Huh?" Nigel asks, taken aback. He looks from Kobe to Lady V and back again.

"No go," confirms Kobe, command tone. He cuts his eyes to his wife, who nods her head once, almost imperceptibly, as if to say, *That's what I'm talkin' about.*

And then the doorbell chimes musically. The fruit plate has finally arrived.

Kobe's suite, the thirtieth floor. Mamacita is gone, whether out shopping or gambling or back home with the girls it is not for me to know. He drags a barstool over to the living room, where there are two sofas and a coffee table, so as not to have to bend his knees so acutely when he sits down. "Ain't gettin' any younger," he explains.

Yesterday, a Sunday with no scheduled Team USA practice, Kobe went to the gym and made five hundred shots. With two balls and two rebounders, he managed to do it in one hour, stopping only long enough to chat with Indiana's legendary coach Bobby Knight. They'd never met before; Kobe was overjoyed — by all accounts, he looked like a kid meeting Kobe for the first time. Then last night, in another Tower suite, he spent two hours signing nine hundred autographs for Upper Deck — a feat made all the more difficult by the heavy "camera pen" that documents the execution of each numbered signature. (Among the items offered: a limited edition of 124 Kobe-inscribed laser-engraved basketballs for $699.99 each.) This morning, he was supposed to be up early working out and doing Pilates, but he canceled.

"You get to a point where you learn to listen to your body and make adjustments from there," he explains. He speaks of his physical self in terms of a finely tuned machine, which of course it is.

I sit on the sofa. He is on the barstool. It is awkward; I feel like I'm sitting at the feet of the Lincoln Memorial. I drag another barstool over to the living room. Now I feel like I'm doing a talk show, with Rico the bodyguard as our audience, sitting quietly in a corner. Kobe is warm and chatty. I've been around awhile, he has become accustomed to me — though I was still not allowed to ride in a car with him or to be with him alone or to spend any unstructured time with him at all. But at least now he's *feelin'* me, as they say in the L. The other day, at the photo shoot, by way of jocular greeting, Kobe's big open palm suddenly whipped down from on high and slapped me pretty hard in the solar plexus. "What up, Mikey?" he said playfully. Luckily, I flexed in time to avoid getting the wind knocked out of me.

For the next ninety minutes, we talk. About how he loves sharks and would like to go down in a shark cage, how he would like to skydive — both of which after he retires. How he grew so fast as an adolescent, he had horrible Osgood-Schlatter disease — so bad, it hurt when someone even breathed on his knees. How he just bought an Akita to go with his two Pomeranians and how having untrained dogs should be a crime, like a form of parental abuse. How Michael Jordan has become a confidant and how his advice "is like getting advice from that Buddha that sits on the top of the mountain, who has everything figured out and passes on some of his knowledge to the next guy who's trying to climb that mountain." How awed he felt one time in Taiwan in this big arena with five thousand screaming kids who had come just to see him run a little clinic. He remembers standing there thinking, *This is weird. This is just insane. I'm goofy. I'm silly. I play basketball.*

We talk about the philosophy of his logo, the Sheath. We talk a bit about baggage, how it's the place you store your energy. About his image in the league, how he got off to a bad start and never recovered. "When I first came into the NBA," he says, "I was one of the first to come out of high school. I was seventeen years old — at the time the NBA was much more grown-up. It wasn't like now. I thought that you come into the NBA, you play basketball all day. The thing I was most excited about was coming to the NBA not having to, you know, not having to worry about writing a paper or doing homework. It was basketball all day, this is awesome.

"The aloofness thing, honestly, I didn't really hear about it until later. A lot of it was just naive, because I didn't read the papers. I didn't watch, like, the news. I had no clue what was going on, what people were saying about me. It sounds silly to say, but it's true. And I think because of that, a lot of people looked at it like, '*Whoa*, he must be arrogant.' But I didn't know what the hell was going on. I had a reporter one day come up to me and ask me about it, you know, 'People think you're arrogant, what's up with that?' And it absolutely just seemed to come out of left field. I was just like, 'What are you talking about?' And he was like, 'Haven't you read the papers?' From that day forward, I started reading the papers."

I ask him about Colorado. He starts to say something and then he stops himself, like maybe he wants to talk but knows he shouldn't. I push him a little bit. He laughs and shakes his head. "I'm not sure I can dive into that one without really *diving* into that one."

"Can you dive into some of it?" I ask.

There is a long silence.

"I . . . uh . . . hum," he says. "I don't know how to touch on that without really sayin' — you know what I'm sayin'?"

What about the whole thing with Shaq, about the whole thing with wanting to be traded from the Lakers?

"If I had to do it all over again, I just never would have said *any-thing* in the press," he says. "Some things need to remain behind closed doors. Do the fans really need to know everything? Do you need to know everything about what goes on in your neighbor's house? Do you even *want* to?

"I just want to continue to push. To just become as good as I possibly can be, to see what other aspects of the game I can get better at. 'Cuz you know, it's fun. I just enjoy doing it, so when you enjoy doing it, you wanna find out new ways to do it. Like the eighty-one game? I had worked extremely hard the summer before that. That game was a culmination of days and days of hard work.

"The thing about that game — and I know it's going in the history books and all that — the best thing about that game is it feels good because we won. It was a tough one. We had lost, like, two or three games in a row; it was just a rough patch. And it was my grandfather's birthday who had passed away not too long ago, and my grandma was at the game, and my wife and daughter were at the game, so it was special, yes, but to me, winning is everything. That's the challenge, the ultimate challenge — how do you get to that elite level as a group? As a whole? Right now, I don't care about points or any of that stuff — it's how do you get to that elite level and remain at that elite level as a unit. What are the things you need to do?

"You have to be open-minded and not be rigid. If you're rigid, that's weakness. All you can do is forget about the bad stuff and then move on. You just kind of roll with it, you just kind of learn. I will not make the same mistakes in the future that I have made in the past. I will make new mistakes, I am sure. And I will learn from them too. You have to be fluid. Your body changes. As that happens, your moves need to change, your training program needs to change, you have to be able to adapt.

"I am going to work extremely hard. I'm not going to cheat the game. I am going to take all the steps and do all the work necessary. It's like, God blessed me with the ability to do this, I'm not going to shortchange that blessing. I'm going to go out there and do the best that I can every single time."

Kobe excuses himself to leave for Vegas's Thomas & Mack arena, a tune-up game for the impending twelve-day international tournament. Over the coming two weeks, Kobe and his USA team will outclass all comers, winning by an average of more than thirty points, clinching a berth in the Olympics, earning the USA its first gold medal in international competition since 2000. And while Kobe will go off for twenty-seven points in the grudge match against Argentina, who won the gold in the last Olympics, throughout the rest of the series, he will distinguish himself with his leadership, his tenacious defense, his artful passing. In every game, he will ask to be assigned to play against the opponent's best scorer. He will hold Brazil's NBA standout, Leandro Barbosa, the tournament's leading scorer, to just four points. Kobe will also be among the leaders in minutes and assists.

He will be the heart of Team USA.

That's what I'm talkin' about.

No Finish Line

FROM SPORTS ILLUSTRATED

DEATH IS one of those things Alberto Salazar used to run into. He'd finish a race and all but perish, as likely from fire as from ice. In 1978, at the end of the 7.1-mile Falmouth (Massachusetts) Road Race, he was read the last rites after collapsing with a body temperature of 108 degrees. After he won the 1982 Boston Marathon, paramedics had to give him six liters of saline solution in an IV drip when his temperature dropped to 88 degrees.

Then, on a Saturday morning four months ago, death came up from behind and tapped Salazar on the shoulder. He was forty-eight. He still logged twenty-five to thirty miles a week. He ate sensibly. He took medicine to control his hereditary high cholesterol and high blood pressure. But at one end of a long greensward on the Nike campus in Beaverton, Oregon, as he ambled along before leading a workout with several young runners he coaches, pain clutched at the back of his neck. Dizzy, Salazar went down on one knee. A former world-record holder in the marathon, a man who once heard testers declare his cardio output to be the greatest they had ever measured, was suffering a heart attack.

"We backed up and gave him space," recalls Josh Rohatinsky, one of the athletes Salazar hopes will create a renaissance in U.S. distance running. "He started gasping, and his face began to turn blue." Rohatinsky ran to the Lance Armstrong Building to look for a defibrillator. Josh's visiting brother, Jared, ran to the field where a football camp was taking place. Galen Rupp, another runner in Salazar's stable, called 911 on his cell phone. "Alberto was on his stomach with his face on the ground," Josh Rohatinsky continues.

"I rolled him over, and the guys from the football field began giving him CPR."

Salazar's heart had stopped. Four minutes is thought to be the most that a human being can survive without a pulse; after six minutes, medical science considers a person to be dead. Salazar's heart did not beat for fourteen minutes.

Members of the Tualatin Valley Fire and Rescue squad arrived within four minutes of Rupp's call. They applied paddles to Salazar — "like they do on TV," Rupp says — and three times tried to shock his heart into beating on its own. They finally succeeded on the fourth try, but in the ambulance his heart stopped again. The printout from the heart monitor, which Salazar has kept, reads like split times from the ultimate interval workout: again on the way to the hospital his heart stopped, and then again, and again. In all it took eight shocks over twenty-six minutes for his heart to beat and blood to flow on their own without interruption. In a cast of heroes, the biggest turned out to be two men working at the football camp: Louis Barahona, a combat medic with the National Guard, and Doug Douglass, an emergency-room doctor who had played outside linebacker at Oregon. Because they immediately began administering CPR, Salazar's brain never went without oxygen. Thus he was spared any brain damage and able to stage an astonishingly quick recovery. From his hospital bed he discussed workouts with his runners, and nine days later he was back with them at the track.

If today Salazar doesn't walk around in a state of abiding wonder, it may be because he has experienced miracles before. In 1990, during a pilgrimage to the Catholic shrine of Medjugorje in Bosnia, he awoke one morning to find that his set of rosary beads had turned from silver to gold. Months before his own heart attack he had given the wife of a neighbor in a coma a crucifix and rosary blessed, respectively, by Pope Benedict XVI and Pope John Paul II. She put them on her husband's nightstand, and he recovered.

After Salazar suffered his heart attack, that woman placed the crucifix by his hospital bed and wrapped the rosary in his hand. They were the first things he saw when he came to. Upon hearing that another woman had survived a heart attack while out running on the day he suffered his, Salazar passed the objects on again. "I gave them to her parents while she was in a coma," he says. She too has recovered.

It's all enough to make one believe in a force greater even than that of the most strong-willed athlete. Which is saying a lot if you consider Salazar that benchmark. As obsessives go, few are more devoted than the anti-Castro Cuban émigré, and Salazar was raised by one. His father, José, had been a schoolmate of Fidel Castro's, serving first in the rebel forces that overthrew the dictator Fulgencio Batista, then as a civil engineer for the new regime. One day in 1960 Che Guevara ordered José to scrap plans for a chapel in a community development project, and Castro upheld the decision, declaring that in the new Cuba there would be no place for religion. "That day my father joined the counterrevolution," Alberto says. "The secret police came for him an hour after he left for Miami."

With the family resettled in New England, Alberto soon threw himself into distance running, training and competing as if nothing less than the secret police were at his heels. For a spell he delivered results commensurate with his intensity. One of the leading high school runners in the country, he went on to Oregon, where he won the 1978 NCAA cross-country championship. Two years later, at age twenty-two, he ran his first marathon, in New York City. In the space on the entry blank for predicted time Salazar put down two hours and ten minutes — a time faster than Bill Rodgers's course record — and then went out and won the race, beating Rodgers, in 2:09:41. Back in town a year later he predicted a world record and delivered, Namath-like. In Boston the following spring he beat Dick Beardsley by ten yards in their epic "Duel in the Sun" and the following fall won his third straight New York City Marathon. He once described the marathon as a chance to take another runner to "the point where he has to give up," and that's the way he ran — as if he were engaging others to subdue them, in a kind of foot-to-foot combat. He spoke matter-of-factly about the heat of his Latin temperament and how he could turn it up to his advantage. To fellow marathoner Amby Burfoot, who gently suggested that he might be entering too many races, he snapped, "Well, I've been doing pretty well at all of them, wouldn't you say?" From his Catholic upbringing he seemed to take all the discipline and sacrifice, but none of the humility. "Running became important to me for its own sake," he says now. "I wanted to be the greatest distance runner in the world. I was twenty-three and a few seconds off the world record in the five- and ten-K and thought I could do it all. Faith definitely became secondary. On Sundays, I was always sure to get my twenty miles in, but I was too tired to go to Mass."

After one too many near-death experiences, his body began to push back. He suffered his first marathon loss in the spring of 1983, finishing fifth in Rotterdam. Three straight times that summer he lost races on his home track in Eugene, Oregon, the high seat of American distance running. He came down with bronchitis before the Worlds in Helsinki that August and, entering the 10,000 meters anyway, finished last. The next summer he finished fifteenth in the marathon at the Los Angeles Olympics. At one point he logged more than one hundred miles a week with a stress fracture. Overtraining led to illness and injury and even, he believes, a suppressed endocrine system. He ran long races, but he wasn't running the long race. "I thought I was going to just push through it," he says, "that it was just a little slump."

Today Salazar the coach practices a restraint that Salazar the competitor never knew. "I needed someone to be strong and firm with me, to hold me back," he says. "Now I coach this young talent and sometimes say, 'You need to take a break.' Whereas Bill [Dellinger, his coach at Oregon] would say, 'Well, okay, Alberto, you're a big boy,' and I'm thinking, he's not telling me no. Runners are so used to pushing through pain, it's very hard sometimes to make rational decisions."

In 2001, with several million dollars from Nike, Salazar launched the Oregon Project, a challenge to the African hegemony in distance running. The program brought to Beaverton a handful of promising U.S. runners and gave them every legal advantage extant, from space-age training aids to the amenities of the Nike campus, which include a fitness center, testing labs, a two-mile woodchip trail, and the soft grass field on which Salazar would eventually collapse. But four years later the Oregon Project had produced only one moderately successful runner, Dan Browne, a 2004 U.S. Olympian in the 10,000 meters and the marathon. The lesson, Salazar says, is that "you can't take mediocre runners and expect them to achieve world-class results."

Salazar has since reconstituted the group, but with a twist. He's trying to develop 5,000- and 10,000-meter runners, and if they happen to be well suited to the marathon, he'll urge them to build up to that distance — but only gradually, at the proper juncture in their careers. Unless a male runner has near-27:30 speed at 10,000 meters, Salazar doesn't regard his potential as world-class and won't take him on.

After his fall from the top in 1983, Salazar explored virtually everything to resurrect his own career: a Finnish masseur; a training pilgrimage to Kenya; a psychologist who believed you could tap into cosmic energy by running with your palms up. Now he channels all his intensity into the hunt for an edge for his heirs. Refinements in form, newfangled treadmills, high-altitude simulators, advances in diet — pick up a second or two per mile from each and, he believes, U.S. distance runners might overcome the disadvantages of affluent sea-level living enough to become competitive after two decades of essential irrelevance. "Any little thing he can find, he'll point out," says Rupp. "Any way he can get a competitive advantage, obviously within the rules, he's willing to do. You want to take advice from other people but at the same time always look for the cutting edge."

Salazar's current charges — in addition to Rupp and Josh Rohatinsky, they include Amy Yoder-Begley and the husband-and-wife team of Kara and Adam Goucher — share other characteristics. They all attend religious services or at least are spiritually inclined. And many have worked through some stretch of debilitating injury, which leads Salazar to believe that a lighter training touch will pay immediate dividends. "All the things that happened to me are a kind of blessing," he says. "People say, 'Salazar, he'll burn people out.' It's just the opposite: Because of what I've been through, [I won't do that]. I believe that if you have enough faith, you can achieve extraordinary things. They don't always come with a bolt out of the blue or some apparition.

"Those guys spent twenty-six minutes trying to get my heart started again. And I wonder, why didn't they just give up?"

In the face of the depth and daunting results of their African counterparts, why don't U.S. distance runners just give up?

No sport renders judgments more ruthlessly than running. "It's your exact time on this exact track," Salazar says. "How you're improving and how you rank is based completely on that stopwatch, and anyone can get on the Internet and see exactly where everyone stands." The Internet tells a brutal truth: last year more than four hundred Kenyans broke two hours, eighteen minutes, in the marathon — and only thirty-one U.S. runners did. Ethiopians, Kenyans, and Moroccans won eight of the twelve medals in the men's distance events at the 2004 Olympics. Not since 1992 has a U.S. runner won an Olympic medal on the track at a distance longer than 800 meters.

Salazar ticks off the ironic circumstances that seem to cast the United States as a Third World country in distance running: "As big as we are, we have fewer people to draw on. In Kenya there are probably a million schoolboys ten to seventeen years old who run ten to twelve miles a day. That's how they get to and from school. The average Kenyan eighteen-year-old has run fifteen thousand to eighteen thousand more miles in his life than the average American — and a lot of that's at altitude. They're motivated because running is a way out. Plus they don't have a lot of other sports for kids to be drawn into. Numbers are what this is all about. In Kenya there are maybe one hundred runners who have hit 2:11 in the marathon — and in the U.S., maybe five."

With those figures, coaches in Kenya can train their athletes to the outer limits of endurance — up to 150 miles a week — without worrying that their pool of talent will be meaningfully depleted. Even if four out of every five runners break down, the fifth will convert that training into performance, at least over the short term. "You can't change where you were born or that you're only starting at fourteen," Salazar says. "But once you understand what you're up against, you can decide not to make it any worse. With the few athletes we get who show talent, we have to do everything right. We can't get impatient. We can't screw up like I did."

Salazar's brother Rick kiddingly offers a solution: send school buses to Kenya. Instead, Alberto adds training volume, but with a built-in margin of safety. Thus his runners train up to 120 miles a week, but only 90 to 100 outside. They get in the other 25 or so on underwater and antigravity treadmills, to lessen the pounding and resultant stress on joints and bones. "Muscularly, very little good happens beyond one hundred miles a week," Salazar says. "You actually lose strength at that point. By doing antigravity and underwater work, you can get the cardiovascular benefits of the extra mileage without the negative muscular effects. It's like lifting weights — at some point you have to allow for recovery."

In addition to employing such Nike-underwritten gadgetry, he obsesses over form. Salazar himself was what's known among runners as a bumblebee, after the insect whose technique suggests that it shouldn't be able to fly. Instead of driving his body forward with every stride, Salazar was a "sitter" who "jammed the ground with each step," as he puts it. "I succeeded despite inefficient form. Eventually my bad mechanics caught up with me." The benefits of good form may seem infinitesimal, but over years, every properly executed footfall and arm pump will save time and reduce stress and ultimately provide a substantial advantage.

Yet even that's not enough. "Even if you have perfect form, you've got to do drills and exercises or you'll lose it," says Salazar, who admiringly watches older African runners follow programs dedicated to maintaining strength and flexibility. "Distance runners used to be known for not being good at other sports. We need to make them athletes. I think I could have run three minutes faster and had a longer career if I'd taken into account the importance of overall fitness. You watch the Ethiopians and Kenyans, and they do drills and drills. They don't just kick the door open and go out and run. Even a good energy drink could give you two or three minutes, and I never ate a good combination of protein and carbohydrates."

Finally, Team Salazar lives in airtight houses and apartments retrofitted with machines that thin the air to simulate the atmosphere at twelve thousand feet. The goal is to fool the body into producing more red blood cells, those Sherpas of oxygen. "Some people say it's a lot of hocus-pocus," Salazar says. "But you know what? We're at sea level, and [Kenyans] are at eight thousand feet; without altitude simulation we'd have no chance to compete at the top level. And the treadmills are keeping our runners healthy. We're using science in an ethical, legal way to have a chance to be competitive."

Salazar draws two lines on a graph. The ascending one describes an athlete's aerobic capacity, which increases with training into one's thirties. (Portugal's Carlos Lopes and Kenya's Paul Tergat, who set world records in the marathon at ages thirty-eight and thirty-four, respectively, are advertisements for a mature cardiovascular system — as was Salazar, who had an astonishing, drought-breaking victory at age thirty-five in the 53.75-mile Comrades Marathon in South Africa in 1994.) The descending line describes speed and power over time — the toll of the road. A runner's great opportunity lies where these two lines intersect.

Salazar sees his challenge as maximizing the aerobic fitness of his athletes while making sure their regimen doesn't so compromise muscular strength that they break down. Despite their history of injuries, none of the runners he has assembled in Oregon — knock wood — has had a lengthy period of debilitation since joining him. "They've all seen it: the program is working," Salazar says.

Indeed, Kara Goucher won a bronze medal in the 10,000 meters at this summer's World Championships in Osaka — the first time a U.S. woman had won a medal in a distance event on the track at the Worlds or Olympics in fifteen years. Then, in late September, in the Great North Run in Newcastle, England, Goucher ran a U.S. best in the half-marathon, beating the women's marathon world-record holder, Britain's Paula Radcliffe, by nearly a minute. At the same event Rohatinsky, the 2006 NCAA cross-country champion (at Brigham Young), finished fifth, only seventeen seconds behind Hendrick Ramaala of South Africa, the victor in the 2004 New York City Marathon. And Rohatinsky had never before competed at such a long distance. Salazar raves about Rohatinsky's potential in the marathon. "Josh has the perfect build and stride," says the coach, who's eager to see how the runner will fare in his first-ever marathon, at the Olympic trials this Saturday in Manhattan's Central Park. "He's not just a speed guy, he's a great hill runner."

Meanwhile Rupp, a junior at Oregon and far too young to be consigned to the marathon, is showing promise on the track. His personal best in the 10,000 meters — 27:33.48 — is the fastest ever run by a U.S.-born collegian. "Galen is only twenty-one," Salazar says. "If he makes a one-minute improvement over the next five years, he can be right there."

Salazar was Rupp's confirmation sponsor. Rohatinsky is a devout Mormon. Amy Yoder-Begley and Kara Goucher were raised Methodists, and Goucher's husband, Adam, has passed along Salazar's talismanic crucifix and rosary to his Roman Catholic father, who's struggling with cancer. Salazar says chatboard charges that he "brainwashes" his athletes are "silly," pointing out that his runners' religious beliefs were formed before he took them on. Still, he does confess to a bias toward runners of religious faith. "Josh's Mormon background is such an important part of why he's so good," Salazar says. "He just does what he's told, completely on faith. Like a good Catholic, he believes that others are put in authority over you and you trust in them. He has stability and mental toughness, and his faith has a lot to do with it. And he's patient, which is what you need as a marathoner.

"Take it from someone who's been there: running by itself isn't necessarily going to make you happy. Happiness has got to come from somewhere else."

Says Rupp, "Alberto and I have that faith that He has a plan for everything, and it helps. We don't ever get too worried that, 'Oh, man, it's going to take so long to catch up with those guys.' If it's His will not to catch them, so be it. It's almost easier for us, not to have to worry about that."

Salazar has a date this late-September afternoon with a team from Portland's Providence Heart and Vascular Institute, the program that treated him after his heart attack. Public-affairs officers want to devote several pages of a guide to heart-healthy living to Salazar's story. After an interview they fan out across the Nike campus, seeking backdrops for a photo of Salazar and the doctors who fixed him up a few months earlier. In whatever grand plan the Lord has for him, Salazar is comfortable with a place in the public square, where he can do for the fight against heart disease what Lance Armstrong is doing to battle cancer: raise awareness and save lives as an athlete turned survivor.

Back in the early 1980s, in the midst of winning race after race, Salazar accepted an invitation to visit the Australian Institute of Sport outside Canberra. It was there that testers measured his cardiac output and declared him to have the most prodigious heart of any elite athlete they had seen. *I guess I'll never have heart trouble,* Salazar told himself at the time.

Only a few years ago he reminded himself of that test Down Under and the longevity it seemed to promise, even though he had lost both grandfathers to heart disease, one at age fifty-two; his father is a survivor of two heart attacks; and his late mother suffered from high blood pressure and diabetes. "I had one of the strongest hearts in the world," he says. "I was so naive to think that." The heart may be a muscle, but it doesn't lend itself to applications of Ben-Gay — and there's all sorts of plumbing that goes with the pump.

After the photo shoot Salazar's cardiologist, Todd Caulfield, pulls him into an empty office for a quick checkup. Salazar peels off a long-sleeved tricot. A Nike swoosh tattoo graces his sleek upper torso, and a defibrillator, installed after the heart attack to treat arrhythmia, bulges like a pack of Luckys beneath the skin on his left breast. Caulfield listens with a stethoscope, then takes a marker to a white board and sketches welters of arteries. He points to the right coronary artery, from which in June he cleared the 70 to 80 percent blockage that had caused Salazar's heart attack. (The cardiologist had to custom-make the stent because of his patient's unusually wide-gauge arteries — which may explain why Salazar had such extraordinary cardio output.) Then Caulfield indicates another obstruction, in the left anterior descending coronary artery, a blockage of 50 to 60 percent. He had left it alone, Caulfield says, because there was less risk in leaving the blockage than in going in to treat it. The best course, Caulfield says, is for Salazar to monitor his own symptoms and come in for "surveillance" stress tests every six months or so.

Caulfield had mentioned the second blockage in the early summer, but there had been so much for Salazar to process that he hadn't entirely grasped its implications. Today he's alarmed. How is he supposed to recognize an imminent heart attack? The onset of his episode in June had been marked not by sharp, angina-like pain but by a much vaguer discomfort. He almost went for a run on the morning he was stricken but didn't, as much because he was running late as because his primary-care physician had told him not to run until an echocardiogram could be taken for his neck pain.

"I'm just supposed to know?" he asks Caulfield.

He's just supposed to know.

The day after the consultation Salazar feels out of sorts. "Crappy," he says. He'd like to think it's because Caulfield dialed back his high-blood-pressure medication. He still feels headachy, and when he runs (with a heart monitor to make sure his pulse never exceeds 130 beats per minute), he feels discomfort again at the back of his neck — the same place he felt it just before the heart attack. "He's not," his wife, Molly, says dryly, "one to call attention to his aches and pains."

The discomfort will persist over the next several weeks. Finally Caulfield schedules an angiogram for October 16. By actually seeing inside the artery with ultrasound, an angiogram can provide the best possible read on the extent of blockage. In the meantime Salazar is on orders not to run at all.

On October 11, in Eugene to meet with Rupp, Salazar parks his car a block and a half from Rupp's apartment and jogs over. "Right then it became apparent," he said later. "I had that uncomfortable feeling in the back of my neck again. Nothing should happen that fast just from a short jog. I knew it wasn't the high-blood-pressure medication." Rupp drives Salazar to Eugene's Sacred Heart Medical Center, where Alberto and Molly's three children — Tony, twenty-five; Alex, twenty-three; and Maria, sixteen — were born. An emergency angiogram reveals that the 50 to 60 percent blockage is actually 90 percent. Doctors insert another stent and tell Salazar that, if not for this intervention, he probably would have suffered another heart attack within twenty-four hours.

So it turns out that there might be virtue not only in imposing one's will but also in submitting it to something else. "It's all reinforced by the events of the last few months," Salazar says. "When it's all over and I'm done coaching, I want my athletes to feel I've helped them running-wise, but life-wise too. I still want them to run well, but not at all costs, where it overpowers everything else. If I were to question Josh's decision not to run on Sundays, I'd deserve to get another heart attack, on the spot."

Marathoning isn't life, as Alberto Salazar once believed. Rather, life is a marathon, and in at least one miraculous instance it ends and, after an interlude the length of a newscast, begins again. Out of respect for the grace of a second chance, you put one foot in front of the other, and by doing so, you signal to the hearts of millions, to say nothing of your own, that you're ready to run into whatever life has left for you.

Not to Get Too Mystical About It

FROM THE NEW YORK TIMES PLAY MAGAZINE

STEVE NASH SAT DOWN on a playground bench in Washington Market Park, like all the other tired Manhattan fathers. It was a summer evening, late in August, and somewhere in the scrum of kids roiling under the monkey bars was one of his three-year-old twin girls, Lola, and her nanny. A rubber ball came bounding by with a pre-K hotshot in hot pursuit. He seemed like the sort of kid who in a few years would be shooting baskets behind a school, pretending he was Steve Nash. *Nash from the corner! Nash driving the lane! Nash in the media room talking to a reporter!*

At the sight of the kid, the wariness melted out of Nash's blue eyes. It was easy to imagine the NBA star himself at that age, before he had his paper route, before the local newspaper clips began to trickle in, and the trophies, and the fans, and the *Sports Illustrated* covers, and the instructional DVDs, and the $11-million-a-year contract, and now the eleven seasons as a pro in which he has enjoyed every success but a championship, his one remaining goal as a professional athlete. The hint of sweetness that crossed his stoic face said he knew how joyful and profound the rapport of a boy and a ball could be. Nearly all the canonical stories of Nash's ascent to the pantheon of NBA point guards feature some kind of ball, whether it is the round mound of wadded-up tape he and his younger brother Martin used to play hall-hockey with, or the basketball he took out to shoot on Christmas Eve in the rain at the junior high school court behind his parents' house in Victoria, British Columbia, or the tennis ball he once dribbled around Santa

Clara University on his way to class, or the soccer ball he once kept aloft for six hundred consecutive kicks until he collapsed. A ball had been the talisman of what he called "my dream."

Then again, maybe what the ball-crazed kid provoked had as much to do with the fact that Nash often found himself in the position of pretending to be Steve Nash too: "Steve Nash" the brand pushing the ball up court on the Wheaties box or hawking watches and sneakers and bottles of Clearly Canadian water; "Steve Nash" the white, nondunking, four-time All-Star whose back-to-back Most Valuable Player Awards won him the unwanted role of minority-race champion in a predominantly black league; "Steve Nash" the self-effacing Canadian long shot whose life story had been puréed into an edifying fable about Chasing Your Dreams and Working Hard and Always Giving Back, and in some parts of his home country had been polished to such a saintly sheen that people called him Can-Je, short for "Canadian Jesus." Nash himself sometimes seemed flustered by this double team of person and persona, struggling to reconcile his sardonic sense of humor and lethal competitive instincts with the humanitarian concerns that obliged him to ladle out all kinds of canned corn at charity events and celebrity appearances. What can you say without playing yourself false, or leaving your body completely, when zoo officials who have paid you the compliment of naming a twelve-pound female Bengal tiger cub in your honor put the razor-clawed kitty-cat in your arms and stick a microphone in your face? (Shrewdly, Nash channeled Tiger Woods: "It's pretty special.") Or for that matter, what about the play-killing questions routinely lobbed by sportswriters after the game?

"It's always the same three questions," Nash said. "'What do you think about the game tonight?' 'How do you feel about the game tomorrow night?' 'What do you think you'll have to do differently next time?' I started off trying to answer honestly, and then I tried being ironic, but that didn't really work either . . ."

In the park, a stranger approached, hand extended.

"Steve Nash!" the man said.

"Hey, man," Nash said, shaking his hand after a quick assessment.

"I love your game."

"Thanks."

Nash's game had been on the shelf for three months, since the

Phoenix Suns were muscled out of the second round of the Western Conference playoffs by the San Antonio Spurs, who went on to win the NBA championship against the overmatched Cleveland Cavaliers. It was a bitter end for the Suns' championship hopes, and for Nash especially. A Game 1 collision with Spurs guard Tony Parker had split his nose so badly that Nash had to leave the court at a crucial moment in the fourth quarter. It took six stitches to close the bloody gash. In Game 4 the Spurs forward Robert Horry forechecked him into the scorer's table, and the ensuing melee cost the Suns their big men when Amare Stoudemire and Boris Diaw were suspended one game each for leaving the bench. Losing the series 4–2 was a defeat that would "forever haunt us," Nash said at the time. In the months since, he'd consoled himself with the distractions of New York, the adopted offseason city where he has spent the last three summers with his wife, Alejandra, and their twins, Lola and Bella.

"I've had a great summer," he was saying now as he stretched out on the bench. He was wearing cargo shorts, a gray T-shirt, and laceless black Converse sneakers. "I watched Tiger Woods and Roger Federer. I went to movies and restaurants. I had great conversations."

He stayed in shape mainly by working out with a trainer and playing soccer at Pier 40 off the Hudson River with a team sponsored by Phebe's Tavern & Grill in the East Village. When he took up basketball in the eighth grade it was for "social reasons," a means of hanging out with his friends. Being able to use his hands felt almost like cheating, because the sport he loved best was soccer. "'Goal' was my first word," he told me, a vintage Nash brand detail found in nearly every profile of him. Nash's English father, John, played soccer professionally in South Africa, where Nash was born; his Welsh mother, Jean, had various careers as an airline ticket agent, secretary, and special education teacher. Sickened by apartheid, they emigrated to Canada when Steve was one, eventually settling in Victoria.

"We had one little TV you had to turn on with tweezers, and even on Christmas Day we would watch the NBA," recalled Joann Nash, who was born after Steve and Martin. "When I was eight, I could recite the audio commentary on the Michael Jordan highlight video. It was burned into my mind." Joann, who recently married Manny

Malhotra, a center for the Columbus Blue Jackets of the National Hockey League, had been captain of the University of Victoria soccer team. Martin still earns his living as a midfielder for the Vancouver Whitecaps, a first-division team in the United Soccer League. In the family, the source of the kids' competitive fervor is not ascribed to their pro-athlete dad but to Mom, who can be counted on to dig deep for victory whether the game is tennis, Pictionary, or simply beating other shoppers to the only open checkout lane at the grocery store.

"Steve makes a mockery of Pictionary," Joann said with a forlorn note in her voice. "He won't take it seriously."

Nash's soul-salving summer had already included a trip to Thailand, and some time back home in July, where he opened a sports club and hosted a charity basketball game in Vancouver. He had spent three days in New Jersey tutoring college and high school point guards at a camp organized by Nike. He also produced a video for Nike, with a crew shooting him as he legged around Manhattan on his skateboard. He sat for an interview with Charlie Rose, confiding in his self-deprecating way that there were other NBA point guards who "are more talented than me physically . . . I say to myself, 'How do I have the same job as this guy?'"

At thirty-three, Nash has defied the actuarial trends of point-guard mortality. He has gotten steadily better with age and insists he is now not just smarter but quicker than when the Phoenix Suns, amid a crescendo of boos, made him the fifteenth pick in the first round of the 1996 NBA draft. The statistical evidence bears him out. Last season Nash put up his finest numbers, better than some of those he posted in his two MVP years. He may not have the obvious physical gifts of some point guards, explosiveness or vertical leap, but his repertoire of inventive shots and ball-handling skills, his breakneck transitions and barn-swallow zigzagging through the tall timber of big men in the paint bespeaks exceptional body control. "His core strength is off the charts," the Phoenix Suns' coach, Mike D'Antoni, told me. "Steve's balance is so good he can stand on an exercise ball."

I'd been struck by Nash's poise, the mental counterpart of his physical balance. Talking to Charlie Rose, the word Nash had picked to describe his ideal state of mind on court was "unflappable." Had he always been able to cast a cool eye at pressure?

"My first and second years in the NBA, I used to get really nervous in a tight game," he said. "But now I wait for that moment when things are really close — that's what I really love. Having the ball in my hands and the responsibility makes me feel calm and open. Not to have that, not to get to that point in a game, would feel really . . ." He paused to find the precise word. ". . . Really confining," he said.

"Was there one shot or game when you first felt that way?"

"Probably it built over time — I don't want it to sound like there's anything too mystical about it."

In a few days he was flying to England to visit relatives and meet with the officers of the Tottenham Hotspurs to discuss business opportunities with the soccer club. "I'd like to be an owner," he says. "It's something I could do for the rest of my life after my little window of popularity dies." In September he was leading a group of NBA players to China for a series of charity events.

We had been talking in the park for almost an hour now, and I was beginning to appreciate the elusive quality that the author Jack McCallum, who spent a year with the Phoenix Suns for his book *:07 Seconds or Less*, described as Nash's "mysterious Canadian reticence." Even though Nash is one of the more introspective and intelligent athletes in the NBA — a player who got a lot of criticism for speaking out against the war in Iraq in 2003, and had the sportswriter fraternity in a dither because his winter reading list included bodice-rippers like *The Communist Manifesto* and Solzhenitsyn's *One Day in the Life of Ivan Denisovich* — it didn't seem that what made him interesting was coming out in conversation. Part of the reason may have been that what made Nash exceptional was his temperamental inclination to downplay what made him exceptional. In interviews he often conveys a mix of humility and politic self-restraint.

As Nash began to fidget on the bench — maybe his back was tightening up, or he was thinking about Lola's supper, or he was just tired of answering questions and the full-court press of chores entailed in being "Steve Nash" — I remembered something his agent, Bill Duffy, had told me: "With Steve it's all about the flow." Flow, of course, being shorthand for that state of mind that artists and athletes strive to enter into, and which in full flood entails an ecstatic expansion of consciousness that releases them from the confines of the self and produces crowning moments of creation and performance — not to get too mystical about it. Maybe the truest picture of Nash depended on seeing him in motion, in the flow; whether he was threading a half-court bounce pass or exploiting his small window of fame to get potable water to Third World villages or practicing surreptitious acts of generosity, like slipping spending money to the coaches to give to his less wealthy basketball teammates at the 2000 Olympics in Sydney. Enacting himself, as it were, as opposed to talking about himself.

Three-Point Land and Beyond

"Hey, rooks," Nash shouted from the back of the bus idling in the garage of the Regent Beijing Hotel. "What time does the 9:30 bus leave?"

It was a trick question, of course, but the "rooks" — D. J. Strawberry Jr. and Alando Tucker, both new members of the Phoenix Suns — froze.

"They told us to go back and get our umbrellas," said Strawberry, a shooting guard and the son of the former New York Mets star outfielder Darryl Strawberry.

"Let's go!" Nash hollered to no one in particular. Apparently more stragglers were still fetching umbrellas. It was nearly 10:00 A.M., a rainy Thursday in mid-September, though in truth you couldn't be sure what time it was from the coal-and-car-fume miasma obscuring China's capital.

Among the two dozen or so passengers on the bus — agents, trainers, friends, a reality-show film crew — were eight NBA players: the rooks Strawberry and Tucker; the twenty-year-old Detroit Pistons forward Amir Johnson; Paul Davis, a twenty-three-year-old center with the L.A. Clippers; Chuck Hayes, a twenty-four-year-old forward with the Houston Rockets; and the established stars like the Suns' Leandro Barbosa (the "Brazilian Blur," who last year won the NBA's Sixth Man Award), Carmelo Anthony, the outstanding forward for the Denver Nuggets who was one of the top scorers in the league last year, and Baron Davis, the street-Shakespeare point guard who led the Golden State Warriors on an improbable run that was the dramatic highlight of the NBA playoffs last spring.

And of course Nash, riding a flow unlike any he'd ever caught on the basketball court, as much a celebrity as an athlete now, his Q-score jacked up by photos with Sharon Stone and Donald Trump and the MVP shout-out in the lyrics of Nelly Furtado's hit "Promiscuous" and the *GQ* "baller of the year" spread featuring an epicene Nash with overly sculpted hair. The fame that had recently produced the tribute of his face stenciled into an Arizona cornfield had also given him the power to "make a difference." Befitting a point guard, he seemed to be feeling his way through celebrity, into that seam between his identity in a profession that had defined his existence since the eighth grade, when he prophetically informed his mother that one day he would play in the NBA, and whatever he might become or do next, out of uniform, away from the confines of the court and the quest for championships.

As the impresario who put the whole China show together, with crucial behind-the-scenes help from Bill Duffy and a team of people from his company, BDA Sports Management, Nash had suspended his mysterious Canadian reticence in hopes of improving the flow of a sightseeing trip to the Forbidden City. Nash broached the idea of the Beijing tour with Yao Ming after a game with the Rockets in Phoenix last March. Yao was thrilled by the prospect of Nash and a pickup crew of players coming to China to help raise money for charity. Bing Hu, the Chinese founder of a high-end architecture development company in Scottsdale, Arizona, had offered to fly the cast to China on his Falcon 900 jet. Eventually an agenda was set, calling for a four-day barnstorm of press conferences, practices, luncheons, a charity auction and black-tie banquet, sightseeing, photo ops, random cultural encounters, and unofficial karaoke pub crawls, along with a televised charity hoops match that would pit Western Hemisphere pros (the Nashionals?) against Yao and the Chinese National team, and would, as it turned out, draw a Chinese TV audience more than three times the size of the horde agglomerated by the Super Bowl.

The Nashionals had landed in China the night before, September 12, and had come shuffling in glassy-eyed from the airport, luggage in tow, to a surreal press conference at the Regent Beijing. Backed by a drop cloth splattered with corporate logos, they sat Last Supper–style along a table onstage, peering out at a bank of eight TV cameras and some sixty Chinese journalists. An earsplitting remix of Queen's "We Will Rock You" pumped through speakers.

"I just want to say that we're here to help out the children in your community," Nash said. He was wearing below-the-knee shorts, a gray shirt, and, as he had in Washington Market Park, black laceless sneakers. "I think so highly of Yao as a person and a player that I asked if he'd be willing to host some of us to come over here and give back. I want to thank the guys for making the long trip."

The proceeds would go to build schools and help impoverished girls in the Xinjiang Kezilesu Keerkzi Autonomous Region, a vast and sparsely settled area in western China, which most people would be hard-pressed to find on a map, much less pronounce. This was Nash's first trip to China, and it wasn't unreasonable to wonder whether his interest in charity work thousands of miles from home in an alien culture where he doesn't understand the language was really a heartfelt reflection of altruistic values. Pieties about the importance of Giving Back are so routinely coughed up you'd think that if NBA stars didn't have such wicked crossover dribbles or a faculty for tomahawk dunks they'd all be following in the footsteps of Albert Schweitzer. The benefits that redound in PR brownie points and IRS income-tax offsets are seldom mentioned.

But Nash often speaks of his interest in "the global village" and doing what he can wherever he can. The Steve Nash Foundation has focused on programs that help "underserved" children and promote worthwhile social and environmental causes, like low-impact development and eco-friendly construction. (The rugs in Nash's new sports club in Vancouver are made of recycled athletic shoelaces.) His foundation has also set up safe drinking water projects in Nicaragua and Guatemala and recently underwrote a hospital ward for neonates in Paraguay, where Nash's wife is from.

Most of the rooks and younger players on the trip were just curious to see a patch of China for the first time; some of the more established stars were eager to enhance their brand visibility in the largest basketball market outside the United States. One-third of all hits to the NBA website come from Chinese Internet users, and in recent years the NBA has made a concerted effort to capitalize on what is already China's multibillion-dollar love affair with basketball, going so far as to publish a partial list of NBA players' Chinese nicknames. (Nash is not on it, for some reason, perhaps because the Chinese haven't solved the conundrum of his mysterious Canadian reticence either. But Carmelo Anthony is known as Sweet Melon, and in what is clearly the most telling evidence of Chinese basketball acumen, Tim Duncan, nemesis of Nash and his fellow Suns, is known as Stone Buddha.)

Nash was as happy to have the good publicity as the next multi-millionaire, but the trip was clearly part of a course in continuing education. He studied sociology at Santa Clara University, where he did enough to get by. "I basically majored in basketball," he told me. He reads during the season when the team is on the road with time to fill, and he is eager to travel abroad during the offseason, pressed, it often seems, by a deep curiosity and thirst for knowledge that the strictures of his NBA dream didn't give him the luxury of indulging as a younger man. Of course it was a two-edged sword. The celebrity that made it possible to come to China also brought the unscholarly and flow-impeding distraction of having to stop every ten seconds to pose for pictures or sign an autograph.

The microphone was passed to all the players, including the rooks. Suddenly flashbulbs went off in the back of the room and a hubbub broke out. Yao Ming, the colossus of Chinese basketball, had unexpectedly arrived. He thundered in wearing a white polo shirt as long as a crib sheet. Photographers herded Nash and Yao together, Nash, six-foot-three, Yao, seven-foot-six. Side by side they looked like a comparative bar graph of Chinese and Canadian economic growth rates.

Now, a day later, fully provisioned with umbrellas, the Nashionals' bus pulled into the traffic of Beijing's Dongcheng district and headed west toward the Forbidden City. Arriving at the Divine Military Genius Gate, the players filed out into the toxic drizzle, and into the vast palace complex that is the heart of Chinese civilization. Nash stepped out of the flow of tourists at one point and stood under an umbrella by a parapet to make a phone call. When he turned around he was ringed by a semicircle of Chinese sightseers, more interested in him than the gargoyles on the Hall of Supreme Harmony. It was to be a recurring theme, the players constantly assembling for pictures with strangers and with one another, the last of the morning a semi-comical group portrait at the Gate of Heavenly Peace, where a giant picture of Mao looked out over Tiananmen Square.

"I'm gonna do that," Baron Davis said. "Buy me some property way out in the middle of nowhere and put up a big-ass picture of myself!"

That night there was a black-tie auction and banquet for six or seven hundred people. When the bus pulled up at the Diaoyutai State Guest House, where Richard Nixon had stayed and met with Premier Chou En-lai on his landmark trip to China in 1972, the Chinese team was milling around the entrance.

"They're probably thinking, 'Goddamn Nash,'" said Nash, who was wearing a gray suit and black shoes. "'If it wasn't for him, we wouldn't have to be standing here doing this stupid stuff.'"

It was a long night, especially for Nash. The suit. The play-by-play of gala stage business in Mandarin. The banquet board of bloodless beef, which, later, on the way back to the hotel, Baron Davis speculated may have been a flank of Snoopy or one of Michael Vick's pit bulls. ("You bite into that meat you gonna be barking! You gonna grow paws!") The jet lag seemed to be catching up with Nash. Arms clasped behind his back, he stood gamely on the stage while the crowd bid in a strangely prolonged and desultory fashion on a basketball holiday from China to Houston and passes to the opening of the 2008 Olympics in Beijing. Somebody bid $60,000 for a special one-off edition of a Yao & Nash–embossed Platinum Visa card.

"Although it is a beautiful card," Nash said, "they don't get to spend our bank accounts."

Nash was bearing up as if he were the true Stone Buddha. He listened earnestly to a musical performance by the Moon, the Sun, and the Star, a Mongolian family trio famous for having had the number-one ring tone in China for six months. Given how the sheer volume of people in China made everyone seem sort of faceless, I wondered if Nash's fortitude, his willingness to stop again and again and again to pose and scribble his name and stretch out his hand, was in some way a measure of his ability to particularize an abstraction — that is, to know that everything he was doing to improve the lives of girls in that all-but-Platonic realm known as the Xinjiang Kezilesu Keerkzi Autonomous Region would give a real and particular child a real and particular book that would sweeten her day, or awaken an idea that would make a difference in her life. Whoever she was . . .

Near midnight Nash climbed wearily aboard the bus and stood in the aisle.

"I know it was a long night, guys," he said. "And the food was rough. But we raised almost a million dollars tonight. So thanks to all of you."

At the Nashionals practice on Friday morning before the game with the Chinese team, Nash and Leandro Barbosa were locked into a fierce H-O-R-S-E battle. It was a test of wits as much as skill. Making a key shot, Nash pumped his fist, as if victory in H-O-R-S-E meant as much as an NBA championship. After the game, Barbosa unleashed a slam-dunk. Nash gave it a college try, but the ball clanged off the iron. Nash's college coach, Dick Davey, had told me he thought he could remember Nash dunking a few times in college, "but only on a really springy floor."

I asked afterward who won the H-O-R-S-E games.

"We kinda split them," Nash said.

"I won two," Barbosa said. "The third one we tied."

When the practice was over and the players were waiting to get on the bus, Yao, who had been practicing with the Nashionals, walked out and crammed himself into the passenger seat of an Audi A-8 sedan with tinted windows. People stared at the car in disbelief. The window came down and there was Yao, head sideways, cervical vertebrae pressed against the roof. He looked like a coal miner in a cave-in.

"It's not my car," Yao said.

The Flow He Knows

The venue for the Yao & Nash Charity Game was an arena in the west of the city called Capital Steel Plant Basketball Center, which looked to seat around six thousand people.

"Why am I so tired?" Nash asked as the bus pulled into the traffic outside the hotel around 5:30 P.M. and immediately lost momentum.

"It's, like, 4:00 A.M. in the morning in Phoenix," said Aaron Nelson, the Suns' trainer.

"It'd be okay if you made a few early turnovers so I have to bench you," said Bill Duffy, a former player himself who was going to coach the Nashionals.

Nash lay down on the backseat and closed his eyes.

Even with the help of a police escort, we reached the arena a scant fifteen minutes before the scheduled 7:30 start of the game. Throngs of people from China's seemingly limitless supply of NBA fans were massed outside around the gate and hanging out of the windows of temporary workers' housing. The game was a sellout, but apparently safety regulations required a certain number of empty seats.

In the visitors' locker room, Nash began to get himself into the flow. He nipped at a basketball with his feet, and before long was booting it back and forth with Barbosa, over a table of bananas and Snickers bars and off the metal ceiling — bang! It was as if Nash and his brother Martin were kids playing hall-hockey and seeing what they could get away with before they broke a lamp or drove Mom buggy. Bang! Nash had told me he always liked to be playing a game within the game, if only to keep alive that spark of whimsy and invention that seemed almost subversively opposed to the business of the pro game.

"When you go in, run around the whole arena," said Duffy.

"Move the needle," cried Bill Sanders, an agent with Duffy's company.

"Remember, guys," said Baron Davis, "this is just a charity game."

After the film star Jackie Chan tossed the opening jump ball, the Chinese team raced out to the lead. The six-foot-nine point guard Sun Yue, who had been drafted by the Lakers, was dunking at will when not deigning to can 3's from downtown. Of course the Chinese hadn't flown halfway around the world, or been out till 5:00 A.M. singing karaoke, or fretting about the provenance of the banquet beef. Nash threw a dilly of a one-handed bounce pass down the lane to a cutting Carmelo Anthony, but Sweet Melon's shot was blocked by Yi Jianlian, the six-foot-eleven first-round draft choice who would be playing for the Milwaukee Bucks in the fall. Every time Yao made a basket, or even touched the ball, six thousand of his countrymen broke into song, singing a little rising-falling ditty: "Yao Ming! Yao Ming!" Yao snared a rebound and held the ball out of reach like a father holding a piñata at a birthday party of leaping three-year-olds. And at the end of the first quarter, the Chinese team led by seventeen points.

But then the Nashionals began to get into the flow. Barbosa the Brazilian Blur got hot from three-point land. Baron "Remember It's Just a Charity Game" Davis went diving into the stands.

Nash drove coast-to-coast and hit one of his acrobatic left-handed lay-ups over Yao, and by the half the Chinese lead had shrunk to 42–37.

Nash's one-handed bounce pass reminded me of a story I'd heard from Dick Davey, the Santa Clara coach, who had been the only man in college basketball interested in recruiting the future two-time MVP. They were having lunch a couple of years ago, and the coach had a bone to pick with his former protégé.

"I said to him, 'Dammit, Steve, you penetrate the paint and you kick the ball out with one hand, you gotta do it with two hands.' And he said, 'If I do it with one hand, it's about three-tenths of a second faster, and my teammate is going to have a better look at the basket.' Do you want to know how smart he is? If he had a guy on the right wing in transition who he knew couldn't shoot the ball, he'd throw a pass that was just good enough to include the guy in the fast break, but just bad enough that the guy wasn't in a position to get off a shot and would have to pass the ball back."

At the start of the third quarter, in front of a CCTV audience estimated at 250 million, Nash stripped off his shorts. He posed a moment in his black compression underwear, as if ready for another *GQ* shoot, and then climbed into a pair of red shorts, thus defecting to the Chinese team. Perhaps he felt it was the most charitable thing he could do, not just for the girls of the Xinjiang Kezilesu Keerkzi Autonomous Region but for all of China. But, alas, all the tension went out of the game. Flow without meaning. By the end, a bunch of players had changed sides, and after a flurry of empty whoop-de-do dunks, the final score of 101–92 in favor of the home team was hardly worth remembering.

Back in street clothes but still drenched in sweat, Yao ducked into the visitors' locker room. "Thank you for doing this for the Chinese people," he said. The Nashionals spontaneously broke into the signature singsong chant: "Yao Ming! Yao Ming!"

Nash had gotten the numbers. "We raised two and a half million dollars," he told the players. "That money will build seventy schools. That's thirty-five thousand kids who'll be able to go to school. So to all of you guys, thanks a lot."

Sweet Melon emerged from the shower with a towel around his waist and said: "I know about five or six schools in Baltimore that need help, y'all."

A Basket with His Arms

I stopped off in Phoenix on my way back from China and spent a few days watching Nash and his Suns teammates scrimmage on the practice court in the US Airways Center. The scrimmages were unofficial, as training camp wouldn't start for a couple of weeks, but there was no shortage of intensity. Among the players running with Nash were Suns regulars Barbosa, Amare Stoudemire, and Marcus Banks, along with their new teammate Grant Hill. There were some good players from Europe trying to catch on. They kept the flow going with a twenty-four-second clock and got into arguments about the score and whether on one possession one team had been unfairly denied an extra four seconds. During breaks when players flopped down onto benches and threw back cups of water, often the only person on the court, practicing shots, was Nash.

Three years ago, newly repatriated to Phoenix, which had traded him to the Dallas Mavericks in 1998, Nash's back went out during practice, the result of a congenital displacement of his fifth lumbar vertebra. To relieve the muscle tightness, he now will often lie on the court during rests and time-outs. And though Nash may be getting better and better as a player, his body doesn't recover from exertion as fast. Nash's preferred method of treating his sore muscles and swollen joints is to lever himself into a fifty-three-degree ice bath, wearing thermal socks to keep the frostbite out of his toes.

"I can't even pull a beer out of water that cold," says the Suns' assistant coach Alvin Gentry.

Over the summer Nash opted not to take a spot on the Canadian Olympic basketball team, wanting to rest and conserve his energy for the upcoming run at the championship he covets. He has two years left on his contract with the Phoenix Suns; barring a catastrophic injury, he could certainly get another deal if he desired. (The Hall of Fame point guard John Stockton, with whom Nash is often compared, played until he was forty-one.) How long he plays in the NBA seems as much a matter of a willing mind as an able body.

"I've always said when Steve retires, I'll retire," Coach Mike D'Antoni said. We were sitting in a little gallery off the practice court watching the scrimmage. "I don't want anyone to be able to figure out whether our success is because of my system or Steve's ability to make it work. There's a period in a player's life where the novelty wears off. You've got kids and money, and sometimes your basketball flame begins to flicker. And then a few years later, you realize you've got a limited amount of time and this is the best it's ever gonna be. I think Steve is one of those guys who has always lived for the game. You can have all the money in the world, but for the great players the only thing that matters is winning a title."

When Nash was done with the scrimmage and some work in the weight room, we headed over to Kincaid's near the US Airways arena to get some lunch. He ordered a couple of salads.

"There are nights when I ask myself, 'Am I really playing basketball?'" Nash said. "But that's mostly from the stuff around the game: talking to the media, taking the bus, getting warmed up. Once I'm out on the court, in the game, the game is great."

I asked what drove him, beyond the obvious goal of a championship.

"I don't know," he said. "I have a lot of energy and a lot of motivation. I have a hard time sitting still. I guess in a way I can't live with the alternative to being driven, which is sitting around being bored. If I'm going to go for something, I'm really going to go for it. I think I realized as a kid that I would keep going when other kids stopped. If my legs are there, if my quickness is there, I can have a good game. If not, I try to find other ways of making plays without being quick. Making smart plays. Making the game simple."

Like he had the last day in China, when the Nashionals were literally mobbed at a fitness-club opening with Yao Ming and Jackie Chan. When they were all safely back on the bus, waiting to be shuttled to the airport for the long flight home, the die-hards in the crowd milled around on the sidewalk, taking pictures and waving at players behind the windows. All except one kid, who was about twelve or thirteen years old. He wore glasses. He wasn't tall. He was draped in a purple-and-white Steve Nash Phoenix Suns jersey, number 13. He stood outside Nash's window and pantomimed jump shot after jump shot, like he was Steve Nash. He had Nash's form down pat — the slight gathering before the jump, the leap straight up, elbows squared, the impeccable wrist-break that left the hand lingering a moment high overhead like it was pleased with itself. Even the way Nash sometimes crimped his lips when he shot. "Look at this dude, he's wiggin' out," one of the players said. Everyone in the bus was falling apart laughing. Again and again, as dogged as a gym rat with a dream, number 13 launched an imaginary ball. *Nash for three from the sidewalk! Nash from half-court! Nash from downtown Beijing!* And then he untied one of his sneakers and began to fire off shots with it, hopping on one foot, form still constant. Nash went to the window and made a basket with his arms.

"Right here, dude!" he said through the glass.

But the kid just slung the sneaker straight up in the air.

"No, right here," Nash said again, tapping the pane, and again he made a basket with his arms. The kid saw what Nash wanted; he jumped and sent his sneaker arcing toward the hoop. If there hadn't been glass in the way, it would have gone in.

"Yeah! Atta boy!" said Nash, and when the bus pulled out, he blew the kid a kiss.

RICK BRAGG

In the Nick of Time

FROM SPORTS ILLUSTRATED

THEY SAY college football is religion in the Deep South, but it's not. Only religion is religion. Anyone who has seen an old man rise from his baptism, his soul all on fire, knows as much, though it is easy to see how people might get confused. But if football were a faith anywhere, it would be here on the Black Warrior River in Tuscaloosa, Alabama. And now has come a great revival.

The stadium strained with expectation. The people who could not find a seat stood on the ramps or squatted in the aisles, as if it were Auburn down there, or Tennessee, and when the crowd roared, the sound really did roll like thunder across the sky. A few blocks away seventy-three-year-old Ken Fowler climbed to his second-story terrace so he could hear it better and stood in the sunlight as that lovely roar fell all around him. He believes in the goodness and rightness of the Crimson Tide the way people who handle snakes believe in the power of God, but in his long lifetime of unconditional love, of Rose Bowl trains, Bobby Marlow up the middle, and the Goal Line Stand, he never heard anything like this. His Alabama was playing before the largest football crowd in state history, and playing only itself. "We had ninety-two thousand," he said, "for a scrimmage."

It felt good. It felt like it used to feel.

They came from Sand Mountain, the wire grass, the Black Belt, the Gulf Coast, and just wide places in the road. They came in motor homes, private jets, $30,000 pickup trucks, $400 cars, and dimestore flip-flops to see Nick Saban walk the sideline of Bryant-Denny Stadium in April.

They have welcomed him as Caesar, as pharaoh, and paid him enough money to burn a wet dog. Now he will take them forward by taking them back to the glory of their past — the twenty-one Southeastern Conference championships, the twelve national championships, the Team of the Twentieth Century (as the *Wall Street Journal* called the Crimson Tide in 2000).

Saban has not promised them so much — "I don't believe in predictions," he says — but they believe. It may take two years, three, more, to be in the discussion again when people talk about the best teams in college football. But they know he will take them home.

"I've been on this roller coaster for a long time," says Fowler, a self-made businessman who could live a lot of places but settled on a house so close to the campus that he can all but see his reflection in the go-go boots of the Crimsonettes as they strut down University Boulevard before the homecoming game. "In the fifties, under coach J. B. (Ears) Whitworth, we went fourteen games without a win, and I watched grown men cry. People said then there would never be another coach here as good as Wallace Wade [who won national championships in 1925, '26, and '30] or Frank Thomas [1934, '41]. They said it was over.

"Then in '58 we hired a coach who could do the things we needed to put us in a position to win SEC championships again and national championships again. People used to stare at him as he stood on the sideline too, like he was about to turn a stick into a snake."

His name was Paul Bryant, and he was popular here. They named an animal after him. How people loved that man. But it is time, past time, to love again.

"There is never anything wrong with remembering the past, but you can't live in it," says Mal Moore, the Alabama athletic director who was all but dragged through saw briars when it appeared that Saban and other marquee names — most notably West Virginia coach Rich Rodriguez — were passing Alabama by. Then on January 3 he brought Saban home with him on the school jet from Miami, where Saban had been coaching the Dolphins. People who had been calling for Moore's resignation praised his leadership.

There is no nice way to say it: the Alabama faithful are done with waiting, with mediocrity, and with disappointment. They are sick of Auburn, which has beaten them five years in a row; bone-weary of

NCAA investigations and probations reaching back to 1993; and finished with coaches who cannot gut out the expectations here, or who might have done well, someday, with more time or a railroad car full of luck.

"We wanted a man who had won a championship, and Nick Saban is that and more," says Moore. "Saban brings a sense of command, a sense of toughness and discipline."

Saban is no rainmaker, no snake oil salesman. The way to his mountaintop is hard and paved with woe. "We can be part of something, build something all these people can be proud of and excited about again," says the fifty-five-year-old coach, who can look intense even when he is not mad and probably looks that way holding a kitten. "I got on our guys in a team meeting. I said, 'I'm tired of hearing all this talk about a national championship when you guys don't know how to get in out of the rain, don't know what to do in the classroom.' It's like you've got little kids in the back seat, saying, 'Are we there yet?'

"The journey itself is important, not just the destination. You have to follow direction. Discipline, offseason recruiting, conditioning, practice, more recruiting, player development, classroom development. I'm not interested in what should be, could be, was. I'm interested in what is, what we control. And when we lose — and we will, one game, two, or more — we have to have a trust that what we are doing will work, trust and belief in who we are. And you get where you're going, one mile marker at a time." People here believe Saban is tough and smart and do not care that he can seem impatient, if not angry, when dealing with the media or hangers-on or just about anybody else, as if he has more important things to do. Like coaching football. In a state where some old men still test their truck's electrical system by grabbing hold of a hot coil wire, football coaches are not supposed to be in touch with their inner child. Saban won a national championship at LSU in 2003, out of a conference where every game can feel like a knife fight in a ditch. No one cares how he did in charm school.

One LSU fan told Alabama fan Sammy Maze that Saban could be, well, a little difficult. "You know he's a son of a bitch?" the LSU fan said.

"Well," Maze said, "he's our son of a bitch now."

Never assume that Alabamans give a damn what others think. "People can write and say that this exemplifies a fanaticism that needs to be curbed," says Fowler, who would have gone to the Tide's intrasquad scrimmage himself if it had not been broadcast live on television. "All Alabama proved, with ninety-two thousand people at a practice, is that nobody loves football better. I don't see how that somehow makes us subhuman. I mean, in some countries they kill soccer players, don't they?"

Saban has yet to coach a down for the Crimson Tide, but people are already naming their children for him. Tim and Hannah Witt of Hartselle, Alabama, named their baby boy, born March 20, Saban Hardin Witt. They already had a son named Tyde. "At first I thought my husband was crazy," says Hannah, "but it grew on me."

In these parts you do not name a child for a coach you expect to go 8–5. The Witts had talked at first about naming their second son Bear.

Hank Williams once said he could throw his cowboy hat onto the stage of the Grand Ole Opry after he finished "Lovesick Blues" and it would get at least one curtain call. It has been that way for decades in Tuscaloosa, except the hat is houndstooth.

Will Nevin, a first-year law student, places an offering the night before every game at the feet of Bryant's statue in front of the football stadium. He and his friends leave a bag of Golden Flake potato chips and an old-fashioned glass bottle of Coca-Cola, the sponsors of Bryant's old TV show. Nevin, twenty one, never saw the show, never saw Bryant on the sideline. But the image of the Bear is alive in his mind's eye. He just knows how it must have been, like hearing someone tell you how sweet an old Mustang used to run, before it was put up on blocks in the barn and covered with a tarp. The most you can do is run your hand over the paint and imagine.

It seems like a dream now: from 1958 through 1982 there were six national championships, thirteen SEC titles, a 232–46–9 overall record, a 19–6 mark against Auburn, and a stable of immortals that included Billy Neighbors, Lee Roy Jordan, Joe Namath, Kenny Stabler, John Hannah, Ozzie Newsome, many others. But the Bryant magic was about more than numbers, more than X's and O's and big ol' boys who would have blocked a pulpwood truck if he'd asked them to. It was about how he could draw every eye in the stadium to him as he leaned against that goalpost during warm-ups, a growling, mumbling golem glued together out of legend, gristle, and a little bit of mean. It was almost cheating, having him on the sideline, like filling your trunk full of cement blocks before a demolition derby.

After a quarter-century of dominance Bryant retired after the 1982 season with a 21–15 win over Illinois at the Liberty Bowl in Memphis, in the freezing cold. Less than a month later he was dead, as if his life was hard-wired to the game. One paper sent reporters to interview the grave digger, and on Bryant's burial day people stood on the overpasses and the roadside, hands over their hearts, to watch a hearse take away one of the best parts of their history.

At any flea market in Dixie, you can still find Bryant commemorative plates. At every roadside bar, church basement rec room, or courthouse café, you can hear this joke:

> Guy gets into heaven. Sees an old man in a houndstooth hat walking on water.
>
> "Hey," he asks Saint Peter, "is that Bear Bryant?"
>
> "Naw," Pete says, "that's God. He just thinks he's Bear Bryant."

Nevin will always love the idea of Bear and always honor his legend, but it is clear that praying to a memory, however fine, has not worked amid so many missing elements. "We want something to celebrate," says Nevin. "By God, it's our right."

In one of the most storied, demanding, and impatient programs in college football, the comparison with Bryant has smothered the coaches who've come after him. With the exception of his protégé, Gene Stallings, who delivered a national championship in '92, schooling trash-talking Miami 34–13 in the Sugar Bowl, men have perished in the shadow of Bear. It is his taped voice, God-like, that still booms across Bryant-Denny Stadium at the start of every home game: "I ain't never been nothin' but a winner."

But Saban totes his own national championship prestige into Tuscaloosa — the first Bryant successor to do so — and a résumé that Alabama was willing to spend a reported $32 million over eight years to procure. "I don't think Saban's afraid of the past," says Kirk McNair, founder and editor of 'Bama magazine, who has covered Crimson Tide football across five decades. "I don't think he cares."

Saban is 91–42–1 as a college coach, in stops at Toledo, Michigan State, and LSU — all rebuilding jobs. LSU had had only three winning seasons in eleven years when he took over in November 1999. Four years later he coached the Tigers to the pinnacle of college football. His forty-eight wins from 2000 through '04 ranked third among major college coaches over that span. The Tigers were SEC champs in '01 and again in '03, when they went on to beat Oklahoma 21–14 to win the BCS national title. Saban builds his teams methodically, on a backbone of conditioning, rigid discipline, and a swarming, ball-stealing defense.

He leads like a tough-minded CEO. Listening to him, you get the feeling you would not want him to decide your fate if your job production was down and your equipment obsolete. The lore of football, the poetry of it, does not complicate his language. But he knows that before the kickoff of Alabama's season opener with Western Carolina on September 1, thousands of Crimson Tide fans, especially the ones who remember, will look to the goalpost and miss the coach who led them so grandly for so long. It should be that way.

"[Bryant] accomplished as much as anybody ever has," says Saban. "He is someone you respect, admire, and appreciate. He established the standard of excellence, him and the players who gave their blood, sweat, and tears.

"That, in itself, has no effect on the future," says Saban, who knows that no ghost, or alumnus, has ever thrown a halfback for a loss. "We have to do the work now."

Saban will not go into great detail about his team, any more than he will discuss his opponents. There is no profit in it. But it is clear that 2007 is a true rebuilding year, with a typically tough SEC schedule. Alabama goes against Vanderbilt, Arkansas, Georgia, and Ole Miss in the first half of its SEC schedule, then Tennessee, LSU, Mississippi State, and Auburn. A September 29 game against Florida State in Jacksonville is not exactly a nonconference breather.

It may be a team unfamiliar to fans used to seeing the Tide carried by a talented defense. Alabama lost too many big, fast, scary people. "If you can't stop the run in the SEC, you're in trouble," says Mitch Dobbs, the assistant editor of *'Bama* magazine, and a lot of the middle is just gone.

But instead of an offense that was too often effective only between the 20s, Alabama may show off a little with junior quarterback John Parker Wilson and a corps of game-breaking receivers. The offensive line, which bore criticism — well, let's face it, scorn — is expected to be less porous. And a redshirt freshman named Terry Grant, a former Mr. Football from Mississippi, runs like something bad is after him.

Concerns that Alabama's defense would be leaner this year materialized in summer practices, but the offense moved the ball smoothly in scrimmages on days when the temperature reached 106 and 107 degrees. No matter how hot it got, however, Alabama players did not complain. Saban and his coaches would not allow their players to even use the word *hot* or *heat* in conversation.

Alabama's athletes could have made Saban's summer a little cooler if they had behaved better off the field. Simeon Castille, an all-SEC cornerback, was arrested early last Sunday in an entertainment district near campus and charged with disorderly conduct. The police were not talking about precisely what Castille had done, and Saban indicated that he will handle the matter internally. Three other players — defensive linemen Brandon Deaderick and Brandon Fanney and running back Roy Upchurch, all reserves — were charged after a disturbance in July.

Saban might not coach the Tide to improbable wins, say Alabama fans. But he will not lose the handle on the games that are winnable and leave Alabama at the ugly end of a soul-killing upset. That is what they want from him, at least right now. In any event, it is unlikely any booster will look into Saban's drill-bit eyes and tell him, "That ain't the way Bear did it."

From the moment Saban was hired, there has been an electricity, a high-stakes poker feel to his every move. In Miami and on the national talk-show circuit he was badmouthed and lambasted for adamantly denying, as the Dolphins' season wound to its 6–10 conclusion, that he would be the Alabama coach, then turning around and taking the job. He was called a liar, a snake, and other pleasantries. Of the firestorm he says, "We gave up a little bit to be here."

Then on April 21 Saban walked onto the field for the intrasquad game to that thunder, the pure and positive manifestation of the expectations at Alabama. "There is something special about this place," he says. It is the only time in almost an hour and a half of discussion about football that Saban does not talk about work ethic, goals, discipline. "It was . . . emotional."

Saban is not surprised that Alabamans agree with his ideas on what it takes to win. He grew up in coal mining country in West Virginia, pumped gas and broke down tires at a filling station his father owned. "The worst I could ever do is go back to West Virginia and pump gas again," he says. "Life's been pretty good to me."

He understands that in Alabama people believe you have to work for what you get. "The best thing about winning the championship at LSU was that it gave people hope, something to be proud of," he says. "I don't wear the ring. It wasn't a personal accomplishment. But I think the people of Alabama understand what it takes to be successful, understand persistence, overcoming adversity, mental and physical toughness."

Saban does not see himself as mean, brusque, or distant: "I think most people who get to know me don't have that feeling." His wife, Terry, told him there might be a slight gap between how he sees himself and how others see him. That, she told him, "is your blind spot. And it's as wide as the Grand Canyon."

"And she wasn't even mad at me," Saban says.

There is no gap between what he wants and what Alabama wants. While "the name of the stadium's not going to change," says McNair, smiling, he believes that Saban, one Saturday at a time, will realign the program with its rich past. "It's been a long, long time since I had this good a feeling."

To find the source of Alabama's hunger, you have to go back further than the Bear. You have to go by train.

It was always a tough room.

Alabama's first coach, E. B. Beaumont, went 2–2 in 1892. "We therefore got rid of him," says the 1894 school yearbook.

It was hard-nosed Wallace Wade who took Alabama to its first recognized national championship, in 1925, when his undefeated team beat Washington 20–19 in the Rose Bowl, the first time a southern team had ever played in the game. Alabama won more national titles — and Rose Bowls — under Wade in '26 and '30. His successor, Frank Thomas, who had learned his football as a quarterback for Knute Rockne at Notre Dame, took Alabama to Pasadena three more times, won a widely recognized national title in '34 — with Paul Bryant playing end — and a still-debated title in

'41. Some fans say Thomas's best team was the undefeated Rose Bowl–winning squad in '45.

They were college boys in suits, but on the trips home from California, across Texas and the lower South, people stood beside the railroad tracks, waving and cheering. It was Faulkner's South, Huey P. Long's and the Klan's. Night riders in sheets still enforced their doomed ideals, and mill workers spun cotton all week for pocket change. Writers from the North and the West would question if it was wise to open the nation's premier bowl game quite so often to the unsophisticated South.

"Columbia or Pennsylvania would make a much better game with the Pacific Coast Conference representative for the 1946 Rose Bowl than would Alabama and, in addition, such a game would have that intangible thing called 'class,' something it can never have with a southern club being one of the participants," wrote Dick Hyland in the *Los Angeles Times*. "Me, I'm kinda tired of hillbillies and swamp students in the Rose Bowl."

But from beside the tracks, people waved and waved. Reconstruction had faded into the Depression, and not much had changed. "It became our culture," says Doug Jones, the former U.S. attorney who successfully prosecuted two Klansmen for the infamous 1963 bombing of the Sixteenth Street Baptist Church in Birmingham. "We were a poor state, with a great darkness in our history, but we took a team by train across the nation and played the best and beat the best."

From 1947 through '54 Harold (Red) Drew kept winning at Alabama, but it is a testament to the expectations here that a coach who went 45–28–7 with berths in the Sugar, Orange, and Cotton Bowls would be considered subpar. Over the next three years, under J. B. Whitworth, it got much worse. He was a nice man, people said, but he was 4–24–2. They needed something else.

Bryant always said his impetus for winning was the fear that he'd have to go home to a plow in Fordyce, Arkansas. In December '57, after having coached at Maryland, Kentucky, and Texas A&M, he came to Alabama. "One year [my family and I] were in Miami, and Auburn happened to be playing the Hurricanes," says Fowler. "I walked out on the beach, and there were all these Auburn people. It was terrible. I looked up as one of these little planes went by pulling a banner, EAT AT JOE'S STONE CRABS, or something, and I got to thinking. The next day the Auburn people were still there, and a plane flies over, and it says ATTENTION AUBURN, THE BEAR LIVES. I don't remember what it cost, but it was pittance for what I got for it."

There was a swagger then. "I had an Auburn friend, Spiro Gregory (Speedy) Mastoras," Fowler says. "He would tell me, after another Auburn loss [to Alabama], 'Wait till year after next.' He knew that next year was out of reach."

What a shame it couldn't last forever.

Except for Stallings, no coach after Bryant lasted more than four years. Bear's successor was Ray Perkins, a wideout on the 1964 and '65 national championship teams, who went 32–15–1 and forever angered fans when he pulled down the tower from which Bryant would watch practice. It went back up after Perkins left. Bill Curry went 26–10 and was never beloved. (An 0–3 record against Auburn didn't help.) Stallings won his title and seventy games, but the record book reads 62–25 after the NCAA stripped eight wins and a tie from the '93 season, when a player was found to have had improper dealings with an agent.

Then came everything but locusts. Mike Dubose, mired in a harassment scandal that the university would settle, went 24–23 as the NCAA investigated booster Logan Young's involvement in the recruitment of a Memphis tackle named Albert Means. Dubose resigned under pressure after he lost homecoming to Central Florida.

Dennis Franchione fled after two years (17–8) as NCAA sanctions became a crippling reality. He left for Texas A&M, and one Alabama fan, Morgan Plott, felt so betrayed that he went to Norman, Oklahoma, to see A&M get whipped 77–0 by the Sooners in 2003. "I wanted to see Coach Fran get beat," says Plott, "but I didn't know it would be that good." Alabama brought in Mike Price, who forgot he was in the Bible Belt and was let go after a visit to a topless bar, having never coached a game for the Tide. Then, in a hurry, Mike Shula was hired.

People liked Shula, who had won a lot of games as a Tide quarterback in the '80s. But, again, this is no business for a nice young man. Hamstrung by probation that was an earlier regime's doing, Shula went 26–23 in four years. He was fired last November, after his fourth straight loss to Auburn. As it became clear that the program was losing ground, fans grew weary of players who talked big and did not do much, talked about realizing their potential and showcasing their talents, and then got beat on the line of scrimmage by Mississippi State.

The expectations are cemented into the architecture. Four bronze giants watch over the promenade in front of Bryant-Denny Stadium. Here stand Wade, Thomas, Stallings, and, of course, Bryant. But because this is Alabama, there is space left for a fifth pedestal. "How could it not be?" says Moore.

Fans expect Saban to take that place. "The brick masons are probably already getting started," says Jim Fuller, who won two national titles as an offensive lineman for Bryant and another as an assistant under Stallings. He has never seen the Alabama legions hungrier or more unified. Why else would ninety-two thousand attend a glorified practice?

"Just so long as he knows that ninety-one thousand of them will be kicking his ass" if things go wrong, Fuller says.

Does he really believe there are one thousand benevolent Alabama fans? "Naw, I was being gracious."

They say college football is a matter of life and death down here, but it's not. Winning only makes life sweeter, and, once in a blue moon, losing can too. Last winter Will Nevin and his father, Randy, who was dying of cancer, took a road trip to Shreveport, Louisiana, to see Alabama play Oklahoma State in the Independence Bowl. "He got cold, and he coughed some, and we lost," Nevin says. "It didn't matter. It was one of the best times we ever had." Randy Nevin died on March 28. At his funeral it was noted that he loved deer hunting, his family, Moundville Nazarene Church, and one football team.

FRANZ LIDZ

Baseball After the Boss

FROM CONDÉ NAST PORTFOLIO

FOR MORE THAN A MONTH, I have been trying to get an audience with George Steinbrenner III, the principal owner of the New York Yankees. His son-in-law and designated heir, the infelicitously named Steve Swindal, was arrested on the night of Valentine's Day for allegedly driving under the influence and is now divorcing his way out of the team hierarchy. I want to ask Steinbrenner who will succeed him at the helm of the most famous franchise in American sports.

But the once bold and blustery Boss, as he often calls himself, has been in nearly silent retreat since fainting at a friend's memorial service in 2003. He has been slowed by a bum knee, and his nearly uncontainable energy has ebbed noticeably, some say alarmingly. At seventy-seven, he attends his club's games less and less frequently. He hasn't been sighted at Yankee Stadium since opening day, April 2, and on that occasion he looked unsteady and hid from public view. The Bronx Bloviator, who used to love sparring with sportswriters as much as bullying employees, now speaks to the media in canned statements issued through his designated mouthpiece, the New York PR guru Howard Rubenstein. Steinbrenner's Howard Hughes–like reclusiveness has fueled rumors that he is, at best, recovering from a mild stroke, at worst, in the early stages of Alzheimer's.

He has only added to the mystery by refusing interview requests and instituting a gag order on the Yankees front office and his relatives. His own publicist declines to discuss him. "Mr. Rubenstein is not available to talk about Mr. Steinbrenner or his team," the

flack's flack told me. "Nor will he be available in the near future."
(Rubenstein later told *Condé Nast Portfolio*, "I speak to George each
day, and he seems okay to me.")

I seek out Tom McEwen, the onetime sports editor of the *Tampa
Tribune*. He and Steinbrenner have been golfing buddies since
1973, the year the Boss bought the Yankees and moved his family
from Cleveland to Tampa, Florida. But they haven't talked to or
seen each other in more than a year. "I've heard all the speculation," McEwen says. "I hope he's okay."

The eighty-four-year-old McEwen doesn't get around much anymore himself. Circulation problems in both legs have confined
him to a wheelchair. Still, he offers to accompany me to Steinbrenner's home, which borders the Palma Ceia Golf and Country
Club in downtown Tampa. "I don't care if George gets mad," he
says. "At this age, what can he do to me?" So on a bright, cloudless
day in June, we pull up to the Steinbrenner compound, a stucco
palace with thick white columns.

As my rental car idles near the entrance, the black wrought-iron
gates part and another car drives out. McEwen says, "Let's go in."
We do. A portly gardener in a Yankees T-shirt leans against a huge
white anchor that dominates the front lawn. McEwen asks him, "Is
George home?"

The gardener nods. "Tell him Tom is here to see him," McEwen
says. The gardener disappears into the house. We park in the circular driveway, and I help McEwen out of the car and into his wheelchair. Then I push him to the front porch. We stare into a dark al-
cove and wait.

Five minutes later, a solitary figure emerges out of the shadows,
limping toward us. It's two in the afternoon, and George Steinbrenner is wearing slippers, silk pajamas, and a terry-cloth robe —
all Yankee blue. A diamond-encrusted World Series ring nearly as
big as a Ritz cracker obscures his wedding ring.

When he sees McEwen, a big, goofy grin spreads across his face.
"Great to see ya, Tommy," he exclaims.

"Great to see you, George," McEwen says. He introduces me as a
writer working on a story and asks about Steinbrenner's wife, Joan.

"Great to see ya, Tommy," Steinbrenner says.

McEwen asks about his sons, Hank and Hal.

"Great to see ya, Tommy," he says.

McEwen asks about his daughters, Jennifer and Jessica.

"Great to see ya, Tommy," he says.

McEwen asks about his health.

Steinbrenner sighs heavily and mutters, "Oh, I'm all right."

He doesn't look all right. In fact, he looks dreadful. His body is bloated; his jawline has slackened into a triple chin; his skin looks as if a dry-cleaner bag has been stretched over it. Steinbrenner's face, pale and swollen, has a curiously undefined look. His features seem frozen in a permanent rictus of careworn disbelief.

McEwen recounts a surreal showdown at a Tampa dog track in which George and Joan cursed each other out in the most obscene language possible. "That's Joan," Steinbrenner says, chuckling. "She's feisty."

I ask Steinbrenner about the Yankees, who are struggling mightily at the time. The grin turns into a snarl. "They'll come around," he snaps. It's the first sign of the old George.

I ask Steinbrenner whom he wants to succeed him. He ignores me. That's the last sign of the old George.

A few minutes later, Steinbrenner starts repeating himself again. "Great to see ya, Tommy," he says in response to every question. "Great to see ya."

Shifting uneasily in his wheelchair, McEwen thanks his old friend for receiving us and says good-bye. Steinbrenner waves and grins. While I wheel McEwen to the car, he whispers, "It's the strangest thing. George didn't want us to go, yet he didn't want us to stay." I look back at the Yankees owner, who is still waving and grinning. "Great to see ya, Tommy," he shouts. "Great to see ya." Then he turns and limps back into the house.

"I'm shocked," McEwen tells me. "George doesn't even seem like the same person. I figured he might be in a bad way, but I never expected this."

Yankee Ingenuity

For thirty-four years, George Steinbrenner has run the New York Yankees the way General Douglas MacArthur ran Japan: somewhat more imperiously than the emperor. By investing all profits in new players and paying them more than any other owner was willing to, he made a dormant team a winner again. Under Steinbrenner's stewardship, the franchise has not only won fifteen division titles, ten pennants, and six world championships but has turned into the biggest attraction in sports. The Yankees' annual revenue exceeds the average team's by $132 million. Sports economist Andrew Zimbalist estimates the Yankees' total value to Major League Baseball at $500 million to $700 million, which is between $50 million and $100 million more than the number-two team, the Boston Red Sox.

Wherever the Yankees play, their games are almost guaranteed sellouts. When they don't make the World Series, ratings plummet. When Steinbrenner has lambasted a player, his rants have become back-page headlines. For four decades, the Yanks have been a three-ring circus, and he has been their clown, their ringmaster, their Barnum. "There is no such thing as apathy when it comes to the Yankees," says Bill Giles, chairman of the Philadelphia Phillies. "He has made his team into something you either love or hate."

The same can be said of Steinbrenner himself. His force of personality is such that he's admired even by some who have reason to despise him. "Les Yankees, c'est moi" is Steinbrenner's attitude. Surely no modern owner is more meddlesome — he has been involved in almost every facet of the team, from negotiating major player deals to running the parking concession for a day — and surely none is more powerful. "Baseball rewrote its collective bargaining agreement in 2002 for the purpose of getting its hands on some of his money," observed *Sports Illustrated* baseball writer Tom Verducci, "both to chip away at his power and to prop up the weaker clubs."

The value of the club Steinbrenner bought thirty-four years ago from CBS for $10 million — his initial equity contribution was $168,000 — has increased to an estimated $1.2 billion, the highest in baseball. The $302 million that the Yankees grossed last season came largely from ticket sales: a team attendance record of 4.2 million fans generated gate receipts of $155 million. Of the $103 million the Yankees pocketed from broadcasting rights, more than half came from the YES network, a regional cable station in which the team has a 35 percent share. The combination of YES money and lucrative marketing deals accounts for how the Yanks lost more than $25 million yet accrued $170 million in value last year. Investment bank Goldman Sachs, which owns a minority stake in YES, has been exploring a possible sale of the network — analysts say it could be worth at least $2 billion. "Goldman is merely testing the market," Rubenstein says. "They do not represent us. The Yankees have no interest in selling their share in YES."

The new $1 billion ballpark set to open in 2009 will make a team that's already the most bankable in sports even more attractive, boosting annual revenue by another $50 million to $60 million from the sale of tickets and luxury suites.

The Yankees will cover 80 percent of the construction and receive a $44 million tax break. Most of their financing comes from a forty-year bond to be paid off in yearly increments of $55 million. If the Yankees don't field a good team, they'll be saddled with some very handsome fixed costs. There will be more pressure than ever on the owner to produce a competitive champion, which is why, in the winter of the patriarch, the person who draws up the flight plan for the Bronx Bombers matters.

Despite his reputation, it has been years since Steinbrenner micromanaged the Yankees. Team president Randy Levine and chief operating officer Lonn Trost have autonomy over business decisions, as does Brian Cashman, the general manager, on the baseball end. "George still calls the shots," says a prominent baseball agent, "but his passion for the game seems to have faded along with his health, and no one is quite sure who's got his ear anymore." Steinbrenner, he notes, loves aphorisms, and one of his favorites is "The speed of the pack is determined by the pace of the leader." "In the past few years, George's pace has slowed considerably. He's been so detached this season that I wonder if he's still in the hunt."

The owner who once crowed, "I will never have a heart attack — I give them," has said that the only way he'll leave the job is horizontally. "George used to talk about turning over the operation to his kids," McEwen says, "but I think he's gonna run the Yankees until the day he dies."

Though Steinbrenner's four children are now middle-aged, he said three years ago that he had never spoken to any of them about the line of succession. In this late inning, with George unwilling to relinquish control, it's doubtful that Hank, Hal, or either of their two sisters will take charge while their father is still in the picture.

Hank has long been George's pick, but in the past, he's shown little interest in the job. Hank's indifference has left the door open for Hal, who clearly wants to be the new Boss.

Regardless of which Steinbrenner leads the Yankees next, the organization is so well managed, the transition will probably be orderly. "This is not Castro dying in Cuba," Zimbalist says.

Steinbrenner's children could band together as a single voting bloc, but Major League Baseball requires that each team pick one managing partner to represent it at league meetings. Over the past three years, Levine has largely performed in that capacity for the Yankees.

Whoever inherits the biggest capital gain in sports history will probably face staggering gift or estate taxes. That could be avoided, temporarily, if Steinbrenner bequeathed his stake in the team, which is now at least 55 percent, to his wife, who owns at least 5 percent herself. But Joan has always kept a low profile, and McEwen is sure she would insist on keeping it that way. (There are at least a dozen other minority partners, but it's unlikely they would play any significant role in the succession. As a previous shareholder once put it, "Nothing is more limited than being George Steinbrenner's limited partner.")

Some Yankees insiders believe that once the Boss is gone, his family will sell its stake to an outsider. Donald Trump has expressed interest, and assuming Rudy Giuliani doesn't land in the White House, the former mayor would be a likely candidate to front a consortium of buyers. But Trump is thought to have too much debt and not enough ready cash. And any billionaire who could afford the Yankees wouldn't appoint someone else to run them — that would be the equivalent of producing a Broadway show and not sitting front-row center on opening night. At a cost of more than a billion dollars, everyone agrees, this would not be about making money. It would strictly be an ego buy.

If the team is sold, the next Big Ego probably would be someone like Cablevision chief executive James Dolan — overlord of the New York Knicks, the New York Rangers, and Madison Square Garden — assuming he has no financial ties to the Cleveland Indians, which are owned by his brother Larry. (Dolan would not comment for this story.) Or it could be a relatively unknown hedge fund manager with a forest of performance fees to burn. Not that the thickest bankroll guarantees success. The nine members of Major League Baseball's ownership committee have absolute say over whom they'll admit to their club, and they tend to be more arbitrary than a Manhattan co-op board. "The committee polices potential investors to protect the game's profitability and reputation," a former high-ranking baseball executive says. The owners don't want a free-spending financier who would try to better a losing team by upping its $200 million payroll to $400 million. In other words, the owners don't want another George Steinbrenner.

A new, more frugal owner could roll back salaries and try to increase profits. That would be foolish, says Zimbalist: "The Yankees play on the world's biggest stage — on Broadway — and they need marquee players. They can't afford to lose their sex appeal." By making the payroll cheaper, an owner would risk devaluing the brand.

Still, we will probably never see another baseball owner with his audacity, chutzpah, and dominant stature. "Steinbrenner's economic legacy is the way he illuminated the synergy between baseball and big cities," Zimbalist says. "He took advantage of the fact that his team was in the country's largest media market and the entertainment capital of the world."

Less a visionary than a canny capitalist, Steinbrenner changed the way baseball owners behaved by refusing to play ball by their rules. As a result, he dramatically increased player salaries around the league, and the other owners hated him for it. In 2002, they tempered his extravagance — and got a piece of his money — by instituting the luxury tax, the proceeds of which form a pool that is shared by all the teams. Last year, other team owners split $105 million in luxury tax and revenue sharing from the Yankees. For most clubs, that $3 million in trickle-down Yankee bucks would cover the cost of a new starting pitcher. For the Yankees, it might fetch a backup catcher and a half-dozen Yankee franks.

Who's the Boss?

"The Yankees are America's team," Hank Steinbrenner once told me. "To put it bluntly, nobody outside of Missouri gives a crap if the St. Louis Cardinals or the Kansas City Royals are in the World Series."

This East 161st Street view of the world is an acquired snobbery.

George and his brood grew up Cleveland Indians fans in Bay Village, Ohio, a lakeside suburb that looks as if it were inspired by a New England greeting card. His own father, Henry George Steinbrenner, was a stern and unyielding shipbuilder who had been a modestly famous scholar-athlete at the Massachusetts Institute of Technology. In 1927, he became the Engineers' first national collegiate track-and-field champion, winning the 220-yard low hurdles.

George was the oldest of three children, and the only son. Raised on a gentleman's farm, the fourteen-year-old followed in his father's goose steps to the Culver Military Academy in Indiana, where he too excelled at the hurdles. He tried hard to impress his old man but rarely did. During one meet, young George won three races, only to be chewed out by Big Hank for losing a fourth. Big Hank, George has said, "always focused on the failures."

George went to Williams College and was a graduate student at Ohio State and an assistant football coach at Northwestern and Purdue. He returned to Cleveland in 1957 to join his family's shipping company, Kinsman Marine Transit. Six years later, he bought out his father and reversed the company's faltering fortunes by switching its principal cargo from ore to grain. In 1967, Kinsman Marine merged with a bigger local rival, American Ship Building, and became the dominant grain carrier on the Great Lakes. Still, Big Hank remained unimpressed. When his son later bought the Yankees, he muttered, "Well, the kid finally did something right."

Which may or may not have been meant as a commentary on George's 1956 marriage to Joan Zieg, the daughter of an Ohio real estate tycoon. Joan (who pronounces her name *Jo-Ann*) and George had met at Ohio State while she was a dental-hygiene student and he was working on his master's in phys ed. They had two children, Hank and Jennifer, but Joan soon found her union to George to be as blissful as a root canal: in July 1962, she filed for divorce. Two months later, the couple reconciled.

As a parent, George tried to be democratic: he browbeat his kids equally. Papa George demanded that his children best their peers at walking, reading, even toilet training. He enrolled all his children at Culver, his alma mater. "Being one of George's kids was not easy," McEwen says. "He rode the boys hard. And he rode Hank hardest of all."

Hank, fifty, was the first and only Steinbrenner to be publicly groomed to follow in his father's footsteps. He stumbled along the way. Though George was Culver's Man of the Year in 1971, Hank wasn't exactly a model cadet. He hated the place. He was constantly getting demerits — for sleeping late, for not shaving, for not cleaning up his room. He would sneak out after taps and climb down the fire escape to rendezvous with his girlfriend. Hank had his serious side too. "While the rest of us guys were out hustling chicks," says a former classmate, "Hank was spending hours studying horses' bloodlines and ballplayers' batting averages."

Eventually, Hank came to think Culver was the "greatest experience" of his life. It wasn't always so. "Hank resented everything the school stood for," says the classmate. "He was very rebellious, always going tooth-and-nail with the superintendent. It always seemed to me that he acted that way to defy his father. Hank loved George and hated him too. His biggest problem was living up to his father's expectations." After graduation, Hank had an argument with George and took off for a couple weeks. Hank turned up at an Ocala motel. "When Hank reappeared," says the classmate, "George softened a lot on him."

Hank didn't go on to Williams. Instead, he made a couple of academic pit stops before settling at tiny Central Methodist in Fayette, Missouri.

"I wasn't more than an average student," Hank once told me. George thought a degree was important; Hank didn't. He dropped out before his senior year and found work at Kinsman Farm, the family's 750-acre Thoroughbred stud farm in Ocala, Florida.

His great passion was researching horses' bloodlines and matching stallions with Kinsman's breeding mares. In 1985, the first crop of foals he bred himself raced as three-year-olds. Hank's track record has been fairly impressive: five Kentucky Derby entrants, though one of them, Bellamy Road, was a big disappointment; the colt started the race as a five-to-two favorite but finished seventh.

In 1986, Hank served a limited apprenticeship with the Yankees. Though he had no title and drew no salary, he traveled with the team, sat in on staff meetings, and manned the phone on conference calls with the club's top brass. Hank's ideas sometimes met with resistance. When he declared that relief pitcher Dave Righetti would be more effective as a starter and should be replaced by Alfonso Pulido, a career minor leaguer, Righetti grumbled, "I don't mind when people I know and whose opinions I respect make suggestions that affect me and my future. But I don't want to hear it from someone who doesn't know what he's talking about." Righetti finished the season with forty-six saves, still the American League record for left-handers. Pulido returned to the minors and was out of baseball entirely by the end of the following season.

Hank also took a lot of high, hard ones from sportswriters. A New York tabloid columnist threw the first knockdown pitch, chastising the twenty-nine-year-old for smoking a cigarette on the field at the Yankees' spring training camp in Fort Lauderdale, Florida. When the Yanks released veteran pitcher Phil Niekro before the '86 season to avoid having to pay a bonus, Hank's sarcastic reaction to the sympathetic reportage didn't charm anyone: "Gee, those Niekro stories really broke my heart." In the press box, he was called Boy George and Damien, after the demon child in *The Omen*.

Like most things Steinbrenner, the nicknames were overblown. Friends of Hank say he is generally mild and terribly shy. In New York, he recoiled from the spotlight and was overshadowed by his dad's despotism. Back in 1986, I was profiling Hank for *Sports Illustrated*. When George found out, he threatened to revoke the magazine's Yankee Stadium press credentials indefinitely. The story never ran. Hank later apologized. "I'm sorry we have to play hardball," he told me.

Before the end of the 1986 season, he returned to the stud farm. He stayed there until 1990, when his father was banned from baseball for the second time, for paying a gambler $40,000 to dig up dirt on star player Dave Winfield, who had sued the Yankees for breach of contract. (The first suspension, in 1974, was for making illegal contributions to Richard Nixon's 1972 campaign fund.) Steinbrenner père nominated Steinbrenner fils to succeed him as the Yankees' general partner. Hank refused the job. "It was pretty obvious to me and everyone else that this wasn't Hank's thing," said Charlotte Witkind, then one of the team's eighteen limited partners.

One of Hank's "things" is drag racing, and he may have come to regret bringing his father into the sport. In 2000, he persuaded George to sponsor a team in the National Hot Rod Association and pledge $10 million over three years. True to form, George constantly pulled rank on Hank and overrode his decisions. And truer to form, Dad wanted to fire the crew chief a few days before the 2001 U.S. Nationals. Eventually, Hank persuaded him not to. "Hank is an intelligent guy — unfortunately, his father is George Steinbrenner," says drag-racing legend Darrell Gwynn, the racing team's co-owner. "I hate to say this, but as long as George is alive, Hank will never blossom as a businessman."

During the 2001 racing season, Gwynn was summoned to Legends Field, the Yankees' spring training base in Tampa, to meet with George and Hank. George announced he was ending his commitment. "We went from $10 million to $3.3 million," Gwynn says. "My screamathon with George lasted four hours, during which I mostly just listened. Then he apologized and said I could have anything I wanted in the Legends Field gift shop." Hank didn't say much of anything. Thirty minutes into the discussion, Gwynn says, he disappeared.

A year ago, worn down by a wrenching divorce, Hank vanished from the family businesses as well. He resurfaced last winter when his brother-in-law Steve Swindal fell from favor. "I'm sure Hank felt George needed him to get on board with the team again," McEwen says. "Either that or George just insisted on it."

This season, Hank has been a fixture at the Yankees team offices in Tampa. George has made a point of trumpeting his son's renewed involvement with the franchise. In May, when Roger Clemens came out of retirement to re-sign with the Yankees, George issued a press release praising the part Hank and brother Hal played in the deal. "The funny thing is that their sister Jenny may be savvier in business," McEwen says. "Yet her name never comes up."

The forty-eight-year-old Jennifer briefly worked in the Yankees public relations department after graduating with honors — she was a Morehead scholar — as a business major at the University of North Carolina. "Even if I wanted to move up in the organization, I would've never been allowed," Jennifer, a mother of two, told the *New York Times* in 2004. "Not in this family." George is such an entrenched chauvinist that in 1995, when trawling for a new general partner, he bypassed Jennifer for her husband, Swindal, a former tugboat company executive.

Swindal's responsibilities ran from acting as a buffer between his father-in-law and general manager Cashman to monitoring the progress of the new stadium. His biggest accomplishment was the amicable way he negotiated manager Joe Torre's three-year, $19.2 million contract extension in 2004 — in stark contrast to the acrimony of '01. Two years ago, Steinbrenner rewarded Swindal by anointing him Boss-to-be. Swindal still has a hand in running Yankees Inc., but few insiders thought that he was ever anything but a pretender to the throne. Swindal is not blood, and George is very big on blood.

That would also seem to rule out Joseph Molloy, the first husband of Jessica Steinbrenner. When George needed a new managing general partner during his second suspension in 1992, he named Molloy, who quickly rose from junior high school basketball coach to vice president in charge of the company's Tampa operations. He is now an assistant middle school principal in Tampa.

A children's book writer with four kids, Jessica, forty-three, has a sociology degree from Sweet Briar College, a solid reputation for co-managing Kinsman Farm with Hank, and, according to McEwen, "absolutely no shot at running the Yankees." She and Molloy divorced in 1998, and she later married his best friend, Felix Lopez. The Cuban-born landscaper had been hired by Molloy to work on the construction of Legends Field. He was tending Jessica's yard when they became an item. He is now a senior vice president of the Yankees, and among other duties, he helps evaluate Latin baseball talent.

The most ambitious of the Bosses-in-waiting is Hank's younger brother, Hal, who at thirty-eight has rotated in and out of the Yankees loop for seventeen years. Known to the Yankees court as Prince Hal, he followed his father to Williams, got an MBA from the University of Florida, and joined the Yanks. George put him through the paces in various departments of the club. Hal, too, clashed early and often with George and bolted from the realm in 1996 to run the family's hotel business. When he turned innkeeper, the Steinbrenners owned three properties. Today, the family has eight.

Though he bears an uncomfortable resemblance to Steinbrenner senior, Hal is keen to show he is his own man. He has become a sort of champion of the Yankees' two hundred employees. After the 2003 season, George wanted to take away their dental coverage; Hal talked his father out of it. Unlike George, Hal seems to disdain players and the media.

Since Swindal's exit, Hal has bunkered down in his office at Legends Field and has taken on many of his ex-brother-in-law's responsibilities. The new Yankee Stadium is the hotelier's pet project. But the question of whether Prince Hal will ascend to the throne may have less to do with his competence than the madness of King George. "I've always thought that Hank was the favorite of the mother, and Hal of the father," McEwen says. "But who knows what George is thinking now? He's got his family in a puzzlement."

Long shots and dark horses aside, the smart money is on Hank, perhaps only because he's the oldest. That's if he even wants the job. Until now, he hasn't.

To be elevated to general partner, Hank would have to win approval from two-thirds of the Yankees' quiescent stockholders. Barring an internecine battle, he would be a shoo-in. Approval by Major League Baseball, on the other hand, will not be automatic. In the past, numerous potential general partners, most notably Eddie DeBartolo of San Francisco 49ers football fame, have been batted down in the rigorous process of interviews and background checks. The nomination must be okayed by three-quarters of team owners. "Being a Steinbrenner should simplify things," says Patrick Courtney, of the baseball commissioner's office. "The family is not unknown."

Though Hank may lack his father's fire and fervor, there's no reason to believe he would be any less of a spendthrift. Five years ago, he argued at a front-office meeting for the team to trade for Raul Mondesi, a famously overpaid and underachieving outfielder. "The Yankees go out and make the big deal!" he told general manager Cashman (as reported in *Sports Illustrated*). "It's what the Yankees do!" Cashman disagreed, but Mondesi became a Yankee and was a colossal bust.

Hank has not talked to reporters about baseball in a very long time, though some twenty years ago, he and I spoke for four hours about his childhood, his father, the team, and all things Yankee. He sat behind a desk in his ballpark office, empty except for a butt-filled ashtray. He wore a monogrammed white shirt, a well-pressed blue pinstriped suit, and a tie with a Yankees insignia. He had a watchful reserve, his hair combed and trimmed with plebe-like precision. The only hint of insouciance was a cigarette cocked Bogart-style in the corner of his mouth. "I don't want to sound conceited," he said in a voice that was almost gentle, "but I'm second in command in this organization."

"What I think Hank means," his father later told me, "is that he's number two at the dinner table." Whether that was confirmation or denial is still debatable.

Though having their father buy the Yankees would be a dream for many kids, Hank initially found it distasteful. "The big salaries repulsed me," he told me. "The fact that guys were playing a kids' game and getting enormous amounts of money seemed illogical. They get millions a year to bitch and moan and be pampered. They ought to try putting on a suit and working behind a desk at IBM for a month instead of jumping around a field." Of course, many people think his father was the cause of all those high salaries, but Hank said, "Dad didn't create the system. He just took advantage of it."

By 1986, Hank had changed his mind and come to think of ball-players as entertainers who should therefore earn as much as rock stars. Until this epiphany, his only professional connection with the game had been a softball team he managed in Tampa, where labor costs weren't so high. Hank told George he would like to learn the business. "It's about time," Dad said.

And what had he learned? "Four big lessons," Hank told me. "My father taught me you've got to out-hustle the competition. He taught me that in business, there's always a time when you can take a risk. And he taught me that if you're not a benevolent dictator, your subjects will take advantage of you every time."

The final lesson — the one that may be most significant if he does become the next Boss — was to ignore public opinion. "The temptation would be to throw up my hands and say, 'Fuck it!'" Hank said. "When my dad bought the Yankees, fans were getting tired of rooting for a piece-of-crap team. I'm certainly not going to sell a club with a strong farm system to some jackass and have him get credit for winning the World Series." Spoken like a true Steinbrenner.

I asked Hank how he would improve the Yankees. He flashed a smile that was broad and diabolical. "Get rid of my father," he cracked.

J. R. MOEHRINGER

Twenty-three Reasons Why a Profile of Pete Carroll Does Not Appear in This Space

FROM LOS ANGELES MAGAZINE

1.

Accepting His Loan of a Shirt Might Have Been an Ethical Violation
(Especially Since I Kept the Shirt as a Souvenir)

PETE CARROLL, HEAD COACH of the football team at the University of Southern California, turns to me one night around 8:00 P.M. and says he's got something to do, somewhere he needs to be. We're standing outside his office at Heritage Hall, the red-brick headquarters of USC's athletic program, the trophy-filled heart of Troy. I ask Carroll where he's going, what he's doing. He doesn't answer.

I ask if I can come along. No, he says, absolutely not. I ask again. Sorry, he says. I stare imploringly. Okay, he says, looking me up and down — but you'd better change. He rummages through a small wardrobe in the corner of his office and finds a white polo, which he flips to me like a screen pass.

Put this on.

How come?

Your shirt, it's blue — you might get shot.

Where the hell are we going?

He walks quickly out of the office.

2.

He Often Wouldn't Let Me Take Notes, So Some Quotations Are Approximations from Memory

While wriggling into Carroll's shirt, I hurry to keep pace. It's not easy. Carroll's normal gait is what others might call a wind sprint. Down some stairs, around a practice field, through a parking lot, we zoom across campus. He tells me to stow my notebook. It might make the people we're meeting uncomfortable.

Who are we meeting?

Look for a blue van, Carroll says.

A *blue van?*

There, he says. Sure enough, a blue van is double-parked at the corner, and beside it stands our driver and escort for the night, a deep-chested, gentle-voiced man named Bo Taylor. I climb into the back seat. Carroll rides shotgun.

Along the way Taylor tells me that he and Carroll do this often. They make late-night journeys through the dicey precincts of Los Angeles. Alone, unarmed, they cruise the desolate, impoverished, crime-ridden streets, meeting as many people (mostly young men) as possible. The mission: let them know that someone busy, someone famous, someone well known for winning, is thinking about them, rooting for them. The young men have hard stories, grim stories, about their everyday lives, and at the very least Carroll's visit gives them a different story to tell tomorrow. Carroll says: "Somebody they would never think would come to them and care about them and worry about them — did. I think it gives them hope."

Few fans of USC, Carroll concedes, know that he spends his nights this way. He's not sure he wants them to know. He's not sure he wants anyone to know. I ask what his wife of thirty-one years, Glena, thinks of these excursions. He doesn't answer. (Days later Glena tells me with a laugh that she doesn't worry about Carroll driving around L.A., but she drew the line when he mentioned visiting Baghdad.)

We start in east South-Central, a block without streetlights, without stores. Broken glass in the gutters. Fog and gloom in the air. We hop out and approach a group of young men bunched on the sidewalk. Glassy-eyed, they're either drunk, stoned, or else just dangerously bored. They recognize Carroll right away. Several look around for news trucks and politicians, and they can't hide their shock when they realize that Carroll is here, relatively speaking, alone.

Carroll shakes hands, asks how everyone's doing. He marches up and down the sidewalk, the same way he marches up and down a sideline — exhorting, pumping his fist. At first the young men are nervous, starstruck, shy. Gradually they relax. They talk about football, of course, but also about the police, about how difficult it is to find a job. They talk about their lives, and their heads snap back when Carroll listens.

A car pulls up. Someone's mother, back from the store. She freezes when she sees who's outside her house. Carroll waves, then helps her with the groceries. He makes several trips, multiple bags in each hand, and the woman yelps with laughter. No, this can't be. This is too much. Pete Carroll? Coach of the roughest, toughest, slickest college football team in the nation, schlepping eggs and soda from her car to her kitchen?

Next we drive to the Jordan Downs housing projects, one of the most dangerous places in L.A. We find a craps game raging between the main buildings. Forty young men huddle in the dark, a different sort of huddle from the ones Carroll typically supervises. They are smoking, cursing, shoving, intent on the game, but most fall silent and come to attention as they realize who's behind them. *Pete Carroll,* someone whispers. *Pete Carroll?* The most famous sports figure in the city, excluding Kobe Bryant? (Maybe *including* Bryant.) Pete Carroll, mentor to Carson Palmer, Matt Leinart, Reggie Bush, LenDale White — here? A sweet-faced teen named Jerome steps away from the game. He stares at Carroll, shakes his head as if to clear it. He says the same thing over and over. *Pete Carroll in the ghetto. Man, this is crazy. Pete Carroll — in the ghetto! Crazy.*

Sometime after midnight Carroll and Taylor head for the van. Time to get back to Heritage Hall, where Carroll will catch a few hours of sleep on his office floor before his assistant coaches start showing up. A young man stops Carroll, takes the coach aside, and becomes emotional while explaining how much this visit has meant to him. He gives Carroll a bracelet, something he made, a symbol of brotherhood and solidarity. Carroll accepts the bracelet as if it were a Rolex. He'll wear it for days, often pushing back his sleeve to admire and play with it. He gives several young men his cell-phone number — something he's never offered me — and tells them to call if they ever need to talk. One, an ex-con, will call early the next morning and confide in Carroll about his struggles feeding his family. Carroll will vow to help find him a job. (So far, Taylor says, Carroll has found part-time jobs for forty young men.)

Driving back to campus, Taylor is bleary-eyed, I'm half asleep, and Carroll looks as if he could go for a brisk 5-K run, then start a big home improvement project. I ask Taylor if people on the streets ever seem suspicious of Carroll. Do they ever think he's grandstanding or recruiting — or crazy? Taylor says he's heard almost no cynicism, though he admits that he was doubtful at first. "Pete was like, 'I want to go through the community with you,'" Taylor says. Sure, Taylor told Carroll, assuming it was just talk. Then, late one night, Taylor's phone rang.

Hey, Bo, what's up?

Not much. Who's this?

Pete.

Pete who?

Pete Carroll. Hey, man, I'm ready, man. When can we go out there?

Taylor was stunned. Not only did Carroll follow through, but there was something in his tone. He was asking to visit neighborhoods where police don't like to go, and he was asking without fear. "He asked like he wasn't afraid," Taylor says. He turns to look at me in the back seat, to make sure I'm sufficiently astonished or to make sure I'm still awake. *"He asked that shit like he was not afraid."*

3.

His Lack of Fear Scared the Hell Out of Me

Carroll gave up fear long ago. He gave it up the way people give up carbs. Fear now has no part in his daily life. Fear is like an old, distant friend. They know each other well, talk once in a while, but they're not close like they used to be.

In meetings, practices, pregame talks, fear is Carroll's theme.

"That's what we're all about," he says, lying back on the leather sofa in his office one night. "Our entire approach is to come to the point where we have the knowing that we're going to win. There's nothing to stop us but ourselves. To do that is to operate in the absence of fear."

Carroll teams are 65–12 over the last six years. They win 84 percent of the time. They win like the sun rises and the Santa Anas blow. Strictly by the numbers — 84 frigging percent — he's the best football coach in the nation, Division I-A or pro. His players, apparently, operate in a fear vacuum. I, on the other hand, operate in the constant presence of fear, the ubiquity of fear. I'm light-headed with dread at the prospect of profiling Carroll, because early on I realize it can't be done, not in any conventional sense. Carroll's the acme of unconventional, and thus a profile of him needs to be radically different. Knowing this creates pressure, a feeling under the ribs that starts like indigestion and becomes a persistent, nagging fear, which is then compounded by Carroll's noticeably absent fear. Even when Carroll says or does something inspiring, a frequent occurrence, part of me feels lifted up, but much of me feels cast down. It's analogous to the way, no matter how fascinating you find them, super-rich people can make you feel sad.

Also, a profile is like a football game. Yes, football is used as a metaphor for just about everything — manhood, America, war, sex, the real estate market — but it's a better-than-average metaphor for writing. (In football, as in writing, your flow is impeded by blocks.) It's especially useful as a metaphor for writing about another person. Football is all about taking something that's not yours, wresting it from someone who'd just as soon keep it. In football the coveted thing is the ball; in journalism it's the subject's self, his interior life, and in a psychic struggle for that prize, Carroll is nearly unbeatable. He's too amorphous, too various — too quick. He walks too fast, talks too fast, runs too deep. Fathoms deep.

His longtime friend Michael Murphy, co-founder of the Esalen Institute, e-mails me from Russia when I plead for help with my profile, but his answer only scares me more. He says Carroll is more complicated than I suspected: "When we talk, we sometimes turn to sports, but more often to philosophy and the amazing possibilities of human nature. For a while we worked together with Russian

coaches and athletes and talked about ending the Cold War . . .
We've discussed Indian philosophy, religious mysticism, parapsy-
chology as a scientific discipline, and various social causes. I've
probably forgotten more topics we've explored than the ones I can
remember."

Carroll is an unnerving inverse of the traditional sportswriter's
dilemma — the athlete who says nothing and has nothing to say.
Carroll says a lot and has a lot to say. The problem, therefore, isn't
lack of information. The problem isn't even too much information. The problem is finding the right template, the right format for all that information. You can't capture a character like
Carroll using that dried-up magazine format — The Profile. (The
opening scene that shows our Subject in a quirky/revealing light;
the writerly riff that makes a claim for the Subject's relevance; the
quotes from friends/family/enemies; the quotes from the Subject
himself; the closing scene that shows the Subject in a setting that
recalls the opening.) With Carroll, I know from the start, this format won't work. It won't feel true. Not even 84 percent true. People will think I never got close to him. People will say: "Damn,
didn't you get any access?"

4.

He Gave Me Total Access

I first meet Carroll just before the season starts. His team is ranked
number one in the nation. We're standing on Howard Jones Field,
a fenced pasture at the center of the sprawling concrete campus,
and I make my pitch. I want to write something distinctive, I tell
him. Comprehensive.

Sure, he says, let's do it. Awesome, he says. (Along with *cool* and
stuff, awesome is one of Carroll's words. He says *awesome* so often that
I anticipate it, hear it, remember it, whether he actually says it or
not. He's forever decreeing people and things to be *awesome,* and
the word is no boilerplate superlative: he means that this person or
thing is filling him to the brim with awe.) He promises me total access, and in the days that follow, he's good to his word. He waves
me into rooms and meetings barred to other reporters. He lets
me eat with him and his assistants. He invites me to watch game

films, sit in on private speeches to players, accompany him on re-cruiting visits, travel with the team — live his life. I'm grateful, of course. I'm aware that a heavy curtain is being drawn back. But I also see that the real VIP area, Carroll's soul, remains behind velvet ropes.

Carroll's specialty, after all, is defense. He knows better than most people how to keep opponents at bay, even while letting them feel as if they're advancing. On the field he favors the bend-but-don't-break style, whereby his teams surrender small nibbles of yardage but never the big bite. I believe that's how he treats a would-be profiler. Not by design, maybe, but by instinct.

In an unguarded moment Carroll confesses that he made up his mind long ago about journalists. They're unavoidable, he says. Like injuries and agents, they come with the job, and it's best to "build relationships" with them. Know your enemy as you know yourself. (Wisdom from Sun Tzu, the ancient Chinese military strategist, one of Carroll's spiritual pillars.) Journalists might help Carroll or flatter him, but they're more likely to wound him, something he learned the hard way in Boston, ten years ago, coaching the New England Patriots. Boston writers were brutal, he says. They blamed Carroll for not being his predecessor, Bill Parcells. They blamed him for not being his successor, Bill Belichick. They blamed him for breathing. Holding back a little, therefore, isn't ungenerous. It's gamesmanship. It's ball control.

5.

There's Nothing in My Notebooks

Even when he's not holding back, Carroll crosses me up by repeating stories and quips to other writers. He's promiscuously quotable, spreading his wit willy-nilly. He doesn't understand, or care, that we're all trying to wring something new out of him. He tells me a great story, never before published, about the time he hit bottom in New England. Unable to sleep, he flipped on the TV and found a movie about Babe Ruth. He watched Bostonians booing Ruth and thought: *Those are the same guys who boo me as I come through the tunnel every Sunday, and they're booing the greatest baseball player of all time!* He was able to laugh, to lighten up, to feel a connection with the Bambino, which got him through the hard times. I write it all down. Days later he gives the same story to the *Boston Globe*.

I can't count the number of times I hear Carroll being pithy with a reporter, e.g., "I always think something really good is about to happen," or, "Sleep is overrated," then say the same thing to another reporter a day or two later. Worse, when he does say something new, something legitimately juicy, he gives my tape recorder the big eye and says — *Off the record.* He goes off the record like Lindsay Lohan goes off the wagon. I like him (another reason I can't profile him, shouldn't profile him), but I'll never forgive him for declaring one particularly delicious rant against a fellow coach — an "asshole" and "a fucking asshole" — off the record.

More confounding, Carroll's conversations and private interactions are note-resistant. Looking through my notebooks, I find page after page of fragments, moments, scenes that seemed poignant or telling at the time and now feel thin. He might be too evanescent, too ephemeral. His essential aura might lie outside the ken of shorthand.

For example, Carroll tells me he suffers from attention deficit disorder. "Self-diagnosed," he says, kidding, but I concur with his joke diagnosis. Besides leaving half his sentences (and meals) unfinished, he's in constant motion, tapping his foot, jiggling his leg, swaying to music, playing drums on tables and dashboards. He's also endearingly absentminded. For the longest time he had no e-mail, because he couldn't remember his password. He misplaces his cell-phone charger. He loses his keys, locks himself out of his office (twice in one twenty-four-hour span). Days after our drive around South-Central, we bump into Taylor at a charity event. Carroll tries to introduce us. We both look at him, bewildered. I gently remind Carroll that the three of us just spent six hours together.

But then this. I'm watching him watching film. In one hand he holds a laser pointer, in the other a remote control, which freezes the action, runs the play backward and forward at different speeds. Without taking his eyes from the screen, he casually asks Nick Holt, his defensive coordinator, how things went at the doctor. Holt, sitting to Carroll's right, grunts that a thing on his skin is precancerous and will need to be removed. Like the players on the screen, Carroll abruptly stops, midmotion. He stares at Holt, unblinking, gauging Holt's level of concern. He stares until Holt lifts his head from what he's reading and looks Carroll straight in the eye. "It's nothing," Carroll says.

"Yeah," Holt says, and shoots Carroll a grateful grin.

No earth-shaking words. No grand gesture. Just a sudden payment of attention, despite an attention debt, because attention is the thing most needed. Just a focus of his personal laser, as in his hand. In my notebook it says:

It's noth —
Doesn't blink. Doesn't jiggle leg
Just stares

In my memory it feels like much more.

6.

There's Nothing on My Tapes

On two separate occasions, though I aim the tape recorder at Carroll's mouth, I later discover nothing on the tape but sibilant mumbles. I hear his voice, then a rustling, then silence, then garble garble — it's spooky. The tape recorder is brand-new. It was the most expensive one they had at Radio Shack. It picks up my voice fine. When Carroll speaks, the recording sounds like an articulate man gagged and locked in the trunk of a car.

7.

I'm Unable to Describe Carroll's Appearance Without Sounding Gay

Most football coaches are bald, pear-shaped sourpusses. They look like southern sheriffs, circa 1954. But Carroll is a Hollywood fever dream, a hybrid of Knute Rockne and a rock star (folk rock). He looks like a man who spends his days in the sun. Not the bad sun, the sun of Marlboro Men and aging soap opera actors, but the good sun, the sun of tennis pros and yachtsmen. He's not leathery, just burnished. His eyes are bright Caribbean blue, and the browner his skin gets, the bluer his eyes turn. His nose is slightly zigzag. It breaks left, then right, a runner in the open field, and his chin is jutting, prominent, always pointing the way forward.

His hair, however, might be his signature feature. A puffy palette of white, silver, and gray, it reminds you sometimes of Bill Clinton, other times of Dick Van Dyke. Now you see follicular intimations of Richard Gere, now you see flashes of Phil Donahue, now a fleck or two of Jack Kemp. A journalist friend, when I mention that I'm writing a profile of Carroll — before I realized I couldn't write a profile of Carroll — says the coach has always seemed to him the paragon of kicked-back cool, the Burt Bacharach of coaches. It's a fine, and fittingly hair-focused, comparison.

He's taller in person than on TV. Stalking a sideline, he's always dwarfed by that phalanx of giants in his private Praetorian Guard, but walking the campus he's taller than most students he passes. He's also in better shape. He dresses in concealing layers — a blousy polo shirt over a white body shirt, khaki pants — but when he changes in his office, when he's standing there shirtless, you notice the definition. A USC strength coach says Carroll is a workout fiend, always looking for new ways to get the heart rate up and the body fat down. He lifts weights, boogie-boards under the pier at Hermosa Beach, and after an exhausting morning of meetings and interviews and speeches, he likes nothing better than to run the floor hard with a pickup basketball team. A doctor told him long ago that his knees are bad, bone-on-bone bad, and he should never play basketball again. He doesn't go to that doctor anymore.

Every year on Carroll's birthday he vows to throw a football as far as he is old. When he turned fifty-six in September, he made a point of going out to the field in the morning and chucking the rock fifty-six yards. He takes visible pride, disarming pride, in telling me that his ball landed with several yards to spare. There is the trace of a smile on his lips as he tells me. There is always the trace of a smile on Carroll's lips. His effectiveness as a motivator begins and ends with that smile, which is sincere, unrestrained, and wide, though he mixes in half smiles and smirks when being sarcastic. More than the smile, it's specifically the prospect of a smile that seems to fuel the many people orbiting Carroll all day. They are prepared to go to great lengths, endure significant pain and inconvenience, to earn one of those Carroll high-beamers, and they brighten visibly upon receipt. They become flustered. They turn the colors of a Pacific sunset. They titter.

Many TV and movie stars hang around Carroll. (On his desk is a Jack Bauer action figure given to him by Kiefer Sutherland for his birthday, and he sometimes plays with it while talking to visitors.) One star, however, is known to giggle uncontrollably around Carroll, according to eyewitnesses. The eyewitnesses don't blame the star, really. Carroll's smile just has that effect.

More than charismatic, more than charming, Carroll's smile represents a break from tradition. Football coaches aren't supposed to smile. There's no crying in baseball? There's no smiling in coaching. Football coaches are supposed to snarl and growl and look chronically constipated. Football coaches are supposed to make Dick Cheney look like Mr. Haney. Football coaches aren't supposed to flash you a smile that makes you go all goosey and forget your dignity. Or your next question.

8.

He Wore Me Down

These are some of the things Carroll doesn't do:

Eat.
Drink.
Sleep.
Pee.
Vacation.
Think negative.

That is, I haven't seen him do any of these things, not the way most people do them, with regularity. I, however, do all these things, sometimes at the same time, and following Carroll around, therefore, doing everything he does, not doing anything he doesn't do, I'm always hungry, tired, thirsty, and need to find a men's room. He pushes me to the limits of my endurance, until I'm barely able to function.

After we've spent the night cruising South-Central, after Carroll has catnapped on the floor of his office, I expect to find him exhausted the next morning. I want to find him exhausted. Instead he looks as if he's slept ten hours, eaten a heart-healthy breakfast, then enjoyed a ninety-minute deep-tissue massage.

It's emotionally as well as physically demoralizing. Under the best of circumstances, emasculation is a major concern when hanging around the USC football team. Heritage Hall is a hypermasculine, phallocentric environment, and with your little notebook, and your nettling questions, and your trick knee, you can't help but feel like Woody Allen's kid brother. It doesn't help that, while interviewing the defensive star, you hold the tape recorder above your head and wish there were a step stool handy. But when the head coach outworks you, outlasts you, when the head coach grinds you into a fine dust, you feel like Dakota Fanning.

If I shut my eyes and try to picture my time with Carroll, one scene comes quickly to mind. It's late. He's pacing outside his office, glancing at a game on TV, tossing a football to himself, talking to me and several assistant coaches all at once. Suddenly and unaccountably he leans against a leather chair and starts doing push-ups. Slumped in a chair, eyelids heavy, I can't help wondering if he might secretly be using crystal meth.

Carroll's wife says that when he does sleep, he sometimes shoots awake in the middle of the night, seized by inspiration. A new play, a new solution to some Xs and Os problem. Carroll likens his mental state to the movie *Phenomenon*. He says he feels something like that John Travolta character, whose mind is racing with ideas and flashes of insight. I remind Carroll that at the end of the movie, doctors discover that Travolta's character has a tumor. Carroll says something to the effect that I'm carrying the metaphor too far.

While watching Carroll in practice one day, I'm vaguely thinking I need to start taking vitamins more regularly. He's smiling, throwing the football, chewing a wad of gum, inspiring everyone, pumping everyone up. He's fourteen years older than I am. His job is harder than mine. His hours are longer. His path is strewn with greater hurdles — Cal and Oregon, to name two. But here he is, on the balls of his feet, running and jumping, leaping through the air while happily blowing his whistle. Baryshnikov as a *Baywatch* lifeguard.

I think: Maybe if I had a whistle.

9.

I Applied Carroll's Coaching Methods to Myself — No Luck

When he's not helping them conquer their fear, Carroll is preaching to his players about fun. He urges them, if they do nothing else, to have fun, because fun is a natural antidote to fear and a prime motive for most of the things we do.

People who know him best invariably seize upon *fun* to describe Carroll, either saying it's fun to be around him or that he's forever having fun. His emphasis on fun comes mainly from his DNA but also from his reading, specifically W. Timothy Gallwey's *The Inner Game of Tennis*, a 122-page book with a cult-like following. (The latest edition features a foreword by Carroll.) Using tennis as a prism through which to view all human endeavor, Gallwey says we focus too narrowly on results. "The three cornerstones of Inner Game," he tells me, "are Performance, Learning, and Enjoyment. Usually people put Performance first, and Learning and Enjoyment are almost absent."

If we focused more on Enjoyment and Learning, Gallwey says, we'd perform better and we'd be a lot happier: "You look at a child. He learns while he plays. Anything he tries to do, or win at, he's playing, he has a wonderful time doing it. They're not separate things for a child. That means to me these things are inherently built into human beings. Most human beings, you have to coach what's already inherent — that is, the drive of excitement to learn and keep learning, and the drive to enjoy. It gets really covered up when winning is everything. I agree with Lombardi: winning is everything. It's just what your definition of winning is."

Defensive end Lawrence Jackson, co-captain of the team, says he struggled last year, recovering from an injury, fighting to play his way back into shape, until Carroll gave him a copy of Gallwey's book. Jackson's game, and his life, changed. "He was telling me to settle down and kind of get back to having fun," Jackson says of Carroll. "Who knew that it was going to come down to 120 pages of a book?"

I study *The Inner Game of Tennis*. I try to have fun with my Carroll profile. But I'm caught in a trap. The more I learn about Carroll, the more there is to learn. The more time I spend with Carroll, the greater the pressure. As pressure increases, enjoyment decreases. As enjoyment decreases, performance plummets.

Sensing my rising tension, Carroll can hardly conceal his pity or his amusement. He asks what my plans are for the week. I tell him I'll be reading about him, thinking about him, trying to figure out how to synthesize all I've seen, heard, and read. He smiles and says something that, unless I'm hearing things, sounds like "Poor guy."

10.

He's Not Finished

Carroll dislikes "goals." He doesn't use the word, makes a face when I use it. So let's say he's undertaken two enormous tasks, and he can't be judged fairly — or profiled — until he succeeds, fails, or quits.

His first task: turn USC into the grandest college dynasty ever. Not this week's number-one team but history's. "To win forever," he says, and before this year he looked to be well on his way. He'd won back-to-back national championships and come within nineteen seconds of another. (He still goes over critical decisions in that 2005 championship game against Texas, when the Trojans had the lead late but couldn't bottle up mighty Vince Young.) He put together a 2007 team that was fast on defense, loaded on offense, the heavy favorite to win the third championship of the Carroll Era.

Then came week five and a series of disturbing setbacks.

There was the inexplicable collapse against Stanford, the most improbable loss by an "overdog" in college football history, according to oddsmakers. There was the flare-up of an old scandal surrounding Bush, the virtuoso former tailback, who stands accused of taking $280,000 in improper payments while a student athlete. (Should Bush be found guilty, the NCAA could levy hefty fines against USC.) There was a rash of injuries on offense, decimating a corps that was supposed to dominate and sidelining John David Booty, the starting quarterback, who cracked a finger on his throwing hand. Suddenly, people were questioning the invincibility of USC and its coach.

Carroll's second task, however, is even more lofty and less likely to be finished soon. Having achieved job security for the first time in his life, he's expanded his work to include the city beyond USC. Some want to save the world — Carroll wants to coach it. He's launched a foundation, A Better L.A., aimed at motivating on a large scale, at ending violence in the inner city, and he now takes time each week to think and talk about problems other than what to call on third and long. With any coach who's still coaching, drawing conclusions can be hard. His legacy is always in flux; it hinges on what happens next Saturday. But when a coach is remaking himself into a social activist, when he's just beginning the task for which he may one day be best remembered, firm statements feel that much more ridiculously premature.

11.

A Profile Will Be Better in Five or Six Years When This Kid Is Actually Playing for USC

On a recruiting swing through the city, Carroll drops in at a private high school. He asks to see a faculty member, a woman whose son is a touted prospect. The mother emerges from her office and frowns. She recognizes Carroll immediately and knows why he's here. She brusquely explains that all the men in her family played for USC's hated rival, Notre Dame, and that's where her boy is almost certainly going. Carroll says he knows all about the boy's Notre Dame pedigree. He's been well briefed. But he came anyway, he tells the mother sheepishly, because he likes a challenge. He smiles. The mother scowls.

Carroll is a master at recruiting. His life is predicated on competition, and he particularly enjoys competing for people, kids, *prospects*, which is how dynasties are made. (College football geeks have ranked Carroll's last five recruiting classes among the best in the nation.) Sometimes, when talking to a recruit and his parents, Carroll can barely contain his enthusiasm. "I know what I'm offering," he tells me. "They can't even conceive. They don't — they can't possibly understand how special —"

Booty remembers his first recruiting visit to USC. Carroll won him over in seconds. "Acted like he'd known me my whole life," Booty says. "Just coming up, giving me a high-five, hugging my parents. It was one of the best experiences I've ever had meeting a college coach. I've met just about every coach — hands down, he was the best."

Before leaving campus Booty knocked at Carroll's door and told him he'd decided to play for USC. "I didn't even go home to think about it. I told my dad, 'This is where I want to be.'"

Carroll tries everything, but the mother refuses to warm up. It's not just that Carroll coaches the Enemy; the mother clearly doesn't like the idea of her son leaving home, ever. She cringes at the thought of handing him over to any coach, no matter the school. He's fourteen, she tells Carroll, pleading. He's a baby, she says. Carroll tries to reassure her. In the soothing voice of a suicide hotline operator, he says that he realizes her boy's young and college is years off. He simply wanted to introduce himself. No big deal, no pressure. But when the time comes to choose a school, he adds, he hopes she'll at least consider USC. Come to the campus for a visit.

The mother nods, thanks Carroll, then walks him — no, escorts him — to the front door. As Carroll crosses the street, the mother yells: *Good luck with the season! Hope you have at least one loss!*

Carroll turns to me.

What'd she say? Hope you have green moss?

Hope you have one loss.

He squints. Still doesn't get it.

In other words, she hopes you lose to Notre Dame.

Really? That's what she said?

We climb back in the car. Ken Norton Jr., Carroll's linebacker coach, drives to the next school. Carroll turns up the radio. Humming along to an R&B song, he stares out the window, lost in thought. All at once he brightens. Hey, he says. At least she wants us to win twelve games! That's what she's saying, right? She hopes we win twelve games. That ain't so bad!

12.

The Three Rules Don't Add Up

Shortly before arriving at USC, Carroll sat down and drew up three rules, three basic imperatives that are central to his view of coaching. The three rules are among the first things a freshman learns when he steps on the USC practice field. The three rules must be memorized, internalized, or the player is out. The three rules are:

1. Protect the team.
2. No whining. No complaining. No excuses.
3. Be early.

No matter how many times I add them up, the three rules look to me like five rules. I feel like a malcontent, a contrarian, for raising the point, for even noticing, but I can't help it.

Also, something inside me rebels against rule number 2 (number 4, by my reckoning). Something inside me bridles at any blanket prohibition of excuses, for reasons that by now should be obvious.

13.

No Matter What I Write, It Will Be Wrong

I could write that Carroll failed as a head coach in the National Football League, that he didn't hit his stride, didn't find himself, until he returned to college ball. It's the most common knock against him, and his NFL record (33–31) *was* less than dazzling. But I could just as easily write that Carroll deserved more time, that he was done in by idiot fans and trigger-happy NFL owners who didn't recognize his strengths. Given more time, Carroll would have become one of the best. "He never really had a chance to establish himself," says Boomer Esiason, who quarterbacked for the New York Jets when Carroll was the coach. Esiason calls the day Carroll got fired "the saddest day of my professional life. I basically went from a PhD to an elementary school education in about fifteen minutes."

I could write that Carroll was too soft on his players in the NFL — it might be the worst charge that could be leveled at a football coach. It's been leveled at Carroll plenty, and he winces when he repeats it. But I could just as easily write that Carroll's positive attitude, his native optimism and idealism, find more receptive ears among young players, who haven't yet become cynical, who don't play for money.

I could write that Carroll's restoration of USC's glory, his resurrection of a prowess and cachet that date back to the 1920s, is one of the most impressive achievements in the annals of college football, so fast and dramatic that it borders on miraculous. Carroll took a team that had become a nonfactor, that hadn't won a national championship in twenty-two years, and turned it into a machine. His stars made a habit of collecting Heismans as if it were their birthright — three winners in four years, a feat no other school has achieved. No one would have dared say I was wrong — until this season. When USC fell to Stanford, you could hear the critics clearing their throats, rehearsing their revisionist histories and eulogies of the Carroll Era. Maybe the magic is gone, they said. Maybe Carroll benefited from a crew of talented assistants, they said, guys like offensive mastermind Norm Chow, who left to become offensive coordinator for the Tennessee Titans, and Lane Kiffin, who left to become head coach of the Oakland Raiders, and Ed Orgeron, who's now coaching the University of Mississippi.

Just wait. Another few losses, another season or two without a championship, and the critics will get louder. Carroll was overrated, they'll say. He got lucky, they'll say. He came along at the same moment as a rare cluster of once-in-a-lifetime players, they'll say. He's lost his Trojan mojo.

Carroll knows what they'll say, and when he hears it, when he feels that he's losing the players, losing the fans, losing momentum, or just losing, he might leave. Regardless of the contract extension he signed in 2005, details of which he declines to discuss, he's not likely to stay where he's not wanted, or where his message is no longer working. "I never want to coach again when it's not like this," he says. "I won't hang on for dear life. I love winning so much that I can't imagine being here when it's any other way."

I could write that, even if he does leave, he'll never go back to the NFL, where he was booed and labeled a failure. "There's no way," he says, and Esiason agrees. "I don't know if there's nirvana for Pete Carroll — but I know it's not in the pros." And yet. When I press Carroll, I can't help feeling that he hedges. "There's no franchise, there's no ownership, there's no philosophy," he says. "The only thing it would give me would be credibility. That you're the best in the world."

14.

I Still Don't Know How to Casually and Smoothly Insert the Obligatory Bio Material, Which Is Why I've Waited This Long

He was born in San Francisco, September 15, 1951, and grew up in nearby Marin County. A boisterous, happy household, by several accounts. His father was a liquor wholesaler, his mother "the life of the party," Carroll recalls. Dad was "competitive," Mom was "loving, really kind." His mother died in 2000, his father in 2001.

He takes after them in equal measure, he says, though at least one friend disagrees. "His mom was really his heart," says Dave Perron, a buddy who played college ball with Carroll. "She just lavished so much love and affection on him that made him feel confident about himself." His father wore the gear, the sweatshirts and hats of every team Carroll ever coached. "Because I got fired and kicked around so much," Carroll says, "he had about eight closets full of stuff." Still, Perron insists, "his core, his soul, comes from his mother."

Carroll attended Redwood High School, where he played three sports. He continued playing football through college, first at the College of Marin, then the University of the Pacific, where he transferred in his junior year. He starred at free safety.

After graduating with a degree in business administration, he went out for the World Football League, but an injured shoulder kept him from making the team. "*They* might not say it was the shoulder," he confesses. He briefly tried his hand at selling roofing materials. He was miserable. When he got wind of a job opening on the coaching staff at his alma mater, he pounced on it. The pay was nothing, but he didn't care. While studying for his master's in sports psychology, Carroll worked as a graduate assistant with the team, coaching the school's receivers and pass defenders. At twenty-five he married Glena, a fellow jock (volleyball). She was one of the first female athletes to earn an athletic scholarship from the University of the Pacific. They have two sons and a daughter.

In 1977, Carroll signed on as a graduate assistant at the University of Arkansas, under Lou Holtz. He soon advanced to the level of assistant coach, first at Iowa State, then Ohio State. In 1980, he caught on as defensive coordinator at North Carolina State. Three years later he returned to Pacific as assistant head coach and offensive coordinator.

Carroll broke into the NFL with the Buffalo Bills, in 1984, coaching the defensive backs. From Buffalo he moved to Minnesota, coaching backs for Bud Grant's Vikings. In 1990, he jumped to the New York Jets, as defensive coordinator, and in 1994, when he was forty-three, he became the team's head coach. He was young for such a big-time job, and the word *wunderkind* got hung on him, sometimes flatteringly, sometimes sarcastically.

The wunderkind went 6–10 his first year and got fired. Carroll recalls sitting across from team owner Leon Hess. It felt, Carroll says, as though he were "staring into the eyes of Satan." He spent the next two years with his hometown 49ers, building a ferocious defense. The playbook was a mess, a mélange of schemes and ideas that went back years, he says. No one could tell where anything had come from, who was the originator of what — like a polygamist's family album. His ability to unravel, decipher, and streamline the book won him praise from many in the organization, including Bill Walsh, his shining hero. (Months after Walsh's death, Carroll keeps a Walsh voice mail in his cell phone and listens to it every time he clicks through his saved messages.)

In 1997, Carroll landed the job of head coach in New England. His first year was his best. The Patriots won ten games and captured the AFC East crown. His next two years saw a slight but steady drop-off. Owner Robert Kraft said publicly that firing Carroll was a tough call, but David Halberstam, in his bestselling book *The Education of a Coach*, says Kraft had grown enamored of Belichick and was eager to shed Carroll.

Most often Carroll sloughs off past failures. Now and then, however, his voice darkens and his tone betrays the residual pain. Over takeout one night — I devour mine, he picks at his like a supermodel — Carroll says his time in Boston inoculated him against criticism. "I've already been dead," he says. "You can't kill a dead man."

It was late 2000, just when he felt he'd recovered from the trauma of New York and New England, that USC fired its coach. The school had been to only one Rose Bowl in ten years. Fans were clamoring for a recognizable name with a sparkling résumé. Carroll knew he was a long shot. School officials had a list of three or four candidates, and he wasn't on it. But to everyone's surprise, Carroll aced his on-campus interview with USC athletic director Mike Garrett. Overnight he was the front-runner.

After weeks of drama and intense public speculation, Garrett introduced Carroll as the new coach shortly before Christmas. The announcement was wildly unpopular with alumni, writers, and fans. "I'm not mad at Pete Carroll," wrote *Los Angeles Times* columnist Bill Plaschke. "I'm mad at USC for hiring him."

A shaky start seemed to validate the anti-Carroll voices. His first season opened with a big wet thud — two wins, five losses. Although Carroll believed this was his last chance at coaching, he didn't panic. As always, he expected something good to happen, and it did. The players began to mesh. The three rules took root. From 2001 until the present, USC has been the nation's dominant team. At one point the Trojans owned a streak of thirty-four straight victories, spread over three seasons. But it was also the way they won. The 2004 muscling of Michigan in the Rose Bowl. The 2005 systematic demolition of Oklahoma. The 2005 "Bush Push" thriller against Notre Dame.

Carroll takes particular pleasure in the change at Los Angeles Memorial Coliseum. For those first few months of his tenure, the stadium was half full. Now every home game brings ninety-two thousand dressed in cardinal and gold, the kind of hard-core fans who make "Tribute to Troy" the ring tone on their cell phones, who know what *Palmam qui meruit ferat* means, who proudly wear pins that read IN PETE WE TRUST.

15.

He Doesn't Speak English

He speaks in Joycean sentences composed of Xs and Os and arrows. He draws up elaborate problems — on dry-erase boards, in a code of symbols and squiggles that might as well be ancient Sumerian — solves them, reconstructs them, then erases them, and starts again. He turns to his assistant coaches one night, all of them sitting in high-backed leather chairs, eating homemade cookies and milk. "How can it be this easy?" he says, drawing up another play to stymie the next opponent. They dunk their cookies, laugh. Thousands of these problems take up the neurons of Carroll's brain. (There are more than nine hundred plays in USC's playbook alone.) The names of the plays convey their esoteric quality, names like "Mash Two Trips Right 99 Y-Stick X-Snap" and "Trips Right Z-Short 12 Track F-Seal." You can't profile someone unless you speak his language, and you can't hope to profile Carroll unless you know the difference between Amigo Burst and Zombie Right, or the relationship between the Mike, the Will, and the Sam, or the glorious history of the Seven Diamond, or why Carroll and his assistants sometimes spontaneously and simultaneously cry out, "Tokyo!" And you can't understand such things without years of study.

One afternoon I watch Carroll enjoy a private eureka moment with his assistant Rocky Seto. While analyzing data on their next opponent, they realize that the defense has a tendency to react the same way every time it's faced with one situation. Leaping to the dry-erase board, Seto points to a series of numbers and says, "They run all their spiders from the right hash!"

You don't say.

On another occasion Carroll lets me sit in a corner as his offensive coordinator, Steve Sarkisian, briefs players about the next defense they face. Everything Sarkisian says is Top Secret, but Carroll knows I might as well sit in on a UN Security Council session without headphones that provide translation. I lose the thread — and, briefly, consciousness — somewhere in the middle of the following Sarkisian speech: "I want to make sure we're clear when we're running seal zone plays and when we're running our regular zones, when we're making slow calls, when we're running power, and when we're blocking with Ds and Cs, and when we're making slappy calls. Big in this game, on first and second downs, guys, is our play action passing, whether it's off the bootleg pass, 13, 12 boot, A 42, A 43, our Nakeds, Rose and Lee, and A 26, and A 27 . . . 80, 90 . . ."

16.

I Can't Conceive Any Explanation for Why This Beautiful Carroll-Orchestrated Moment Wasn't National News, Which Makes Me Question All My Judgments About Carroll

The first quarter of the first game of 2007. Carroll's team is preoccupied, heavy-hearted, mourning their beloved place kicker, Mario Danelo, who died in January after falling from a cliff in San Pedro. (Danelo was drunk, but police still don't know why he fell.) The players have honored Danelo with an emotional pregame ceremony and with a moment of silence before kickoff, but it's not enough. After USC scores its first touchdown, Carroll sends just ten men onto the field to kick the point after. One man is missing — Danelo.

Slowly the crowd realizes what's happening. They see the holder kneeling in an empty backfield — a sort of missing man formation. Murmurs ripple through the crowd, then a cheer goes up. It grows louder. The play clock runs down, the refs whistle the play dead. USC is penalized for delay of game. The ball is moved back five yards. At last Danelo's replacement trots onto the field and boots the ball through the uprights. The symbolic gesture, which perhaps has given some extra comfort to Danelo's family, sends chills around the Coliseum and further cements the bond between coach and players.

17.

I Can't Explain the American Fascination with Football Coaches, a Prerequisite for Putting Carroll in His Proper Historical and Cultural Context

Americans have always felt a deep reverence for their Lombardis and Halases, their Landrys and Bryants, their Rocknes and Strams. The American love of coaches goes back 110 years, and it says something about who we are and where we stand as a culture, the way we lap up gossip about them, chart their up-and-down careers, YouTube their tantrums. We thrill to watch them throw clipboards, pound lecterns, grab face masks, berate writers — so long as they win. Hell, we love them even if they don't win, so long as they're good and crazy. When Mike Gundy, head coach of Oklahoma State, suffered a public nervous breakdown in September, when he spent his weekly press conference bullying a female columnist for something fairly innocent, I expected him to be hospitalized. Instead he was lionized. Writers and fans praised Gundy for "backing" his players. Recruitment at Oklahoma State spiked. Parents wanted to pack up their sons and send them to live with this lunatic.

Maybe we love coaches because deep down we long to be coached. Whatever we do, we'd like to do it better, and we go weak at the knees for the man of passion who vows to kick our ass until we do our best. Even some of our cultural icons are actually coaches in disguise. What is Oprah but a coach to tens of millions of women?

Or maybe some deep, virulent strain of cultural bellicosity underlies our football coach fetish. We're a warlike nation, on a war footing, and if football is our weekend simulacrum of war, football coaches are our stand-ins for four-star generals — and God knows we swoon over generals. (More than one in four U.S. presidents was a former general.) Given our atavistic fondness for field marshals and chieftains, it's a wonder more coaches don't run for high office. Then again, why would they voluntarily submit to such a drastic cut in pay and a still sharper decrease in power?

Carroll believes he knows why we love coaches, why the epic coaches have become American icons. "They were themselves," he says. Great coaches, he says excitedly, *know themselves.* What about coaches who fail? "They don't know themselves," he says. "So they act in accordance with what they think they should be acting like, as opposed to finding out who they are so they can act directly in connection with the essence of who they are."

18.

Carroll Might Be God, or Thor, and Everyone Knows That Neither God nor Thor Can Be Profiled

While coaching the Jets, Carroll got his hands on some strange reading material, stuff that was really "out there," he says. He was seeking the philosophers' stone, the idea or set of ideas that would help him reach players and also find meaning in his life. He befriended a blind woman, a "futurist," who read crystals in her spare time and experienced strong visions whenever Carroll was near. "We had kind of a cool friendship. I was learning about Native American stuff."

Carroll stumbled on a concept called "Long Body," a way the Iroquois thought of the tribe. One feels pain, all feel pain. One triumphs, all triumph. Long Body. He began applying this idea to football. "Things were occurring," he says. "I didn't know — I had a meeting with players and coaches, and I was telling them about this Iroquois concept. Connection of the tribe. They live together, they hunt together. They become one. So I'm telling them about this concept — *this is really far out* — and I say, 'As we go through this camp, go through this season, we're going to get so close, we're going to connect in this true fashion. Long Body. It's going to take us to places we've never been before.' And at the end of my talk I say, 'As we get through it, I'll explain it more to you, and I know this to be true so much right now that thunder will strike —'"

At that moment, Carroll says, he struck a table with his fist and a clap of thunder shook the building.

His coaches, he says, turned white.

I turn a little pale myself.

"At bed check," he says, laughing, "I found guys curled up, reading their Bibles."

As with many gods, and most holy men, Carroll endured the archetypal Time of Suffering, followed by the mandatory Period of Exile, then the classic Journey Through the Wilderness, culminating with the all-changing Epiphany. It happened this way. After being fired by New England, Carroll retreated to his office in Massachusetts, to read and reflect. He thought his coaching career might be over. That is, he did and he didn't. He still believed, deep down, something good was about to happen. He still believed he was a winner who simply hadn't won yet. John Wooden told him so. Carroll read one of the UCLA basketball coach's books and learned that the man who won ten national championships in twelve years didn't win any in the first sixteen years of his career. His dry spell gave Carroll comfort.

During his exile, Carroll also tried his hand at a column for the NFL's website. Something about the discipline of writing every day made him look inward, a thousand miles inward. A logjam loosened; the universe got clearer. Eventually it all came pouring out, his principles, his beliefs. He wrote and wrote, page after page, caught in the grip of inspiration. He laid out the Carroll Doctrine, a battle plan, a battle cry, a manifesto, stressing the value of Fun, Competition, and Practice in helping athletes "self-actualize." In other words, know themselves. An athlete who knows himself, Carroll says, is unstoppable. The Soul is the Zone that every athlete must strive to enter. Before a big game, Carroll is likely to remind his players to be themselves. "Be who we are. Don't make shit up, ever!" He says this to his men before their game against Nebraska, a street fight in which they put forty-nine points on a stunned Husker team that thought it had improved.

I ask Carroll if I can read this manifesto. Carroll says he has no idea where it is. He might not have written it, per se.

What?

It might have been a dream, he says. What matters is that he woke one day and knew himself. He had himself down cold. He was ready to go forth. He was ready to win.

19.

To Write a Profile That's Accurate, I'd Be Obligated to Describe a
Bizarre and Humiliating Contest of Wills Between the Coach and Me

Carroll is part camel. It's the only explanation. After a morning of meetings, followed by a speech to a booster group, we return to campus. It's unseasonably warm. I fantasize about a dozen glasses of cool water lined up before me. Looking at my watch, I calculate eighteen hours since he's ingested any type of liquid. I couldn't be more parched if I were trailing around after T. E. Lawrence. I mention my ravenous, desperate thirst to Carroll. He sighs, guides me to a mini-fridge in the assistant coaches' locker room, grabs me a cold Gatorade. My mouth waters as I start to unscrew the cap.

Aren't you going to have one? I ask.

Nah.

Really?

I hesitate.

Well, I say, I'm not having one until you do. I set down the Gatorade.

He warns me not to make it a competition. If I make it a competition, he'll die before he takes another drink. (Later he explains it this way: "What I am is a competitor. That's what I am. My whole life, everything I can ever remember, I've been competitive — competitive for friendships, competitive for love, competitive for sports, competitive for heroship, competitive for everything and battling for everything. When I throw my gum away, I'm trying to land it on the line.") Clearly I don't want to get into a thirst-off with this man. Nothing good can come of that. I take a sip of Gatorade. The cool orange flavor runs down the back of my throat, and I almost weep with pleasure.

That night I get a text message. I don't recognize the number. But it doesn't take long to figure out who it's from.

still haven't had anything to drink.

20.

I Couldn't Figure Out How to Work This Image into the Top of a Profile, So I Could Return to It Later, Establishing It as an Evocative Symbol of Carroll's Ethos

He loves music. The computer in his office is always playing something, usually his favorite radio station, KFOG, in San Francisco. He lives from song to song — John Legend, Stevie Wonder, the Grateful Dead — so it's perfect that Heritage Hall sits twenty feet from USC's music school. Whenever Carroll walks to or from practice he passes through a wall of music.

Not music, actually, but scales, exercises. Students sit outside at all hours, rehearsing on their cellos and oboes and French horns. They unwittingly provide a sense of perpetual overture and underscore a central tenet of Carroll's coaching — practice, practice, practice.

"One thing I've learned, which I was taught a long time ago but didn't grasp at the time, is the power of practice," Carroll says. "The discipline that comes from practice, that allows you to transcend the early stages of learning and take you to a point where you're freefloating and totally improvising. Through the discipline, the repetition, you become free."

21.

He Already Has His Own Personal Boswell Profiling Him Minute-to-Minute

Ben Malcolmson, a twenty-two-year-old former player, sits at a tiny Bob Cratchit desk outside Carroll's office, ready to drop everything and follow Carroll to the next talk, practice, team meeting. Malcolmson takes careful note of everything Carroll says, then blogs it instantly, with photos, on his popular website, uscripsit.com, which he launched earlier this year with Carroll's help. Thousands of people visit the site every day.

It's an experiment few coaches would be open enough to permit, and it's a life-changing adventure for Malcolmson, who might be the most ardent Carroll fan of them all. "I've learned a lot from

him about eliminating all negatives," Malcolmson says. "That's
something that's going to stick with me the rest of my life."

Malcolmson recalls last season, when USC lost to Oregon State,
the team's first regular season loss in three years. No one knew
what to do, what to feel. Everyone looked to Carroll to tell them, to
guide them through the pain: "I was thinking — I can't wait to get
[there] Monday, to know how to feel."

22.

At Some Point, I Lost the Capacity for Cynicism

Carroll is standing in Salon E at the Omaha Marriott, the night before the Nebraska game, when he spots fourteen-year-old Ryan
Davidson. (A USC alum introduced them four years ago.) Carroll
hugs Ryan, asks how he's feeling, then invites him to sit up front
with the offensive linemen while Carroll addresses the team.

Davidson looks painfully small, wedged between linemen who
outweigh him by two hundred pounds. But they all pat him on the
back, talk with him, go out of their way to make him feel welcome.
He beams. He radiates joy.

This is precisely why Ryan's father, Kirby, brought the boy here,
all the way from their home in Sun Prairie, Wisconsin. Ryan is due
to have surgery in four days, Kirby says. Doctors will remove two
new tumors on his brain, a third recurrence of the brain cancer
first diagnosed when he was six. "We found out two months ago it
had come back," Kirby says.

Carroll bounds to the front of the room. Before talking about tomorrow's game, before giving the team its last-minute instructions,
he asks them to welcome their honored guest. The players give
Ryan a thunderous ovation, which can be heard down the hall and
out in the lobby.

At the game, Ryan and Kirby are Carroll's guests on the USC
sideline. They watch alongside Will Ferrell and Keanu Reeves. During the postgame press conference, they try to stay out of the way,
but again Carroll spots Ryan.

Hey, Carroll says. Come up here, Ryan. I need you up here with
me.

While answering questions, Carroll wraps an arm around Ryan.

"He was up there with Coach a good ten minutes," Kirby says later. "Anybody I've shown that videotape to — you can just tell the feeling Coach Carroll has for Ryan. He held on to him really tight and never let go."

23.

My Reaction to the Stanford Defeat May Disqualify Me as an Objective Observer, Even More Than My Acceptance of a Free Shirt

Seated next to me at the black-tie event is a USC student. He takes a call on his cell phone, then closes it and turns to me. USC lost, he says.

No, I say. Impossible.

My friend just called me, the young man insists. Final score — Stanford 24, USC 23.

We both stare at the floor. The first home loss in thirty-five games? To a forty-one-point underdog?

I'm surprised by how the news affects me.

The next day I watch clips of Carroll's press conference. He calls the loss "crushing." I blanch. That's not the Carroll I know. That's not a word I've ever heard him use. If Carroll is crushed, I'm further than ever from understanding him. More important, if Carroll is crushed, we're all in trouble. If Carroll is crushed, if his ideas about Fun, Competition, and Practice can be swept away by one loss, what chance do the rest of us have to connect with our inner Carroll, to coach ourselves, to inspire ourselves, to go forth and win?

I drop by Heritage Hall weeks later. Middle of the night. I find Carroll huddled in the war room, watching film with his assistants. He gives me a big smile and seems to be in better spirits. His players are getting healthy, and they've just delivered a mega-statement in South Bend, skunking Notre Dame, 38–0, for the first time since 1933.

He takes me into his office, asks me how the profile's coming. I tell him that I decided I couldn't write a profile of him, so I wrote about all the reasons why I couldn't. He laughs — as if he's won something. Which makes me laugh.

He asks when we saw each other last. Before Stanford, I remind him. His face changes. No more laughter. No more smile. Stanford. Not even the trace of a smile. Stanford. He starts replaying the game for me, describing the interceptions, the fatal miscues, the wrongheaded decisions. Stanford. He reaches for a black baseball bat and tests its weight, swings it hard at a phantom fastball as he recounts the final harrowing plays. The fourth-down conversion. The stomach-churning touchdown.

I was so pissed off, he says. I'm still pissed off. I'll always be pissed off.

Really?

Well — he smiles. I want to feel pissed off. I harvest that pissed-off feeling.

He talks excitedly about the next opponents, the remaining schedule. The smile grows. The bat slices quicker through the air. He lists the things that are about to start falling into place, the good things that are about to happen. I lean back. I listen. I smile.

I don't know if I believe. But, hard as I try, I can't think of a single reason not to.

Contributors' Notes

Notable Sports Writing of 2007

Contributors' Notes

A *Washington Post* columnist since 1984, THOMAS BOSWELL is best known for the many books he has written on baseball, including *How Life Imitates the World Series*. In 1994 he served as guest editor for *The Best American Sports Writing*.

RICK BRAGG is the author of *Somebody Told Me, Ava's Man*, and *All Over but the Shoutin'*. A former reporter for the *New York Times*, for which he won the Pulitzer Prize, Bragg teaches at the University of Alabama.

A writer at large for *Runner's World*, JOHN BRANT is making his third appearance in *The Best American Sports Writing*. Charlie Butler and David Willey were his editors for the three selections. Brant is a frequent contributor to *Play, Inc., Best Life,* and *Men's Health,* and the author of *Duel in the Sun: Alberto Salazar, Dick Beardsley, and America's Greatest Marathon*. He lives in Portland, Oregon, with his wife and two children.

From 1979 to 1985 CHIP BROWN was a staff writer with the *Washington Post*. In 1985 he moved to New York and began a magazine freelance career, writing for over thirty national magazines, among them the *New York Times Magazine, The New Yorker, Harper's, Outside, Vanity Fair, Men's Journal, Vogue, GQ, Condé Nast Traveler,* and *National Geographic Adventure*. A former contributing editor at *Esquire* and correspondent for *Outside*, he is currently a contributing editor at *Men's Journal*. He has won many journalism awards, including the 1989 National Magazine Award for feature writing.

TOM CLYNES is a journalist and photographer who covers environmental issues, science, and adventure travel. He is a contributing editor for *National Geographic Adventure* and *Popular Science* and author of the book *Wild Planet*.

TOMMY CRAGGS is a writer in New York and a native of Urbana, Illinois. This is his second appearance in *The Best American Sports Writing*.

STEVE FRIEDMAN is the author of three books and is writer-at-large for *Backpacker*, *Bicycling*, and *Runner's World*. His stories have been published in many national titles and anthologies, including *The Best American Travel Writing*. A St. Louis native and graduate of Stanford University, Friedman lives in New York City. This is his seventh appearance in *The Best American Sports Writing*.

PATRICK HRUBY is a "Page 2" columnist and occasional contributor to other sections of ESPN.com. A resident of Washington, D.C., he holds degrees from Georgetown and Northwestern and previously wrote about sports for the *Washington Times*.

DAN JENKINS is a native of Fort Worth, Texas, and a graduate of Texas Christian University. After working for the *Fort Worth Herald* and the *Dallas Times Herald*, Jenkins was for many years a senior writer at *Sports Illustrated*. He writes a regular column for *Golf Digest* and is the author of numerous books, including *Semi-Tough* and *Dead Solid Perfect*. He lives in Texas.

MARK KRAM JR. is making his fifth appearance in *The Best American Sports Writing*. A sportswriter for the *Philadelphia Daily News*, he also worked at the *Detroit Free Press* and the *Baltimore News American*. He appears regularly on Comcast on the Emmy Award–winning program *Daily News Live*. Kram lives in Haddonfield, New Jersey, with his wife and two daughters.

JEANNE MARIE LASKAS is a *GQ* correspondent and a National Magazine Award finalist. She is the author of five books, including the award-winning memoirs *Fifty Acres and a Poodle* and *The Exact Same Moon*. She is a columnist for the *Washington Post Magazine*, where her "Significant Others" essays appear weekly. A professor in the creative writing program at the University of Pittsburgh, she lives with her husband and daughters at Sweetwater Farm in Scenery Hill, Pennsylvania. Her newest book, *Hidden America*, stories of coal miners and oil drillers and cowboys, is forthcoming from Putnam.

MICHAEL LEWIS is the author of *The New New Thing*, *Liar's Poker*, *Moneyball*, *Coach*, and *The Blind Side*. In 2006 he served as guest editor for *The Best American Sports Writing*.

FRANZ LIDZ is a frequent contributor to *Condé Nast Portfolio* and writes "The Windup" column for Portfolio.com. He is the author of *Unstrung Heroes* and *Ghosty Men: The Strange but True Story of the Collyer Brothers and*

My Uncle Arthur, New York's Greatest Hoarders and the golf memoir *Fairway to Hell*. He was a senior writer at *Sports Illustrated* from 1980 to 2007.

MARK LUCIUS is director of corporate and public relations for Northwestern Mutual, where he has worked for twenty-six years. He spent eleven years there as speechwriter to the CEO and saw his work published in many publications, including *Vital Speeches in America*. Previously he worked at the University of Wisconsin at Milwaukee, where he earned a BA in journalism and an MA in mass communication. He is also a songwriter. He lives in Milwaukee with his wife, Barbara, and daughter, Anna.

J. R. MOEHRINGER is a former Nieman Fellow at Harvard University. He was the winner of the Pulitzer Prize for feature writing in 2000 and a Pulitzer finalist for feature writing in 1998 for his magazine piece "Resurrecting the Champ," which was recently adapted for a film starring Samuel L. Jackson and Josh Hartnett. He is the author of the memoir *The Tender Bar.*

TIM NEVILLE is a freelance writer who started his magazine career after working on the travel desk at *Outside,* where he remains a frequent contributor. When he was eighteen years old, he left home on the Eastern Shore of Maryland to live in Switzerland. There he fell in love with mountain sports and French. Now a correspondent for *Skiing,* Neville has traveled to more than fifty countries, speaks four languages, and returns as often as he can to the Alps. He lives in Bend, Oregon, with his wife.

JOE POSNANSKI has been a sports columnist at the *Kansas City Star* since 1996. He has twice been named the best sports columnist in America by the Associated Press Sports Editors. He has also been nominated for fifteen awards by the APSE, and has won first-place national awards in feature and project writing. He is the author of two books, *The Good Stuff,* a collection of columns, and *The Soul of Baseball: A Road Trip Through Buck O'Neil's America.*

S. L. PRICE has been a senior writer at *Sports Illustrated* since 1994 and is the author of several books, including *Far Afield: A Sports Writing Odyssey.* His forthcoming book, *Heart of the Game,* which examines the life and death of Mike Coolbaugh and the state of Minor League America, will be published in April 2009.

After twenty-three years with *Sports Illustrated,* RICK REILLY has recently joined ESPN. Guest editor of *The Best American Sports Writing 2002,* Reilly, a native of Boulder, Colorado, is the author of *Hate Mail from Cheerleaders and Other Adventures from the Life of Reilly*, a collection of his columns for *Sports Illustrated*.

MIKE SAGER is the author of two bestselling collections of magazine journalism, *Scary Monsters and Super Freaks* and *Revenge of the Donut Boys*, and a novel, *Deviant Behavior*. A former *Washington Post* reporter and *Rolling Stone* contributing editor, he is currently a writer-at-large for *Esquire*.

ELI SASLOW is a staff writer for the *Washington Post* and was a Nieman Fellow at Harvard University.

SAM SHAW is a graduate of Harvard College and the Iowa Writers' Workshop. His nonfiction and fiction have appeared in numerous magazines and anthologies, including *The Best American Nonrequired Reading* and *The Best American Mystery Stories*. He lives in Brooklyn, New York.

T. J. SIMERS has been an award-winning sports columnist for the *Los Angeles Times* since 2000.

PAUL SOLOTAROFF is a contributing editor for *Men's Journal*.

RICK TELANDER is a native of Peoria, Illinois, and attended Northwestern University on a football scholarship. He is a columnist for the *Chicago Sun-Times*.

WRIGHT THOMPSON is a senior writer for ESPN.com and *ESPN the Magazine*. He and his wife, Sonia, live in Oxford, Mississippi. This is his third appearance in *The Best American Sports Writing*.

MICHAEL WEINREB is the author of *The Kings of New York: A Year Among the Geeks, Oddballs, and Geniuses Who Make Up America's Top High School Chess Team*, which won the Quill Award as the best sports book of 2007. A former staff writer for the *Akron Beacon Journal* and *Newsday*, Weinreb has also authored a short-story collection, *Girl Boy Etc*. He has a BA in journalism from Penn State University and an MA in creative writing from Boston University, lives in Brooklyn with his girlfriend, and is working on a book about sports in the 1980s.

ALEC WILKINSON has been a writer at *The New Yorker* since 1980. He has published eight books, the most recent of which is *The Happiest Man in the World*, about a man who built a raft from things he found on the streets of New York City and then sailed it across the Atlantic.

ALEXANDER WOLFF is a writer for *Sports Illustrated* and owner of the Vermont Frost Heaves of the American Basketball Association. The author of *Big Game, Small World*, he lives in Vermont.

Notable Sports Writing of 2007

SELECTED BY GLENN STOUT

THE BEST AMERICAN SERIES®

THE BEST AMERICAN SHORT STORIES® 2008
Salman Rushdie, editor, Heidi Pitlor, series editor
ISBN: 978-0-618-78876-7 $28.00 CL
ISBN: 978-0-618-78877-4 $14.00 PA

THE BEST AMERICAN NONREQUIRED READING™ 2008
Edited by Dave Eggers, introduction by Judy Blume
ISBN: 978-0-618-90282-8 $28.00 CL
ISBN: 978-0-618-90283-5 $14.00 PA

THE BEST AMERICAN COMICS™ 2008
Lynda Barry, editor, Jessica Abel and Matt Madden, series editors
ISBN: 978-0-618-98976-8 $22.00 POB

THE BEST AMERICAN ESSAYS® 2008
Adam Gopnik, editor, Robert Atwan, series editor
ISBN: 978-0-618-98331-5 $28.00 CL
ISBN: 978-0-618-98322-3 $14.00 PA

THE BEST AMERICAN MYSTERY STORIES™ 2008
George Pelecanos, editor, Otto Penzler, series editor
ISBN: 978-0-618-81266-0 $28.00 CL
ISBN: 978-0-618-81267-7 $14.00 PA

THE BEST AMERICAN SPORTS WRITING™ 2008
William Nack, editor, Glenn Stout, series editor
ISBN: 978-0-618-75117-4 $28.00 CL
ISBN: 978-0-618-75118-1 $14.00 PA

THE BEST AMERICAN TRAVEL WRITING™ 2008
Anthony Bourdain, editor, Jason Wilson, series editor
ISBN: 978-0-618-85863-7 $28.00 CL
ISBN: 978-0-618-85864-4 $14.00 PA

THE BEST AMERICAN SCIENCE AND NATURE WRITING™ 2008
Jerome Groopman, editor, Tim Folger, series editor
ISBN: 978-0-618-83446-4 $28.00 CL
ISBN: 978-0-618-83447-1 $14.00 PA

THE BEST AMERICAN SPIRITUAL WRITING™ 2008
Edited by Philip Zaleski, introduction by Jimmy Carter
ISBN: 978-0-618-83374-0 $28.00 CL
ISBN: 978-0-618-83375-7 $14.00 PA